JOINING TOGETHER

Group Theory
And Group Skills

JOINING TOGETHER

Group Theory And Group Skills

Second Edition

DAVID W. JOHNSON
The University of Minnesota

FRANK P. JOHNSON
The University of Maryland

Prentice-Hall, Inc., Englewood Cliffs, New Jersey 07632

Library of Congress Cataloging in Publication Data

JOHNSON, DAVID W.,
 Joining together.

 Bibliography: p.
 Includes index.
 1. Social groups. 2. Leadership. 3. Group
relations training. I. Johnson, Frank P.,
II. Title.
HM131.J613 1982   302.3'4   81–21028
ISBN 0-13-510396-7   AACR2

Printed in the United States of America

10 9 8 7 6

Editorial/production supervision
 and interior design by Virginia Cavanagh Neri
Cover design by Diane Saxe
Manufacturing buyer: Edmund W. Leone

ISBN 0-13-510396-7

Prentice-Hall International, Inc., *London*
Prentice-Hall of Australia Pty. Limited, *Sydney*
Prentice-Hall of Canada, Ltd., *Toronto*
Prentice-Hall of India Private Limited, *New Delhi*
Prentice-Hall of Japan, Inc., *Tokyo*
Prentice-Hall of Southeast Asia Pte. Ltd., *Singapore*
Whitehall Books Limited, *Wellington, New Zealand*

This book is dedicated to our parents,
who created the basic group
to which we first belonged.

CONTENTS

List of Exercises

Preface

Joining Together seeks to provide the theory and experiences necessary to develop an understanding of group dynamics and effective group skills. It is more than a book reviewing current social psychological knowledge in the area of small groups, and it is more than a book of group exercises. The theory and exercises are integrated into an inquiry or experiential approach to learning about the dynamics of small groups.

The authors wish to thank many people for their help in writing this book and in preparing the manuscript. Our younger sister, Edythe Johnson Holubec, contributed most of the questions the reader will find in the text. Special thanks go to our brother-in-law Buddy Holubec who, at great personal risk, made Edythe get up at 6:30 a.m. every morning so she could do the preliminary editing of the manuscript. We owe much to the social psychologists who have influenced our theorizing and to the colleagues with whom we have conducted various types of laboratory-training experiences. We have tried to acknowledge sources of the exercises included in this book whenever possible. Some of the exercises presented are so commonly used that the originators are not traceable. If we have inadvertently missed giving recognition to anyone, we apologize. Special thanks are extended to our wives, Linda Mulholland Johnson and Jane Miley Johnson, who contributed their support to the development and writing of this book. All photographs were taken by David W. Johnson and Thomas Allen. We wish to thank Nancy Valin Waller, who drew the cartoon figures appearing in the book.

D. W. J.
F. P. J.

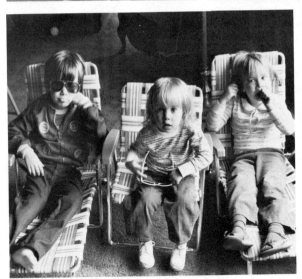

Group Dynamics

BASIC CONCEPTS TO BE COVERED IN THIS CHAPTER

In this chapter a number of concepts are defined and discussed. The major ones are listed below. The procedure for learning these concepts is as follows:

1. The class forms groups of four. These groups should be as heterogeneous as possible.
2. Each group divides into two pairs.
3. The task for each pair is to:
   a. define each concept, noting the page on which it is defined and discussed.
   b. make sure that both members of the pair understand the meaning of each concept.
4. In each group, members compare the answers of the two pairs. If there is disagreement, the members look up the concept in the chapter and clarify it until they all agree on the definition and understand it.

Concepts

1. group
2. group dynamics
3. group effectiveness
4. group skill
5. action theory
6. experiential learning
7. Kurt Lewin
8. role playing
9. process observation
10. feedback
11. learning contract

THE IMPORTANCE OF GROUPS

All day long we interact first in one group and then in another. We live in a dwelling as part of a group, we learn in groups contained in the same classroom, we work in groups, we interact with friends in groups, and we spend much of our leisure time in groups. Our family life, our leisure time, our friendships, and our careers are all filled with groups. In fact, if a person from outer space conducted a study of the people of Earth, group membership would probably be the dominant characteristic noted. We are born into a group called the family, and we would not survive the first few minutes, the first few weeks, or even the first few years of our lives without membership in this group. It is within our family and peer groups that we are socialized into ways of behaving and thinking, educated, and taught to have certain perspectives on ourselves and our world. Our personal identity is derived from the way in which we are perceived and treated by other members of our groups. We learn, work, worship, and play in groups. As humans we have a inherent social nature: Our life is filled with groups from the moment of our birth to the moment of our death.

The ubiquitousness of groups and the inevitability of being in them make groups one of the most important factors in our lives. In business, government, and the military there is great interest in improving the productivity of groups. There is great concern in our society with strengthening the family. Educators are striving to better understand how the classroom functions as a group. Drug abuse, delinquency and crime, and mental illness are all being treated through group procedures, and there is continued concern with making those procedures more effective. As the effectiveness of groups goes, our quality of life goes. The more effective our family, career, and educational groups, the higher the quality of our lives. The effectiveness of our groups depends both on our knowledge of group processes and on our ability to behave effectively within groups. This book, therefore, has two purposes: to provide you with a systematic analysis of group effectiveness and to provide you with exercises that will help you develop competent group skills.

Despite the incalculable importance of groups, there are many puzzling contradictions in the findings of those who have studied groups. Performing a task in the presence of others can under certain conditions create anxiety and apprehension and under different conditions inspire and energize. Under some conditions people avoid close physical contact with others; under different conditions they seek it out. People like to be part of groups, but they also enjoy being different and distinct from others. People seek out crowded situations at certain times and avoid them at others. There is nothing particularly simple about the way in which human groups function.

The importance of groups for humans has led a number of social scientists to perceive groups as the salvation or the bane of our species. To some social scientists groups are the basis for everything that is good in our lives. For other social scientists groups are destructive influences on our lives. Both views are oversimplified: groups can have constructive or destructive effects depending on how they are used. The more you understand the dynamics of groups, the more you will be able to maximize the constructive aspects of groups and minimize the destructive ones. When it comes to group functioning, knowledge does give power. But knowledge of group dynamics in and of itself is not sufficient to promote effective group functioning; social skills are also required. To promote effective group functioning, then, you must both know what an effective group is and have the social skills necessary to actualize group effectiveness.

In this chapter the concept *group* is defined. Effective and ineffective groups are then differentiated. A brief history of the study of group dynamics is given. Experiential learning and the procedures for learning group skills are explained. Finally, the nature of this book and how to use it are explained.

WHAT IS A GROUP EXERCISE

There has been considerable controversy as to what a group is. The purpose of this exercise is to structure a critical examination of the different definitions. The procedure is as follows:

1. The class forms groups of seven members.
2. Each member receives a sheet containing one of the seven definitions that appear on the following pages. Without interacting with the other group members, each member is to:
   a. study his or her definition until it is thoroughly understood.
   b. plan how to teach the definition to the other members of the group.
   c. name three examples of groups that meet the criterion contained in the definition.
   d. name three examples of two or more people in close proximity who do not meet the criterion contained in the definition.
   e. explain in what way(s) his or her group (doing this exercise) meets the criterion contained in the definition.
   About ten minutes are allowed for this phase of the exercise.
3. Each group meets to derive a single definition of the concept *group*. Up to twenty minutes are allowed for this phase.
4. Each group reads its definition to the entire class.
5. If there is substantial disagreement, the class forms new groups (composed of one member from each of the previous groups). The task of the new group is to arrive at one definition of the concept *group,* each member representing the definition of his or her former group.
6. Each group reads its definition to the entire class.

Interpersonal Interaction

A *group* may be defined as a collection of individuals who are interacting with one another. According to this definition, the individuals are not a group unless they are interacting with one another. Three psychologists who have defined *group* in this way are Bonner, Stogdill, and Homans:

> A group is a number of people in interaction with one another, and it is this interaction process that distinguishes the group from an aggregate (Bonner, 1959, p. 4).

> A group may be regarded as an open interaction system in which actions determine the structure of the system and successive interactions exert coequal effects upon the identity of the system (Stogdill, 1959, p. 18).

> We mean by a group a number of persons who communicate with one another often over a span of time, and who are few enough so that each person is able to communicate with all the others, not at secondhand, through other people, but face-to-face (Homans, 1950, p. 1).

All three of these definitions stress that the primary defining characteristic of a group is interpersonal interaction. It is questionable that a group can exist without its members interacting with one another.

Perceptions of Membership

A *group* may be defined as a social unit consisting of two or more persons who perceive themselves as belonging to a group. According to this definition, the persons are not a group unless they perceive themselves to be part of a group. Two psychologists who have defined *group* in this way are Bales and Smith:

> A small group is defined as any number of persons engaged in interaction with one another in a single face-to-face meeting or series of such meetings, in which each member receives some impression or perception of each other member distinct enough so that he can, either at the time or in later questioning, give some reaction to each of the others as an individual person, even though it be only to recall that the other was present (Bales, 1950, p. 33).

> We may define a social group as a unit consisting of a plural number of separate organisms (agents) who have a collective perception of their unity and who have the ability to act and/or are acting in a unitary manner toward their environment (Smith, 1945, p. 227).

Both of these definitions stress that the primary defining characteristic of a group is that the members perceive themselves to be part of a group. It is questionable that a group could exist without its members being aware that they are members of a group.

Interdependency

A *group* may be defined as a collection of individuals who are interdependent. According to this definition, the individuals are not a group unless an event that affects one of them affects them all. Four psychologists who have defined *group* in this way are Cartwright and Zander, Fiedler, and Lewin:

> A group is a collection of individuals who have relations to one another that make them interdependent to some significant degree. As so defined, the term group refers to a class of social entities having in common the property of interdependence among their constituent members (Cartwright and Zander, 1968, p. 46).

> By this term [group] we generally mean a set of individuals who share a common fate, that is, who are *interdependent* in the sense that an event which affects one member is likely to affect all (Fiedler, 1967, p. 6).

> Conceiving of a group as a dynamic whole should include a definition of group which is based on interdependence of the members (or better, of the subparts of the group) (Lewin, 1951, p. 146).

All three of these definitions stress that the primary defining characteristic of a group is that the members are interdependent in some way. It is questionable that a group could exist without its members being interdependent.

Goals

A *group* may be defined as a collection of individuals who join together to achieve a goal. According to this definition, the individuals are not a group unless they are trying to achieve a mutual goal. Three psychologists who have defined *group* this way are Mills, Deutsch, and Freeman:

> To put it simply, they [small groups] are units composed of two or more persons who come into contact for a purpose and who consider the contact meaningful (Mills, 1967, p. 2).

> A psychological group exists (has unity) to the extent that the individuals composing it perceive themselves as pursuing promotively interdependent goals (Deutsch, 1949, p. 136).

> Freeman, as early as 1936, pointed out that people join groups in order to achieve common goals.

These definitions stress that the primary defining characteristic of a group is the striving of its members to achieve a mutual goal. It is questionable whether a group could exist unless there was a mutual goal that its members were trying to achieve.

Motivation

A *group* may be defined as a collection of individuals who are all trying to satisfy some personal need through their joint association. According to this definition, the individuals are not a group unless they are motivated by some personal reason to be part of a group. Two psychologists who have defined *group* in this way are Bass and Cattell:

> We define "group" as a collection of individuals whose existence as a collection is rewarding to the individuals (Bass, 1960, p. 39).

> The definition which seems most essential is that a group is a collection of organisms in which the existence of all (in their given relationships) is necessary to the satisfaction of certain individual needs in each (Cattell, 1951, p. 167).

Both of these definitions stress that the primary defining characteristic of a group is that its members belong to the group in order to obtain needed rewards or to satisfy other personal needs. It is questionable that a group could exist without its members' needs being satisfied by their membership.

Structured Relationships

A *group* may be defined as a collection of individuals whose interactions are structured by a set of roles and norms. According to this definition, the individuals are not a group unless their interactions are structured by a set of role definitions and norms. Two sets of psychologists who have defined *group* in this way are McDavid and Harari and Sherif and Sherif:

> A social-psychological group is an organized system of two or more individuals who are interrelated so that the system performs some function, has a standard set of role relationships among its members, and has a set of norms that regulate the function of the group and each of its members (McDavid and Harari, 1968, p. 237).

> A group is a social unit which consists of a number of individuals who stand in (more or less) definite status and role relationships to one another and which possesses a set of values or norms of its own regulating the behavior of individual members, at least in matters of consequence to the group (Sherif and Sherif, 1956, p. 144).

Both of these definitions stress that the primary defining characteristic of a group is that the interaction of its members is structured by role definitions and norms. It is questionable whether a group could exist unless role definitions and norms structured the interaction of its members.

Mutual Influence

A *group* may be defined as a collection of individuals who influence each other. According to this definition, the individuals are not a group unless they are affecting and being affected by each other. Shaw (1976, p. 11) defined *group* in this way:

A group is defined as two or more persons who are interacting with one another in such a manner that each person influences and is influenced by each other person.

This definition stresses that the primary defining characteristic of a group is interpersonal influence. It is questionable that a group could exist without its members influencing each other.

WHAT IS A GROUP?

How do you tell when you are a member of a group? As you have learned from the preceding exercise, there are many different definitions of the concept *group*. The social scientists who have tried to define what a group is seem much like the blind men trying to describe an elephant. Each social scientist has taken some aspect of a group and assumed that that aspect revealed the essence of a group.

One solution to the profusion of definitions is to combine them all into one definition. A *group* may be defined as two or more individuals who (a) interact with each other, (b) are interdependent, (c) define themselves and are defined by others as belonging to the group, (d) share norms concerning matters of common interest and participate in a system of interlocking roles, (e) influence each other, (f) find the group rewarding, and (g) pursue common goals. Not all of these characteristics are equally important, and while it is impossible to gain consensus among social scientists as to which characteristics are most important, the authors prefer the following definition: A *group* is two or more individuals in face-to-face interaction, each aware of his or her membership in the group, each aware of the others who belong to the group, and each aware of their positive interdependence as they strive to achieve mutual goals. Though there may be some groups that do not fully fit this definition, the most commonly recognized examples of groups do.

Based upon the above definition of a group, is an audience at a concert a group? Are the people traveling in the same airplane a group? Are the children waiting in the same line to talk to Santa Claus a group? Are all twenty-one-year-old males in our society a group?

EFFECTIVE GROUPS AND EFFECTIVE GROUP SKILLS

Group dynamics is the area of social psychology that focuses on advancing our knowledge about the nature of group life. It emphasizes theoretically significant empirical research and the potential applicability of its findings to the improvement of group effectiveness. Before examining group dynamics as a field of inquiry and practice, we need a definition of group effectiveness and ineffectiveness.

Any effective group has three core activities: (1) accomplishing its goals, (2) maintaining itself internally, and (3) developing and changing in ways that improve its effectiveness. A successful group has the quality and kind of interaction among members that integrates these three core activities. Group members must have the skills to eliminate barriers to the accomplishment of the group's goals, to solve problems in maintaining high-quality interaction among members, and to overcome obstacles to the development of a more effective group. To be an effective group member, you need an understanding of what group effectiveness is and how your behavior can contribute to this effectiveness.

There are several dimensions of group effectiveness that relate to these three core activities, and together they make up a model that can be used to evaluate how well a group is functioning. This model provides a sense of direction to the building of a productive group by stating what, ideally, the group should be. An awareness of the difference between the ideal model and the way in which their group is functioning will motivate group members to improve their effectiveness. These dimensions, discussed in detail in later chapters, are as follows:

1. Group goals must be clearly understood, be relevant to the needs of group members, highlight the positive interdependence of members, and evoke from every member a high level of commitment to their accomplishment.

2. Group members must communicate their ideas and feelings accurately and clearly. Effective, two-way communication is the basis of all group functioning and interaction among group members.

3. Participation and leadership must be distributed among members. All should participate, and all should be listened to. As leadership needs arise, members should all feel responsibility for meeting them. The equalization of participation and leadership makes certain that all members will be involved in the group's work, committed to implementing the group's decisions, and satisfied with their membership. It also assures that the resources of every member will be fully utilized, and increases the cohesiveness of the group.

4. Appropriate decision-making procedures must be used flexibly if they are to be matched with the needs of the situation. There must be a balance between the availability of time and resources (such as members' skills) and the method of decision making used. Another balance must be struck among the size and seriousness of the decision, the commitment needed to put it into practice, and the method used for making the decision. The most effective way of making a decision is usually by consensus (unanimous agreement). Consensus promotes distributed participation, the equaliza-

tion of power, productive controversy, cohesion, involvement, and commitment.

5. Power and influence need to be approximately equal throughout the group. They should be based on expertise, ability, and access to information, not on authority. Coalitions that help fulfill personal goals should be formed among group members on the basis of mutual influence and interdependence.

6. Conflicts arising from opposing ideas and opinions (controversy) are to be encouraged. Controversies promote involvement in the group's work, quality and creativity in decision making, and commitment to implementing the group's decisions. Minority opinions should be accepted and used. Conflicts prompted by incompatible needs or goals, by the scarcity of a resource (money or power), and by competitiveness must be negotiated in a manner that is mutually satisfying and does not weaken the cooperative interdependence of group members.

7. Group cohesion needs to be high. Cohesion is based on members liking each other, each member's desire to continue as part of the group, the satisfaction of members with their group membership, and the level of acceptance, support, and trust among the members. Group norms supporting psychological safety, individuality, creativeness, conflicts of ideas, and growth and change need to be encouraged.

8. Problem-solving adequacy should be high. Problems must be resolved with minimal energy and in a way that eliminates them permanently. Procedures should exist for sensing the existence of problems, inventing and implementing solutions, and evaluating the effectiveness of the solutions. When problems are dealt with adequately, the problem-solving ability of the group is increased, innovation is encouraged, and group effectiveness is improved.

9. The interpersonal effectiveness of members needs to be high. Interpersonal effectiveness is a measure of how well the consequences of your behavior match your intentions. Johnson (1981) has focused on this subject, and therefore it will not be discussed at length in this book.

These aspects of group effectiveness are summarized in Table 1.1, and each is subsequently discussed at length in a separate chapter. Building effective work groups and leading discussion and growth groups are briefly covered in further chapters. Specific instructions for leading skill-training exercises may be found in Appendix A.

DEVELOPING AN EFFECTIVE GROUP EXERCISE

The purpose of this exercise is to give participants some practice in planning how to develop an effective group. The procedure for the exercise is as follows:

1. The class forms groups of four.
2. Groups read and discuss the paragraph below, and then answer the following questions about the situation:
   a. What should the goals of the group be?
   b. How should leadership be managed?
   c. Who should have the most power in making decisions?
   d. What decision-making procedure should be used?
   e. How should conflicts be managed?
3. Each group decides whether its answers to the above questions are indicative of an effective or an ineffective group.
4. Each group shares its answers with the rest of the class.

Sinking Boat Situation

On a dark summer night seven persons cling to a swamped and slowly sinking boat on a black tropical sea. They are not alone. A large shark glides below them, and soon, perhaps, there will be more. With fear thick in their salt-swollen throats, the seven are faced with a difficult choice. If they kick in unison, they may be able to fight the fierce current and tides driving them away from the shore and all make it to safety; if they all stick together they have an equal chance to survive or drown. If they split up, each going it alone, one or two of the stronger swimmers might make it to safety, but the majority will certainly drown or be devoured by sharks.

Which alternative would you choose if you were there? What kind of people would you want as companions in such a situation?

KURT LEWIN AND THE FIELD OF GROUP DYNAMICS

Group dynamics is a relatively young field, one that is rooted in a wide range of traditionally separate fields. Although the earliest existing philosophical literature contains a great deal of wisdom about the nature of groups, and although the basic assumptions that guide the field of group dynamics were discussed from the sixteenth through the nineteenth centuries, the field of group dynamics is strictly a twentieth-century development.

Early in the 1900s a number of psychologists investigated the effects of having several persons take part simultaneously in a variety of standard psychological experiments to see if an individual's normal solitary performance occurred when others were present (Allport, 1924; Moede, 1920). A related line of research compared the performance of individuals and groups to determine which were more productive (Gordon, 1924; Watson, 1928; Shaw, 1932).

At the end of the 1930s a rapid advance in the field took place, due largely to the efforts of three sociologists. Sherif (1936) studied the impact of group norms on perception of an ambiguous stimulus. In an ingenious

TABLE 1.1 Comparison of effective and ineffective groups.

Effective Groups	Ineffective Groups
Goals are clarified and changed so that the best possible match between individual goals and the group's goals may be achieved; goals are cooperatively structured.	Members accept imposed goals; goals are competitively structured.
Communication is two-way, and the open and accurate expression of both ideas and feelings is emphasized.	Communication is one-way and only ideas are expressed; feelings are suppressed or ignored.
Participation and leadership are distributed among all group members; goal accomplishment, internal maintenance, and developmental change are underscored.	Leadership is delegated and based upon authority; membership participation is unequal, with high-authority members dominating; only goal accomplishment is emphasized.
Ability and information determine influence and power; contracts are built to make sure individual goals and needs are fulfilled; power is equalized and shared.	Position determines influence and power; power is concentrated in the authority positions; obedience to authority is the rule.
Decision-making procedures are matched with the situation; different methods are used at different times; consensus is sought for important decisions; involvement and group discussions are encouraged.	Decisions are always made by the highest authority; there is little group discussion; members' involvement is minimal.
Controversy and conflict are seen as a positive key to members' involvement, the quality and originality of decisions, and the continuance of the group in good working condition.	Controversy and conflict are ignored, denied, avoided, or suppressed.
Interpersonal, group, and intergroup behavior are stressed; cohesion is advanced through high levels of inclusion, affection, acceptance, support, and trust. Individuality is endorsed.	The functions performed by members are emphasized; cohesion is ignored and members are controlled by force. Rigid conformity is promoted.
Problem-solving adequacy is high.	Problem-solving adequacy is low.
Members evaluate the effectiveness of the group and decide how to improve its functioning; goal accomplishment, internal maintenance, and development are all considered important.	The highest authority evaluates the group's effectiveness and decides how goal accomplishment may be improved; internal maintenance and development are ignored as much as possible; stability is affirmed.
Interpersonal effectiveness, self-actualization, and innovation are encouraged.	"Organizational persons" who desire order, stability, and structure are encouraged.

experiment he demonstrated that the judgments made by individuals were influenced by the judgments of their fellow group members. During the years 1935–39, Newcomb (1943) conducted a field study investigating the impact of social norms concerning political issues on the students at Bennington College. Most of the students came from politically conservative homes, but the prevailing political attitudes among them were liberal. Newcomb documented how the interaction of the students changed their attitudes so that they became more congruent with the prevailing norms of the peer group. In 1937 W. F. Whyte moved into one of the slums of Boston and began a three-and-a-half-year study of social clubs, political organizations, and racketeering. Whyte (1943) reported in vivid detail the structure, culture, and functioning of the Norton Street gang and the Italian Community Club. His study dramatized the great significance of groups in the lives of individuals and in the functioning of larger social systems.

By far the most influential study of group dynamics in the late 1930s, however, was that of three psychologists, Lewin, Lippitt, and White (1939). They studied the influences on groups and group members of different leadership patterns. Groups of ten- and eleven-year-old children met regularly for several weeks under the leadership of an adult, who behaved in one of three ways: democratically, autocratically, or in a laissez-faire manner. The effects of these leadership styles on the behavior of group members were large and dramatic. Severe forms of scapegoating, for example, occurred in the autocratic groups, and at the end of the experiment the children in some of those groups destroyed the things they had constructed. This study made it clear that important social issues could be produced in the laboratory and studied experimentally.

Almost immediately Lewin and his students and associates began a number of research studies aimed at developing a theory of group dynamics. French (1941) conducted a laboratory experiment comparing the effects of fear and frustration on organized versus unorganized groups. Bavelas (1942) conducted an experiment to determine whether the behavior of leaders of youth groups could be significantly modified through training. With the entry of the United States into the Second World War, Lewin, French, and Marrow (Marrow, 1956) explored group-decision procedures as a means of improving industrial production, and Lewin, Radke, and others (Lewin, 1943; Radke and Klisurich, 1947) conducted a number of experiments on group decision as a means of changing eating habits related to wartime food shortages.

In the 1940s, after a worldwide depression, the rise of dictatorship in Europe, and the Second World War, most Americans were worried about the fate of their country and the future of democracy. There was general agreement that a better understanding was needed of how democratic organizations could be made to function more effectively. Scientists had helped win the war, many people said, and now research should improve democracy. The field of group dynamics was thought to have significant potential for improving democracy. The health of a democratic society was seen as depending on the effectiveness of its component groups. Strengthening the family, the community, and the multitude of groups within our society was viewed as the primary means of ensuring the vitality of our democracy. At the same time, the notion that the scientific method could be employed in the task of improving group life gained popularity. People began to see that the scientific method could be applied to important social issues involving the functioning of groups—for example, leadership, decision making, and productivity. The belief that the solution of social problems could be facilitated by systematic research gained acceptance.

The drive to strengthen democracy by using the scientific method to strengthen groups resulted in two movements within psychology. The first was the scientific study of group dynamics. Social psychologists (a newly arrived group of specialists) began to conduct studies of group discussion, group productivity, attitude change, and leadership. They developed experimental methods of studying group dynamics, hoping thereby to find ways of strengthening democracy. Concurrently, the second movement began deriving methods for training leaders and group members in the social skills they would need in order to promote the effective functioning of democratic groups.

At the head of both movements was one of the most important psychologists of the twentieth century, Kurt Lewin. Lewin was born on September 9, 1890, in the tiny village of Mogilno in the Prussian province of Posen (now part of Poland), where his father owned and operated a general store. In 1910 Lewin began studying for a doctorate in philosophy and psychology at the University of Berlin. After finishing his doctoral work in 1914 he entered the Kaiser's army as a private and fought for four years in World War I in the infantry. He left the army as a lieutenant with an Iron Cross, and returned to the University of Berlin to teach. There he became part of the Psychological Institute, where Max Wertheimer, Kurt Koffka, and Wolfgang Kohler were formulating their Gestalt theory. Lewin become one of the Gestaltists, but he was never an orthodox follower of their early leaders. His interests were in the area of motivation, and his work was directed more to practical application than to understanding for its own sake. In 1933, as Hitler was rising to power, Lewin migrated to the United States. He subsequently worked at Cornell University, the University of Iowa, and M.I.T., where he set up and headed the famous Research Center for Group Dynamics. On February 11, 1947, he died unexpectedly of a heart attack.

It was Lewin more than anyone else who stressed the importance of applying existing knowledge to the training of leaders and members in order to promote effective functioning of democratic groups. In 1942, for example, the Second World War had just begun for America, and travel was restricted. The Society for the Psychological Study of Social Issues had canceled its annual convention and was holding a single dinner session for members who lived in the Washington area. On that warm September evening, Kurt Lewin spoke to an audience deeply concerned about the fate of their country and the future of democracy. His listeners welcomed his brave prediction:

> Although the scientific investigations of group work are but a few years old, I don't hesitate to predict that group work—that is, the handling of human beings not as isolated individuals, but in the social setting of groups—will soon be one of the most important theoretical and practical fields. . . . There is no hope for creating a better world without a deeper scientific insight into the function of leadership and culture, and of other essentials of group life. (Lewin, 1943)

Lewin's prediction came true. From 1890 to 1940 there had been a gradual growth in the number of published studies on group behavior from 1 per year to approximately 30 per year. By the late 1940s 55 studies were being published annually, and by the end of the 1950s the rate had skyrocketed to about 150. During the 1960s and 1970s the rate of research studies on group dynamics persisted at about 125 per year.

The interest in applied psychology and social reform evident in Lewin's early work continued throughout his life. He believed that social psychology could provide the information and understanding required for the solution of society's fundamental problems. In his advocacy of the study of group dynamics Lewin was noted for three things: his early championing of the use of experimental methodology, his development of theory, and his insistence that theory and research be relevant to social practice.

Lewin had a genius for thinking of ways to study ideas experimentally, and he inspired in his students something of this ability. It was Lewin's study of different leadership strategies that proved that complex social phenomena could be studied with experimental methods. Lewin was convinced that the use of experimental methods in researching the dynamics of groups would revolutionize the field, and he was right.

Lewin, however, was above all a theorist. Throughout his career he was concerned primarily with the problem of constructing an empirically based theory of human behavior. He did not see his commitment to theory as irrelevant to, or in any way incompatible with, his concern for the solution of social problems. He was convinced that the interests of the theorist and the practitioner were inextricably interrelated. Lewin assumed that every field of science must be concerned primarily with theory, since it is theory that illuminates the causal structure of the empirical world. He believed that social psychological theory should do more than advance knowledge: it should also provide the sort of understanding required for action. In order to advance knowledge and solve social problems, however, the theorist and the practitioner must work together. As Lewin (1951, p. 169) stated, close cooperation between theorists and practitioners "can be accomplished . . . if the theorist does not look toward applied problems with highbrow aversion or with a fear of social problems, and if the applied psychologist realizes that there is nothing so practical as a good theory."

Lewin saw clearly that theorists and practitioners share a common interest in understanding reality and acting competently. He viewed them as having interdependent tasks: practitioners identify significant problems to be solved, theorists develop a valid view of reality that contains the keys for solving the problems, and practitioners apply the theory. Practitioners keep theorists in contact with social reality, and theorists provide practitioners with a deeper understanding of the social problems that confront them. Lewin believed that theorists have a special obligation: to provide the kind of theory that can be used in solving social problems. Lewin was a doer, and he wanted to conduct and inspire research that made a difference in the real world of human affairs. He was constantly suggesting ways to bridge the gap between theoretical science and public policies and practices. And the particular applications he suggested were infused with democratic values. He had a profound faith in democracy, which to him was much more than just a political system. It was also a way of life, based on mutual participation and continual interaction in decision making for purposeful change.

Lewin was in his element with an informal seminar group. He was not at his best in a formal lecture, as he was not highly organized. But he had an enthusiasm for psychological analysis that was contagious. His contacts with his students were so strong that sometimes an afternoon discussion would last beyond midnight. Informal group discussions reflected not only Lewin's style of interacting with other people but also his beliefs in democracy. Given his style of working with groups, his interests in social action, and his concern for democratic decision making, it was not surprising that Lewin turned increasingly to the study of group dynamics in his years in America. Although Lewin did not create the field of group dynamics (it was the result of many developments that occurred over a period of several years and in several different disciplines and professions), he was the major link between much of the theorizing and much of the practical application in the field. The contents of this book as well as the entire field of group dynamics are heavily influenced by Lewin and his work.

The use of experiential procedures to learn about behavior in groups was greatly influenced by Lewin. His colleagues and students have been the chief promoters of experiential learning in the area of group theory and group skills. One of Lewin's characteristics was to discover valuable concepts and principles by observing his own and other people's experiences. The most trivial event, the most casual comment, might spark a thought in Lewin's mind that would result in a new theoretical breakthrough in the social psychology of groups. Those associating with Lewin never knew when he might make an important discovery, and this produced an excitement rare in a relationship with a colleague or teacher. Students and colleagues learned from Lewin how important it is to examine one's own experiences for potential principles about the way in which groups develop and work. Thus, Lewin's personal style focused on experiential learning.

Much of Lewin's research highlighted the importance of active participation in groups in order to learn new skills, develop new attitudes, and obtain new knowledge about groups. His research demonstrated that learning is achieved most productively in groups whose members can interact and then reflect on their mutual experiences. In this way members are able to spark one another's creativity in deriving conclusions about group dynamics. From Lewin, therefore, came an emphasis on studying one's own experiences in order to learn about group dynamics, on discussing mutual experiences with associates in order to increase mutual creativity and learning, and on behaving democratically in structuring learning situations.

Because an experiential approach to learning about group theory and developing group skills is taken in this book, it is necessary to explain what is meant by action theories and experiential learning, how they relate to skill learning, and what motivates students to learn experientially. Two important aspects of experiential learning, role playing and the use of observation procedures, are also explained in this chapter. The chapter concludes with a procedure for reflecting on your behavior in groups, and a learning contract for you to sign.

ACTION THEORIES

All humans need to become competent in taking action and simultaneously reflecting on their action in order to learn from it. Integrating thought with action requires that we plan our behavior, engage in it, and then reflect on how effective we were. When we learn a pattern of behavior that effectively deals with a recurrent situation, we tend to repeat it over and over until it functions automatically. Such habitual behavioral patterns are based on theories of action. An *action theory* is a theory as to what actions are needed to achieve a desired consequence in a given situation. All theories have an "if . . . then . . ." form. An action theory states that in a given situation if we do *x*, then *y* will result. Our theories of action are normative: they state what we ought to do if we wish to achieve certain results. Examples of action theories can be found in almost everything we do. If we smile and say hello, then others will return our smile and greeting. If we apologize, then the other person will excuse us. If we steal, then we will be punished. If a person shoves us, then we should shove back. All our behavior is based on theories that connect our actions with certain consequences.

As children we are taught action theories by parents and other socializing agents. As we grow older we learn how to modify our action theories and develop new ones. We learn to try to anticipate what actions will lead to what consequences, to try out and experiment with new behaviors, to experience the consequences, and then to reflect on our experiences to determine whether our action theory is valid or needs modification. Experiential learning is a procedure based on the systematic development and modification of action theories.

We all have many action theories, one for every type of situation we regularly find ourselves in. This does not mean that we are aware of our action theories. An action is usually based on tacit knowledge—knowledge that we are not always able to put into words. Since most of our action theories function automatically, we are rarely conscious of our assumed connections between actions and their consequences. One of the purposes of this book is to help you become more conscious of the action theories that guide how you behave in small-group situations, test these theories against reality, and modify them to make them more effective.

EXPERIENTIAL LEARNING

We all learn from our experiences. From touching a hot stove we learn to avoid heated objects. By dating we learn about male–female relationships. Every day we have experiences we learn from. Many aspects of group dynamics can be learned only by experience. Hearing a lecture on resisting group pressure is not the same as actually experiencing group pressure. Seeing a movie about the benefits of controversy is not the same as engaging in a controversy. Reading a description of leadership is not the same as experiencing leadership. It takes more than listening to explanations to learn group skills.

Experiential learning affects the learner in three ways: (1) the learner's cognitive structures are altered, (2) the learner's attitudes are modified, and (3) the learner's repertoire of behavior skills is expanded. To be affected in these three ways, learners must pay attention to their action theories, knowledge, attitudes, perceptions of self and social environment, and behavior patterns. To learn leadership skills, for example, the learner must develop a concept of what leadership is (knowledge), an action theory concerning what leadership behaviors will lead to effective group functioning, positive attitudes toward new leadership procedures, and perceptions that the new leadership actions are appropriate and that she is capable of performing them. Finally, she must develop the skills needed to perform the new leadership actions.

The process of experiential learning is shown in Figure 1.1. When you generate an action theory from your own experiences and then continually modify it to improve its effectiveness, you are learning experientially. Experiential learning can be conceived of in a simplified way as a three-stage cycle: (1) The learner takes action by trying out the strategies and procedures in his action theory; (2) the learner experiences the consequences of his ac-

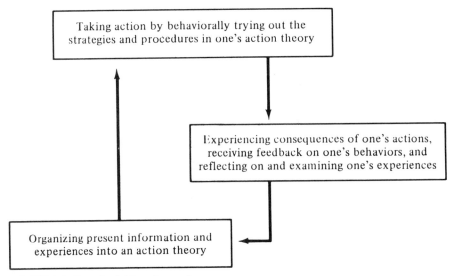

FIGURE 1.1 Experiential learning cycle.

tions, receives feedback on his behavior, and examines and reflects on his experiences; and (3) the learner organizes present information and experiences into an action theory. As the learner formulates his action theory, tests it out behaviorally, reflects on the results, and modifies and extends the theory, he must perceive himself as capable of implementing the procedures and strategies contained in the theory, perceive these procedures and strategies as being appropriate to his social world, and develop positive attitudes toward the theory and its implementation.

There are a number of principles of experiential learning that need to be understood and followed. These principles are based on the work and theorizing of Kurt Lewin (Lewin, 1935; Lewin and Grabbe, 1945).

principle 1. Effective experiential learning will affect the learner's cognitive structures (action theories), attitudes and values, perceptions and behavioral patterns. To alter his action theories, modify his attitudes, and expand his repertoire of concrete skills, the learner must pay attention to his action theories, knowledge, attitudes, perceptions of self and social world, and behavioral patterns. To learn to be a more effective decision maker, for example, the learner must develop a concept of what decision making is (knowledge), an action theory concerning what decision making behaviors will lead to effective group decision making, positive attitudes toward new decision making procedures, perceptions that the new decision making actions are situationally appropriate and that one is capable of performing them, and the behavioral skills needed to perform the new decision making actions.

principle 2. A person will believe more in knowledge she has discovered herself than in knowledge she is presented with by others. Lewin was a great believer in experimental procedures whereby a person behaviorally validates or disproves a theory. He believed that such procedures needed to be introduced into the educational process so that students could test alternative behavioral patterns within controlled conditions. An approach to learning based on inquiry and discovery has been found to increase students' motivation to learn and their commitment to implement their conclusions in the future.

principle 3. Learning is more effective when it is an active rather than a passive process. When a learner can take a theory, concept, or practice and "try it on for size," he will understand it more completely, integrate it more effectively with past learnings, and retain it longer. There are many concepts (such as mathematical procedures) that are never really learned until one uses them.

principle 4. Acceptance of new action theories, attitudes, and behavioral patterns cannot be brought about by a piecemeal approach—one's whole cognitive-affective-behavioral system has to change. The three elements are interconnected, and change as a whole rather than as separate parts. Like any system, a cognitive-affective-behavioral system demands coherence, consistency, orderliness, and simplicity. Trying to change part of the system will not be effective. The need for consistency creates resistance to the item-by-item approach to new learning. Only when the whole system changes will the new learning be fully accepted and integrated.

principle 5. It takes more than information to change action theories, attitudes, and behavioral patterns. Telling people about the desirability of change does not mean that they will change. Providing a rationale for change is not sufficient to motivate people to change. Reading a book or listening to a lecture does not result in mastery and retention of the material, does not promote attitude change, and does not increase behavioral skills. Information does generate interest in learning more about the desired changes.

principle 6. It takes more than firsthand experience to generate valid knowledge. Lewin used to state that thousands of years of human experience with falling bodies did not bring humans to a correct theory of gravity. Besides experience there needs to be a theoretical system that the experience tests out, and reflection on the meaning of the experience.

principle 7. Behavior changes will be temporary unless the action theories and attitudes underlying them are changed. New behavioral skills may be practiced and mastered, but without changes in the person's action theories and attitudes the new behavior patterns will fade away.

principle 8. Changes in perceptions of oneself and one's social environment are necessary before changes in action theories, attitudes, and behavior patterns will take place. A learner must perceive herself as capable of doing the needed behaviors and must see the behaviors as being appropriate to the situation before she will engage in them. Lewin believed that behavior, action theories, and attitudes are all steered by perception. Your perceptions of yourself and your immediate situation affect how you behave, what you believe, and how you feel.

principle 9. The more supportive, accepting, and caring the social environment, the freer a person is to experiment with new behaviors, attitudes, and action theories. As the need to justify oneself and protect oneself against rejection decreases, it becomes easier to experiment with new ways of behaving, thinking, and valuing.

principle 10. In order for changes in behavior patterns, attitudes, and action theories to be permanent, both the person and the social environment have to change. The person's role definitions, the expectations of him held by colleagues and friends, and the general values of career and social settings all must change if the person is to maintain his changed behaviors, attitudes, and action theories. Team training is more effective than individual training because it changes both individuals and their social environment at the same time.

principle 11. It is easier to change a person's action theories, attitudes, and behavioral patterns in a group context than in an individual context. The discussion and consensual validation that takes place within a group provides a personal commitment and encouragement for change that is not present when only one person is being changed.

principle 12. A person accepts a new system of action theories, attitudes, and behavioral patterns when she accepts membership in a new group. New groups with new role definitions and expectations for appropriate behavior are helpful in educational efforts. A person becomes socialized by internalizing the normative culture of the groups to which she belongs. As the person gains membership in a new group, a new normative culture is accepted and internalized.

In experiential learning the responsibility for your learning lies with you, not with the teacher or the coordinator. In experiential learning situations you need to become active and aggressive in your learning role and give direction to the construction of your action theories. Experiential exercises are structured so that you can experiment with your behavior, try things out, see what works, build skills, and build action theories out of your own experiences. Appropriate theory is then presented so that you can summarize your learning and build conceptual frameworks within which you can organize what you know. Although experiential learning is a stimulating and involving activity, it is important to always remember that experience alone is not beneficial: you learn from the combination of experience and the conceptualization of your experiences.

Experiential learning procedures are especially useful when you want to learn new skills. In the next section we shall review how skills are learned.

LEARNING GROUP SKILLS

You are not born with group skills, nor do they magically appear when you need them. You have to learn them. Group skills are learned just as any other skill is learned. Learning how to lead a group is no different from learning how to play the piano or throw a football. All skills are learned the same way, according to the following steps:

1. *Understand why the skill is important and how it will be of value to you.* To want to learn a skill, you must see a need for it.

2. *Understand what the skill is and what are the component behaviors you have to engage in to perform the skill.* To learn a skill, you must have a clear idea of what the skill is and you must know how to perform it. Often it is helpful to observe someone who has already mastered the skill perform it several times while describing it step by step.

3. *Find situations in which you can practice the skill.* To master a skill, you have to practice it again and again. Try practicing the skill for a short time each day for several days until you are sure you have mastered it completely.

4. *Get someone to watch you and tell you how well you are performing the skill.* Getting feedback is necessary for correcting mistakes in learning a skill and for identifying problems you are having in mastering the skill. Through feedback you find out how much progress you are making in mastering the skill. Feedback lets you compare how well you are doing with how well you want to do.

5. *Keep practicing!* In the learning of most skills there is a period of slow learning, then a period of fast improvement, then a period in which performance remains about the same (a plateau), then another period of fast improvement, then another plateau, and so forth. Plateaus are quite common in skill learning; you just have to stick with them until the next period of rapid improvement begins.

6. *Load your practice toward success.* Set up practice units that you can easily master. It always helps to feel like a success as you practice a skill.

7. *Get friends to encourage you to use the skill.* Your friends can help you learn by giving you encouragement to do so. The more encouragement you receive, the easier it will be for you to practice the skill.

8. *Practice until it feels real.* The more you use a skill, the more natural it feels. While learning a skill you may feel self-conscious and awkward. Practicing a skill is like role playing—it does not feel like *real* behavior. But you should not let this awkwardness stop you from mastering the skill. Ever try learning to type by only typing when it feels natural? It is through role playing and drill that all skills are learned. If you keep practicing, the awkwardness will pass and soon you will become comfortable and *natural* in using the skill.

While you engage in skill-building exercises you may sometimes feel that the process is somewhat mechanical and unreal. But this is true of every kind of skill development. Learning how to play the piano, for example, also involves the mechanical practice of specific behaviors, which seem unreal compared with the performance of a beautiful piano concerto. It is when you apply your new skills to real situations that they will gain the fire and life that may sometimes be lacking when you practice.

This book is designed to provide you with information about the nature of and the need for the group skills discussed. The behaviors needed to engage in the skills are specified. Questions that test your comprehension and understanding of the material presented are included in most chapters. You are given instructions for participating in exercises that provide you with a chance to practice the skills and receive feedback on how well you are mastering them. It is up to you, after engaging in the exercises, to practice the skills until you feel comfortable performing them. At the end of most chapters you will be asked to evaluate the extent to which you have mastered the skills presented in the chapter.

In short, this book provides you with guidance for increasing your group skills. It is up to you to take advantage of the material and exercises presented and use them in ways that will increase your group skills. The extent of your learning and skill development rests entirely on your commitment to use this book in fruitful ways.

EXPERIENTIAL LEARNING AND MOTIVATION

What motivates you to learn concepts and skills? If someone offered you the opportunity either to earn a great deal of money or to experience a basic sense of accomplishment and satisfaction from learning a skill, which would you choose? Some educators seem to believe that students must be forced or persuaded into learning; others seem to believe that learning is fun and enjoyable in its own right. What do you believe? Experiential learning stresses the intrinsic sense of success of accomplishment in learning. Motivation is based upon what you see as desirable learning goals and the method you choose to accomplish them. The goal-directed aspect of motivation places an emphasis upon your feelings of success or failure in the learning situation. What leads to a psychological feeling of success in a learning situation? Kurt Lewin and his associates (1944) came up with four factors. They found evidence that you will experience psychological success (as opposed to psychological failure) if:

1. you are able to define your own goals.
2. the goals are related to your central needs and values.
3. you are able to define the paths that lead to the accomplishment of the goals.
4. the goals represent a realistic level of aspiration for you—neither too high nor too low, but high enough to test your capabilities.

Feelings of success will be promoted when you are encouraged to take as much responsibility for your own behavior as you can handle. You must believe that you are in control of (or at least have some influence over) your learning in order to feel psychological success. Experiential learning offers the opportunity for experiencing success by allowing you freedom to decide what aspects of your experience you wish to focus upon, what skills you wish to develop, and how you conceptualize the conclusions drawn from your experience. This is quite different from the traditional lecture approach to learning, in which you are a passive listener and the control of the material being presented is in the hands of the instructor. When an instructor decides what material will be presented and how it will be presented without letting learners have any influence over the decision, learners will experience psychological failure no matter how entertaining the presentation is.

Although the primary motivation for learning in experiential situations is psychological success, there are extrinsic factors that will encourage further learning. The approval and support of other learners is an example of extrinsic motivators that facilitate learning without interfering with intrinsic motivators, such as a sense of accomplishment. As you participate in the exercises in this book, your learning will accelerate if other participants give you approval and recognition for successful learning. You should consciously try to give approval to other readers who are seriously trying to increase their group skills. Few influences on our behavior are more powerful than the support and approval of a group of friends or acquaintances. Using such group influences to help individuals learn is one of the most constructive ways of assuring the development of group skills and knowledge.

ROLE PLAYING

In this and the following sections two important procedures for experiential learning are briefly discussed: role playing and observation of the dynamics of a group. *Role playing* is a tool for bringing a specific skill and its consequences into focus, and thus is vital for experiential learning. It is a way in which you can experience concretely the type of interaction under examination. An imaginary life situation is set up in which you act and react in terms of the assumptions you are asked to adopt, the beliefs they are asked to hold, and the character you are asked to play. Role playing is intended to give you experience in practicing skills and in discussing and identifying effective and ineffective behavior. The outcome of a role-playing situation is not determined in advance, and the situation is not rehearsed. Initial instructions are given, and the role players determine what happens. When participating in a role-playing exercise, remain yourself and act as you would in the situation described. You do not have to be a good actor or actress to play a role; you need only accept the initial assumptions, beliefs, background, or assigned behaviors and then let your feelings, attitudes, and behavior change as circumstances seem to require. The role-playing instructions describe the point of departure and the beginning frame of reference; you and the situation then take over.

What happens in group role playing may lead you to change behaviors and attitudes, and you may have emotional experiences that you did not expect when the role playing began. The more real the role playing and the more effective the exercise, the more emotional involvement you will feel and the more you will learn. That role playing can simulate real-life situations makes it possible for you to try new ways of handling situations without suffering any serious consequences if the methods fail.

In role playing, questions may be raised in discussion that are not covered by the instructions given in this book. When this happens, role players are free to make up facts or experiences that accord with the circumstances; they should avoid making up experiences or facts that do not fit the role. In participating in a role-playing exercise you should not consult or look at your role instructions after you have used them to start the action; you should be yourself. You should not act the way you feel a person described in the instructions should behave; you should act as naturally as possible merely by following the instructions.

The coordinator of the exercise should help involve the role players in the situation by introducing it in such a way that the players are emotionally stimulated. Using name tags and asking the players questions to help them get a feeling for the part are helpful. Introduce the scene to the role players and the observers. Always "de-role" after the role playing has ended.

PROCESS OBSERVATION

Within a group a distinction can be made between the *content* the group is discussing and the *process* by which the discussion is being conducted. Group process involves such things as leadership, decision making, communication, and controversy. Content is *what* is being discussed; process is *how* the group is functioning. To observe the group process is to observe how the group is functioning. A person highly skilled in process observation can both participate in group work and observe group process at the same time, thus becoming a *participant-observer*.

Observation procedures are aimed at describing and recording behavior as it occurs. From the behavior of group members an observer can make inferences about the group process—the way in which the group is functioning. Five steps are usually involved in observation, the first being to decide which aspects of a group process you wish to observe. The model of effective groups presented in Figure 1.1 covers the basic aspects of group process that you will be interested in observing. By the time you finish this book you will have a clear understanding of the aspects of group process that are important to observe.

The second step in observation is to find or construct an observation sheet that specifies observable and countable behaviors reflecting the aspect of group process to be studied. Numerous observation sheets are included in this book. The third step is to observe the group and count the number of members engaged in one of the specified behaviors. When there is more than one observer, you may be able to focus only on some of the group members. The fourth step is to look at the frequency with which group members are engaged in the specified behaviors and then infer how well the group is functioning in that aspect of the group process under observation. The final step is to summarize the observations in a manner that is clear and useful to the group members and then present the summary to the group as feedback. The group can then discuss the observations and revise the group process to make it more effective.

The purpose of process observation is to clarify and improve the ways in which the group is presently functioning through an objective assessment of its group process. Information about group process is collected and then openly discussed so that modifications in group procedures and members' behavior can be made in order to improve the group's effectiveness.

By the time you finish this book you will have developed skills in observing group process. At first the observation tasks specified in the exercises will seem difficult, but gradually you will find them easier and more helpful as your skills develop. As effective future behavior depends upon awareness of the nature and consequences of current behavior, there is no substitute for direct observation in skill development and in the facilitation of group effectiveness. Any effective group member must be aware of group process while participating in the group, and it is through observation practice that such skills are developed.

NATURE OF THIS BOOK AND HOW TO USE IT

This is not a book that you can read with detachment. It is written to involve you with its contents. By reading this book you will not only be able to learn the theoretical and empirical knowledge now available on group dynamics, but you will also learn to apply this knowledge in practical ways within the groups to which you belong. Often in the past, group dynamics practitioners did not pay attention to the research literature, and group dynamics researchers neglected to specify how their findings could be applied. Thus, the knowledge about effective groups and the learning of group skills was often divided. In this book we directly apply existing theory and research to the learning and application of effective group skills. As you participate in the exercises, use diagnostic procedures for assessing your current skill levels, and discuss the relevant theory and research provided, you will bridge the gap between theory and practice.

In selecting exercises to include in this book, we tried to include exercises that were original, short, relevant to the theory and research being discussed, clear and simple, and easy to prepare. We intended each exercise to be like a supporting actor; it should do its work effectively, unobtrusively, and without upstaging the theory and research being presented. Each exercise is also aimed at promoting the development of group skills. The book defines the skills needed for effective group functioning and provides opportunities for readers to practice the skills for themselves and to receive feedback on their performance.

The purpose of this book is to bring together the theory and research on group dynamics and structured exercises aimed at building practical group skills and illuminating the meaning of the theory and research presented. The central aim of each chapter is to review the most important theory and research, analyze basic issues in group dynamics, and provide structured skill-building exercises and other instructional aids. The format of each chapter is based on sound pedagogy and the principles of experiential learning. Most chapters begin with a discussion task involving the concepts presented in the chapter. At the beginning of most chapters is a short diagnostic instrument that will help you become more aware of your current behavior in the area discussed in the chapter. Also in most chapters is a controversy in which you and your classmates argue different sides of one of the central issues of the chapter. Exercises aimed at developing skills and understanding in the topic of the chapter are then provided. The relevant theory and research is presented. At the end of many of the chapters there is a procedure for examining the changes in your knowledge and skills.

In using this book you should diagnose your present knowledge and skills in the areas that are covered, actively participate in the exercises, reflect on your experiences, read the chapters carefully, and integrate the information and experiences into action theories related to group dynamics. You should then plan how to continue your skill- and knowledge-building activities after you have finished the book.

As you read this book you may wish to keep a personal diary in which you record what you are learning about yourself and how you behave in interpersonal and group situations. Such a diary will be of great interest after you have finished the book. You may also wish to include specific information you have learned about the social psychology of groups, effective behavior in groups, and the extent to which you have developed the group skills you want.

QUIZ

Now, check your understanding of the information presented in this chapter by answering the following questions. Answers are at the end of the chapter.

1. Name the six components included in the author's definition of a group:

   a. _____

   b. _____

   c. _____

   d. _____

   e. _____

   f. _____

2. The core activities of an effective group are:
   a. accomplishing goals.
   b. maintaining itself internally.
   c. developing and changing to improve.
   d. all of the above.

3. Group goals must:
   a. be clearly understood.
   b. be relevant to the needs of group members.
   c. highlight the positive interdependence among members.
   d. evoke from every member a high level of commitment.
   e. all of the above.

4. The basis of effective interactions among group members is:

   a. willingness to participate.
   b. two-way communication.
   c. a positive goal.
   d. group interdependence.

5. Group leadership should be:
   a. distributed among group members.
   b. delegated to one person.
   c. taken from the powerful and given to the weak.
   d. handled by the powerful.

6. If everyone participates equally in the group, members will be:
   a. satisfied with their membership.
   b. committed to implementing group decisions.
   c. frustrated by lack of leadership.
   d. a and b

7. Decision making procedures must be:
   a. by consensus.
   b. handled by the group leader.
   c. flexible to meet the needs of the situation.
   d. beat into reluctant participants.

8. In the consensus method of decision making:
   a. everyone must agree with the decision.
   b. equalization of power is promoted.
   c. productive controversy is promoted.
   d. all of the above

9. Power and influence in the group should be:
   a. based on authority.
   b. based on who's the strongest.
   c. based on expertise, ability, and information access.
   d. unequal within the group.

10. Conflicts among opposing ideas and opinions:
   a. should be encouraged.
   b. should be avoided.
   c. promotes involvement in the group's work.
   d. weakens the quality of the decision.
   e. a and c
   f. b and d

11. Group norms should encourage:
   a. psychological safety.
   b. individuality and creativeness.
   c. conflicts among ideas.
   d. growth and change.
   e. all of the above
   f. a and d only

12. If you are interpersonally effective:

    a. you always know what you should do in the group.
    b. the outcome of your behavior matches your intentions.
    c. you are elected the group leader.
    d. you are qualified to write this book.

13. The field of group dynamics developed in the:
    a. sixteenth century.
    b. nineteenth century.
    c. twentieth century.
    d. it has not developed yet.

14. In a classic study of the effects of democratic, autocratic, and laissez-faire leaders, Lewin, Lippitt, and White found that:
    a. important social issues could be studied experimentally.
    b. autocratic leadership is productive.
    c. scapegoating occurs with democratic leadership.
    d. laissez-faire leaders are out to lunch.

15. Kurt Lewin was noted for:
    a. championing the use of experimental methods of study.
    b. developing theory.
    c. insisting that theory and research be relevant to social practice.
    d. all of the above
    e. none of the above

16. Lewin was good at:
    a. being organized.
    b. formal lecturing.
    c. theoretical breakthroughs.
    d. all of the above

17. Lewin's research demonstrated that learning is most productive in:
    a. groups that interact and then reflect.
    b. groups that have a structured leader.
    c. individual interactions with materials.
    d. individually reading and answering these questions.

18. Learning is more effective when:
    a. it is discovered by the student.
    b. the process is active rather than passive.
    c. both the person and social environment change.
    d. it is done in the company of others.
    e. all of the above

19. Role playing is helpful because it gives you a chance to:
    a. practice new skills.
    b. identify effective and ineffective behaviors.
    c. act like someone else rather than like yourself.
    d. a and b

20. Process observation involves being concerned with:
    a. what the group is discussing.

b. how the group interacts.

c. what the group decision is.

d. all of the above

ARE GROUPS BENEFICIAL OR HARMFUL EXERCISE

This exercise consists of a structured controversy over the possible constructiveness or destructiveness of group membership. The objective of the exercise is to promote a thoughtful examination of the benefits and costs of being a member of a group, whether it is a learning, career, family, friendship, or leisure group. The procedure for the exercise is as follows:

1. The class forms groups of four.

2. Each group is ultimately to write a report summarizing its position on whether groups are constructive or destructive. The report is to contain the group's overall conclusion and the facts and rationale supporting its position. The supporting facts and rationale may be obtained from the accompanying briefing sheets, the entire book, and outside reading.

3. First, each group divides into two pairs. One pair is assigned the position that groups are beneficial and the other pair the position that groups are harmful. The coordinator gives each pair the appropriate briefing sheet, explains the procedure, and reviews the rules for constructive controversy listed below.

4. The pairs meet separately to prepare as forceful a presentation of their position as possible. They are to make sure that both members have contributed to building a persuasive case for their position and that it includes as many facts and research findings as possible. Both members need to master all the rationale supporting their position. About ten minutes should be allowed for this phase of the exercise.

5. The group of four meets. Each pair presents its position, being as forceful and persuasive as possible, while the other pair takes notes and asks for clarification of anything that is not fully understood. Each pair has about three minutes to present its position.

6. The group of four has an open discussion on whether groups are harmful or beneficial. Each side should present as many facts and research findings as it can to support its point of view. Members should listen critically to the opposing position, asking for facts that support any conclusions advanced by the opposing pair. All the facts supporting each side should be brought out and discussed. The rules for constructive controversy appearing at the end of the exercise should be followed. About ten minutes should be allowed for this phase.

7. The perspectives in each group are now reversed, each pair arguing the opposing pair's position. Members should be as forceful and persuasive as they can in arguing for the opposing pair's position. They should elaborate on the opposing position, seeing if they can think of any new arguments or facts that the opposing pair did not present. Each pair has about three minutes for its presentation.

8. Each group of four should come to a group position that all members can agree on. The members should summarize the best arguments for each point of view, detailing what they know about the benefits and costs of group membership. When they have consensus in their group they should organize their arguments for presenta-

tion to the rest of the class. Since other groups will have other conclusions, each group may need to explain the validity of its position to the class. About ten minutes should be allowed for this phase.

9. The coordinator samples the decisions made by the groups of four by having several of them report briefly (not more than two minutes) to the class. The class then discusses similarities and differences.
10. The coordinator summarizes what participants have learned about the benefits and costs of group membership.

Rules for Constructive Controversy

1. I am critical of ideas, not individuals. I challenge and refute the ideas of the opposing pair, but I do *not* indicate that I personally reject the members of the pair.
2. I focus on coming to the best decision possible, not on "winning." I remember that we are all in this together.
3. I encourage everyone to participate and to master all the relevant information.
4. I listen to everyone's ideas, even if I don't agree.
5. I paraphrase or restate what someone has said if it is not clear to me.
6. I first bring out *all* the ideas and facts supporting both sides, and then I try to put them together in a way that makes sense.
7. I try to understand both sides of the issue.
8. I change my mind when the evidence indicates that I should do so.

Briefing Sheet: Groups Are Good for Humans

Groups are good for humans. The following overview of important research in social psychology clearly supports this point of view.

1. Under most conditions, the productivity of groups is higher than the productivity of individuals working alone.
2. Groups make more effective decisions and solve problems more effectively than individuals working alone.
3. It is through group membership that the values of altruism, kindness, consideration for others, responsibility, and so forth, are socialized in us.
4. The quality of emotional life in terms of friendship, love, camaraderie, excitement, joy, fulfillment, and achievement is greater for members of groups than for individuals functioning alone.
5. The quality of everyday life is greater in groups due to the advantages of specialization and division of labor. Our material standard of living, for example—our housing, food, clothing, transportation, entertainment, and so forth—would not be possible for a person living outside of a society.
6. Conflicts are managed more productively in groups. Social influence is better managed in groups. Without group standards, social values, and laws, civilization would be impossible.
7. A person's identity, self-esteem, and social competencies are shaped by the groups of significance to him or her.

8. Without cooperation, social organization, and groups of various kinds, humans would not survive. Humans have a basic social nature, and our survival and evolution are the results of the effectiveness of our groups.

Briefing Sheet: Groups Are Not *Good for Humans*

Groups are *not* good for humans. The following overview of important social-psychological research clearly supports this point of view.

1. People in groups are more likely to take greater risks than they would alone. Groups tend to take more extreme positions and indulge in more extreme behavior than their members would alone.
2. In groups there is sometimes a diffusion of responsibility such that members take less responsibility for providing assistance to someone in need or for rewarding good service.
3. In large groups individuals can become anonymous and therefore feel freer to engage in rowdy, shocking, and illegal behavior. When one member engages in impulsive and antisocial behavior, others may do likewise. Riots are often initiated and worsened by such modeling effects.
4. Being identified as part of a group may increase the tendency of nonmembers to treat one in impersonal and inhumane ways. It is easier, for example, to drop a bomb on the "enemy" than on a person.
5. Group contagion often gives rise to collective panic.
6. Millions of persons have been swept into mass political movements only to become unhappy victims of their distorted visions of the leaders.
7. Groups often influence their members to conform. One type of conformity, obedience to authority, can cause a person to act in cruel and inhumane ways to others. The identity of the individual can be threatened when conformity is too extreme.

LEARNING CONTRACT

Before beginning the next chapter, we would like to propose a learning contract. The contract is as follows:

I understand that I will be taking an experiential approach to learning about the social psychology of groups and to developing the skills needed to function effectively in groups. I willingly commit myself to the statements hereunder:

1. I will use the structured experiences in this book to learn from. This means I am willing to engage in specified behaviors, seek out feedback about the impact of my behavior on others, and analyze my interpersonal interactions with other class members in order to make the most of my learning.
2. I will make the most of my own learning by (a) engaging in specified behaviors and in being open about my feelings and reactions to what is taking place in order that others may have information to react to in giving me feedback and in building conclusions about the area of study, (b) setting personal learning goals that I will work actively to accomplish—which means that I will take responsibility for my own learning and not wait around for someone

else to "make me grow," (c) being willing to experiment with new behavior and to practice new skills, (d) seeking out and being receptive to feedback, and (e) building conclusions about the experiences highlighted in the exercises.

3. I will help others make the most of their learning by: (a) providing feedback in constructive ways, (b) helping to build the conditions (such as openness, trust, acceptance, and support) under which others can experiment and take risks with their behavior, and (c) contributing to the formulation of conclusions about the experiences highlighted in the exercises.

4. I will use professional judgment in keeping what happens among group members in the exercises appropriately confidential.

Signed: _____

YOUR SKILL LEVEL

Before going on, it will be useful for you to assess your current group skill level. Answer the following questions, describing yourself as accurately as you can:

1. How do you see yourself as a group member? What is your style of functioning within groups?

2. What are your strengths in functioning in groups? How do they fit into how you see yourself as a group member?

3. What situations within groups do you have trouble with and why? How do you feel when faced with them? How do you handle them? How would you like to handle them?

4. In what group skills do you wish to grow and develop? What changes would you like to make in your present group behavior? What new strengths in group behavior would you care to develop? What new group skills would you like to acquire?

You now have a basic understanding of what makes a group and what group dynamics is. You are prepared for the experiential kind of learning expected of you and know when a group is beneficial or harmful. In the next chapter you will learn how to define and develop leadership skills needed in a group.

ANSWERS

Page 27—1. two or more people, face-to-face interaction, aware of his or her membership, aware of others' membership, aware of positive interdependence, and mutual goals;

2. d; 3. e; 4. b; 5. a; 6. d; 7. c; 8. d; 9. c; 10. e; 11. e; 12. b; 13. c; 14. a; 15. d; 16. c; 17. a; 18. e; 19. d; 20. b.

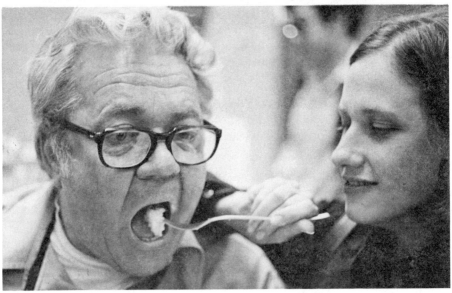

2

Leadership

BASIC CONCEPTS TO BE COVERED IN THIS CHAPTER

In this chapter a number of concepts are defined and discussed. The major ones are listed below. The procedure for learning these concepts is as follows:

1. The class forms groups of four. These groups should be as heterogeneous as possible.
2. Each group divides into two pairs.
3. The task for each pair is to:
   a. define each concept, noting the page on which it is defined and discussed.
   b. make sure that both members of the pair understand the meaning of each concept.
4. In each group, members compare the answers of the two pairs. If there is disagreement, the members look up the concept in the chapter and clarify it until they all agree on the definition and understand it.

Concepts

1. trait approach to leadership
2. charismatic leadership
3. Machiavellian leadership
4. leadership-styles
5. initiating structure
6. influence approach to leadership
7. position approach to leadership
8. distributed-actions definition of leadership
9. task behavior
10. relationship behavior
11. member maturity
12. telling
13. selling
14. participating
15. delegating

WHAT IS LEADERSHIP?

What is a leader? What is leadership? Are leaders born, or are they made? Does effective leadership originate in a person or in a set of actions and behaviors? The concepts *leader* and *leadership* have been defined in more different ways than almost any other concept associated with group structure. Curiosity about leaders is not contained to social scientists. A preoccupation with leadership occurs throughout countries with an Anglo-Saxon heritage. The *Oxford English Dictionary* notes the appearance of the word *leader* in the English language as early as 1300. The word *leadership,* however, did not appear until about 1800. When one reads the historical as well as the current literature on leaders and leadership it seems as if there are as many different definitions as there are persons who have attempted to define the concepts. Perhaps an example will help clarify who a leader and what leadership is.

Before Benjamin Franklin reached thirty years of age he had been chosen public printer for the colony of Pennsylvania, had founded the famous and influential Junto Club, and created and published *Poor Richard's Almanac* (the most widely read publication in America), had founded the first circulating library, and had been elected grand master of the Freemasons Lodge of Pennsylvania. The next year he inaugurated the first fire-fighting company in Pennsylvania and was chosen clerk of the Pennsylvania Assembly. He was one of the most successful businessmen in the colonies, but had enough interest in scholarship and research to be the founder (at age thirty-seven) of the American Philosophical Society. He continued to serve in a variety of leadership posts in politics, the army, science, diplomacy, and education (founding the academy that became the University of Pennsylvania). At eighty he led the group enterprise of writing the Constitution of the United States. A biographer noted, "Nobody could approach him without being charmed by his conversation, humor, wisdom, and kindness" (Fay, 1929).

How would you explain Benjamin Franklin's success as a leader? Was it due to his (pick only one):

1. inborn, genetic traits?
2. style of leadership?
3. abilty to influence others?
4. occupation of positions of authority?
5. ability to provide helpful behaviors in diverse situations?

In selecting one of these alternatives, you have decided on a theory of leadership. In this chapter we shall review each of these theories.

THE NATURE OF LEADERSHIP EXERCISE

There has been considerable controversy as to the nature of leadership. The purpose of this exercise is to structure a critical discussion of the different views of leadership.

The procedure is as follows:

1. The class forms groups of four.
2. Each group is ultimately to write a report summarizing its position on the nature of leadership. The report is to contain the group's overall conclusions and the facts and rationale supporting its position. The supporting facts and rationale may be obtained from the accompanying briefing sheets, the entire book, and outside reading.
3. The sequence of the exercise contains two controversies:
   a. Are leaders pawns of history or are they origins (creators and controllers) of history?
   b. Are leaders born or made?
   For each controversy two briefing sheets are given, one representing one side of the argument and one the other.
4. Each group divides into pairs. One pair is assigned the position that leaders are pawns of history and the other pair the position that leaders are the origins of history. The coordinator gives each pair the appropriate briefing sheet, explains the procedure, and reviews the rules for constructive controversy (p. 31).
5. The pairs meet separately to prepare as forceful a three-minute presentation of their position as possible. They are to make sure that both members have contributed to building a persuasive case for their position and that it includes as many facts and research findings as possible. Both members need to master all the rationale supporting their position. About ten minutes should be allowed for this phase of the exercise.
6. The group of four meets. Each pair presents its position, being as forceful and persuasive as possible, while the other pair takes notes and asks for clarification of anything that is not fully understood. Each pair has about three minutes to present its position.
7. The group of four has an open discussion on whether leaders are pawns or origins. Each side should present as many facts and research findings as it can to support its point of view. Members should listen critically to the opposing position, asking for facts to support any conclusions made by the opposing pair. Participants should ensure that all the facts supporting both sides are brought out and discussed. The rules for constructive controversy should be followed. About ten minutes should be allowed for this phase.
8. The perspectives in each group are now reversed, each pair arguing the opposing pair's position. Members should be as forceful and persuasive as they can in arguing for the opposing pair's position. They should elaborate on the opposing position, seeing if they can think of any new arguments or facts that the opposing pair did not present. Each pair has about three minutes for its presentation.
9. Each group of four should come to a group position that all members can agree on. The members should summarize the best arguments from each position. Detailing as many facts as they can on whether leaders are pawns or origins. When they have consensus in their group they should organize their arguments for presentation to the rest of the class. Since other groups will have other conclusions, each group may need to explain the validity of its position to the class. About ten minutes should be allowed for this phase.

10. The coordinator samples the decisions made by the groups of four by having several of them present their position to the class. The class then discusses similarities and differences, and the coordinator summarizes what participants have learned about leadership.

11. Steps 1–10 are repeated for the issue of whether leaders are born or made.

12. The coordinator summarizes what the participants have learned from the two controversies.

Briefing Sheet: Leaders Control Fortune

Your position is that leaders basically control fortune and that it really matters who is elected president of the United States or president of General Motors, as they determine the future. To support your position, use the following quotations from *The Prince* by Machiavelli and any material from this chapter that is applicable.

> . . . one who adapts his policy to the times prospers, and likewise . . . one whose policy clashes with the demands of the times does not.

> It can be observed that men use various methods in pursuing their own personal objectives, such as glory and riches. One man proceeds with circumspection, another impetuously; one uses violence, another strategem; one man goes about things patiently, another does the opposite; and yet everyone for all this diversity of method, can reach his objective.

> It can also be observed that with two circumspect men, one will achieve his end, the other not; and likewise two men succeed equally well with different methods, one of them being circumspect and the other impetuous. This results from nothing else except the extent to which their methods are or are not suited to the nature of the times.

> . . . if a man behaves with patience and circumspection and the time and circumstances are such that this method is called for, he will prosper; but if the time and circumstances change he will be ruined because he does not change his policy.

> Thus a man who is circumspect, when circumstances demand impetuous behavior, is unequal to the task, and so he comes to grief. If he changed his character according to the time and circumstances, then his fortune [i.e., prosperity] would change.

Briefing Sheet: Leaders Are Pawns of Fortune

Your position is that leaders are basically pawns of fortune and that it does not really matter who is president of the United States or president of General Motors, because the future turns out the same regardless of who is in charge. To support your position, use the following quotations from *War and Peace* by Leo Tolstoy and any material from the chapter that seems applicable.

Man lives consciously for himself, but is an unconscious instrument in the attainment of the historic, universal, aims of humanity. . . . The higher a man stands on the social ladder, the more people he is connected with and the more power he has over others, the more evident is the predestination and inevitability of his every action.

A king is history's slave.

History . . . uses every moment of the life of kings as a tool for its own purposes.

Briefing Sheet: Leaders Are Born, Not Made

Your position is that leaders are basically born, not made. To support your position, use the information given below, any material from this chapter or the rest of the book that seems applicable, and any information from your outside reading that is appropriate.

Throughout history there has been a continuing popular belief that leaders possess unique, inborn traits. Aristotle, for example, once remarked, "From the moment of their birth, some are marked for subjugation and others for command." There are individuals who seem to dominate others through the force of their personality and what they stand for. Some individuals seem to rise to leadership in a range of settings. Woods (1913) studied fourteen nations over periods of five to ten centuries. The conditions of each reign were found to reflect the ruler's capabilities. The brothers of the more successful kings, furthermore, were found to be men of power and influence in their time. Woods concluded that the person makes the nation and shapes it in accordance with his or her abilities. Wiggam (1931) concluded that the survival of the fittest and marriage among them produce an aristocratic class that differs biologically from the lower classes. Thus, an adequate supply of superior leaders depends on a proportionately high birth rate among the abler classes. The best predictor of leadership ability, therefore, may be family background.

Briefing Sheet: Leaders Are Made, Not Born

Your position is that leaders are basically made, not born. To support your position, use the information given below, any material from this chapter or the rest of the book that seems applicable, and any information from your outside reading that is relevant.

Leadership competencies and skills are learned, and anyone with certain minimal requirements can acquire them. A number of studies have demonstrated that schoolchildren are more successful and effective leaders after receiving training in leadership skills (Cassel and Shafer, 1961; Eichler and Merrill, 1931; Zeleny, 1940). It is not uncommon for individuals to practice and master the skills of leadership needed by the groups to which they belong. Schneider (1937) found that the number of great military leaders in England was proportional to the number of conflicts in which the nation engaged. Since leadership skills can be taught and individuals can become more successful leaders through training, and since individuals may deliberately develop the leadership competencies needed by the groups to which they belong, it may be concluded that leaders are made, not born.

OUR IDEAL LEADERS EXERCISE

The purpose of this exercise is to identify the traits possessed by ideal leaders in our society. The procedure for the exercise is as follows.

1. The class forms heterogeneous groups of four.
2. Each group is to:
   a. read the assignment sheet that appears below.
   b. pick at least five great leaders who have lived in the last fifty years.
   c. list the qualities of each that made him or her great.
   d. decide by consensus the ten most important traits of a great leader.
3. Each group reads its list to the class. Note differences and similarities.
4. Compare the qualities identified by the groups with the material in this chapter.

Ideal Leaders Assignment Sheet

Every society identifies traits characteristic of its ideal leaders. The ancient Egyptians, for example, attributed three qualities of divinity to their king (Frankfort, Frankfort, Wilson, and Jacobsen, 1949): "Authoritative utterance is in thy mouth, perception is in thy heart, and thy tongue is the shrine of justice." An analysis of leaders in Homer's *Iliad* resulted in four sets of ideal leadership qualities admired by ancient Greeks (Sarachek, 1968): (1) justice and judgment (Agamemnon), (2) wisdom and counsel (Nestor), (3) shrewdness and cunning (Odysseus), and (4) valor and action (Achilles). What are the qualities we most admire in our outstanding leaders?

TRAIT THEORIES OF LEADERSHIP

Throughout history many people have believed that leaders are born, not made, and that great leaders are discovered, not developed. Especially in times of great social upheaval and trouble many people have looked for a great leader who has unique, inborn traits. This is the "great-man" or "great-woman" theory of leadership. Royalty, members of elite social classes, older siblings, and early maturing children and adolescents are likely to believe in this approach to leadership. They would state that Benjamin Franklin was one of the greatest leaders of the eighteenth century because he was genetically superior to his contemporaries. One of the strongest advocates of this theory of leadership was Aristotle, who once stated, "From the moment of their birth, some are marked for subjugation and others for command." There do seem to be individuals who dominate others through the force of their personality, their charisma, what they stand for, or their ability to manipulate others. And there have been historical periods when the prevailing ideology was that leaders are superior to other human beings.

In the early twentieth century there were many strong advocates of the

40

trait theories of leadership. Wiggam (1931), for example, concluded that the survival of the fittest and marriage among them produce an aristocratic class that differs biologically from the lower classes. Advocating the social Darwinism that was popular at that time, Wiggam took the position that an adequate supply of superior leaders depended on a proportionately high birth rate among the abler classes.

Hundreds of research studies have been conducted to identify the personal attributes of leaders. In one of the more interesting ones Frederick Adams Wood (1913), an early-twentieth-century American historian, examined 386 rulers in fourteen countries in western Europe who lived between A.D. 1000 and the French Revolution. All of these rulers had absolute power over their kingdom. Each was classified as strong, weak, or mediocre on the basis of knowledge about his or her intellectual and personal characteristics (which were presumably independent of the strength or weakness of the nation at that time). The condition of each country was also classified—as prosperous, declining, or lacking a clear indication of either. (This classification was based on the country's economic and political status, not on its artistic, educational, and scientific development.) Wood found a relationship between the monarchs' personalities and the state of their countries. He summarized his results as follows: "Strong, mediocre, and weak monarchs are associated with strong, mediocre, and weak periods respectively" (p. 246). Although the correlation coefficient was reasonably strong (between +.60 and +.70), as with any correlation we cannot infer a direct relationship between cause and effect. However, Wood clearly favored the interpretation that strong leaders cause their countries to flourish.

The typical research studies on trait theories have compared the characteristics of a leader (defined as an individual holding a position of authority, such as the president of the United States) with the characteristics of a follower (defined as an individual *not* holding a position of authority, such as a low-level government employee). The findings of these studies are somewhat contradictory and inconclusive. Mann (1959) reviewed 125 studies of leadership and personality characteristics representing over 700 findings (see Table 2.1). He concluded that intelligence and personal adjustment seem to be correlated with leadership.

There may be leaders who are more intelligent than nonleaders, yet it is evident that many of the most intelligent people never obtain positions of leadership. Intelligence may have been a prerequisite for Benjamin Franklin's type of leadership, but it is doubtful whether Franklin or John Adams or George Washington possessed the highest IQ of his period (Cox, 1926). A follow-up study of one thousand highly intelligent children from California showed that in twenty-five years relatively few of them had reached the roster of famous leaders (Terman and Odor, 1947). None had attained high political office or the presidency of a corporation or college. Only 5 percent were in *Who's Who* and only 13 percent were in *American Men of Science*. And despite the findings that leaders are better adjusted psychologically than nonleaders, many leaders (such as Adolf Hilter) showed signs of being emotionally disturbed.

TABLE 2.1 Percentage of significant relationships reported in a positive or negative direction for 125 studies, representing 751 findings on the relationship of various personality characteristics and leadership. (After Mann, 1959)

Personality Factors and Number of Studies of Each	Number of Findings	Percent Yielding Sig. Positive Relationship	Percent Yielding Sig. Negative Relationship	Percent Yielding Neither
Intelligence— 28	(196)	46% (91)	1%° (1)	53% (104)
Adjustment— 22	(164)	30% (50)	2%° (2)	68% (112)
Extroversion— 22	(119)	31% (37)	5% (6)	64% (76)
Dominance— 12	(39)	38% (15)	15% (6)	46% (18)
Masculinity— 9	(70)	16% (11)	1%° (1)	83% (58)
Conservatism— 17	(62)	5% (3)	27% (17)	68% (42)
Sensitivity— 15	(101)	15% (15)	1%° (1)	84% (85)

° Rounded upward.

Source: Mann, R., "A Review of the Relationship between Personality and Performance in Small Groups." *Psychological Bulletin*, 1959, *56*, 241–270. Reprinted by permission.

Stimulated by the personnel-testing and selection programs began during the First World War, social scientists attempted to identify the distinguishing traits of leaders. On these tests leaders were found to score higher than followers on a wide variety of characteristics, including intelligence and aptitude, personality, task motivation and performance, and social competence (Stogdill, 1974). Despite the great ingenuity displayed in the development of tests to measure these characteristics, however, such instruments have not proved reliably useful in the selection of leaders.

Although the correlations between individual traits and leadership measures are not large, some conclusions may be made. Stogdill (1974) divided the research on this subject into two periods: studies conducted between 1904 and 1947 and studies conducted between 1948 and 1970. The former body of research, he noted, revealed that leaders who participated actively in organizing cooperative tasks and carrying them through to completion were characterized by intelligence, alertness to the needs and motives of others, insight into situations, and such habits as responsibility, initiative, persistence, and self-confidence. The trait studies conducted between 1948 and 1970 indicated that leaders who have the capacity for organizing and expediting cooperative effort are characterized by a strong drive for responsibility and task completion, vigor and persistence in pursuit of goals, venturesomeness and originality in problem solving, a drive to exercise initiative in social situations, self-confidence and a sense of personal identity, willingness to accept the consequences of decisions and actions, readiness to absorb interpersonal stress, readiness to tolerate frustration and delay, ability to influence the behavior of others, and the capacity to structure social systems according to the purpose at hand.

These characteristics seem to differentiate (1) leaders from nonleaders, (2) effective from ineffective leaders, and (3) higher-echelon from lower-echelon leaders. Stogdill (1974) added, however, that when these characteristics are considered singly they hold little diagnostic or predictive significance. In combination they appear to be advantageous to the person seeking the responsibilities of leadership. Stogdill also noted that whether any one person with these characteristics rises to a leadership position depends considerably on chance: one must not only have the traits but also be in the right place at the right time. Perhaps the safest conclusion to draw from the trait and personality studies of leadership is that individuals who have the energy, drive, self-confidence, and determination to succeed will become leaders, because they work hard to get leadership positions.

The best predictor of leadership success is prior success in leadership roles (Stogdill, 1974). But a previously successful leader may fail when placed in a situation that imposes demands incompatible with his or her personality or stabilized pattern of interaction and performance. Leader characteristics and situational demands seem to interact to determine the extent to which a given leader will prove successful in a group.

Besides the extensive research trying to differentiate leaders from non-leaders on the basis of personal attributes, there has been considerable discussion and research on two major traits of some leaders: charisma and Machiavellianism. Let's take a brief look at these traits.

Charismatic Leaders

One of the dictionary definitions of *charisma* is "an extraordinary power, as of working miracles." Sometimes charismatic leaders seem to inspire their followers to love and be passionately devoted to them. Other times charismatic leaders offer their followers the promise and hope of deliverance from distress. Charismatic leaders are saviors who say in essence, "I will make you safe," "I will give you identity," or "I will give your life significance and meaning."

Charisma does not seem to be correlated with any one personality type. The personalities of Alexander, Julius Caesar, George Washington, Robespierre, Bolivar, Sun Yat-sen, and Gandhi were widely different, yet all of these individuals were all able to inspire confidence in their followers and to demand from them the sacrifice even of life itself. Garibaldi won the loyalty of his Roman soldiers with an unusual appeal: "What I have to offer you is fatigue, danger, struggle, and death; the chill of the cold night in the fall air, and heat under the burning sun; no lodgings, no provisions, but forced marches, dangerous watchposts, and the continual struggle with the bayonet against batteries—those who love freedom and their country may follow me!" Winston Churchill offered "blood, sweat, and tears," but sustained the faith and courage of millions.

Attempts to define charisma specifically and to measure the degree of charisma possessed by various leaders have failed. In general, however, to be charismatic a leader must have (1) an extraordinary power or vision and be able to communicate it to others, or (2) unusual powers of practical leadership that will enable her to achieve the goals that will alleviate followers' distress. The charismatic leader must have a sense of mission, a belief in the social-change movement she leads, and confidence in herself as the chosen instrument to lead the movement to its destination. She must appear extremely self-confident in order to inspire others with the faith that the movement she leads will, without fail, prevail and ultimately reduce their distress.

Machiavellianism

Current theories of leadership ignore not only the irrational aspects of leadership and followership reflected in charisma but also the realities of how power is often handled. If charismatic leaders found social movements and bring them to power, it is the Machiavellian leaders who consolidate and wield the power the charismatic leaders obtain. The essence of Machiavellian leadership is believing (1) that people are basically weak, fallible, and gullible, and not particularly trustworthy; (2) that others are impersonal objects; and (3) that one should manipulate others whenever it is necessary in order to achieve one's ends.

Niccolò Machiavelli (1469–1527) was a Florentine statesman whose treatise *The Prince* advocated the use of craft, duplicity, and cunning by rulers as political principles for increasing their power and success. He did not originate such as an approach. Throughout history there have been theorists who conceived of leadership essentially in terms of the possession and exercise of power for self-enhancement. After analyzing the historical literature on how political leaders should govern, Richard Christie (Christie and Geis, 1970) concluded that Machiavellian leaders who manipulate their followers for political and personal reasons have four characteristics. First, they have little emotional involvement in their interpersonal relationships, as it is easier to manipulate others if they are viewed as objects rather than as fellow humans. Second, since they take a utilitarian rather than a moral view of their interactions with others, they are not concerned with conventional morality. Third, since successful manipulation of followers depends on an accurate perception of their needs and of "reality" in general, they will not be grossly psychopathological. Finally, since the essence of successful manipulation is a focus on getting things done rather than achieving long-term ideological goals, Machiavellian leaders will have a low degree of ideological commitment.

INTERPERSONAL PATTERNS EXERCISE

This exercise focuses on your interaction with other members of your group. It may help you think about how you conduct yourself in a group. The procedure for the exercise is as follows:

1. The class divides into groups of three. Each person fills out the adjective checklist below.
2. Analyze the meaning of the adjectives you checked by following the instructions below the checklist.
3. Share with the other two members of your triad the results of the exercise, and ask for their comments on whether they perceive you in the same way or differently.

The twenty verbs listed below describe some of the ways people feel and act from time to time. Think of your behavior in groups. How do you feel and act in groups? Check the five verbs that best describe your behavior in groups as you see it.

____ acquiesce	____ disapprove
____ advise	____ evade
____ agree	____ initiate
____ analyze	____ judge
____ assist	____ lead
____ concede	____ oblige
____ concur	____ relinquish
____ coordinate	____ resist
____ criticize	____ retreat
____ direct	____ withdraw

There are two underlying patterns of interpersonal behavior represented in the list of objectives: *dominance* (authority or control) and *sociability* (intimacy or friendliness). Most individuals tend either to like to control things (high dominance) or to let others control things (low dominance). Similarly, most persons tend either to be warm and personal (high sociability) or to be somewhat cold and impersonal (low sociability). In the following diagram, circle the five verbs you used to describe yourself in group activities. The set of ten verbs—horizontal for the dominance dimension and vertical for the sociability dimension—in which three or more are circled represents your tendency in that pattern of interpersonal behavior.

	HIGH DOMINANCE	LOW DOMINANCE
HIGH SOCIABILITY	advises coordinates directs initiates leads	acquiesces agrees assists complies obliges
LOW SOCIABILITY	analyzes criticizes disapproves judges resists	concedes evades relinquishes retreats withdraws

LEADERSHIP STYLES

Perhaps Benjamin Franklin became a leader through his style of relating to others. Franklin was noted for his charm, conversational skills, humor, wisdom, and kindness. But was Franklin's leadership style the same as George Washington's or Thomas Jefferson's? Even casual observation of leaders in action reveals marked differences in their styles of leadership. Some leaders seem autocratic: they dictate orders and determine all policy without involving group members in decision making. Some leaders seem democratic: they set policies through group discussion and decision, encouraging and helping group members to interact, requesting the cooperation of others, and being considerate of members' feelings and needs. Finally, some leaders take a laissez-faire approach: they do not participate in their groups decision making at all. It seems obvious that such differences in leadership style should affect group productivity and the attitudes of group members.

        The pioneering study of whether leadership styles do in fact make a difference in group functioning was conducted by Lewin, Lippitt, and White (1939). Although the study has many shortcomings, it demonstrated strikingly that the same group of individuals will behave in markedly different ways under leaders who behave differently. As we have seen in Chapter 1, groups of ten- and eleven-year-olds were run by three adult leaders who adopted each of three leadership styles for a specified period: autocratic, democratic, or laissez-faire. When the groups were under an autocratic leader, they were more dependent on the leader and more egocentric in their peer relationships. When rotated to a democratic style of leadership, the same children evidenced more initiative, friendliness, and responsibility, and continued to work even when the leader was out of the room. Their interest in their work and in the quality of their product was higher. Aggressive acts were more frequent under autocratic and laissez-faire leaders than they were under a democratic leader. Hostility was thirty times as great in the autocratic as in the democratic groups. There was more scapegoating in the autocratic groups than in either of the other two: frequently one group member was made the target of hostility and aggression until he left the group, and then another member would be chosen to perform the same function. Nineteen of twenty members liked the democratic leader better than the autocrat, and seven of ten liked the laissez-faire leader better than the autocrat.

Since this classic study a number of researchers have investigated the relative impact of democratic and autocratic leaders on group functioning. In reviewing these studies Stogdill (1974) noted that neither democratic nor autocratic leadership can be advocated as a method for increasing productivity, but that member satisfaction is associated with a democratic style of leadership. Satisfaction with democratic leadership tends to be highest in small, interaction-oriented groups. Members are more satisfied with autocratic leadership in large, task-oriented groups. Other studies have compared permissive, follower-oriented, participative, and considerate leadership styles with restrictive, task-oriented, directive, socially distant, and structured leadership styles. After reviewing the studies in each of these areas Stogdill (1974) made the following conclusions:

1. Person-oriented styles of leadership are not consistently related to productivity.
2. Among the work-oriented leadership styles, socially distant, directive, and structured leader behaviors that tend to maintain role differentiation and let members know what to expect are consistently related to group productivity.
3. Among the person-oriented leadership styles, only those providing for member participation in decision making and showing concern for members' welfare and comfort are consistently related to group cohesiveness.
4. Among the work-oriented leadership styles, only the structuring of member expectations is uniformly related to group cohesiveness.
5. All of the person-oriented leadership styles tend to be related to member satisfaction.
6. Only the structuring of member expectations is related positively to member satisfaction among the work-oriented leadership styles.

Initiating structure by clearly defining one's role as a leader and what one expects from the other members of the group is the single style of leadership that contributes positively to group productivity, cohesiveness, and satisfaction. The most effective leaders may be those who show concern for the well-being and contributions of group members and at the same time structure members' role responsibilities.

The Lewin, Lippitt, and White (1939) study, along with research conducted by Lewin and his colleagues, helped inspire and initiate the training programs in applied group dynamics conducted for the past thirty years at Bethel, Maine, by the National Training Laboratories Institute of Applied Behavioral Science. Immediately after the Second World War a group of adult educators and Kurt Lewin and his associates began conducting workshops aimed at developing the leadership competencies of participants. These workshops formed the basis for the explosion of small-group methods for personal and organizational change that took place during the 1960s and the growth in the number of consultants concerned with improving the development and planned change of organizations.

The major shortcoming of the leadership-style approach is that different styles are effective under different conditions. Certain conditions exist, for example, under which autocratic leadership seems most effective (such as when an urgent decision has to be made). In other conditions a democratic style may be most effective (such as when considerable member commitment to the implementation of the decision needs to be built). There are even conditions in which the laissez-faire style seems best (such as when the group is committed to a decision, has the resources to implement it, and needs a minimum of interference to work effectively). Because different leadership styles seem to be required in different situations, even with the same group, the attention of many social psychologists has moved to situational approaches to leadership. But before considering such approaches, let's turn briefly to two other theories of leadership.

THE INFLUENCE THEORY OF LEADERSHIP

Benjamin Franklin may have been an outstanding leader because he knew how to influence people. A *leader* may be defined as a group member who exerts more influence on other members than they exert on him. A number of studies have examined the factors affecting the amount of influence a leader has on the attitudes and behaviors of groupmates. Michener and Burt (1975), for example, found that the compliance of members is greater when a leader justifies his demands as being good for the group, has the power to punish members who do not do as he has asked, and has a legitimate right to make demands of subordinates. The success or failure of the group does not seem to affect a leader's ability to influence, nor does approval of him by subordinates.

An influence approach to leadership implies that there is a reciprocal role relationship between leaders and followers in which an exchange, or transaction, takes place. Without followers there can be no leader, and without a leader there can be no followers. The leader and the followers both give something to and receive something from each other. As Homans stated, "Influence over others is purchased at the price of allowing oneself to be influenced by others" (1961, p. 286). While leadership may be defined as the successful influencing of other group members, the followers also influence the leader. The leader receives status, recognition, esteem, and other reinforcement for contributing her resources to the accomplishment of the group's goals. The followers obtain the leader's resources and ability to structure the group's activities toward the attainment of a goal. The leader provides structure, direction, and resources. The followers provide deference and reinforcement. Since both the leader and the followers control resources that the other desires, they can each influence the other's behavior.

The interdependence of leader and followers has been demonstrated by a number of studies. Research indicates, for example, that leaders tend both to talk more than other group members and to receive more communications than do other group members (Zander, 1979). When a person is reinforced and encouraged by other group members to engage in active leadership behaviors, the person's proportion of talking time increases as his perceived leadership status increases (Bavelas, Hastorf, Gross and Kite, 1965; Zdep and Oakes, 1967). Pepinsky and his associates (1958) demonstrated that individuals who had previously exhibited few leadership behaviors were influenced to behave far more actively in such behaviors by the group's evident support for their assertions; individuals who had previously exhibited many leadership behaviors in earlier situations were affected in precisely the opposite way by the group's evident disagreement with their statements. From these and other studies it may be concluded that (1) the amount of participation and influence by a leader affects members' perceptions of her leadership, and (2) the amount of encouragement and support by followers affects the amount of a person's participation and perceived leadership status.

Viewing leadership as a reciprocal influence between a leader and a set of followers does not necessarily mean that leadership is based on domination. Influence is directed toward persuading group members to cooperate in setting and achieving goals. Leadership, then, becomes the art of ensuring that group members work together with the least friction and the most cooperation. This often means that the leader needs to persuade and inspire members to follow her view of what needs to be done in order to achieve the group's goals.

THE POSITION APPROACH TO LEADERSHIP

Another approach to the question Who is a leader? focuses on high-authority positions within organizations. The approach would suggest that Franklin was known as a leader simply because he was appointed to various leadership positions. Leadership within organizations begins with the formal role system (for example, president, vice-president, manager, supervisor, worker), which, among other things, defines the hierarchy of authority. Authority is legitimate power, power vested in a particular position to ensure that individuals in subordinate positions meet the requirements of their organizational role. A supervisor, for example, is given the authority to ensure that workers are doing their job. Because organizational law demands that subordinates obey their supervisors in matters of role performance, a person with authority will influence his or her subordinates. A person who is directly above you in the authority hierarchy, therefore, is your leader. The trouble with the position approach to leadership theory is that it is unclear how certain individuals are placed in high-authority positions to begin with. All of their behavior is certainly not leadership behavior. Group members other than the designated leader influence the behavior of the group members, furthermore, and there is no way to take this fact into account when leadership is defined as a position of authority.

YOUR LEADERSHIP BEHAVIOR EXERCISE (I)

Any action that helps a group complete its task is a leadership action. Any action that helps a group maintain effective working relationships among its members is a leadership action. When you are a member of a group, what leadership actions do you engage in? How do you influence other group members to complete the task and maintain collaborative relationships? This exercise has two purposes: (1) to make you more aware of your typical leadership actions, and (2) to make your group more aware of its patterns of leadership. The procedure for the exercise is as follows:

1. Working by yourself, complete the following questionnaire.
2. Determine your score and place it on the task-maintenance grid in Figure 2.1.
3. In your group, place all members' scores on the task-maintenance grid. With the other members of your group, write a description of the leadership pattern of your group. Then write a description of how this pattern may be improved.

Understanding Your Leadership Actions Questionnaire

Each of the following items describes a leadership action. In the space next to each item write 5 if you *always* behave that way, 4 if you *frequently* behave that way, 3 if you *occasionally* behave that way, 2 if you *seldom* behave that way, and 1 if you *never* behave that way.

When I am a member of a group:

_____ **1.** I offer facts and give my opinions, ideas, feelings, and information in order to help the group discussion.

_____ **2.** I warmly encourage all members of the group to participate. I am open to their ideas. I let them know I value their contributions to the group.

_____ **3.** I ask for facts, information, opinions, ideas, and feelings from the other group members in order to help the group discussion.

_____ **4.** I help communication among group members by using good communication skills. I make sure that each group member understands what the others say.

_____ **5.** I give direction to the group by planning how to go on with the group work and by calling attention to the tasks that need to be done. I assign responsibilities to different group members.

_____ **6.** I tell jokes and suggest interesting ways of doing the work in order to reduce tension in the group and increase the fun we have working together.

_____ **7.** I pull together related ideas or suggestions made by group members and restate and summarize the major points discussed by the group.

_____ **8.** I observe the way the group is working and use my observations to help discuss how the group can work together better.

_____ **9.** I give the group energy. I encourage group members to work hard to achieve our goals.

_____ **10.** I promote the open discussion of conflicts among group members in order to resolve disagreements and increase group cohesiveness. I mediate conflicts among members when they seem unable to resolve them directly.

_____ **11.** I ask others to summarize what the group has been discussing in order to ensure that they understand group decisions and comprehend the material being discussed by the group.

_____ **12.** I express support, acceptance, and liking for other members of the group and give appropriate praise when another member has taken a constructive action in the group.

In order to obtain a total score for task actions and maintenance actions, write the score for each item in the appropriate column and then add the columns.

Task Actions	Maintenance Actions
_____ **1.** information and opinion giver	_____ **2.** encourager of participation
_____ **3.** information and opinion seeker	_____ **4.** communication facilitator
_____ **5.** direction and role definer	_____ **6.** tension reliever
_____ **7.** summarizer	_____ **8.** process observer

	Task Actions		Maintenance Actions
___	**9.** energizer	___	**10.** interpersonal problem solver
___	**11.** comprehension checker	___	**12.** supporter and praiser
___	Total for Task Actions	___	Total for Maintenance Actions

Description of Task–Maintenance Patterns

(6,6) Only a minimum effort is given to getting the required work done. There is general noninvolvement with other group members. The person with this score may well be saying "To hell with it all." Or he or she may be so inactive in the group as to have no influence whatsoever on other group members.

(6,30) High value is placed on keeping good relationships within the group. Thoughtful attention is given to the needs of other members. The person with this score helps create a comfortable, friendly atmosphere and work tempo. However, he or she may never help the group get any work accomplished.

(30,6) Getting the job done is emphasized in a way that shows very little concern with group maintenance. Work is seen as important, and relationships among group members are ignored. The person with this score may take an army-drillmaster approach to leadership.

(18,18) The task and maintenance needs of the group are balanced. The person with this score continually makes compromises between task needs and maintenance needs. Though a great compromiser, this person does not look for or find ways to creatively integrate task and maintenance activities for optimal productivity.

(30,30) When everyone plans and makes decisions together, all the members become committed to getting the task done as they build relationships of trust and respect.

FIGURE 2.1 Task–maintenance grid.

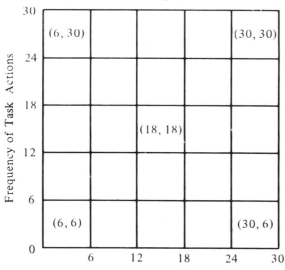

A high value is placed on sound, creative decisions that result in understanding and agreement. Ideas and opinions are sought and listened to, even when they differ from one's own. The group as a whole defines the task and works to get it done. The creative combining of both task and maintenance needs is encouraged.

Matching Exercise 1

To help you learn the task and maintenance actions, match the following terms with their definitions (answers on page 82).

Task Actions

____ **1.** Information and Opinion Giver
____ **2.** Information and Opinion Seeker
____ **3.** Direction and Role Definer
____ **4.** Summarizer
____ **5.** Energizer
____ **6.** Comprehension Checker

Maintenance Actions

____ **7.** Encourager of Participation
____ **8.** Communication Facilitator
____ **9.** Tension Releaser
____ **10.** Process Observer
____ **11.** Interpersonal Problem-Solver
____ **12.** Supporter and Praiser

a. Makes sure all group members understand what each other says.

b. Pulls together related ideas or suggestions and restates them.

c. Offers facts, opinions, ideas, feelings, and information.

d. Expresses acceptance and liking for group members.

e. Uses observations of how the group is working to help discuss how the group can improve.

f. Lets members know their contributions are valued.

g. Asks for facts, opinions, ideas, feelings, and information.

h. Asks others to summarize discussion to make sure they understand.

i. Encourages group members to work hard to achieve goals.

j. Calls attention to tasks that need to be done and assigns responsibilities.

k. Helps resolve and mediate conflicts.

l. Tells jokes and increases the group fun.

Matching Exercise 2

Match the following statements with the task or maintenance action they best seem to fill (answers on page 82).

Task Actions

_____ **1.** Information and Opinion Giver

_____ **2.** Information and Opinion Seeker

_____ **3.** Direction and Role Definer

_____ **4.** Summarizer

_____ **5.** Energizer

_____ **6.** Comprehension Checker

Maintenance Actions

_____ **7.** Encourager of Participation

_____ **8.** Communication Facilitator

_____ **9.** Tension Releaser

_____ **10.** Process Observer

_____ **11.** Interpersonal Problem-Solver

_____ **12.** Supporter and Praiser

a. "Does everyone in the group understand Helen's idea?"

b. "How about giving our report on yoga while standing on our heads?"

c. "Edye's idea seems like Buddy's; I think they could be combined."

d. "I think we should openly discuss the conflict between Dave and Linda to help resolve it."

e. "Before we go on, let me tell you how other groups have solved this task."

f. "We need a time-keeper. Keith, why don't you do that?"

g. "I really enjoy this group. I especially enjoy Roger's sense of humor."

h. "I think we'd find a good solution if we put a little more work into it."

i. "Frank, tell us what we've said so far to see if you understand it correctly."

j. "We seem to be suggesting solutions before we're ready. Let's define the problem first."

k. "I don't understand. What do you mean?"

l. "Helen, I'd like to hear what you think about this; you have such good ideas."

SITUATIONAL THEORIES OF LEADERSHIP

Perhaps Benjamin Franklin became a renowned leader because he was able to vary his behavior systematically from situation to situation so as to provide the appropriate leadership actions at the appropriate time. There is currently a consensus among social scientists that leadership skills and competencies are not inherited from one's ancestors, that they do not magically appear when a person is assigned to a leadership position, and that the same set of competencies will not provide adequate leadership in every situation. Different situations require different approaches to leadership. We shall discuss four situational theories in this chapter: the distributed-actions theory, Bale's interaction-process analysis, Fiedler's situational theory, and Hersey and Blanchard's situational theory.

The Distributed-Actions Theory of Leadership

Groups have at least two basic obectives: to complete a task and to maintain effective collaborative relationships among the members. The distributed-actions theory of leadership emphasizes that certain functions need to be filled if a group is to meet these two objectives. It defines *leadership* as the performance of acts that help the group to complete its task and to maintain effective working relationships among its members. For a group to successfully complete its task, group members must obtain, organize, and use information to make a decision. In doing this they require certain task-leadership actions. Members have to contribute, ask for, summarize, and coordinate the information. They have to structure and give direction to the group's efforts and provide the energy to motivate efforts to make the decision. For any group to be successful, such task-leadership actions have to be provided.

But it does no good to complete a task if the manner of doing so alienates several group members. If a number of group members refuse to come to the next meeting, the group has not been successful. Thus, members must pay attention to maintaining good working relationships while working on the task. The task must be completed in a way that increases the ability of group members to work together effectively in the future. For this to happen, certain maintenance-leadership actions are needed. Members have to encourage one another to participate. They have to relieve tension when it gets too high, facilitate communication among themselves, and evaluate the emotional climate of the group. They have to discuss how the group's work can be improved, and they have to listen carefully and respectfully to one another. These leadership actions are necessary for the maintenance of friendly relationships among members and indeed, for the success of the group.

The distributed-actions theory of leadership includes two basic ideas: (1) any member of a group may become a leader by taking actions that help the group complete its task and maintain effective collaborative relationships; (2) any leadership function may be fulfilled by different members performing a variety of relevant behaviors. Leadership, therefore, is specific to a particular group in a particular situation. Under specific circumstances any given behavior may or may not serve a group function. Under one set of conditions a particular behavior may be helpful; under another set it may impair the effectiveness of the group. For example, when a group is trying to define a problem, suggesting a possible solution may not be helpful; however, when the group is making various solutions to a defined problem, suggesting a possible solution may indeed be helpful.

From the perspective of this theory, leadership is a learned set of skills that anyone with certain minimal requirements can acquire. Responsible group membership and leadership both depend on flexible behavior, the ability to diagnose what behaviors are needed at a particular time in order for the group to function most efficiently, and the ability to fulfill these behaviors or to get other members to fulfill them. A skilled member or leader, therefore, has to have diagnostic skills in order to be aware that a given function is needed in the group, and he or she must be sufficiently adaptive to provide the diverse types of behaviors needed for different conditions. In addition, an effective group member or leader must be able to utilize the abilities of other group members in providing the actions needed by the group.

For at least three reasons, it is usually considered necessary for the behaviors that fulfill group functions to be distributed among group members. First, if members do not participate, then their ideas, skills, and information are not being contributed. This hurts the group's effectiveness. The second reason is that members are committed to what they help build. Members who participate become more committed to the group and what the group has done. Members who remain silent tend not to care about the group and its effectiveness. The more members feel they have influenced the group and contributed to its work, the more committed they will be to the group. The third reason is that active members often become worried or annoyed about the silent members and view them as unconcerned about task completion. Unequal patterns of participation can create maintenance problems within the group.

Sometimes actions within a group not only help it to operate but serve oneself as well. Such individually oriented behavior sometimes involves issues of personal identity (Who am I in this group? Where do I fit in?), personal goals and needs (What do I want from this group? Are the group's goals consistent with my personal goals?), power and control (Who will control what we do? How much power and influence do I have?), and intimacy (How close will we get to each other? How much can I trust the other group members?).

The distributed-actions theory of leadership is one of the most concrete and direct approaches available for improving a person's leadership skills and for improving the effectiveness of a group. People can be taught the diagnostic skills and behaviors that help a group accomplish its task and maintain effective collaborative relationships among its members. There is, however, some criticism of the approach. There are so many different actions members can take to help in task achievement and group maintenance that specific ones are hard to pin down. What constitutes leadership then depends on the view of the person who is listing the leadership behaviors.

Interaction-Process Analysis

If you put five strangers together and assign them a task that requires them to cooperate, something quite remarkable but very predictable happens: the social interaction among them becomes patterned and a leadership structure emerges. One of the common forms this leadership structure takes is for one person to assume a task-leadership role that includes behaviors oriented primarily to task achievement (such as directing, summarizing, and providing ideas) and another person to assume a social-emotional-leadership role that includes behaviors oriented primarily to the expressive, interpersonal affairs of the group (such as alleviating frustrations, resolving tensions, and mediating conflicts).

Robert Bales (1950, 1952, 1955), in a series of studies in the late 1940s and early 1950s, was among the first to focus on task and social-emotional leadership. His work has been corroborated and extended by Burke (1972). The basic interaction-process theory consists of the following points:

1. When a group has a task to complete, its members engage in task-related behaviors on an unequal basis.
2. The members who are high on task behaviors tend to create some tension and hostility on the part of members who are less committed to the task.
3. There is a need for actions that help maintain effective working relationships among members.
4. Social-emotional actions are engaged in by members other than those high on task actions.
5. These differentiated roles (task and social-emotional) are stabilized and synchronized as the task and social-emotional leaders reinforce and support each other.

When the group has no task to achieve, or no commitment to achieve its assigned task, a task leader is not needed and will not appear. Correspondingly, with no commitment to a goal there is no need to maintain relationships among members and a social-emotional leader will not evolve.

In his research Bales developed an observational instrument for identifying task and social-emotional behaviors within a small group (Figures 2.2 and 2.3). The instrument consists of several categories that are designed to allow a systematic classification of all the acts of participation in a group. As you can see in Figure 2.2, the categories are polarized: category 1 is the

FIGURE 2.2 Bales's system of categories used in observation.

Social-Emotional Area: Positive
   1. Shows solidarity, raises others' status, gives help, rewards

---

   2. Shows tension release, jokes, laughs, shows satisfaction

---

   3. Agrees, shows passive acceptance, understands, concurs, complies

---

Task Area: Neutral
   4. Gives suggestions, direction, implying autonomy for others

---

   5. Gives opinions, evaluation, analysis: expresses feeling, wishes

---

   6. Gives orientation, information; repeats, clarifies, confirms

---

Task Area: Neutral
   7. Asks for orientation, information, repetition, confirmation

---

   8. Asks for opinions, evaluation, analysis, expressions of feeling

---

   9. Asks for suggestions, direction, possible ways of action

---

Social-Emotional Area: Negative
   10. Disagrees; shows passive rejection, formality; withholds help

---

   11. Shows tension, asks for help, withdraws, leaves the field

---

   12. Shows antagonism, deflates others' status, defends or asserts self

---

Bales, R., *Interaction Process Analysis.* Reading, Ma.: Addison-Wesley, 1950.

opposite of category 12, 2 is the opposite of 11, and so on. The first three categories are positive emotions, the last three negative emotions. Categories 7, 8, and 9 request aid, whereas categories 4, 5, and 6 offer it.

Bales's research indicates that positive emotions (categories 1, 2, and 3) are usually expressed more than twice as often as negative emotions (10, 11, and 12). Opinions and information are much more often volunteered (46 percent of all participant behaviors observed) than asked for (7 percent). Problem-solving groups tend to progress through three stages: orientation (What is the problem?), evaluation (How do we feel about it?), and control (What should we do about it?). As the discussion moves from the intellectual examination of the problem (the orientation phase) to evaluation and decision (the control phase), emotions are expressed more often.

Bales's observation form may be found in Figure 2.3. Why not try using it to observe a number of group meetings?

Fiedler's Situational Theory of Leadership

Social psychologist Fred Fiedler did a series of studies on leadership (1964, 1967, 1969) in many different situations and groups. Defining a leader's effec-

FIGURE 2.3 Cumulative interaction form.

Date _____ Group _____ Time: _____ to _____ Observer _____

Members

BEHAVIOR													TOTALS
Shows solidarity													
Shows tension release													
Agrees													
Gives suggestions													
Gives opinions													
Give orientation													
Asks for orientation													
Asks for opinions													
Asks for suggestions													
Disagrees													
Shows tension													
Shows antagonism													
TOTALS													

POSITIVE EMOTIONS

TASK

NEGATIVE EMOTIONS

tiveness in terms of his group's performance in achieving its goals, Fiedler divided leaders into those who were task-oriented and those who were mainte-nance-oriented. He found no consistent relationship between group effective-ness and leadership behaviors, the reason being that maintenance-oriented leaders were more effective in certain situations and task-oriented leaders more effective in other situations.

A task-oriented leader is effective under two sets of conditions. Under the first she is on very good terms with the group members, the task is clearly structured, and she has a position of high authority and power. Under such conditions the group is ready to be directed and is willing to be told what to do. Under the second set of conditions she is on poor terms with group members, the task is ambiguous, and she has a position of low authority and power. Under these conditions she can also be effective in taking responsi-bility for making decisions and directing group members. When moderately good or poor relations exist between the leader and the group members, when the leader has a position of moderate authority and power, and when the task is moderately clear, the maintenance-oriented leader who emphasizes member participation in decision making seems to be the most effective type of leader.

Fiedler's results imply that the distributed-functions theory of leadership needs to be modified to take into account the situational conditions influencing the impact of leadership style upon a group. There are some difficulties with this theory, however. For example, how can a person tell if the situational conditions of leader–member relations, task clarity, and leader power are high, moderate, or low? Almost all group situations fall into the moderate range; in only the most extreme cases are the sets of conditions in the high or low categories. A second difficulty is that although the theory is more complex than the outdated leadership-style theory, which held that a leader should always be democratic, it may not be complex enough. A good leader is always paying attention to the situational conditions that influence the group, modifying his behavior to make it effective. Moreover, leader–member relations, task–clarity, and leader power may be only three of many different situational factors that group leaders should be aware of.

Hersey and Blanchard's Theory of Situational Leadership

On the basis of studies of leadership conducted at Ohio State University, Paul Hersey and Kenneth Blanchard (1977) concluded that they can classify most of the activities of leaders into two distinct behavioral dimensions: initia-tion of structure (task actions) and consideration of group members (relation-ship of maintenance actions). They define *task behavior* as the extent to which a leader engages in one-way communication by explaining that each follower is to do as well as when, where, and how tasks are to be accomplished. They define *relationship behavior* as the extent to which a leader engages in two-way communication by providing emotional support and facilitating behaviors. According to Hersey and Blanchard, the Ohio State University studies found that some leaders focus mainly on directing task-accomplishment-related activities for their followers, whereas other leaders concentrate on providing emotional support through relationships with their followers. Still other leaders engage in both task and relationship behaviors, or in neither. Hersey and Blanchard determined that task and relationship behaviors are two separate dimensions, which can be portrayed as in Figure 2.4.

Hersey and Blanchard's situational-leadership theory assumes that any of the four combinations of leadership behaviors shown in Figure 2.4 may be ineffective or effective depending on the situation. Which combination of behaviors is appropriate depends on the level of maturity of the group. They define *maturity* as the capacity to set high but attainable goals (achievement motivation), willingness and ability to take responsibility, and the educa-

FIGURE 2.4 Situational leadership.

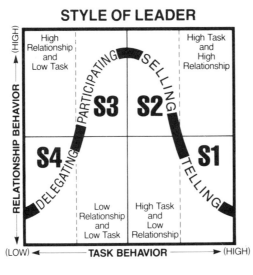

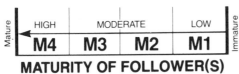

Hersey, P., & Blanchard, K. *Management of Organizational Behavior: Utilizing Human Resources* (3rd Edition). Englewood Cliffs, N.J.: Prentice-Hall, Inc., 1977. Reprinted by permission.

tion and/or experience of group members. Maturity is determined only in relation to a specific task to be performed. On one task a member may have high maturity, on another task low maturity.

The essence of Hersey and Blanchard's theory is that when group members have low maturity in terms of accomplishing a specific task, the leader should engage in high task and low relationship behaviors. When members are moderately mature, the leader moves to high task and high relationship behaviors and then to high relationship and low task behaviors. When group members are highly mature in terms of accomplishing a specific task, then low task and low relationship behaviors are needed. Hersey and Blanchard refer to *high-task/low-relationship leadership behavior* as *telling*, because it is characterized by one-way communication in which the leader defines the roles of group members and tells them how, when, and where to do various tasks. As the members' experience and understanding of the task goes up, so does their task maturity. *High-task/high-relationship leadership behavior* is referred to as *selling*, because while providing clear direction as to role responsibilities the leader also attempts through two-way communication and socio-emotional support to get the group members to psychologically buy into decisions that have to be made. As group members' commitment to the task increases, so does their maturity. *Low/task/high-relationship leadership behavior* is referred to as *participating*, because the leader and group members share in decision making through two-way communication and considerable facilitating behavior from the leader, since the group members have the ability and knowledge to complete the task. Finally, *low-task/low-relationship leadership behavior* is referred to as *delegating*, because the leader allows group members considerable autonomy in completing the task, since they are both willing and able to take responsibility for directing their own task behavior.

GROUP STRUCTURE AND LEADERSHIP

Whenever two or more individuals join together to achieve a goal, a group structure develops. The group structure consists of role definitions and group norms that structure the interaction among group members. A *role* is a set of expected behaviors associated with a position within a group. A *norm* is essentially a rule that specifies acceptable behavior in the group. Once a formal structure is established, it is largely independent of the particular individuals who compose the group. Part of the group structure organizes the way in which members influence one another while trying to reach the desired goals. When two or more group members who depend on one another to reach the group's goals influence one another, leadership exists. Leadership is one aspect of the structure of the group.

Check your understanding of the information presented by answering the following questions. Answers are at the end of the chapter. Match the following statements with the theories of leadership they describe or define:

_____ 1. Helen was born to be great; it's inherited from her family background.

_____ 2. Jane is leader because she changes her behavior according to the situation.

_____ 3. People blindly follow Roger because his engaging personality inspires confidence.

_____ 4. Dale lets the group do whatever they want, providing little or no guidance.

_____ 5. Frank is successful because he knows how to manipulate others to get what he wants.

_____ 6. Dave is the group leader because he affects the group members more than they affect him.

_____ 7. Edye is a leader because she is president of the corporation.

_____ 8. Keith determines what the group should do and then gives them orders.

_____ 9. The group determines policy, aided by the leader.

_____ 10. There are three types of leadership; the most effective is the democratic type.

a. Trait
b. Charismatic
c. Machiavellian
d. Leadership Style
e. Influence
f. Position
g. Distributed Actions
h. Laissez-faire
i. Democratic
j. Autocratic

Match the following leadership styles with the conditions most effective for its use:

_____ 11. A decision has to be made immediately.

a. Democratic
b. Autocratic

_____ **12.** Member commitment to implementing the decision is
needed.

_____ **13.** The group is committed, re-
sourceful, and works well.

c. Laissez-faire

Match how the Distributed Actions Theory would label the following
behaviors:

_____ **14.** Helen always does the decision making in a group.

_____ **15.** Dave tells a pig joke in the
middle of a discussion.

_____ **16.** Edye gets others to contribute their ideas.

_____ **17.** Frank figures which behaviors the group needs and
then does them.

_____ **18.** Keith is usually silent in a
group.

a. Effective

b. Ineffective

Using Fiedler's situational theory of leadership, match which type of
leader is found to be most effective in the following circumstances:

_____ **19.** She is on good terms with
group members, the task is
clearly structured, and she
has a position of high authority and power.

_____ **20.** She has moderately good relations with group mem-
bers, the task is moderately
clear, and she has a position
of moderate authority and
power.

_____ **21.** He is on poor terms with
group members, the task is
ambiguous, and he has a position of low authority and
power.

a. Task-oriented

b. Maintenance-oriented

Match Hersey's and Blanchard's leadership categories with their descriptions:

_____ 22. Participating

_____ 23. Delegating

_____ 24. Selling

_____ 25. Telling

_____ 26. Leader defines roles and jobs of members

_____ 27. Leader defines roles and elicits support

_____ 28. Leader encourages group autonomy and responsibility

_____ 29. Leader is facilitative and shares decision-making

_____ 30. Used when the group has highest maturity

a. High Task/Low Relationship

b. High Task/High Relationship

c. Low Task/High Relationship

d. Low Task/Low Relationship

_____ 31. Which of the following are characteristics of Machiavellian leaders?
  a. They have little emotional involvement with their followers.
  b. They are not concerned with conventional morality.
  c. They are out of touch with reality.
  d. They have a high level of ideological commitment.
  e. a and b
  f. all of the above

_____ 32. Which of the following are characteristics of democratic groups?
  a. Much less hostility than autocratic groups.
  b. More scapegoating than autocratic groups.
  c. Increased productivity.
  d. Increased member satisfaction.
  e. a and d
  f. a, c, and d

_____ 33. In the Distributed Actions Theory, leadership is defined as acting in which of the following ways:
  a. Helping the group complete the task.
  b. Helping maintain effective working relationships among members.
  c. Influencing the others to follow directions.
  d. a and b
  e. all of the above

—— **34.** In the Distributed Actions Theory of leadership:
    a. Anyone can learn to be a leader.
    b. Leadership is distributed by genetics.
    c. Leadership depends on personal maturity.
    d. a and c
    e. all of the above

—— **35.** Why should leadership functions be distributed among the members of a group?:
    a. So everyone's ideas and skills are made available.
    b. So members will be more committed to the group actions.
    c. So silent members will not be viewed with suspicion.
    d. a and b
    e. all of the above

—— **36.** Bales found that a problem-solving group goes through which of the following stages:
    a. orientation, evaluation, solution
    b. orientation, evaluation, control
    c. orientation, control, solution
    d. orientation, discussion, control

—— **37.** How do Hersey and Blanchard define "maturity"?
    a. Capacity to set high but attainable goals.
    b. Willingness and ability to take responsibility.
    c. Education and/or experience.
    d. Age.
    e. a, b, and c
    f. all of the above

T F   **38.** Mann concluded that intelligence and personal adjustment seem to be correlated with leadership.

T F   **39.** A follow-up study of 1,000 high I.Q. children showed that many of them had become well-known leaders.

T F   **40.** Stogdill concluded that being an effective, upper-level leader is a combination of leadership traits and luck.

T F   **41.** Although the best predictor of leadership success is prior success in leadership roles, an effective leader may fail when placed in a situation incompatible with his previous success pattern.

T F   **42.** The 1939 study by Lewin, Lippitt and White demonstrated that people in a group behave the same way no matter what style of leadership is used.

T F   **43.** Group members should encourage everyone in the group to participate in the decision making if they want them to help implement it.

T   F   **44.**   Research indicates that a person with high leadership skills will emerge as leader even if the group does not agree or follow his ideas.

T   F   **45.**   Bales found that when some members pushed hard for getting the job done, others became committed to helping maintain relationships.

T   F   **46.**   Bales found that emotions are more often expressed during the early stages of a group than during later stages.

T   F   **47.**   Hersey and Blanchard describe task behavior as one-way communication and relationship behavior as two-way.

THE FURNITURE FACTORY EXERCISE

The purpose of this exercise is to give participants an opportunity to observe task-leadership and maintenance-leadership actions within a decision-making group. The procedure is as follows:

1. The class divides into groups of seven. Two members should volunteer to be observers. The task of the observers is to record the frequency of task and maintenance actions within the group. The observation sheets to be used are on pages 69–70.

2. The task of each group is to read and discuss the problem description that follows and rank the five possible solutions on the basis of how effective they would be in ensuring the least resistance to the proposed changes in work procedures. Each member of the group must be willing to sign the group answer sheet, indicating that he agrees with the group's ranking and can explain the rationale for ranking the possible solutions in the order that the group did so.

3. After deciding how the possible solutions are to be ranked, members discuss the nature of leadership within the group. The following questions may be used as a starter:
   a. What leadership actions were present and absent in the group?
   b. What leadership actions did each member engage in?
   c. How do the members feel about their participation in the group?
   d. How might the task effectiveness of the group be improved?
   e. How might the relationships among group members be improved?

4. Each group shares its conclusions with the class.

5. The ranking of possible solutions by experts on organizational change appears in Appendix D on page 473.

Problem Description: Furniture Factory Exercise

Lazy-Days Manufacturing Company is located in a small northern town. This small, family-owned business manufactures school furniture. Because of the opportunities for work available in a larger town located about fifty miles away, Lazy-Days must attract whomever it can and train them to do the job. Most of the 400 workers are women and young people just out of high school. Lazy-Days also hires some physically handicapped and mentally retarded adults as part of a special community program.

Until now, Lazy-Days has manufactured school furniture but, due to a tightening of the economy, management has realized a dire need to diversify its manufacturing capabilities. After a study of the market, the decision was made to add showroom display cases as a new product. If well-made, this line will bring increased income and security to Lazy-Days Manufacturing.

Because of the difficulties in getting new workers, particularly trained ones, Lazy-Days would like to divert current personnel to the new jobs. However, the current workers are very set in their ways and are highly resistant to and suspicious of changes at work. The last time changes were needed, workers demanded higher wages, threatened to unionize, and a few key people quit. If the new line is successful, Lazy-Days could raise wages, but this is not possible under current conditions that require using available income to help purchase the new equipment and finance necessary remodeling to accommodate the new equipment.

Michael Days, President of Lazy-Days, has listed several ways of approaching the workers about the needed changes. He has asked you to decide which alternative to use. As a group, rank these alternatives from 1 to 5 in terms of their effectiveness in bringing about the desired changes with the least resistance from the workers. Number

Observation Sheet for Task Actions

actions	Group Members				
Information and Opinion Giver					
Information and Opinion Seeker					
Direction and Role Definer					
Summarizer					
Energizer					
Comprehension Checker					

1 would be the most effective, 2 the next most effective, and so on through 5, the least effective. Remember, your decision can make the difference between the success or failure of Lazy-Days Manufacturing Company.

_____ **a.** Mr. Days would send a written memo to all employees that would tell them about the needed changes. He would then make the changes and layoff any employees who did not comply with the changes in their jobs.

_____ **b.** Mr. Days would meet with small groups of employees. He would explain the need for the changes and the reasoning behind the changes. He would then ask everyone to help in designing and implementing the new jobs.

_____ **c.** Mr. Days would meet with large groups of his employees. He would enthusiastically describe the needed changes and present multicolored charts and film-clips to make his points dramatically and forcefully. He would then implement the changes.

_____ **d.** Mr. Days would send a written memo to all employees that would explain the need for the changes and ask the employees to go along with the changes for the good of the company.

_____ **e.** Mr. Days would meet with large groups of his employees. He would explain the need for the changes and the reasoning behind the changes. He would then have the employees select representatives to work with him in designing and implementing the new jobs.

Observation Sheet for Maintenance Actions

actions	Group Members				
Encourager of Participation					
Communication Facilitator					
Tension Releaser					
Process Observer					
Interpersonal Problem-Solver					
Supporter and Praiser					

Observation Sheet for Task and Maintenance Actions

actions	Group Members				
Information and Opinion Giver					
Information and Opinion Seeker					
Direction and Role Definer					
Summarizer					
Energizer					
Comprehension Checker					
Encourager of Participation					
Communication Facilitator					
Tension Releaser					
Process Observer					
Interpersonal Problem-Solver					
Supporter and Praiser					

TOWER BUILDING EXERCISE

This exercise is aimed at providing participants with an opportunity to observe leadership behavior in a situation of intergroup competition in which verbal communication is not allowed. Several groups are needed for this exercise, all of which should have at least seven members. The task of each group is to build a tower from supplied materials. A large room is needed so that the groups can work separately (but within sight of one another). The time needed to complete the exercise is approximately one hour. The procedure is as follows:

1. Two judges are selected to determine which one tower is (1) the highest, (2) the strongest, (3) the most beautiful, and (4) the cleverest.
2. The class forms groups of at least seven members.
3. Each group selects two of its members to observe leadership in the group. The observers (using the observation sheets on pages 69–70) are to note:
   a. how the group organizes for work.
   b. how decisions are made by the group.
   c. whether participation and influence is distributed throughout the group, or whether a few members dominate.
   d. what task and maintenance actions are needed to improve the functioning of the group.
   e. how the group reacts to winning or losing.
4. Each group receives a box of supplies containing construction paper, newsprint, tape, magazines, crayons, pipe cleaners, scissors, and glue.
5. The groups have twenty minutes to build their towers. This is a *nonverbal* exercise: *no talking among group members or between groups is allowed.*
6. During the twenty minutes the judges meet to decide how they will evaluate the towers on the basis of the four criteria given above. At the end of the twenty minutes the judges decide which tower wins and award a box of candy (provided by the person conducting the exercise) to the winning group.
7. The groups meet with their observers and discuss the exercise. All impressions concerning how the group functioned and what leadership patterns were present and absent should be presented and reviewed.

SELECTING A CITY EXERCISE

The purposes of this exercise are for participants to develop through role playing an understanding of the distributed-actions theory of leadership and to observe task and maintenance actions in a decision-making group. Instructions for the coordinator are as follows:

1. Introduce the exercise by stating the objectives. Then explain the following leadership actions (see page 52 for definitions):
   a. information and opinion giver
   b. information and opinion seeker
   c. direction and role definer
   d. summarizer
   e. encourager of participation
   f. communication facilitator
   g. process observer
   h. tension reliever

2. Form heterogeneous groups of eight. Two members from each group should volunteer to be observers.

3. Explain the task-behavior and maintenance-behavior observation form to the observers and instruct them to look for:
   a. what leadership actions are present and absent in the group.
   b. how well participation is distributed among group members.
   c. what specific leadership actions each group member provides.

4. Place a large envelope containing role-playing-instruction envelopes in the center of each group; give no further instructions or information.

5. After the exercise has been completed, instruct each group to discuss its experience, using the following questions as a starter:
   a. What leadership actions was each member supposed to role-play, and how were they carried out?
   b. What leadership actions were present and absent in the group decision making, and what were the consequences of the presence or absence of these actions?
   c. What were the feelings and reactions of the group members?
   d. What conclusions about leadership and group functioning can be drawn from this exercise?

6. Have each group share its conclusions with the class.

Envelope Instructions

Instructions written on the large envelope, which contains all other envelopes:
Enclosed you will find three envelopes containing directions for the phases of this group session. You are to open the first one (labeled Envelope I) at once. Later instructions will tell you when to open the second (Envelope II) and third (Envelope III).

Envelope I contains the following directions:
Directions for Envelope I:
Time allowed: fifteen minutes.
Special instructions: Each member is to take one of the enclosed envelopes and follow the individual role-playing instructions contained in it.
Task: The group is to select a city.
DO NOT LET ANYONE ELSE SEE *YOUR* INSTRUCTIONS!
(After fifteen minutes go on to the next envelope.)

Envelope II contains the following directions:
Directions for Envelope II:
Time allowed: five minutes
Task: You are to choose a group chairperson.
(After five minutes go on to the next envelope.)

Envelope III contains the following directions:
Directions for Envelope III:
Time allowed: ten minutes.
Task: You are to evaluate the first phase of this group session.
Special instructions for the second phase: The newly selected chairperson will lead a discussion on the roles and actions of group members in the process of decision making

and their feelings and reactions to that process. The discussion should begin with the report of the observers.
(After ten minutes return the directions to their respective envelopes and prepare for a general discussion of the exercise.)

Role-Playing-Instruction Envelopes For Phase I

Here are the contents of the six individual-instruction envelopes to be used in the first phase of the exercise. Each envelope contains an assigned leadership action and a position concerning which city to select. Two of the envelopes also contain special knowledge concerning the selection process.

1. *Leadership Action:* Direction and Role Definer
   Position: Introduce and support Albuquerque. Oppose San Diego.
2. *Leadership Action:* Encourager of Participation
   Position: Introduce and support San Diego. Oppose Albuquerque.

Selecting a City Exercise Observation Sheet

actions	Group Members					
Information and Opinion Giver						
Information and Opinion Seeker						
Direction and Role Definer						
Summarizer						
Encourager of Participation						
Communication Facilitator						
Process Observer						
Tension Reliever						

Special Knowledge: The group is going to select a chairperson later in the exercise. You are to conduct yourself in such a manner that they will select you.

3. *Leadership Action:* Information and Opinion Seeker
   Position: Introduce and support New York City.

4. *Leadership Actions:* Summarizer and Process Observer
   Position: Oppose New York City.

5. *Leadership Action:* Communication Facilitator
   Position: When there seems to be a clear polarity in the discussion, suggest a compromise city, such as Minneapolis or Frameswitch, Texas.

6. *Leadership Action:* Tension Reliever
   Position: Support San Diego.
   Special Knowledge: The group is going to select a chairperson later in the exercise. You are to conduct yourself in such a manner that they will select you.

7. (if needed) *Leadership Action:* Any
   Position: any

ARE GROUPS RUN BY GREAT PERSONS EXERCISE

The purpose of this exercise is to compare two opposing theories of leadership: the great-person theory and the interaction-process-analysis theory. According to the great person theory, the leader is the best-liked member of the group and is perceived as being the most important member for achieving the group's goals. The interaction-process-analysis theory suggests that task-actions and maintenance-actions are ordinarily executed by different persons, so that a group will usually have two complementary leaders. The procedure for the exercise is as follows:

1. Each participant locates a group that has worked together for some time and has a stable group structure. The group should be small enough so that every member knows every other member well enough to evaluate them on likeability and task ability.

2. Give every member of the group a questionnaire consisting of two items:
   a. Rank order the members of the group from best to worst at helping the group complete its tasks.
   b. Rank order the members of the group from most to least likeable.

3. Construct two sociometric matrices for the group. The task-ability matrix is constructed by:
   a. Listing the names of the group members down the left-hand side of the matrix and also across the top of the matrix.
   b. Listing the rankings given by each group member to all other members on task ability in the rows. Each column then represents the rankings received for one member by all the other members of the group.
   c. Compute the mean rank of each member.

4. Repeat this process for the likeability rankings.

5. By graphing the mean ranking of the members on the two dimensions the answer to which theory holds in that group can be determined. If the two sets of rankings

correspond, the graph should resemble a straight line, and the great-person theory of leadership is confirmed. If any pattern other than a straight line results, the theory of two complementary leaders or another theory of leadership is supported.

6. The class divides into groups of five. Share with each other your graphs. Discuss the following questions:

a. How do the graphs of the different groups compare with one another?

b. What overall conclusions concerning group leadership can be made from the five graphs?

EXAMPLE OF SOCIOMETRIC TASK-ABILITY MATRIX

Members Being Ranked

Members Doing Ranking	John	Sue	Fred	Ralph	Betsy	Helen
John						
Sue						
Fred						
Ralph						
Betsy						
Helen						
Mean Ranking						

EXAMPLE OF SOCIOMETRIC GRAPH

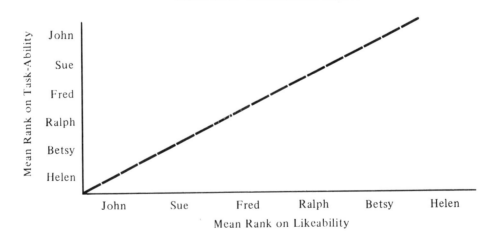

c. What have you learned about leadership be analyzing and comparing the leadership patterns of the five groups?

HOLLOW SQUARE EXERCISE

The Hollow Square Exercise is a problem-solving situation in which you can observe leadership functions. You can see the processes of group planning, the problems of communication between a planning group and an implementing group, and the problems with which an implementing group must cope when carrying out a plan it did not make itself, all of which requires effective leadership behavior. The specific objectives for the exercise are to provide a problem-solving task in which you can observe leadership behavior, to increase your awareness of the problems involved in using a formal hierarchy in group problem solving, and to give you practice in observing groups and in giving the group feedback on your observations.

The exercise is carried out in clusters of ten to twelve persons. Each cluster is divided into three subgroups: four persons are planners, four are implementers, and the rest observers. The planners decide how they will instruct the implementers to do a task, the implementers carry through the task as best they can, and the observers watch the process of both groups in the two phases. Here is the specific procedure for the coordinator of the exercise:

1. Tell the participants the objectives of the exercise and divide them into four-person planning teams, four-person implementing teams, and observers. Each team goes to a separate room or different parts of a large room (out of earshot) to await instructions.

2. Hand out the appropriate instruction sheets to each team. Give them adequate time to read them, then review them with each team. The observers should be fully briefed first, the planners next, and the implementers last.

3. The planners are given the general diagram sheet and the pieces of the puzzle and are instructed to begin Phase I. Each planner is given four pieces of the puzzle. The exact distribution of the pieces is not crucial, but they should not have any labels marked on them. Phase I lasts forty-five minutes. All information the planners need to know is on their briefing sheet. The answer as to how the puzzle fits together is on page 473, Appendix D.

4. At the end of Phase I the planning team gives the implementing team its instructions. The planners are then prohibited from giving any further help; they must remain silent and uninvolved as the implementing team works.

5. Implementers are to finish the task, Phase II, according to their instructions, taking as much time as necessary.

6. When the task is completed a discussion is held involving all the members of each cluster. This discussion is to include reports from the observers, planners, and implementers, and a comparison of similarities between the exercise and other organizational and group experiences of the members. Questions for the discussion should include:
   a. What leadership functions were present and absent in the planning and implementing teams? What were the consequences of the functions being present or absent?

b. What leadership functions were needed for each type of activity?

c. How could the functioning of each team have been improved?

d. Were the leadership functions distributed among all the team members? Was participation and influence evenly distributed throughout the team?

e. How was communication between the planning and implementing teams handled? How could it have been improved?

f. What did it feel like to wait for the planners' instructions, and what did it feel like to watch the implementers carry them out?

7. The major points of the discussion should be summarized with an emphasis placed upon the conclusions about the leadership functions being present, absent, and distributed within the teams. Other types of learnings that typically take place during the exercise are:

a. Planners often place limitations on team behavior that do not appear in the instructions, thereby making their task harder. They could, for example, ask the implementing team to observe their planning meeting.

b. There is considerable frustration in planning something that others will carry out without yourself being involved. The commitment to implement a plan is usually built through the planning process, and when the planners cannot put the plan into effect they often experience frustration.

c. Planning is so interesting and absorbing that planners can forget what their implementing team is experiencing. Implementers can become anxious because they do not know what the task will be, though this concern does not usually enter the minds of the planners.

d. Planners often fail to use all the resources at their disposal to solve the problem, such as getting the silent members of the planning team to participate.

e. Planners can spend so much time planning the task that they do not allow enough time to communicate their plans adequately to the implementers, which results in wasting much of their effort.

f. In communicating their plan to the implementing team the planning team often does not take into account the implementers' anxieties, their needs for being physically comfortable, and so on. Their preoccupation with giving information under pressure blinds them to the needs of the members of the implementing team, which reduces the effectiveness of the communication.

g. Implementers usually develop some feelings of antagonism or hostility toward their planners while they are waiting for their instructions. This antagonism increases if they are given complex instructions in a short amount of time and left confused as they take responsibility for finishing the task.

Instruction Sheet for Observers

You will be observing a situation in which a planning team decides how to solve a problem and gives instructions to an implementing team. The problem consists of assembling sixteen flat pieces into a square containing an empty square in its middle. The planning team is supplied with a general diagram of the assembled pieces. The planners are *not* allowed to put the puzzle together themselves; they are to instruct the implementing team on how to assemble the pieces in minimum time. You will be silent observers throughout the process. Half of you should observe the planners throughout the entire exercise and half of you should observe the implementers. Observation sheets focusing upon task and maintenance leadership behaviors are provided to help you observe. Make sure you understand the behavioral roles before you begin. Some suggestions for observers are:

1. Each observer should watch the general patterns of leadership behavior.
2. During Phase I, consider the following questions:
   a. What kinds of behavior block or help the process?
   b. Are the team members participating equally?
   c. How does the planning team divide its time between planning and instructing?
   d. What group functions are not provided by the group members?
3. During the instructing process, note these behavioral questions:
   a. At the beginning of the instruction, how do the planners orient the implementers to their task?
   b. What assumptions made by the planning team are not communicated to the implementing team?
   c. How effective are the instructions?
   d. Does the implementing team appear to feel free to ask questions of the planners?
   e. What leadership functions are present and absent?
4. During the assembling period, seek answers to the following questions:
   a. How does the implementing team show that instructions were clearly understood or misunderstood?
   b. What nonverbal reactions do planning team members show as they watch their plans being implemented or distorted?
   c. What leadership functions are present and absent?
5. You should each have two copies of the observation sheets, one for Phase I and one for Phase II.

Instruction Sheet for Planners

Each of you will be given a packet containing four pieces of a puzzle. When all the pieces from all four packets are properly assembled, they will form a large square containing an empty place in the middle. A sheet bearing a diagram of the completed puzzle is provided for your team. Your task is to:

1. Plan how the sixteen pieces distributed among you can be assembled to solve the puzzle.
2. Decide on a plan for instructing your implementing team on how to carry out your plan for putting the puzzle together.

3. Call the implementing team and begin instructing them at any time during the next forty minutes.

4. Give them at least five minutes of instructions; the implementing team must begin assembling the puzzle forty-five minutes from now.

Before you begin, read these rules:

1. During planning:
   a. Keep the pieces from your packet in front of you at all times.
   b. Do not touch the pieces nor trade any with other persons, either now or during the instruction period.
   c. Do not assemble the square; that is the implementers' job.
   d. Do not mark any of the pieces.
2. During instruction:
   a. Give all instructions in words. Do not show the diagram to the implementers; hide it. Do not draw any diagrams yourselves, either on paper or in the air with gestures. You may give your instructions orally or on paper.

Hollow Square Pattern

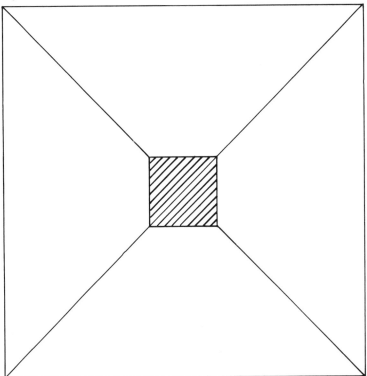

b. The implementing team must not move the pieces until the signal is given to start Phase II.

c. Do not show any diagram to the implementers.

d. After the signal is given for the assembly to begin, you may *not* give any further instructions; stand back and observe. You may not touch the pieces or in any way join in the implementers' work.

Instruction Sheet for Implementers

1. Your team will have the responsibility of carrying out a task in accordance with instructions given you by your planning team.

2. Your task will begin forty minutes from now.

3. Your planning team may call you in for instruction at any time during the next forty minutes.

4. If they do not call you during the next forty minutes, you must report to them on your own at the end of that time.

5. You may send notes to the planners and they may send notes in reply.

6. Once you have begun the task of assembling the puzzle, your planning team will not be allowed to give you any further instructions. Finish the assigned task as quickly as possible.

7. While you wait for a call from your planning team, do the following:

   a. Individually, write on a piece of paper the concerns you feel while waiting for instructions.

   b. As a group, think of anything you can that might help you follow instructions or keep you from doing so. Write actions that will help you on one sheet of paper and those that will hinder you on another.

   c. Make notes on how the four of you can organize as a team to receive and follow the instructions.

   d. Keep handy the sheets on which you have written these notes. You may find them useful during the discussion that takes place after you have completed the task.

OTHER LEADERSHIP EXERCISES

1. An exercise for an ongoing group is to place the task and maintenance functions singly on three-by-five-inch cards, shuffle the cards, and deal each member one or two of them face down. During a meeting of the group, each member then practices the task or maintenance function on the card he or she received. There must be at least two observers. After the meeting the group discusses which functions different members fulfilled and which ones they were trying to fulfill.

2. The class groups forms groups of six. Each group chooses a leader and then analyzes why it selected that person.
3. Members lie on the floor with their heads toward the center of the group and begin a group fantasy about what the perfect leader for this group would have to be like. When the fantasy is over the group reviews the experience.
4. Working as a group, members paint or draw a picture of the perfect leader for their group. Members then discuss both the process of making the picture and the picture itself.

YOUR LEADERSHIP BEHAVIOR EXERCISE (II)

Now that you have completed some or all of the exercises in this chapter and have read some or all of the information presented, it may be helpful for you to again take stock of your leadership behavior. Here is a procedure for doing so:

1. Describe the task and maintenance actions you usually engage in.
2. Describe the task and maintenance actions you would like to practice and become better at.
3. Ask other members of your group to describe your usual task and maintenance actions and help you decide which ones would be helpful for you to practice.
4. Plan how you can practice being a process observer in order to determine which task and maintenance actions would be most helpful for the group to focus on.
5. Plan how you can encourage other group members to engage in needed task and maintenance actions.

SUMMARY

Now you have learned about the different theories of leadership and assessed your own style of leadership. You are probably aware of some group actions you would like to improve your skill in. Continue to practice these areas as you learn about decision-making, the subject of the next chapter.

ANSWERS

Page 54—1. c; 2. g; 3. j; 4. b; 5. i; 6. h; 7. f; 8. a; 9. l; 10. e; 11. k; 12. d.

Page 55—1. e; 2. k; 3. j; 4. c; 5. h; 6. a; 7. l; 8. i; 9. b; 10. f; 11. d; 12. g.

Page 64—1. a;   2. g;   3. b;   4. h;   5. c;   6. e;   7. f;   8. j;   9. i;   10. d;   11. b;   12. a;   13. c;   14. b;   15. b;   16. a;   17. a;   18. b;   19. a;   20. b; 21. a;   22. c;   23. d;   24. b;   25. a;   26. a;   27. b;   28. d;   29. c; 30. d;   31. e;   32. e;   33. d;   34. a;   35. e;   36. b;   37. e;   38. true;   39. false;   40. true;   41. true;   42. false;   43. true;   44. false;   45. true;   46. false;   47. true.

3

DECISION MAKING

BASIC CONCEPTS TO BE COVERED IN THIS CHAPTER

In this chapter a number of concepts are defined and discussed. The major ones are listed below. The procedure for learning these concepts is as follows:

1. The class forms groups of four. These groups should be as heterogeneous as possible.
2. Each group divides into two pairs.
3. The task for each pair is to:
   a. define each concept, noting the page on which it is defined and discussed.
   b. make sure that both members of the pair understand the meaning of each concept.
4. In each group, members compare the answers of the two pairs. If there is disagreement, the members look up the concept in the chapter and clarify it until they all agree on the definition and understand it.

Concepts

1. decision
2. effective decision
3. consensus
4. majority vote
5. minority control
6. expertise
7. averaging opinions
8. defensive avoidance
9. vigilant information processing
10. social facilitation
11. perspective taking
12. group polarization
13. egocentrism
14. dissonance reduction
15. concurrence seeking
16. authority rule

"Corona is nice looking and his clothes are neat—and a killer, to have killed twenty-five men in the manner that these were killed, wouldn't look or act like Corona looks and acts . . . would he?" (p. 113)

"I bet you didn't hear half the evidence and half of that didn't register and you think he's guilty because you hate Mexicans!" (p. 120)

"I still can't bridge within my soul from thinking he's guilty to saying and voting that, yes, he's guilty." (p. 129)

In 1972 Juan Corona was placed on trial for the savage murder of twenty-five men, all skid-row bums who had no real homes or families (Villasenor, 1977). At the time, this case represented the largest mass murder charged to one person in the history of the United States. The jury consisted of ten men and two women ranging in age from twenty-six to sixty-six, all of them citizens of Fairfield, California. The jurors included retired military personnel, a teacher, a grocer, a welder, a janitor, and a machinist. For four months they heard the testimony of 117 witnesses and saw 980 exhibits. When the time came for their deliberations, they were sequestered so that they would have no contact with the media. On the eighth day of their deliberations they reached a verdict. This trial was vividly documented in Victor Villasenor's (1977) account of the jury's deliberations from which the preceding comments of the jurors were taken.

A jury is only one of the small groups in our society that have to make vital decisions. Most of the important decisions made in our society are made by small groups. How good the decisions are depends on how effective the group is. Groups are continually making decisions, some as important as whether a peer accused of a crime will live or die, others as ordinary as when and where the group will meet, what course of action it will take toward accomplishing goals, and what procedures it will use in discussions.

The purpose of group decision making is to decide upon well-considered, well-understood, realistic action toward goals every member wishes to achieve. A *decision* implies that some agreement prevails among group members as to which of several courses of action is most desirable for achieving the group's goals. Making a decision is just one step in the more general problem-solving process of goal-directed groups—but it is a crucial one. After defining a problem or issue, thinking over alternative courses of action, and weighing the advantages and disadvantages of each, a group will decide which course is the most desirable for them to implement.

Typically, groups try to make their decisions as effective as possible. There are five major characteristics of an *effective decision:*

1. the resources of group members are fully utilized,
2. time is well used,

3. the decision is correct, or of high quality,

4. the decision is implemented fully by all the required group members,

5. the problem-solving ability of the group is enhanced, or at least not lessened.

A decision is effective to the extent that these five criteria are met; if all five are not met, the decision has not been made effectively.

Some groups have a difficult time making decisions; members do not agree on what the decision should be. There are several reasons for indecisiveness—fear of the consequences of the decision, members' loyalties to other groups that undermine their commitment to making good decisions, conflicts among members that destroy their ability to reach decisions cooperatively and implement them, and rigid methods of decision making that do not fit the immediate situation. To help assure that their group will arrive at effective decisions, members must not only pay attention to the factors that may block effective decision making but also take advantage of the factors that facilitate effective decision making.

In this chapter we shall discuss the comparative effectiveness of individual and group decision making. Then we shall consider the factors that facilitate and hinder an effective group discussion. We next explain the different methods a group can use to arrive at a decision, under what circumstances each method is useful and productive, and what the likely outcomes are for these methods. The next topic is the effects on group members of their involvement in the group's decision making. Finally, we detail a process groups may use to ensure effective decision making.

QUIZ

Review the previous information by seeing how well you can answer the following questions. Answers are on page 134.

1. If you want to determine whether a group decision is effective, what five criteria should you use?

  a. group members reach agreement easily.

  b. the resources of group members are fully utilized.

  c. time is well used.

  d. the decision is correct or of high quality.

  e. the group members are in full agreement.

  f. the decision is implemented fully by all necessary group members.

  g. the problem solving ability of the group is enhanced or not lessened.

2. If your group has difficulty reaching a decision, what four reasons should you first examine to find an explanation?

a. fear of the consequences of the decision.
b. lack of importance of the problem.
c. conflicting membership loyalties to other groups.
d. unresolved conflicts among group members.
e. lack of understanding of the problem.
f. the decision-making method used doesn't fit the situation.
g. not having read this book.

INDIVIDUAL VERSUS GROUP DECISION MAKING EXERCISE

There has been some controversy over whether individual or group decision making is more effective. The purpose of this exercise is to structure a critical discussion of the issue. The procedure is as follows:

1. The class forms groups of four.
2. Each group is ultimately to write a report summarizing its position on whether individual or group decision making is more effective. The report is to contain the group's overall conclusions and the facts and rationale supporting its position. The supporting facts and rationale may be obtained from the accompanying briefing sheets, the entire book, and outside reading.
3. First each group divides into pairs. One pair is assigned the position that individuals are superior to groups in making decisions, and the other pair the position that groups are superior to individuals in making decisions. Each pair takes the appropriate briefing sheet and reviews the procedure and the rules for constructive controversy (p. 31).
4. The pairs meet separately to prepare as forceful a three-minute presentation of their position as possible. They are to make sure that both members have contributed to building a persuasive case for their position and that it includes as many facts and research findings as possible. Both members need to master all the rationale supporting their position. Ten minutes is allowed for this phase.
5. The group of four meets. Each pair presents its position, being as forceful and persuasive as possible, while the other pair takes notes and asks for clarification of anything that is not fully understood. Each pair is allowed about three minutes to present its position.
6. The group of four has an open discussion of whether individuals or groups make the best decisions. Each side should present as many facts and research findings as it can to support its point of view. Members should listen critically to the opposing position, asking for facts to support any conclusions made by the opposing pair. Participants should ensure that all the facts supporting both sides are brought out and discussed, and should follow the rules for constructive controversy. About ten minutes are allowed for this phase.
7. The perspectives in each group are now reversed, each pair arguing the opposing pair's position. Members should be as forceful and persuasive as they can in arguing

for the opposing pair's position. They should elaborate on the opposing position, seeing if they can think of any new arguments or facts that the opposing pair did not present. Each pair has about three minutes for its presentation.

8. Each group of four should derive a position that all members can agree on. The members should summarize the best arguments from both positions, detailing as many facts as they can on whether individuals or groups make the best decisions. When they have consensus in their group they should organize their arguments for presentation to the rest of the class. Since other groups will have other conclusions, each group may need to explain the validity of its position to the class. About ten minutes are allowed for this phase.

9. The coordinator samples the decisions made by the groups of four by having several of them present their position to the class. The class then discusses similarities and differences.

10. The coordinator summarizes what participants have learned about decision making.

Briefing Sheet: Individuals Make Superior Decisions

Your position is that individuals make higher-quality decisions than groups. To support your position, use the two quotations below, any material from this chapter that is applicable, and what you know from your outside reading.

> If anything, group membership blunts ethical perception and fetters moral imagination, because we then uncritically and passively let others think for us.
>
> Weston LaBarre (1972, p. 14)

> When a hundred clever heads join a group, one big nincompoop is the result, because every individual is trammelled by the otherness of the others.
>
> C. G. Jung (Illing, 1957, p. 80)

Briefing Sheet: Groups Make Superior Decisions

Your position is that groups make higher-quality decisions than individuals. To support your position, use the quotation below, any material from this chapter that is applicable, and what you know from your outside reading.

> Group operations have two kinds of potential advantage over action by a single individual. One is the caliber of thinking, the range of resources, and the critical scrutiny which enter the problem solving. The other is the willingness with which people carry out decisions they have helped to make. . . . Groups may sometimes be more sane, moderate, well-balanced and wise than their average member. . . . A thoughtful group may make its members more rational, more self-critical, and more ready to revise personal prejudices in the light of objective evidence, than these members would be if they were studying alone.
>
> Watson and Johnson (1972, pp. 130–131)

INDIVIDUAL VERSUS GROUP DECISION MAKING

We humans have gained control of steam power, internal-combustion engines, electric motors, and nuclear fission and fusion. Extraordinary advances in the physical sciences have enabled us to utilize the immense potential of our physical world. Yet our skill in utilizing the immense potential of human cooperation has advanced very little from prehistoric times until now. The field of group dynamics has opened the way to better utilization of the creative energy of collaborative efforts among humans, but there is still a long way to go.

There is, for example, considerable evidence that small groups make more effective decisions than individuals working alone (Johnson, Maruyama, Johnson, Nelson, and Skon, 1981; Johnson, 1980; Watson and Johnson, 1972). But over the years there have been notably few sound efforts to explain what goes on when groups are making decisions or solving problems. The failure to develop theories in this area is noteworthy because many groups exist to solve or to decide in our society. Thousands of small groups are making vital decisions every day, yet we still know little about the internal dynamics of small groups that make effective decisions.

Two distinctions need to be made before the research on individual versus group decision making is discussed. First, certain decision-making situations that are labeled group decision making in fact do not allow members to interact with one another. Making decisions by decree of the designated leader (without group discussion), by edict of an expert, or by averaging members' opinions does not require any group interaction. The Delphi method of group decision making, in which members generate ideas independently, read a summary of the ideas of other members, and then vote, is another example. The evidence supporting the superiority of group decision making to individual decision making is based primarily on situations in which group members do interact with one another.

The second distinction that needs to be made is between groups in which members have the necessary skills and motivation to work collaboratively with one another and those that do not. Obviously, when members cannot communicate or manage conflicts constructively, or when they deliberately sabotage the efforts of the group, the group's decisions may not be superior to those made by individuals.

One of the earliest studies to compare individual and group decision making was conducted by Goodwin Watson (1931). He used three equivalent forms of an intelligence test, each consisting of nine tasks suited to bright adults. Sixty-eight graduate students participated in the study. Each student took the first test alone, students then joined with one another in groups of four or five to solve the second test cooperatively. The third form of the test was taken by each individual alone. The two individual performances were averaged. Groups had no previous practice in working together, and were allowed only ten minutes per task. Eleven of the fifteen groups excelled their *average* member in score; six of the fifteen excelled their *best* individual performer. The typical group attained a level of effective intellectual performance of about the seventieth percentile of its members. The subsequent research generally confirms Watson's findings.

There are a number of reasons why group decision making may be better than individual decision making. These factors include the exchange and utilization of diverse information, increased motivation, cognitive processing of information, the gaining of insight into diverse perspectives from which to view the decision, and a willingness to adopt more extreme positions.

Information Exchange

In most decision-making groups, members with incomplete information interact with others who have different facts and perspectives relevant to the decision. The quality of decision making in such a situation depends on the processes of information exchange. If a high-quality decision is to be made, the resources of each member have to be judged correctly, the participation of all members has to be encouraged, all contributors must be listened to carefully, and the complementary knowledge must be coordinated properly. Thus, the pooling of resources results in a better decision (Laughlin, Branch, and Johnson, 1969; Goldman, 1965).

Within a group, chance errors among members can be corrected (Ziller, 1957). Some members may overestimate and some members may underestimate the advantages of a solution; if these estimates are averaged, the result will be more accurate than the estimate of the typical individual. Blind spots may also be corrected in a group. It is usually easier for us to see others' mistakes than our own. In a group other members can remedy our mistakes and we can remedy theirs. Bekhterev (1924) briefly showed a picture to groups. Members then wrote down all the details they could remember from the picture. A discussion period followed in which the group tried to reach a consensus about each item. The group decision corrected many of the mistaken recollections of the members. Villasenor (1977) notes that the jurors in the Juan Corona trial remembered far more collectively about the evidence and the testimony than they did individually. Shaw (1932), furthermore, concluded from a study on group decision making that a group is better able to recognize and reject incorrect solutions and suggestions than are individuals working alone.

Finally, group discussion often stimulates ideas that might not occur to the individual working alone. In a musical jam session, for example, each member responds continuously to the stimulation of others in building a creative product. Barnlund (1959) found that after a group discussion, decisions surpassed both the average of the decisions of individual members and the best individual answers. A number of studies have found that groups discussing problems derive more crucial insights into how best to solve the problems than do individuals working alone (Johnson, Skon, and Johnson, 1980; Skon, Johnson, and Johnson, 1981). Falk and Johnson (1977) found that group discussions led to decisions that none of the participants had thought of before the discussion.

Motivation to Make a High-Quality Decision

Individuals working in groups often tend to be more motivated to make a high-quality decision than do individuals working alone. There is considerable evidence that a person working in the presence of others often performs better than when working alone (Zajonc, 1980), providing he or she knows well the information on which the decision is based. Groups may benefit from such social-facilitation effects. Working in a group also allows members to imitate the actions of more highly motivated members (Bandura, 1965) and to compare contributions with those of other members (Festinger, 1954), both of which inspire greater efforts.

In cooperative decision-making groups there is usually more support and encouragement for contributing to high-quality decision making than when individuals are working alone (Johnson, 1980). This social encouragement and accountability may be the reason that members of groups, compared with individuals working alone, are more optimistic that a successful decision will be made, are more intrinsically motivated to make a high-quality decision, and are more emotionally involved in the decision-making process (Johnson, 1980).

Finally, there is much evidence that discussing a problem with fellow members of a collaborative group will result in considerably more motivation to rethink a decision and to obtain more information about the problem when one's fellow members disagree with one's conclusions (Johnson, 1980). This aspect of motivation will be discussed more thoroughly in Chapter 6.

Cognitive Processing and Perspective Taking

A group discussion usually results in the cognitive processing of relevant information in a way that increases its understanding and integration by group members. The rehearsal of information relevant to the decision and the elaboration of the information's meaning both increase members' comprehension, deeper-level understanding, and retention of the information being discussed (Johnson, 1979).

The more able a person is to take a variety of perspectives on the decision to be made, the more effective the decision will tend to be (Falk and Johnson, 1977; Johnson, 1977). There is considerably more likelihood that individuals will be challenged by opposing perspectives and build an understanding of diverse ways of viewing the decision to be made when they are part of a collaborative group than when they are working alone. Less fixation on a prominent alternative course of action and more attention to information other than what supports one's initial conclusions may result.

Group Polarization

Groups seem to be more secure than individuals in adopting positions that are more liberal or conservative than those originally held by the members (Myers and Lamm, 1976). A group discussion can polarize decisions by causing the group to adopt a position more extreme than those of the individual members beforehand. This is an advantage when the highest-quality decision requires extreme action. When members show some disagreement at the beginning of a discussion, and the decision has implications for socially accepted behaviors and attitudes, the discussion results in exposure to new information and persuasive arguments, the rehearsal and elaboration of arguments, and the active commitment of members to the position of the group. Thus, group discussion leads to an enhancement of participants' involvement with the issues and their confidence that the group decision is the correct one (Moscovici and Doise, 1974; Moscovici and Zavalloni, 1969).

Conclusions

Some of the factors contributing to the superior decisions made by groups are the increased exchange and utilization of diverse information, the increased motivation of members to make a high-quality decision, the rehearsal and elaboration of information crucial to the making of a high-quality decision, the gaining of insight into a variety of ways of viewing the decision, and the willingness of groups to adopt more extreme positions when necessary. There are, however, a variety of factors that can hamper effective group decision making. It is to these factors that we now turn.

FACTORS HAMPERING EFFECTIVE GROUP DECISION MAKING

As we saw in the previous section, six of the fifteen groups in the Watson (1931) study excelled the decision of their best member. There are a number of possible reasons why more of the groups did not do so: lack of group development or maturity, conflicting goals of group members, failure of members to communicate effectively with one another and utilize one another's information, egocentrism of group members, concurrence seeking within the group, lack of sufficient heterogeneity among members, members interfering with one another's thinking, inappropriate group size, no need for deliberation, loafing by members, power differences and distrust among members, premature closure and dissonance reduction, and lack of sufficient time. Each of these potential hamperers of group-decision-making effectiveness is briefly discussed below.

Lack of Group Maturity

In the study conducted by Watson (1931) and in most of the other studies conducted on group decision making, college students are assigned to groups in which they know none of the other members and in which they stay together for only one hour or so. Such temporary, ad hoc groups do not have time to develop enough maturity to function with full effectiveness. Group members need time and experience working together to develop into an effective decision-making team.

Conflicting Goals of Group Members

Members bring to a group a variety of motives. Some may wish, consciously or unconsciously, to sabotage the group effort. Others have self-oriented needs that may interfere with attention to making an effective decision. Members may be competing with one another in ways that reduce their effectiveness in working together. Even when members are genuinely work-oriented and anxious to achieve results, they may have different ideas about how to proceed.

Failure to Communicate and Utilize Information

Not all members participate equally in a group, and not all contributions are listened to carefully by group members. In many decision-making groups, members fail to communicate through shyness or reluctance to participate. Lack of communication skills may add further problems.

Egocentrism of Group Members

A critical aspect of effective decision making is the ability to view the issues being discussed from a variety of points of view. When members egocentrically present their opinions and coldly evaluate the extent to which the information and conclusions of other members agree with their own, a competition over whose ideas are going to dominate develops. A number of studies indicate that an egocentric approach to decision making results in lower-quality decisions than an approach emphasizing understanding of other members' perspectives (Falk and Johnson, 1977; Johnson, 1972, 1977). The more members are embedded in their own perspective and the more they refuse to consider the perspectives of others, the lower the quality of the group's decisions will be.

Concurrence Seeking Within the Group

Concurrence seeking occurs when members of a group inhibit discussion in order to avoid any disagreement or arguments, emphasize agreement, and avoid realistic appraisal of alternative ideas and courses of action. Quick compromises and censorship of disagreement are characteristic of groups dominated by concurrence seeking. Concurrence seeking typically results in poor decision making, a fact that will be discussed thoroughly in Chapter 6.

Lack of Sufficient Heterogeneity

Whether a group will be optimally productive depends on how fully the necessary information, skills, and viewpoints are represented. The more homogeneous the participants, the less each member adds to the resources present in the others. In general, homogeneous groups make less effective decisions than heterogeneous groups (Johnson, 1980).

Interference

Because only one person can talk (and be heard by all the others) at any one time, participants in a discussion often have to wait to make their point. Sometimes the delay is so long that the whole course of the discussion has changed before the would-be speaker gets a chance to be heard. He or she may then drop the idea entirely, which deprives the group, or may bring up the idea belatedly, which causes the others to backtrack from the issues they have moved on to. There are times when the participation of one member may interfere with the participation of other members and lower the decision-making effectiveness of the group.

Inappropriate Group Size

Some decisions require that a large number of persons participate; other decisions need only one or two individuals. An inappropriate group size may interfere with effective group decision making. In groups of more than eight or nine members, a few participants are likely to dominate and others are likely to remain passive (Watson and Johnson, 1972). It is important that decision-making groups be large enough so that needed resources and diversity are present, but small enough so that everyone's resources are fully utilized, participation is high, acceptance and support by all members is possible, and coordination is easy (Johnson, 1980).

No Need for Deliberations

When the correct decision is already known by one or more members, the process of decision making becomes less an aspect of problem solving and more a persuasive situation. Laughlin (1980) has noted that when one person in a group knows the answer to a problem, members who do not know the answer often do not agree to the correct solution.

Leaving Work to Others

The "let George do it" attitude illustrates the tendency in some groups to assume that someone else will take the necessary responsibility. There are certain types of tasks on which many persons seem to loaf when they are part of a group. Cheering and clapping after a performance, for example, becomes less intense when others in the audience are also cheering and clapping (Latane, Williams, and Harkings, 1979).

Power Differences and Distrust

The quality of group decision making often suffers because of differences in power among members and lack of trust in what the high-power person will do if other members actively disagree with him or her. Those in high-power positions can talk freely and be listened to, but often this is a one-way affair. Many groups have explicit or implicit power structures that impede free communication. Torrance (1954), for example, studied the decision making of B-26 combat crews, in which the pilot was the commanding officer, the navigator was a commissioned officer, and the gunner was an enlisted man inferior in status to the two officers. He found that when one of the men had the right answer and the other two were mistaken, the pilots were almost always successful in persuading the other two to accept their view (94 percent), the navigators not quite as successful (80 percent), and the gunners much less persuasive (63 percent). It is not uncommon in decision-making groups for a low-power person to have a critical insight or piece of information and be ignored.

Premature Closure and Dissonance Reduction

Making a decision prematurely and then reducing any dissonance felt by group members can contribute to ineffective decision making. According to dissonance theory, any time one is forced to choose between two attractive options, postdecision dissonance is present (Festinger, 1957). Cognitive dissonance exists when a person possesses two cognitions that contradict each other. Dissonance exists, for example, if a group member knows the group selected one alternative as the most desirable option when other attractive alternatives also exist. A state of dissonance is assumed to motivate group members to reduce or eliminate it. One way to reduce the dissonance is to increase the perceived desirability of the decision made and decrease the perceived desirability of the alternatives that were not adopted. The more difficult or important the decision, the more likely group members are to find reasons that support the choice that was made and to minimize the attractive qualities of the foregone choice. This spreads apart the alternatives so that the one chosen is viewed as more attractive (in comparison with the other alternatives) after the decision than before it. If the group needs to reconsider the decision or reopen the decision making, dissonance reduction may interfere with their doing so.

Lack of Sufficient Time

The superiority of group to individual decision making depends in part on having enough time. A short work period favors the individual response; it takes time for group members to become adjusted to one another, to express ideas, to assimilate one another's contributions, to interact, to criticize, and to integrate proposals. The larger the group, the longer the time required. Groups need enough time to thoroughly discuss the issues, especially when their task does not have a clear answer (Fox and Lorge, 1962; South, 1927).

Summary

Although groups tend to make higher-quality decisions than individuals working alone, there is nothing magical about groups. In order for high-quality decision making to take place within a group, the group needs to work together long enough to mature and to develop effective patterns of interaction among members. Conflicting goals of individual members need to be resolved. All members need to participate and have the necessary social skills to present their information and ensure that it is incorporated into the group's deliberations. Egocentric refusal to consider any ideas but one's own needs to be avoided by group members. Avoidance and suppression of conflict and disagreement must also be avoided. A group needs sufficient heterogeneity among its members to ensure that different viewpoints and resources will be contributed to the discussion. Participation of members needs to be managed so that all members contribute without interfering with one another's thinking processes. Group size needs to be appropriate to the problem, the problem has to be important to group members, and there needs to be sufficient time to deal with the problem. Power within the group needs to be managed constructively, and members' motivation needs to be sustained. Quick decisions and premature closure need to avoided.

QUIZ

Check your comprehension of the previous section by answering the following questions. Answers are on page 134.

1. Ann organizes her workforce into groups because she knows that decisions made by a group can be superior to an individual's decisions since groups contribute to (check five):
   a. increased exchange and use of diverse information.
   b. increased motivation of members to make a high-quality decision.
   c. increased complication of the task and thus a more detailed solution.
   d. rehearsal and elaboration of information crucial to high quality decisions.
   e. gaining of insight into a variety of ways to view the decision.
   f. willingness to go along with the expert in the group.
   g. willingness to adopt more extreme positions when necessary.

2. Ann is also careful about the details of the group's organization because she knows that decisions made by a group can be inferior if (check eight):
   a. the leader is extensively trained.
   b. the group has not worked together long enough to develop maturity and effective interaction patterns.
   c. members have conflicting goals.
   d. members refuse to consider ideas other than their own.
   e. conflict and disagreement are avoided or suppressed.
   f. there is not enough heterogeneity to ensure different viewpoints and resources.
   g. the group size does not fit the needs of the problem.
   h. there is not enough time.
   i. there is too much time.
   j. unequal power is equalized.
   k. decisions are made quickly and prematurely.

THE BEAN JAR EXERCISE (I)

The purpose of this exercise is to compare the reactions of group members to the seven methods of decision making discussed in the next section of this chapter. A large jar full of a known quantity of beans is required for the exercise. The procedure for the coordinator is as follows:

1. Set a large jar of beans in front of the participants. You need to know exactly how many beans are in the jar. Inform the participants that they will be asked to estimate how many beans the jar contains.

2. Divide the participants into heterogeneous groups of six. Seven groups are ideal for this exercise. Appoint one member of the group to be the recorder. After the group has made its decision and all group members have completed the postdecision questionnaire (at the end of the exercise), the recorder collects the results and computes a group average for each question by totaling the individual scores for each question and dividing the sum by the number of members in the group.

3. State that each group has to estimate the number of beans the jar contains. Assign one method of decision making to each group. The instructions for each method are as follows:

a. The member with the most authority makes the decision: One member is appointed leader by the coordinator. This person should exercise control by such means as telling the group how to sit while waiting for the decision to be made and how to use their time while she is deciding. The leader then estimates how many beans are in the jar and announces her decision to the group. All members of the group then complete the postdecision questionnaire.

b. The member with the most expertise makes the decision: The coordinator appoints the member with the most training in mathematics to be the leader. The expert then considers how many beans are in the jar, makes a decision, and announces it to the group. All group members then complete the postdecision questionnaire.

c. The opinions of the individual members are averaged: Each member of the group backs away from the group so that he cannot see the answers of other group members and they cannot see his answer. Each member independently estimates the number of beans in the jar without interacting with the other group members. The recorder then asks each member for his estimate, adds the estimates, and divides the sum by the number of members. The resulting number is announced as the group's decision. All group members then complete the postdecision questionnaire.

d. The member with the most authority makes the decision following a group discussion: One member is appointed leader by the coordinator, and she calls the meeting to order. She asks the group to discuss how many beans are in the jar. When she thinks she knows how many beans are in the jar she announces her decision to the group. This is not consensus or majority vote—the leader has full responsibility and makes the decision he thinks is best. All members of the group then complete the postdecision questionnaire.

e. A minority of group members makes the decision: The coordinator appoints an executive committee of two members. The committee meets away from the group to decide how many beans are in the jar. They announce their decision to the group. All group members then complete the postdecision questionnaire.

f. Majority vote: Each group member estimates the number of beans in the jar, and the group then votes on which estimate is to be its decision. When the majority of members agree on an estimate, the group decision is made. All group members then complete the postdecision questionnaire.

g. Consensus: All members of the group participate in a discussion as to how many beans are in the jar. Discuss the issue until all members of the group can live with and support the group's estimate. Follow the basic guidelines for consensual decision making given on page 106. When an estimate is agreed on, all members of the group complete the postdecision questionnaire.

4. Collect the results from the postdecision questionnaires and enter them in the summary table below. Instruct each group to make four conclusions as to what is to be learned from these results. Have each group share its conclusions with the class. Then conduct a class discussion on how the conclusions agree or disagree with the material presented in this chapter. Point out the following relationships:

a. The extent to which a member feels understood and influential in the group is related to how well his or her resources are utilized.

b. The extent to which a member is committed to the decision and responsible for its implementation is related to his or her commitment to implement the decision.

c. The extent to which a member is satisfied with his or her participation and the positiveness of the atmosphere of the group is related to the future problem-solving ability of the group.

5. Note how accurate each group's estimate was. Usually, the more group members directly involved in the decision making the more effective the decision is.

Postdecision Questionnaire

On a sheet of paper record your answers to the following questions. Then hand the paper to the recorder in your group.

1. How understood and listened to did you feel in your group?
Not at all 1 : 2 : 3 : 4 : 5 : 6 : 7 : 8 : 9 Completely

2. How much influence do you feel you had in your group's decision making?
None 1 : 2 : 3 : 4 : 5 : 6 : 7 : 8 : 9 A great deal

3. How committed do you feel to the decision your group made?
Very uncommitted 1 : 2 : 3 : 4 : 5 : 6 : 7 : 8 : 9 Very committed

4. How much responsibility do you feel for making the decision work?
None 1 : 2 : 3 : 4 : 5 : 6 : 7 : 8 : 9 A great deal

5. How satisfied do you feel with the amount and quality of your participation in your group's decision making?
Very dissatisfied 1 : 2 : 3 : 4 : 5 : 6 : 7 : 8 : 9 Very satisfied

6. Write one adjective that describes the atmosphere in your group during the decision making. _____

METHODS OF DECISION MAKING

Think about the groups to which you belong. How do they make decisions? Do different groups use different methods? Does your family use the same procedure for making decisions that you and your friends do? Among the alternatives listed below, which decision-making method would you prefer for the groups to which you belong?

1. Rely on the person in charge of the group because she should have the power to make the decision she believes is best, no matter what the rest of the group members think. The designated leader has the responsibility; she should also have the power to make the decisions.

2. Postpone making a decision and wait it out. Time takes care of everything; with a little luck a decision will never have to be made if the group waits long enough.

Results of Postdecision Questionnaire

Method of Decision Making	Understanding	Influence	Committment	Responsibility	Satisfaction	Atmosphere
Decision by authority without discussion						
Expert member						
Average member						
Decision by authority after discussion						
Minority rule						
Majority vote						
Consensus						

3. Let the expert make the decision. Give the person with the most expertise in the group the authority to make whatever decision he thinks best.

4. Find out what each member thinks, and then choose the most popular alternative. With this method the group does not even have to meet; members are polled individually.

5. Flip a coin, roll the dice, or pick a number out of a hat.

6. Rely on the person in charge of the group to make the decision, but only after the group has thoroughly discussed the issue with that person.

7. Put the decision in the hands of a knowledgeable and qualified committee that will look at the issues, decide what the group should do, and tell the group members its decision.

8. Take a vote and let the majority rule. The issues should be presented to the group, discussed, and then a vote held with the majority deciding.

9. Ask the group next door what it is going to do and then do just the opposite.

10. Obtain a basic agreement among everyone in the group as to what the decision should be. The issues should be thoroughly discussed, each member participating, until all agree on what the group should do.

There are many ways in which a group can make a decision. We shall take up seven of the major ones. Do not judge which methods are desirable and undesirable. Each decision-making method has its uses and is appropriate under certain circumstances. Each also has its particular consequences for the group's future operation. An effective group understands each method of decision making well enough to choose the method that is best for:

1. the type of decision to be made.
2. the amount of time and resources available.
3. the history of the group.
4. the nature of the task being worked on.
5. the kind of climate the group wishes to establish.
6. the type of setting in which the group is working.

The seven methods of decision making to be discussed below result in decisions being made by:

1. the member with the most authority, without a group discussion.
2. the member with the most expertise, without a group discussion.
3. averaging the opinions of individual group members, without a group discussion.
4. the member with the most authority, following a group discussion.

5. a minority of group members, without the consultation of the entire group.

6. a majority vote following a group discussion.

7. consensus, or agreement of the entire group following a group discussion.

Method 1: Decision by Authority Without Group Discussion

In this method the designated leader makes all the decisions without consulting the group members in any way. This method is quite common in organizations. It is an efficient method in the sense that it can take a short time to execute, but it is not very effective. Even if the designated leader is a good listener who sorts out the correct information upon which to make his decision, it is still the group that has to act on the decision, and under this method the involvement of the other group members is very small. Furthermore, when the designated leader makes the decision, not all members of the group may understand what it is; they may not, therefore, be able to implement it. And if they disagree with it, they may not want to implement it. Under this method, how well the decision is implemented is particularly crucial.

Method 2: Decision by Expert

Group decisions can be made by letting the most expert member in the group decide what the group should do. The procedure for this method is to select the expert, let her consider the issues, and then have her tell the group what the decision is. The group does not discuss the issue, but rather lets the expert decide on her own.

There is one major problem with this method: how to tell which member has the most expertise. On most complex issues, individuals disagree as to what the best approach is, and this makes it difficult for them to identify the expert among them. Personal popularity and the amount of power a person has over the group members often interfere with the selection of the most expert member. The classic illustration of this point is the story of the general with a high-school education and several captains with Ph.D.'s in engineering discussing how a bridge should be built. Needless to say, it is the general who designs the bridge, simply because he has the most power. Individuals with a lot of power are notorious for overestimating their expertise while underestimating that of others. Unless there is a clear and effective way to determine who the expert is, this method does not work very well. Moreover, it too fails to win the involvement of other group members, which is necessary for implementing the decision.

Method 3: Decision by Averaging Individuals' Opinions

This method consists of separately asking each group member her opinion and then averaging the results. When a chairwoman of a group, for example, calls each member on the telephone, asks what the member's opinion is, and then takes the most popular opinion as the group's decision, she is using the averaging method. This procedure is like majority voting, except that the group's decision may be determined by less than 50 percent of the members (the most common opinion is not necessarily the opinion of more than half of the members) and no direct discussion is held among members as to what decision the group should make.

Because individual errors and extreme opinions tend to cancel themselves out under this method, it is usually a better procedure to follow than the designated-leader method (without a group discussion). At least members are consulted in this method. The disadvantage of the method is that the opinions of the least knowledgeable members may annul the opinions of the most knowledgeable members. Letting the most expert member make the decision is always better than using a group average to decide. And although group members are consulted before the decision is made, they are still little involved in the decision making itself. Consequently their commitment to the decision is not very strong. If implementation of a decision made by this method requires the efforts of all group members, the effectiveness of the decision will probably be slight.

Method 4: Decision by Authority After Group Discussion

Many groups have an authority structure that clearly indicates that the designated leader will make the decisions. Groups that function within organizations such as businesses and government agencies usually employ this method of decision making. The group does originate ideas and hold discussions, but it is the designated leader who makes the final decision. Under this method the designated leader calls a meeting of the group, presents the issues, listens to the discussion until he is sure of what he thinks the decision should be, and then announces his decision to the group.

Listening to a group discussion will usually improve the accuracy of a decision made by the group's leader. The greater the designated leader's skill as a listener, the greater will be the benefits of the group discussion. But although members can become involved in the discussion, they have no part in the decision making, which does not help the decision's effectiveness. As a result, the group members tend to either compete to impress the leader or tell the leader what they think he wants to hear.

Method 5: Decision by Minority

A minority—two or more members who constitute less than 50 percent of the group—can make the group's decisions in several ways, some legitimate and some illegitimate. One legitimate method is for the minority to act as an executive committee composed of only a few members, making all but the most important decisions for the group. Another is for the minority to act as a temporary committee that considers special problems and decides what action the group should take. The illegitimate methods involve railroading. For instance, two or more members may come to a quick agreement on a course of action, challenge the rest of the group with a sudden "Does anyone object?" and, if no one replies fast enough, proceed with a "Let's go ahead, then." Or a minority may forcibly recommend a course of action—implying that anyone who disagrees is in for a fight—and then move ahead before other members can consider the issue carefully. We shall focus on the legitimate methods of minority decision making; group members should be able to tell when they are being railroaded.

The minority members who make the decision may be committed to it, but the majority may not only be uncommitted, they may even want to keep the decision from being implemented. When a few members railroad a decision, furthermore, they seem to assume that persons who are silent agree. But often a majority of group members need more time to organize their thoughts against a proposal, or sometimes members keep silent because they are afraid they are the only ones who disagree. When a group has a large number of decisions to be made and not enough time to deal with them all, decision-making committees can be efficient. This method may also be effective if a large number of decisions do not need member involvement in order to be implemented. In general, however, decision by minority is not a good method of decision making.

Method 6: Decision by Majority Vote

Majority vote is the method of group decision making most commonly used in the United States. Its procedure is to discuss an issue only as long as it takes at least 51 percent of the members to decide on a course of action. This method is so common in our society—indeed, it is almost a ritual—that it is often taken for granted as the natural way for any group to make decisions. And it is certainly one of the methods that is used most often. On the surface, majority voting resembles our election system, but there are critical differences between elections and the use of majority vote in most groups. In our political system minority rights are carefully protected through the Bill of Rights and the Constitution, and political minorities always have the right to compete on equal terms in the next election in order to become a majority. In most groups, however, minority opinions are not always safeguarded. Thus, majority voting often splits a group into "winners" and "losers," encourages "either/or" thinking (when there may be other ways of looking at a problem), and fosters blind argument rather than rational discussion. A minority that has often been outvoted is not contributing its resources toward influencing the decision. This circumstance not only reduces the quality of the decision but often creates coalitions of individuals who resent losing the vote and who try to regroup, pick up support, and overturn the decision. When a task needs the support of everyone in the group, when the lack of support, or sabotage, by one or more members could seriously damage the undertaking, a decision by vote can be dangerous. Where commitment by everyone is not essential, of course, a majority vote can serve very well. If majority voting is to be used, however, the group must be sure that it has created a climate in which members feel they have had their day in court and will feel obliged to support the majority decision.

Method 7: Decision by Consensus

Consensus is the most effective method of group decision making, but it also takes the most time. Perfect consensus means that everyone agrees what the decision should be. Unanimity, however, is often impossible to achieve. There are degrees of consensus, all of which bring about a higher-quality decision than majority vote or other methods of decision making. Consensus is more commonly defined as a collective opinion arrived at by a group of individuals working together under conditions that permit communications to be sufficiently open—and the group climate to be sufficiently supportive—for everyone in the group to feel that he has had his fair chance to influence the decision. When a decision is made by consensus, all members understand the decision and are prepared to support it. In operation, consensus means that all members can rephrase the decision to show that they understand it, that all members have had a chance to tell the group how they feel about the decision, and that those members who continue to disagree or have doubts will nevertheless say publicly that they are willing to give the decision a try for a period of time.

To achieve consensus, members must have enough time to state their views and, in particular, their opposition to other members' views. By the time the decision is made they should be feeling that others really do understand them. Group members, therefore, must listen carefully and communicate effectively. Decisions made by consensus are sometimes referred to as synergistic decisions, because the group members working together arrive at a decision of higher quality than the decision they would obtain if each one worked separately. In reaching consensus, group members need to see differences of opinion as a way of (1) gathering additional information, (2) clarifying issues, and (3) forcing the group to seek better alternatives.

The basic guidelines for consensual decision making are as follows:

1. Avoid arguing blindly for your own opinions. Present your position as clearly and logically as possible, but listen to other members' reactions and consider them carefully before you press your point.

2. Avoid changing your mind *only* to reach agreement and avoid conflict.

Support only solutions with which you are at least somewhat able to agree. Yield only to positions that have objective and logically sound foundations.

3. Avoid conflict-reducing procedures such as majority voting, tossing a coin, averaging, and bargaining.

4. Seek out differences of opinion. They are natural and expected. Try to involve everyone in the decision process. Disagreements can improve the group's decision because they present a wide range of information and opinions, thereby creating a better chance for the group to hit upon more adequate solutions.

5. Do not assume that someone must win and someone must lose when discussion reaches a stalemate. Instead, look for the next most acceptable alternative for all members.

6. Discuss underlying assumptions, listen carefully to one another, and encourage the participation of *all* members.

Consensus is the best method for producing an innovative, creative, and high-quality decision that (1) all members will be committed to implementing, (2) uses the resources of all group members, and (3) increases the future decision-making effectiveness of the group. Consensus is not easy to achieve (Kerr et al., 1976), but is worth the time and trouble as it is characterized by more conflict among members, more shifts of opinion, a longer time to reach a conclusion, and more confidence by members in the correctness of their decision (Nemeth, 1977). Consensus requires a fairly sophisticated understanding of the dynamics of controversy, distributed participation and leadership, communication, and all other group and interpersonal skills. All group members must participate actively, and power must be distributed evenly among them.

Decisions by consensus take a great deal of time and member motivation, and often prove frustrating to designated leaders. But in terms of the future ability of the group to make high-quality decisions, consensus productively resolves controversies and conflicts—which majority vote, minority rule, and all other methods of decision making do not. Research shows that the more effective groups tend to have designated leaders who allow greater participation, and more differences of opinions and who express greater acceptance of different decisions (Torrance, 1957). Effective leaders have been shown to encourage minority opinions and conflict to a greater extent than less effective leaders (Maier and Solem, 1952). Groups members with little influence over a decision not only fail to contribute their resources to it, but usually are less likely to carry it out when action is required (Coch and French, 1948). If consensus is to be used effectively, all group members must contribute their views on the issue and their reactions to proposed alternatives for group action; no one should be allowed to remain silent. For a group to achieve consensus, furthermore, time must be allowed for everybody to state her opposition fully enough to feel that the others understand her—a procedure that requires careful listening and effective communication by the group members.

The advantages and disadvantages of consensus and the other six methods of decision making discussed above are summarized in Table 3.1.

TABLE 3.1 Advantages and disadvantages of decision-making methods

Method of Decision Making	Disadvantages	Advantages
1. Decision by authority without discussion	One person is not a good resource for every decision; advantages of group interaction are lost; no commitment to implementing the decision is developed among other group members; resentment and disagreement may result in sabotage and deterioration of group effectiveness; resources of other members are not used	Applies more to administrative needs; useful for simple, routine decisions; should be used when very little time is available to make the decision, when group members expect the designated leader to make the decision, and when group members lack the skills and information to make the decision any other way.
2. Expert member	It is difficult to determine who the expert is; no commitment to implement the decision is built; advantages of group interaction are lost; resentment and disagreement may result in sabotage and deterioration of group effectiveness; resources of other members are not used.	Useful when the expertise of one person is so far superior to that of all other group members that little is to be gained by discussion; should be used when the need for membership action in implementing the decision is slight.
3. Average of members' opinions	There is not enough interaction among group members for them to gain from each other's resources and from the benefits of group discussion; no commitment to implement the decision is built; unresolved conflict and controversy may damage group effectiveness in the future.	Useful when it is difficult to get group members together to talk, when the decision is so urgent that there is no time for group discussion, when member commitment is not necessary for implementing the decision, and when group members lack the skills and information to make the decision any other way; applicable to simple, routine decisions.
4. Decision by authority after discussion	Does not develop commitment to implement the decision; does not resolve the controversies and conflicts among group members; tends to create situations in which group members either compete to impress the designated leader or tell the leader what they think he or she wants to hear.	Uses the resources of the group members more than previous methods; gains some of the benefits of group discussion.

Method of Decision Making	Disadvantages	Advantages
5. Majority control	Usually leaves an alienated minority, which damages future group effectiveness; relevant resources of many group members may be lost; full commitment to implement the decision is absent; full benefit of group interaction is not obtained.	Can be used when sufficient time is lacking for decision by consensus or when the decision is not so important that consensus needs to be used, and when complete member commitment is not necessary for implementing the decision; closes discussion on issues that are not highly important for the group.
6. Minority control	Does not utilize the resources of many group members; does not establish widespread commitment to implement the decision; unresolved conflict and controversy may damage future group effectiveness; not much benefit from group interaction.	Can be used when everyone cannot meet to make a decision, when the group is under such time pressure that it must delegate responsibility to a committee, when only a few members have any relevant resources, and when broad member commitment is not needed to implement the decision; useful for simple, routine decisions.
7. Consensus	Takes a great deal of time and psychological energy and a high level of member skill; time pressure must be minimal, and there must be no emergency in progress.	Produces an innovative, creative, and high-quality decision; elicits commitment by all members to implement the decision; uses the resources of all members; the future decision-making ability of the group is enhanced; useful in making serious, important, and complex decisions to which all members are to be committed.

THE RELATION BETWEEN TIME AND DECISION METHOD

Every method of decision making takes a different amount of time to carry out. Obviously, methods that involve group discussion take more time than methods that do not. Usually, the more persons involved in the decision making the longer it will take to reach a decision. Figure 3.1 summarizes the relationship among the number of persons involved, the type of method used, the quality of the decision, and the time needed to arrive at a decision. If the time needed for both making and implementing a decision is considered, however, the time factor becomes less clear. Often the extra time taken to make a consensual decision will greatly reduce the time needed to implement it. Thus, many group authorities insist that if the whole process of decision making and implementation is considered, consensus is the *least* time-consuming method.

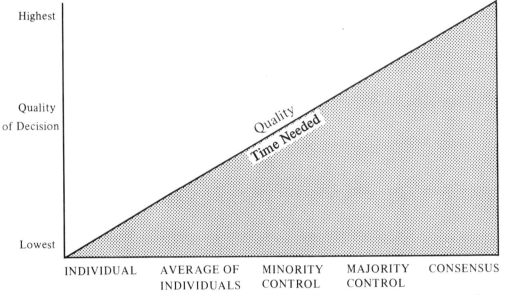

FIGURE 3.1 Quality of decision and time needed, as a function of number of decision makers.

QUIZ

Check your reading of the previous section by answering the following matching and true-false questions. Answers are on page 135.

_____ 1. Leader makes decision

_____ 2. Everyone must agree

_____ 3. At least 51% of the members must agree

_____ 4. Leader makes decision after listening to group

_____ 5. The one who knows the most makes the decision

_____ 6. Leader polls members; decision is the most popular response

_____ 7. A small subgroup makes the decision

a. Consensus
b. Majority vote
c. Minority
d. Averaging
e. Expert
f. Authority with discussion
g. Authority without discussion

____ **8.** Considered to take the most time

____ **9.** Considered to take the least time

____ **10.** Considered the highest quality decision

____ **11.** Considered the lowest quality decision

____ **12.** Useful when members cannot meet

____ **13.** Usually leaves an alienated minority

____ **14.** Group members may compete to impress the leader

____ **15.** Useful in serious, important, and complex decisions

____ **16.** You are a superintendent of a small, traditional school system. You would like to introduce new methods of teaching. What decision-making method should you use to get the teachers to change?

____ **17.** You are a teacher. A student is tardy to class. What decision-making method should you use to determine the proper punishment?

True   False   **18.** The extra time needed to make a consensual decision is offset by the lesser time it takes to implement it.

True   False   **19.** There is one decision making method which should be used constantly while the others should be avoided.

True   False   **20.** People with a lot of power usually overestimate their own expertise and underestimate the expertise of others.

WINTER SURVIVAL EXERCISE

The purpose of this exercise is to compare the effectiveness of five different methods of making decisions. Three of the methods do not utilize group discussion; the others do. The methods compared are: (1) decision by a designated leader before a discussion, (2) decision by averaging members' opinions, (3) decision by expert member, (4) decision by a designated leader after a discussion, and (5) decision by consensus. At least four groups of eight to twelve members each should take part. Inasmuch as the results are very predictable, however, fewer groups with fewer members may be used if necessary. The exercise takes approximately two hours. The materials needed are as follows:

instructions for observers

a description of the situation and a decision form

a group summary sheet

instructions for groups that decide by consensus

instructions for groups whose leader decides

a summary table

The coordinator for the exercise should use the following procedure:

1. State that the purpose of the exercise is to compare several different methods of decision making. Set the stage by pointing out that group decision making is one of the most significant aspects of group functioning, that most consequential decisions are made by groups rather than individuals, that though many decisions are routine others are extremely crucial, and that participants in this exercise are now in a situation where the decisions they make as a group may determine whether or not they survive.

2. Divide the participants into groups of approximately eight members—six participants and two observers. Give each group a number or name for purposes of identification, ask the observers to meet at a central place to be briefed, and then distribute the description and decision forms to the participants. Review the situation with the participants, again emphasizing that their survival depends upon the quality of their decision. In half the groups designate one person as the leader; in the other groups make no mention of leadership. Then instruct the participants to complete the decision form quietly and by themselves so that the results indicate their own decisions. They have fifteen minutes to complete the decision form and make a duplicate copy of their ranking. The designated group leaders should write "leader" on their duplicate copy, and all participants must write their group designation on their duplicate copy. At the end of the fifteen minutes collect the duplicate copies.

3. While the participants are completing their decision forms, brief the observers. Give each a copy of the instructions for observers and copies of the description and decision form (to orient them to the group task). Review the instructions to make sure the observers understand their task.

4. Distribute one copy of the group summary sheet and the appropriate instruction sheet to each participant. The groups with a leader their instruction sheet and the groups without a leader the other instruction sheet. Observers should also receive a copy of the instructions for their group. The groups should be placed far enough apart so that they cannot hear each other's discussions or be aware that they have different instructions. The groups have forty-five minutes to decide upon a group ranking of the items on the decision form. They are to make a copy of their group ranking with their group designation clearly written on the top.

5. While the groups are working on their rankings, score the individual decision forms in the following way:

    a. Score the net difference between the participant's answer and the correct answer. For example, if the participant's answer was 9 and the correct answer is 12, the net difference is 3. Disregard all plus or minus signs; find only the net difference for each item. (The correct ranking appears in Appendix D.)

    b. Total these scores; the result is the participant's score. The lower the score the more accurate the ranking.

    c. To arrive at an average member score, total all members' scores for each group and divide by the number of members.

    d. Put the scores in order from best to worst for each group. This ranking will be used to compare how many members, if any, had more accurate scores than the group's score.

    e. In the summary table that follows the instruction sheets for the groups, enter the average member's score for each group and the score of the most accurate group member. Then, for the groups with a designated leader, enter the score of that person.

6. At the end of forty minutes, give a five-minute warning. After forty-five minutes instruct the groups to complete their ranking in the next thirty seconds and, with the group number or name clearly marked on the paper, to turn in their group ranking. Quickly score the groups' rankings and enter them in the appropriate place in the summary table. Recruit one or two observers to help if you need them.

7. In a session with all the participants, give the correct ranking and the rationale for each item. The correct ranking and the rationale appears on pages 474 to 477, Appendix D. Then explain how the rankings are scored so that each person can determine his or her score.

8. Present the data in the summary table, preferably on a blackboard or a sheet of newsprint so that everyone can see it. Review the purpose of the exercise (to compare five different methods of making decisions), and then present the data in this order:

    a. State that one way to make a decision is to have the designated leader make it, and that this is a very common practice in most organizations. Write in the leader scores, and compare them to see which group had the most accurate leader.

    b. Move on to the next column, which is reserved for another way in which to make a decision: to poll the group and take the average opinion. Enter these data in the table and compare them with the leader scores. Usually the group average will be better than the designated leader's scores.

    c. Refer to the third column as a third decision-making method: to let the most expert member make the decision. Enter the scores of the most accurate group members in the summary table and compare with the other two methods. The expert score is usually far superior to the other two. The problem, however, is that it is often hard to identify who the most expert member of the group is; the person with the most power often believes he or she is the most expert.

    d. Point out that these first three methods represent decision procedures that do not require group interaction, that the next two procedures do involve interaction among group members and discussion as to what the decision should be, and that research on decision making overwhelmingly indicates that under most conditions discussion methods are better than nondiscussion methods.

e. Review the instructions to the "leader" groups. Then state that a fourth way of making decisions is to have a designated leader make the decision after a group discussion. This method is also very common in most organizations. Enter the relevant data and compare them with the first three methods.

f. Explain that the fifth column represents another way of making decisions: by group consensus. Review the instructions for the "consensus" groups. Enter the appropriate data and compare with the other four methods. When a group is functioning well, the consensus score should be better than the scores resulting from all the other methods.

9. Give the groups twenty minutes to discuss the data presented and the way in which they functioned, using as a basis of their discussions the notations of the observers. Ask each group to write out on newsprint a list of conclusions that they can share with the other groups. Here are some questions the group might discuss:

a. How well did the group use its resources? Was there anyone who had valuable information who could not persuade others to his or her point of view? If so, why? How were silent members treated by the group: were they encouraged to participate or left alone?

b. What factors caused the group to use its resources well—or not well? Who behaved in what ways to influence group functioning?

c. Was there anyone who forced his or her opinion on the group? If so, why was he or she able to do this?

d. Did the group follow its instructions in making decisions? What influence did the instructions have on the way the group functioned?

e. What were the personal reactions of one particular group member to the group decision making? How did this person feel? What was he or she thinking?

f. How similar were the behaviors in this exercise to those in other group sessions? What implications does this exercise have for group meetings?

10. Share the conclusions of each group in a general session and discuss the material on decision making included in this chapter.

Instructions to Observers

This exercise looks at the process by which groups make decisions. Crucial issues are how well the group uses the resources of its members, how much commitment to implement the decision is mustered, how the future decision-making ability of the group is affected, and how members feel about and react to what is taking place. As an observer, you may wish to focus on the following issues:

1. Who does and does not participate in the discussion? Who participates the most?

2. Who influences the decision and who does not? How is influence determined (expertise, sex, loudness of voice)?

3. Who is involved and who is uninvolved?

4. What are the dominant feelings of the group members? How would you describe the group atmosphere during the meeting?

5. What leadership behaviors are present and absent in the group? You may wish to use the task-behavior and maintenance-behavior observation sheets on pp. 69–70.

6. What are the basic causes for the members' resources being used or not being used?

Winter Survival Exercise: The Situation

You have just crash-landed in the woods of northern Minnesota and southern Manitoba. It is 11:32 A.M. in mid-January. The light plane in which you were traveling crashed on a lake. The pilot and copilot were killed. Shortly after the crash the plane sank completely into the lake with the pilot's and copilot's bodies inside. None of you are seriously injured and you are all dry.

The crash came suddenly, before the pilot had time to radio for help or inform anyone of your position. Since your pilot was trying to avoid a storm, you know the plane was considerably off course. The pilot announced shortly before the crash that you were twenty miles northwest of a small town that is the nearest known habitation.

You are in a wilderness area made up of thick woods broken by many lakes and streams. The snow depth varies from above the ankles in windswept areas to knee-deep where it has drifted. The last weather report indicated that the temperature would reach minus twenty-five degrees Fahrenheit in the daytime and minus forty at night. There is plenty of dead wood and twigs in the immediate area. You are dressed in winter clothing appropriate for city wear—suits, pantsuits, street shoes, and overcoats.

While escaping from the plane the several members of your group salvaged twelve items. Your task is to rank these items according to their importance to your survival, starting with *1* for the most important item and ending with *12* for the least important one.

You may assume that the number of passengers is the same as the number of persons in your group, and that the group has agreed to stick together.

Winter Survival Decision Form

Rank the following items according to their importance to your survival, starting with *1* for the most important one and proceeding to *12* for the least important one.

_____ Ball of steel wool

_____ Newspapers (one per person)

_____ Compass

_____ Hand ax

_____ Cigarette lighter (without fluid)

_____ Loaded .45-caliber pistol

_____ Sectional air map made of plastic

_____ Twenty-by-twenty-foot piece of heavy-duty canvas

_____ Extra shirt and pants for each survivor

_____ Can of shortening

_____ Quart of 100-proof whiskey

_____ Family-size chocolate bar (one per person)

Winter Survival: Group Summary Sheet

Item	Members						Summary
	1	2	3	4	5	6	
Ball of steel wool							
Newspapers							
Compass							
Hand ax							
Cigarette lighter							
.45-caliber pistol							
Sectional air map							
Canvas							
Shirt and pants							
Shortening							
Whiskey							
Chocolate bars							

Instructions for Groups Without a Leader

This is an exercise in group decision making. Your group is to employ the method of group consensus in reaching its decision. This means that the ranking for each of the twelve survival items *must* be agreed upon by each group member before it becomes a part of the group decision. Consensus is difficult to reach. Therefore, not every ranking will meet with everyone's complete approval. Try, as a group, to make each ranking one with which all group members can at least partially agree. Here are some guidelines to use in reaching consensus:

1. Avoid arguing *blindly* for your own opinions. Present your position as clearly and logically as possible, but listen to other members' reactions and consider them carefully before you press your point.

2. Avoid changing your mind just to reach agreement and avoid conflict. Support only solutions with which you are able to agree to at least some degree. Yield only to positions that have objective and logically sound foundations.

Summary Table: Accuracy of Decisions

| group | Before Group Discussion | | | After Group Discussion | | | | | |
	designated leader's score	average member's score	most accurate member's score	leader-group score	consensus-group score	gain or loss over designated leader's score	gain or loss over average member's score	gain or loss over most accurate member's score	number of members superior to group score
1									
2									
3									
4									

3. Avoid conflict-reducing procedures such as majority voting, tossing a coin, averaging, and bargaining.

4. Seek out differences of opinion. They are natural and expected. Try to involve everyone in the decision process. Disagreements can improve the group's decision because a wide range of information and opinions improves the chances of the group to hit upon more adequate solutions.

5. Do not assume that someone must win and someone must lose when discussion reaches a stalemate. Instead, look for the next most acceptable alternative for all members.

6. Discuss underlying assumptions, listen carefully to one another, and encourage the participation of *all* members—the especially important factors in reaching decisions by consensus.

Instructions for Groups with a Leader

This is an exercise in how a leader makes decisions after participating in a group discussion. Your group is to discuss what the ranking of the survival items should be, but the final decision rests with the designated leader of your group. At the end of forty-five minutes your group's leader will hand in what he or she considers to be the best ranking of the items. The role of the group members is to provide as much help as the leader wants in trying to determine how the items should be ranked.

DANGERS OF SOME COMMON DRUGS EXERCISE

The purpose of this exercise is to compare the effectiveness of three different methods of making decisions: (1) Decision by averaging members' opinions, (2) decision by expert member, and (3) decision by group consensus. The procedure for the exercise is as follows:

1. Each class member individually completes the following ranking task on the relative dangers of some common drugs. Answers are to be written on a separate sheet of paper.

2. The class divides into groups of six. One member in each group should volunteer to be an observer. The task of the observer is to record the nature of decision-making and leadership behavior in the group by using the observation instructions given for the Winter Survival Exercise.

3. The task of the group is to arrive by consensus to one ranking of the relative dangers of the common drugs listed. Each member of the group has to be willing to sign the group answer sheet, indicating that she agrees with the group's ranking and can explain the rationale for ranking the drugs as the group has done so.

4. When the task is completed the group members:
   a. Score their original individual rankings using the answer key in Appendix D (page 477).
   b. Identify the most accurate member's score.

c. Average the individual prediscussion scores so that a group average score is derived.

d. Score the group's ranking.

e. Enter the results in the Summary Table.

5. When all groups have entered their results in the Summary Table, discuss as a class the three types of decision making.

6. Each group discusses how well they functioned using the following questions as a starter:

a. How well did the group use its resources? (If the consensual score was lower than the expert or average-opinion score, the group did not fully utilize the resources of its members.)

b. What factors caused the group to use its resources well or not well?

c. What patterns of leadership existed in the group during the decision-making task?

d. How do members feel about the decision-making process and experience?

e. What conclusions about decision-making can be made from the group's experience?

*Dangers of Some Common Drugs Ranking Sheet**

A noted expert has ranked several common drugs by their relative dangers. He based his judgments on the drug's overall potential for (in order of less severe to more severe):

being used repeatedly or compulsively

being taken intravenously

producing physical dependence

impairing judgment

causing social deterioration (such as not being able to hold a job)

producing irreversible tissue damage and disease

causing accidental death from overdose

Below are listed nine drugs. Your task is to rank the nine drugs in the same order of danger as the expert did. Place the number "1" by the most dangerous drug, the number "2" by the next most dangerous drug, and so forth.

_____ alcohol

_____ barbiturates and hypnotics

_____ tobacco smoking

_____ glue sniffing

_____ speed (methamphetamine and dexedrine)

_____ heroin, codine, morphine, and other opiates

_____ marijuana

_____ cocaine

_____ LSD and other hallucinogens

* The authors do not recommend the use of these or any other drugs.

Summary Table: Accuracy of Decisions

Group	Average Member's Score	Most Accurate Member's Score	Consensus Group Score	Gain or Loss Over Average Score	Gain or Loss Over Expert Score	Number of Members Superior to Consensus
1						
2						
3						
4						
5						
6						

This exercise uses the same procedure as the Winter Survival Exercise and the Dangers of Some Common Drugs Exercise.

They'll Never Take Us Alive Ranking Sheet

In a recent survey *Dun's Review* lists the most perilous products or activities in the United States, based on annual death statistics. Below are listed fifteen of these death causing hazards. Your task is to rank them in order of dangerousness according to the number of deaths caused each year. Place the number "1" by the most dangerous, the number "2" by the next most dangerous, and so forth:

_____ swimming

_____ railroads

_____ police work

_____ home appliances

_____ alcohol

_____ nuclear power

_____ smoking

_____ motor vehicles

_____ pesticides

_____ handguns

_____ bicycles

_____ firefighting

_____ mountain climbing

_____ vaccinations

_____ surgery

INVOLVEMENT IN DECISION MAKING

There are at least three important reasons for involving all group members in decision making: to improve the quality of the decision, to increase members' allegiance to the group, and to increase the commitment of group members to implement the decision. In general, the more group members participating in the making of a decision, the more effective the decision will be. High involvement in decision making increases the use of the members' resources, which in turn increases the quality of the decision. The members responsible for implementing the decision, furthermore, may be especially knowledgeable about what the decision should be. Many groups, while deliberating over what the decision should be, ignore those members who have to carry out the decision, thus losing their special expertise. Involvement in decision making also tends to increase members' allegiance to the group.

One of the most famous research studies of the 1940s dealt with involving workers in decisions about how their work should be conducted. An associate of Kurt Lewin and the personnel manager of a clothing factory teamed up to do a study on overcoming the resistance of workers to changes in their work activities (French and Coch, 1948). The workers in question resisted management's changes in work activities by quitting their jobs, lowering their level of production, and expressing verbal hostility toward the plant and co-workers. French and Coch decided to try out three methods of instituting changes in job duties. One group of workers was simply told about the planned changes in their jobs and what was expected of them; they did not participate in the decision making. The second group appointed representatives from among themselves to meet with management to consider problems involved in changing work methods. All members of the third group met with management, participated actively in discussions, shared many suggestions, and helped plan the most efficient methods for mastering the new jobs. The differences in outcome were dramatic. Average production in the nonparticipating group dropped 20 percent immediately and did not regain the prechange level. Nine percent of the group quit. Morale fell sharply, as evidenced by marked hostility toward the supervisor, by slowdowns, by complaints to the union, and by other instances of aggressive behavior. The group that participated through representatives required two weeks to recover its prechange output. Their attitude was cooperative, and none of the members quit their jobs. The consequences in the total-participation group were even more positive. Members of this group regained the prechange output after only two days, and then climbed steadily until they reached a level of about 14 percent above the earlier average. No one quit, all members of the group worked well with their supervisors, and there were no signs of aggression. Zander and Armstrong (1972), furthermore, found that when work groups in a slipper factory were asked to set their own daily-production goals, they tended to aim for goals even higher than the standard set by the manager.

Perhaps the only times decisions should be made by one or a few persons are (1) when the decisions are about matters that do not need committed action by most members of the group, (2) when the decisions are so simple that coordination among group members and understanding of what to do are easy, and (3) when the decisions have to be made quickly.

CHANGING BEHAVIORAL PATTERNS AND ATTITUDES

Participating in a decision-making discussion within a group can have an impact on a person's subsequent behavior and attitudes. The classic experiments demonstrating this were conducted by Kurt Lewin and his associates.

During World War II there was considerable concern in the U.S. government about the reactions of the public to food rationing and the need to promote the use of foods not ordinarily eaten by U.S. citizens. Lewin was persuaded to come to Washington and help. He and his associates conducted a series of experiments to determine (1) what procedures were most effective in changing behavioral patterns and attitudes and (2) what methods of persuading citizens to eat foods they consider undesirable to recommend to the government. In the first study Lewin (1943) attempted to encourage housewives to use less popular meat products, such as kidneys and sweetbreads. The subjects were six groups of Red Cross volunteers ranging from thirteen to seventeen members each. Half of the groups were given an interesting lecture arguing for greater use of these meat products, and the other half were led through a group discussion that developed the same arguments as those presented in the lecture. At the end of the group discussion, the group leader asked for a show of hands by those willing to try one of the undesirable meat products. A follow-up survey revealed that only 3 percent of those in the lecture groups had served one of these meats, whereas 32 percent of those in the group-decision groups had served them.

A second study was conducted with six groups of housewives, ranging from six to nine members (Radke and Klishurich, 1947). The attempt in this study was to increase the consumption of milk. The groups were temporary and the same person served as both lecturer and group-decision leader. Again, an interesting lecture was given to half of the groups and the other half participated in a group discussion about the use of milk. A follow-up was made after two weeks and again after four weeks. In both cases the increase in the use of milk was greater among those in the group-decision situation.

A third study was conducted in which an attempt was made to increase the consumption of orange juice and cod-liver oil by babies (Radke and Klishurich, 1947). In this study farm mothers with their first baby either examined interesting materials on the use of orange juice and cod-liver oil or participated in group discussions covering the same material. Again, the group-decision procedure was more effective in getting the mothers to actually use more orange juice and cod-liver oil.

A number of studies have confirmed the findings of Lewin and his associates (Kostick, 1957; Levine and Butler, 1952), although subsequent work indicates that later use of the foods may have been influenced by the commitment of the public to use them and the degree of perceived consensus in the group as well as by participation in the discussion (Bennett, 1955; Pelz, 1958; Pennington, Hararey, and Bass, 1958). In a related study Preston and Heintz (1949) compared the impact of participatory- and supervisory-leadership roles on students' attitudes. The participatory leader was told to be sure that each member of his or her group was considered, to encourage all members to take part in the discussion, to discourage chance methods of decision making, and to complete the group's assigned work in the allotted time. The supervisory leader was instructed not to participate in the discussion and to limit his or her responsibility to seeing that the work was done in the allotted time. The results showed that participatory leadership was more effective than supervisory leadership in changing students' attitudes. Participatory-group members also were more satisfied with their group's decision than members of the supervisory groups, found the task more interesting and meaningful, and rated their group discussions as more friendly and enjoyable.

Overall, the results of these and other studies indicate that if you wish to change people's behaviors and attitudes, you should involve them in group discussions that lead to public commitment to (1) the new behaviors and attitudes and (2) the perception that all members of the group support the new behaviors and attitudes. A participatory-leadership pattern may facilitate this process.

TWO PROBLEMS WITH THE THEORIZING ON DECISION MAKING

There are at least two major problems with the theorizing and research on decision making in small groups (Janis and Mann, 1977). The first is that much of the research has focused on whether the decisions made by groups are of high or low quality. In the real world many decisions cannot be objectively evaluated in terms of success or failure because their long-term effects cannot be fully measured. To evaluate long-term success or failure, one would need to take into account the negative consequences of the decision made, the positive consequences that would have resulted if each of the other alternatives had been adopted as the decision, the positive consequences of the decision, and the negative consequences that would have resulted if each of the other alternatives had been adopted. Obviously, it is difficult if not impossible to quantify these factors.

The second problem is that much of the theorizing and research on decision making has assumed that decision makers are completely informed (that they know all the possible courses of action and the potential outcomes of each), infinitely sensitive (they see each alternative in all its complexity), and always rational (they always maximize the outcomes of their action). Real-life decision makers, however, are *not* always completely informed (they do not or cannot know all courses of action and their potential outcomes), do not understand fully the intricacies of various alternatives, and are rarely completely rational. Real-life decision makers often seem beset by conflicts, doubts, and worries: they struggle with conflicting loyalties, antipathies, and longings and engage in procrastination, rationalization, and denial of responsibility for their decisions. Instead of determining the solution that maximizes their outcomes, many decision makers look only for the alternative that meets a minimal set of requirements (this is called satisficing) and make quick decisions (Hoffman, 1961; Simon, 1976). Ineffective groups seem to operate under a variety of decision-making rules, such as "Tell a qualified expert about the problem and do whatever he or she says—that will be good enough" and "Do what we did last time if it worked, and the opposite if it didn't work." Real-life decision makers also realize how expensive it is in time, effort, and money to collect and dissect the huge amounts of information a group needs in order to use an ideal form of decision making.

Researchers can alleviate these two problems by studying the process of decision making rather than focusing on quality, and by specifying procedures that encourage real-life decision makers to become more systematic and rational in their decision making. In the next section we shall deal with both of these approaches.

EFFECTIVE DECISION-MAKING PROCESSES

Janis and Mann (1977) reviewed the theory and research on decision making and developed a seven-step process of effective decision making. They were then able to rate the quality of decision making not on the basis of the decision but rather on the basis of how the observed procedures used by groups compared with their seven-step ideal process, which they call "vigilant information processing." The seven steps taken by effective decision makers are as follows:

1. They thoroughly canvass a wide range of possible courses of action.
2. They survey the full range of objectives to be fulfilled and the values implied by the decision.
3. They carefully weigh whatever they know about the costs and risks of the negative consequences that could flow from each alternative.
4. They search intensively for new information relevant to further evaluation of the alternatives.
5. They correctly assimilate any new information or expert judgment to which they are exposed, even when the information or judgment does not support the course of action they initially prefer.
6. They reexamine the positive and negative consequences of all known alternatives, including those originally regarded as unacceptable, before making a final choice.
7. They make detailed provisions for implementing the chosen course of action, paying special attention to contingency plans that might be required if various risks were to materialize.

The more adequately each step is performed, the less likely serious miscalculations will be made and the better the ultimate decision.

Janis and Mann (1977) single out *systematic evaluation* as the strongest influence on the occurrence of vigilant information processing. Systematic evaluation is a procedure whereby decision makers explore the full range of alternatives and analyze the advantages and disadvantages of each before they make a final decision. The more explicit the systematic evaluation, the less likely that an alternative will be overlooked or rationalized away. If decision makers know what the alternatives are and have correctly diagnosed their inherent advantages and disadvantages, they will not choose a certain course of action unless its advantages are expected to exceed its disadvantages. This approach is supported by the research of Maier and Thurber (1969), who found that groups often lose good solutions not because they did not think of them but because they did a poor job of evaluating and choosing among them.

One of the major barriers to vigilant information processing is defensive avoidance (Janis and Mann, 1977). This phenomenon, which always causes defects in information processing, appears in at least three patterns: selective inattention to indications of the seriousness of the problem, such that the decision makers become convinced that action is not really necessary; the shifting of responsibility to other groups or persons; and the bolstering of the desirability of one alternative by ignoring or developing rationalizations against evidence indicating that potentially undesirable consequences will result if that alternative is adopted.

Janis and Mann (1977) recommend that to eliminate the possibility of defensive avoidance and to ensure that vigilant information processing takes place, a group systematically evaluates each alternative on the basis of the following four factors:

1. the tangible gains and losses for the group.
2. the tangible gains and losses for significant others.
3. group self-approval or self-disapproval (Will we feel proud or ashamed if we make this choice?)
4. the approval or disapproval of the group by significant others (Will important persons we are connected with think we made the right decision?)

The procedure Janis and Mann (1977) developed to ensure that these factors are thought about and discussed for each alternative is as follows. First, a balance sheet (Figure 3.2) is completed for each course of action being considered. Second, the group is instructed to rate the importance of each of the four factors, using a seven-point scale ranging from "hardly important" to "extremely important." Finally, the group studies the completed balance sheets and then ranks all the alternatives from "most desirable" to "least desirable." Using a balance sheet to ensure systematic evaluation has been found to be related to level of satisfaction with a decision, commitment

FIGURE 3.2 Balance sheet for group decision making.

Decision_____	Alternative_____	
	advantages/gains	*disadvantages/losses*
1. Tangible gains and losses for group		
2. Tangible gains and losses for significant others		
3. Group self-approval or self-disapproval		
4. Approval or disapproval by significant others		

to a decision, and security about the correctness of a decision (Janis and Mann, 1977).

Janis and Mann (1977) also suggest that decision-making groups use the following procedures to ensure that they make high-quality decisions:

1. By not stating preferences and expectations at the outset and without advocating specific proposals, the leader should allow members to develop an atmosphere of open inquiry and to explore impartially a wide range of policy alternatives.
2. The leader should assign each member the role of critical evaluator, giving high priority to the airing of objections and doubts and accepting criticism of judgments in order to discourage group members from soft-pedaling their disagreements.
3. The group should choose a member to represent unpopular positions in the group.
4. The group should regularly divide into two subgroups, each of which makes a decision, and then rejoin and remake the decision as one group.
5. Immediately following a preliminary consensus on what seems to be the best course of action, the group should hold a "second-chance" meeting in which every member is expected to express as vividly as he can all his residual doubts and to rethink the entire issue before making a definitive choice.
6. Outside experts should be invited to group meetings and asked to challenge the views of the group members.

Finally, a skilled leader can increase the effectiveness of a decision-making group by using disagreement and conflict constructively. Groups generate better ideas when they structure themselves to retard speedy decisions and to be problem- rather than solution-oriented. Groups make more effective decisions when they take time to locate facts and potential obstacles. Conflict in the group can delay premature acceptance of an obvious solution and promote the search for alternative solutions. Controversy has an important function in decision making, and we will consider it in detail in Chapter 6.

ORGANIZATIONAL DECISION MAKING

Effective decision making is one of the most significant determinants of organizational success. Almost all organizational decision making occurs in small groups, and therefore all the material in this chapter applies to organizational decision making. It may be helpful to note, however, that several characteristics of organizations influence the decision-making process.

The first of these characteristics is that some decisions within organizations are routine and programmable, based primarily upon technical factors, and apply to highly structured situations. Other decisions apply to problem situations that are less structured, and here interpersonal factors greatly influence the decision-making process. As decisions become less routine and programmable, the relationships among group members become more crucial.

A second characteristic is that no single person in an organization can expect to have all the information necessary to make a decision. Most decisions must be handled by groups because each individual will have only a certain amount of the information necessary to make a valid decision. As a result, the accuracy of the information received by the key decision-making group is of utmost importance. Mutual dependence among organizational group members for precise information underscores the importance of communication—the subject of Chapter 5.

Even when group members have all the information they need to make a good decision, group-process factors can either help or hurt effective decision making. A high level of interpersonal and group skill is needed by group members in order for decision making to proceed effectively. The resources of all group members must be properly identified and well utilized by the group.

Another important characteristic is that a decision made by one group within an organization often has implications for other parts of the organization, and vice versa. This interdependence creates a need for coordination of organizational decisions. In order to harmonize decisions, an organization must develop a "problem-finding mechanism" that helps it to identify problems, establish priorities, and regulate group decisions made about the problems.

Finally, the decisions made in organizations affect all members of the organization, both directly and indirectly. As a consequence, people's feelings, reactions, and relationships with other members are often as important in making a good decision as facts and logic. The effectiveness of a decision depends upon both logical soundness and the level of psychological commitment to the decision by the members who have to implement it. Individuals uninvolved in the decision-making group may withhold information the group needs in order to arrive at a high-quality decision, and may put forth only a minimum effort to implement it. A logical decision to which people are uncommitted is not an effective decision.

QUIZ

Check your reading of this section by answering the following questions. Answers are on page 135.

1. Barbara Lee involves all group members in decision making because she knows the likely results are (check three):
   a. increased recognition by higher-ups.
   b. improved quality of the decision.
   c. increased allegiance to the group.
   d. increased dissatisfaction with the group leader.
   e. increased commitment to implementing the decision.
2. Paula knows that decisions should be made by only one or a few people when (check three):
   a. the decision doesn't need commitment from group members.
   b. matters are too complicated for the average group member to understand.
   c. matters are simple and easily understood.
   d. the decision must be made quickly.
   e. there is an established hierarchy in the organization.
3. Melanie, a school principal, is an effective decision maker. She and her group use the vigilant information process of Janis and Mann, which includes (check seven):
   a. thoroughly canvasing a wide range of alternative courses of action.
   b. surveying the full range of objectives to be filled and the values implied by the decision.
   c. carefully weighing whatever is known about the costs and risks of the negative consequences that could flow from each alternative.
   d. intensively searching for new information relevant to further evaluation of the alternative.
   e. personally attending to each detail of the implementation of the decision and holding others accountable for their actions.

    f. correctly considering new information, even when it does not support the favored course of action.

    g. conferring at length with others on how to best implement this decision when it is made.

    h. reexamining the positive and negative consequences of all known alternatives, including originally unacceptable ones, before making a final choice.

    i. making detailed provisions for implementing the course of action, with contingency plans to use if risks materialize.

4. Mindy knows that her group has a tendency to practice defensive avoidance, so she watches to avert these group patterns (check three):

    a. selective inattention to threat cues so they become convinced that action is not really necessary.

    b. letting one person do all the work while the group takes all the credit for it.

    c. passing the buck and shifting the responsibility to other groups or people.

    d. finding excuses to avoid attending meetings, thus avoiding working on the problem.

    e. ignoring evidence that shows undesirable consequences to the alternative favored by the group.

5. Kathy is trying to break her group of defensive avoidance so she insists that her group use the recommendations of Janis and Mann and evaluate each alternative on the following factors (check four):

    a. the tangible gains and losses for the group.

    b. the tangible gains and losses for significant others.

    c. the tangible gains and losses for all others.

    d. the group self-approval or disaproval.

    e. the approval or disapproval of the group by significant others.

    f. the approval or disapproval of the group by all others.

6. As group leader, Esther wants to ensure high quality decisions, so she uses the following procedures (check six):

    a. she allows members to explore a wide range of alternatives without stating her own preferences and expectations at the outset.

    b. she assigns the role of critical evaluator to each member and encourages expression of objections and doubts.

    c. she assigns the role of devil's advocate to a group member to represent unpopular positions in the group.

    d. she regularly divides the group into two subgroups to make a decision, then calls them together to remake the decision as a total group.

    e. after a preliminary decision is made, she holds a second chance meeting where every member is expected to express doubts and rethink the issue.

f. she assigns a role of compromiser to one member to pull together everyone's ideas into a composite decision.

g. she invites outside experts to the group meeting to challenge the views of the members.

h. she takes responsibility for the consequences of the decision after it has been made by the group.

True False   **7.** The more people involved in decision making, the longer it takes to reach a decision.

True False   **8.** The fewer people involved in decision making, the higher the quality of the decision.

True False   **9.** Supervisory leadership is more effective in changing attitudes than participatory leadership.

True False   **10.** Members of groups with participatory leadership are more likely to be satisfied with the decision and happier with the group than those with supervisory leadership.

True False   **11.** It is not difficult in real life to evaluate the quality of a decision.

True False   **12.** Many decision makers only look for an alternative that meets minimal requirements and then make a quick decision.

True False   **13.** Groups often lose good solutions not because they do not think of them but because they do a poor job of evaluating and choosing.

True False   **14.** Using a decisional balance sheet makes groups more satisfied, committed, and secure about a decision.

True False   **15.** Conflict and disagreement will keep a group from making an effective decision.

True False   **16.** When there is an obvious solution, groups should make the decision quickly and use the saved time to work on a more complex problem.

True False   **17.** Groups should be "solution" rather than "problem" oriented.

True False   **18.** Most people within an organization have the information needed to make decisions individually and should do so.

True False   **19.** In order for decisions to be made effectively, the group members should have highly developed interpersonal and group skills.

True False   **20.** Considering people's feelings, reactions, and relationships is just as important as facts and logic in making a good decision.

THE BEAN JAR EXERCISE (II)

The purpose of this exercise is to show that the involvement of more persons in the decision-making process affects the accuracy of the decision. The exercise can be done in an hour, and it requires only a large jar full of a known quantity of beans. The procedure for the coordinator is as follows:

1. Explain that the exercise focuses on the accuracy of the decisions made by different combinations of individuals. Then set a large jar of beans in front of the participants. You need to know exactly how many beans are in the jar. Tell the participants they will be asked to estimate how many beans the jar contains.
2. Have each person estimate the number of beans, working alone. Record the estimates.
3. Have each participant pick a partner. Have the two-person teams work out a system for estimating how many beans are in the jar, and record their estimates.
4. Have each pair pick another twosome and the four-person teams estimate the number of beans. Record their estimates.
5. Have each quartet pick another foursome and the eight-member groups estimate the number of beans. Record their estimates.
6. Have each octet pick another group and the sixteen-member groups estimate the number of beans. Record their estimates.
7. Ask for the final estimates and then tell the participants the number of beans in the jar. Have the class form groups of eight and discuss their experience, how they felt during the decision making, and the way in which they operated in the groups. Finally, ask the groups of eight to build a set of conclusions about the effect that an increasing number of members has on the accuracy of the decision and why the number of members influenced decision accuracy in the way it did. Have each group share its conclusions with the rest of the participants, and then have a class discussion of the conclusions.

YOUR DECISION–MAKING BEHAVIOR EXERCISE

Before this chapter ends it might be useful for you to consider your decision-making behavior. How do you usually behave in a decision-making group? How would you like to behave? Here is a closing exercise for you to do in a group with two of your classmates:

1. Throw all your loose change into the center of the group. Decide (using consensus) how to use the money. Then look at the group decision in terms of the behaviors of each member. How did each of you behave? What task and maintenance functions did you yourself fulfill? How did you feel about your participation? How did your usual behavior reveal itself in the group decision making?
2. Review as a group the task and maintenance functions listed in the previous chapter. Discuss what other functions could be added. Examples are:
   a. *Clarification or elaboration:* interpret or reflect ideas or suggestions; clear up confusion; bring up alternatives and new issues before the group; give examples.

b. *Summarization:* pull together related ideas; restate suggestions after the group has discussed them.

c. *Consensus testing:* check with the group to see how much agreement has been reached; test to see if the group is nearing a decision.

d. *Communication of feeling:* express your feelings about the issues the group is discussing and the way in which it is functioning.

e. *Verification of feeling:* ask other members how they are feeling; check to see if your perception of their feelings is correct.

Pick the task and maintenance functions you usually engage in; pick those you would like to perform better. Give one another feedback about each member's behavior.

3. Have you received any feedback on your behavior that has increased your awareness of how you behave? How would you now describe your behavior in decision-making situations?

4. Decide as a group when to end this exercise.

How I Behave Questionnaire

The purpose of this questionnaire is to help you look at how you behave in a group that is making a decision. Different persons act in different ways when they are members of groups that are making decisions. Moreover, the same person may act differently at different times, depending on the group, the decision to be made, and the circumstances. But in general, how do you act when a group in which you are a member is making a decision? In each of the following three statements, choose the best description of the way in which you behave when a group to which you belong is making a decision. Be as objective and honest as you can; the results are for your use only.

1. When my group is making a decision, I:

_____ passively defer to others.

_____ work for a decision that satisfies everyone without worrying about how good it is.

_____ look entirely at the merits of the alternatives without thinking about how the members of the group feel or how satisfied they are.

_____ look for alternatives that work, though I might not personally think they are the best.

_____ work for a strong, creative decision having a common basis of understanding among group members.

2. When my group is facing a decision, I:

_____ show little interest in the decision or the other group members.

_____ think mostly about how the members of the group are getting along, without worrying about what the decision will be.

_____ push for a really good decision and view the other members only as contributors of resources that will help make a better decision.

_____ work for good relations among the members and a good solution, though I am willing to sacrifice a little of each to get the job done.

_____ avoid compromise and try to get everyone to agree to and be satisfied with a decision that is based upon looking at the situation in a realistic way.

3. When my group is making a decision, I:

_____ wait for the group to tell me what to do and accept what they recommend for me.

_____ help others participate by giving them moral support and by testing to see if members can agree.

_____ give information, evaluate how well the group is working toward completing the task, set ground rules for behavior, and see that everyone stays at the task.

_____ summarize periodically what has been discussed, call for things to be made clearer, and encourage members to compromise.

_____ help the group think of alternatives, discuss how practical the alternatives are, and work out ways in which the group can come to an agreement.

You can plot this self-assessment on the task–maintenance grid in Figure 2.4. Each of the preceding statements can be completed in five possible ways. The first alternative for each statement is a (6,6) response; it shows that this person has little or no interest in either maintaining the group or helping it accomplish its task of making a decision. The second alternative is a (6,30) response, showing that this member emphasizes group maintenance while ignoring the task. The third alternative is a (30,6) response; here the person focuses on getting the task done but ignores group maintenance. The fourth alternative is an (18,18) response, indicating a member who compromises on both task and maintenance in order to reach a decision. The fifth alternative for each question is a (30,30) response; this person tries to achieve a creative, consensual decision, and emphasizes both the task and maintenance functions of the group.

Look at your three responses. Locate each on the task–maintenance grid. Then discuss the results in groups of three, comparing your responses here with those you gave on the leadership surveys in the previous chapter, and with the way you would like to act in groups.

SUMMARY

This chapter dealt with effective decision making and gave you practice in skills needed for being an effective group decision maker. The next chapter will help you learn the importance of group goals and give you practice in setting them.

ANSWERS

Page 87—1. b, c, d, f, g; 2. a, c, d, f.

Page 97—1. a, b, d, e, g; 2. b, c, d, e, f, g, h, k.

Page 110—1. g; 2. a; 3. b; 4. f; 5. e; 6. d; 7. c; 8. a; 9. g; 10. a; 11. g; 12. d; 13. b; 14. f; 15. a; 16. a; 17. g; 18. true; 19. false; 20. true.

Page 129—1. b, c, e; 2. a, c, d; 3. a, b, c, d, f, h, i; 4. a, c, e; 5. a, b, d, e; 6. a, b, c, d, e, g; 7. true; 8. false; 9. false; 10. true; 11. false; 12. true; 13. true; 14. true; 15. false; 16. false; 17. false; 18. false; 19. true; 20. true.

4

Group Goals

BASIC CONCEPTS TO BE COVERED IN THIS CHAPTER

In this chapter a number of concepts are defined and discussed. The major ones are listed below. The procedure for learning these concepts is as follows:

1. The class forms heterogeneous groups of four.
2. Each group divides into two pairs.
3. The task for each pair is to:
   a. define each concept, noting the page on which it is defined and discussed.
   b. make sure that both members of the pair understand the meaning of each concept.
4. In each group, members compare the answers of the two pairs. If there is disagreement, the members look up the concept in the chapter and clarify it until they all agree on the definition and understand it.

Concepts

1. Goal
2. Group goal
3. Ambiguous goal
4. Operational goal
5. Hidden agenda
6. Cooperation
7. Goal structure
8. Competition
9. Individualistic
10. Distributive justice
11. Merit system of distributive justice
12. Equality system of distributive justice
13. Need system of distributive justice
14. Goals as motivators

WHAT IS A GROUP GOAL?

No wind favors him who has no destined port.

Montaigne

Every group has at least one goal. The goal may be to build a better mousetrap, to climb a mountain, to get the most pay for the least amount of work, or to apply the material being presented in this book. Ever since there were two humans on earth, we have joined together to achieve mutual goals and to maximize our joint welfare. Every group has a reason for being and for doing what it does. A group cannot exist unless it has at least one goal that is understood by some of its members. One of the most important aspects of group effectiveness is the group's ability to define its goals and achieve them successfully. In this chapter we shall focus on the formation of group goals, the importance of clarity in doing so, and the cooperation among group members that is essential for the achievement of group goals.

What is a goal, and what is a group goal? The essence of a *goal* is that it is an ideal: It is a desired place toward which people are working, a state of affairs that people value. A *group goal* is a future state of affairs desired by enough members of a group to motivate the group to work towards its achievement. A group goal, for example, might be to learn more about group effectiveness, and if enough members of a group want to learn about group effectiveness they will behave in ways they hope will achieve their purpose! Three aspects of goal achievement need to be stressed: (1) the group goal itself, (2) the tasks the group must perform in order to achieve the goal, and (3) the processes of interaction among members that are necessary for achieving the goal. Thus, the group's goal may be to plan a camping trip, the tasks may be to gather the necessary information and equipment, and the processes of interaction among members might consist of a division of labor, a sharing of ideas and materials, and a constructive resolution of conflicts.

Most groups have several goals, some immediate and some long-range. It is usually the immediate goals that are of greatest significance: the activities of group members are directly related to short-term goals and only indirectly related to long-range goals. The immediate goals are stepping stones to the long-range ones. If group members are clear about the immediate objectives that lie along a path toward a long-range goal, they can avoid misunderstanding about their final destination. In setting goals it is important to choose immediate ones that can be easily recognized when achieved and that can be reached in a specified, reasonable length of time.

In the next section we shall discuss the importance of group goals. We shall then move on to the relationship between the goals of individual members and the group's goals. We shall then discuss the issues of structuring goals to ensure adequate collaboration among members and selecting goals that are clear and workable.

QUIZ

Check your reading of this section by answering the following questions. Answers are on page 176.

1. What is a group goal?
   a. An ideal.
   b. A desired place or objective toward which people are working.
   c. A state of affairs that people value.
   d. all of the above
2. In setting group goals, it is important to choose immediate ones:
   a. that can be reached in a specified, reasonable length of time.
   b. that can be easily recognized when achieved.
   c. as stepping stones to long-range goals.
   d. all of the above

ARE GROUP GOALS NECESSARY EXERCISE

There has been some controversy over whether group goals are necessary. The purpose of this exercise is to structure a critical discussion of the issue. The procedure is as follows:

1. The class forms groups of four.
2. Each group is ultimately to write a report summarizing its position on whether group goals are necessary for a group to be effective. The report is to contain the group's overall conclusions and the facts and rationale supporting its position. The supporting facts and rationale may be obtained from the accompanying briefing sheets, the entire book, and outside reading.
3. First, each group divides into pairs. One pair is assigned the position that group goals are of no use and the other pair the position that groups cannot function without goals. Each pair reviews the appropriate briefing sheet, the procedure for the exercise, and the rules for constructive controversy (p. 31).
4. The pairs meet separately to prepare as forceful a three-minute presentation of their position as possible. They are to make sure that both members have contributed to building a persuasive case for their position and that it includes as many facts and research findings as possible. Both members need to master all the rationale supporting their position. Ten minutes are allowed for this phase.
5. The group of four meets. Each pair presents its position, being as forceful and persuasive as possible, while the other pair takes notes and asks for clarification of anything

that is not fully understood. Each pair is allowed about three minutes to present its position.

6. The group of four has an open discussion on whether group goals are necessary for a group to be effective. Each side presents as many facts and research findings as it can to support its point of view. Members listen critically to the opposing position and ask for facts to support any conclusions made by the opposing pair. Participants should ensure that all the facts supporting both sides are brought out and discussed, and should follow the rules for constructive controversy on page 31. About ten minutes are allowed for this phase.

7. The perspectives in each group are now reversed, each pair arguing the opposing pair's position. Members should be as forceful and persuasive as they can in arguing for the opposing pair's position. They should elaborate on the opposing position, seeing if they can think of any new arguments or facts that the opposing pair did not present. Each pair has about three minutes for its presentation.

8. Each group of four should derive a position that all members can agree to. The members should summarize the best arguments from each position, detailing as many facts as they can on whether group goals are necessary for a group to be effective. When they have consensus in their group, they should organize their arguments for presentation to the rest of the class. Since other groups will have other conclusions, each group may need to explain the validity of its position to the class. About ten minutes are allowed for this phase.

9. The coordinator samples the decisions made by the groups of four by having several of them present their position to the class. The class then discusses similarities and differences, and the coordinator summarizes what the participants have learned about group goals.

Briefing Sheet: Groups Cannot Function Without Goals

Your position is that a group cannot function without having at least one goal understood and accepted by several of its members. To support your position, use the rationale given below, any material from this chapter that is applicable, and what you know from your outside reading.

The rationale for your position is as follows: Group goals guide the actions of members and allow them to plan and coordinate their efforts. Group goals direct, channel, motivate, coordinate, energize, and guide the behavior of group members. Groups cannot exist unless the activities of their members are directed toward achieving something (a goal). It is the power of goals to influence members to engage in needed behaviors that makes goals essential to an effective group.

Briefing Sheet: Group Goals Are of No Use

Your position is that a goal is never useful to a group and may even be a concept that has no basis in reality. To support your position, use the rationale given below, any material from this chapter that is applicable, and what you know from your outside reading.

The rationale for your position is as follows: Group goals are often stated in such vague terms that they could not possibly be effective guides for the actions of members. Many members of groups, furthermore, cannot accurately describe the goals of their group when asked, and thus the goals can have no impact on these persons. In certain cases goals are not determiners of members' efforts because they do not come close to describing what is being done in the group. Appraisals of group progress, moreover, usually reveal that groups have fallen short of their goals, which suggests that the goals are not being closely followed. It may even be that groups do not try to accomplish anything; they just exist and use up resources. All in all, it is not useful to try to describe the goals of a group.

WHY ARE GOALS IMPORTANT?

There are a number of reasons why group goals are important. First, goals are guides for action, and it is through group goals that the efforts of group members are planned and coordinated. Roles and responsibilities are assigned to members on the basis of what needs to be done in order for the group's goals to be accomplished. Second, the efficiency and usefulness of group procedures are evaluated on the basis of how they facilitate goal accomplishment. The third reason why group goals are important is that conflicts among group members are resolved on the basis of what helps the group achieve its goals.

Most important, goals are the motivation for the behavior of group members. Without group goals members would not be motivated to take any action. All group-goal accomplishment is based on the members' commitment to engage in the activities necessary to achieve the goal. It is the group's goals that direct and motivate members' behavior. As members commit themselves to achieving a goal, an inner tension is aroused that continues until the goal has been accomplished or until some sort of psychological closure is achieved concerning the goal. It is this internal tension that motivates group members to work toward goal accomplishment. Thus, when group members commit themselves to the group goal of planning a camping trip, internal tension arises that makes them restless and dissatisfied until the group completes its plans. Members' commitment to accomplishing a group goal depends on several factors, such as:

1. how desirable the goal seems
2. how likely it seems that the group can accomplish the goal
3. how challenging the goal is (a moderate risk of failure is more challenging than a high or low risk of failure)
4. being able to tell when the goal has been achieved
5. the satisfaction or reward the member expects to feel or receive when the goal is achieved

6. the ways in which the member will relate to other members in working toward the accomplishment of the goal (some ways of relating to other members are more fun and involving than others)

The more cohesive a group, furthermore, the more its members will be motivated to achieve its goals.

The motivation of members to work for the achievement of their group's goals is heightened by their participation in setting the goals. This increase in motivation comes in part from the fact that participation produces: (1) a better matching of the group goals to the motives of members, which brings about greater acceptance of the goals, (2) a better understanding of the group actions needed to achieve the goals, and (3) a better appreciation of how individual behavior contributes to the necessary group action.

Finally, it is the awareness of group goals that solidifies cooperation among group members, because a goal helps members judge what actions by colleagues are for the good of the group and in what ways each member depends on the others.

If they are accepted, understood, and desired by group members, group goals direct, channel, motivate, coordinate, energize, and guide the behavior of group members. The goals of a group, therefore, are the beginning point in evaluating a group's effectiveness.

QUIZ

Check your reading of this section by answering the following questions. Answers are on page 176.

1. Goals are important because they are (choose four):
    a. guides for action.
    b. a necessary motivating force.
    c. the basis for evaluation of the group procedures.
    d. aids in resolving conflict.
    e. helpful in keeping the members from getting too personal.
    f. the only motivation to read this book.
2. Commitment by group members to accomplishing a goal depends on (choose six):
    a. how attractive or desirable the goal seems.
    b. how likely it seems that the group can accomplish the goal.
    c. how easily the goal can be achieved with a minimum of effort.
    d. how challenging the goal is.
    e. being able to tell when the goal has been achieved.
    f. the expected satisfaction or reward from achieving the goal.

g. how attractive or desirable the members of the group are.

h. the ways in which members relate to one another.

3. How does participation in setting the goals help motivate members (choose three)?

    a. Members better understand what they need to do to achieve their goals.

    b. Members better understand the hidden dynamics of the goal.

    c. The goals fit the members better.

    d. Members feel more amply rewarded when they achieve the goal.

    e. Members better appreciate how individual actions contribute to the group.

True   False   **4.** A high risk of failure is more challenging than a moderate or low risk of failure.

True   False   **5.** The more cohesive the group, the less likely it is that the members will be motivated to achieve the group's goals.

YOUR GOAL-RELATED BEHAVIOR EXERCISE (I)

The purpose of this exercise is to allow you to examine your group-goal-related behavior in problem-solving groups. Working by yourself, answer the following three questions. Be honest. Check as many responses to each question as are characteristic of your usual and regular behavior. Then form a group with two of your classmates and discuss your answers to the questions and why you answered them as you did. Try to develop as much awareness of your behavior in goal-related situations as possible.

1. When I am a member of a group that does not seem to have a clear awareness of what its goals are or how they are to be achieved, I usually:

    _____ ask the group to stop and discuss its goals until all group members clearly understand what they are and what actions the group needs to take to accomplish them.

    _____ feel disgusted and refuse to attend meetings.

    _____ state as specifically as possible what I consider the goals of the group to be, and comment on how the present actions of the group relate to goal accomplishment.

    _____ ask the designated leader to stop messing around and tell the group what it is supposed to be doing.

2. When I am a member of a group that has a clear understanding of its goals but seems to have little commitment to accomplishing them, I usually:

    _____ try to shame other group members into being more motivated.

    _____ blame the designated leader for being incompetent.

    _____ ask the group members to look at how meaningful, relevant, and acceptable the goals are to them.

_____ try to change the group's goals in order to make them more relevant to the members' needs and motives.

_____ point out the sacrifices some members have made in the past toward goal accomplishment and hope that all members become more committed.

3. When I am a member of a group that has conflicting opinions on what its goals should be, or that has members with conflicting needs and motives, I usually:

_____ figure out how much cooperative and competitive behavior exists in the group and give the group feedback based on my observations in an attempt to increase cooperativeness among its members.

_____ start a group discussion on the personal goals, needs, and motives of each group member in order to determine the extent to which there are competing goals among them.

_____ declare one member of the group to be the winner and ask all other group members to work toward accomplishing the person's goals.

_____ ask the group to determine how the members' actions can become more coordinated.

_____ form a secret coalition with several other group members so that our goals will become dominant in the group.

GROUP GOALS AND INDIVIDUAL MEMBERS' GOALS

Do groups have goals? Or are there only the various individual goals of the group's members? As dry as these questions may seem, social psychologists have hotly debated this issue for decades. Emmy Pepitone (1980), for example, insists that group goals can be identified, that they function as an important source of member interdependence in groups, and that they denote a common, central focus that is present most of the time and is readily identifiable as an objective reality. She states that group goals provide an aspect of unity, of a common fate, that one cannot readily convey simply by noting the individual goals of group members. Lewin (1944) noted that there are situations in which group members do seem to act to maximize joint outcomes or accomplish group goals rather than to maximize their individual outcomes or achieve their individual goals. Both Horwitz (1954) and Pepitone (1952) conducted studies that indicated that group members become motivated to have their group achieve its goal and are personally satisfied when the group does so. The success of the group, rather than their personal gain, seems to be the major source of their satisfaction. Numerous other studies have demonstrated that individuals do focus on joint outcomes rather than individual outcomes when they are placed in situations requiring cooperation with others.

The dominant view in social psychology today, however, is that a group goal is a combination of the individual goals of all group members. From this point of view it is the individual members who set the goals for the group. People become group members because they have certain goals and motives that they wish to express or fulfill through group membership. In other words, each person brings to the group a wish to satisfy personal goals. These goals are not always clearly known to the member: she may be completely aware, partially aware, or totally unaware of her goals and motives during a group meeting.

The group goals agreed upon by the group members must be relevant to the individual needs of the members. Group members try usually to achieve both individual and group goals, and the degree to which they can accomplish this through the same activities determines how effective the group will be in attaining its goals. The situation is further complicated by the fact that different members value different goals at different times and even the same member places different values on the same goal at different times.

The personal goals of the group members can be homogeneous (alike) or heterogeneous (different). Homogeneity of individual members' goals (or consensus about what the group's goals should be) usually helps group functioning, whereas heterogeneity of individual members' goals (or disagreement about what the group's goals should be) usually interferes with group functioning. Individual group members with homogeneous goals are usually happier with the group and its tasks than members of groups with heterogeneous individual goals. Heterogeneous goals may easily become *hidden agendas*—personal goals that are unknown to all the other group members and are at cross-purposes with the dominant group goals. Hidden agendas can greatly hinder, indeed destroy, group effectiveness. Yet they are present in almost every group. A group, therefore, must both increase consensus among group members on what the group's goals should be and decrease disagreement among different members' goals. Some procedures for doing this are as follows:

1. When you first form a group, thoroughly discuss its goals, even when they are prescribed by superiors or by the constitution of the group. Such a discussion will clarify the members' understanding of the goals and help clear away any misunderstandings concerning the tasks necessary to reach them. During the discussion the group should reword, reorganize, and review the goals until the majority of members feel a sense of "ownership" toward them.

2. As the group progresses in its activities, remember that it is continuously working on two levels at once: toward the achievement of the group's goals and toward the achievement and satisfaction of the individual members' goals and motives. Look for hidden agendas. The recognition of a group problem is the first step in diagnosing and solving it.

3. Bear in mind that there are conditions under which hidden agendas should be brought to the surface and rectified, and conditions under which they should be left undisturbed. A judgment must be made about the consequences of bringing hidden agendas to the attention of the entire group.

One way in which to tell how willing other group members are to deal with hidden agendas is to initiate a discussion on the subject, taking care not to force anyone into admitting their own hidden agendas. A statement like this one may be helpful: "I wonder if we've said all that we feel like saying about the issue. Maybe we should take time to go around the table so that any further thoughts can be brought up."

4. Do not scold or pressure the other group members when hidden agendas are recognized. They are present and legitimate and must be worked on in much the same manner that group tasks are. Hidden agendas should be given different amounts of attention at different times, depending upon their influence on the group's effectiveness and upon the nature of the group and its members.

5. Spend some time evaluating the ability of the group to deal productively with hidden agendas. Each experience the group has should reveal better ways in which to handle agendas more openly. As groups mature, hidden agendas are reduced.

Zander (1980) notes that there are several factors that influence group members to choose a personal goal that reflects the goals of other group members. These factors include how much a person likes the other members, how important it is to the other members that one adopt a similar goal, the extent to which the person's activities are relevant of the achievement of the other members' goals, and whether the goal represents a moderate challenge (rather than a difficult one). Zander (1980) also notes that any goals adopted by the group reflect the value system of the group's organizers.

Thus far this chapter has covered what a goal is, why group goals are important, and whether or not group goals really exist. Whether goals reside in individuals or in groups, how the goals are structured and how clearly members understand them have a significant impact upon group effectiveness.

QUIZ

Check your reading of this section by answering the following questions. Answers are on page 176.

True	False	1. The current dominant view in social psychology is that a group goal is a combination of the individual goals of all the group members.
True	False	2. Individual members are normally aware of their personal goals and motives in a group.
True	False	3. Homogeneity of individual members' goals usually hinders group functioning.

True False **4.** Hidden agendas are at cross-purposes with the dominant group goals.

True False **5.** Hidden agendas can be minimized if a group has discussed the goals enough to know them.

True False **6.** Hidden agendas can be minimized if there is group concern for satisfying individual goals as well as group goals.

True False **7.** A group cannot be effective unless the hidden agendas in the group are brought out.

True False **8.** Group members should be pressured into disclosing and working out their hidden agendas for the good of the group.

True False **9.** As groups mature, hidden agendas are reduced.

True False **10.** A group member will be influenced to choose a personal goal that reflects the goals of the other group members if she likes them.

PLANE WRECK EXERCISE

The purpose of this exercise is to provide participants with an opportunity to experience cooperation based on a division of labor as well as a joint goal. The procedure is as follows:

1. The class forms groups of three. One member plays the role of observer, another member the role of *A,* and the third member *B.*
2. Each group of three needs the following materials:
   a. a blindfold
   b. five or six odd-sized pieces of cardboard
   c. a roll of cellophane tape or masking tape
   d. a piece of rope at least three feet long
3. *The situation: A* and *B* were flying a plane, which suddenly developed engine trouble and crashed on a desert island with no water. They will be rescued in a few days, but they must have water if they are to survive. They have some materials for making a container to hold rainwater. The only problem is that *B* received a heavy blow on her head and is now both blind and mute. *A* burned both his hands badly and is not able to use them at all. But they must build the container if they are to live: A rain cloud is quickly approaching, and they must have the container finished before it reaches the island. A few drops are already beginning to fall.
4. The observer ties *A*'s hands behind his back and blindfolds *B. B* is not to say a word during the entire building process.
5. The observer takes notes on how well the two persons work together. How good are the directions? How well are they carried out? How cooperative are the two persons? What communication problems exist? What could they have done differently?
6. If the container is not finished in twenty minutes, the two persons stop. The group

then combines with another group of three and the two groups discuss the following questions:

   a. How did the person playing *A* feel?

   b. How did the person playing *B* feel?

   c. What does the container look like? If it were made of wood and nails instead of cardboard and tape, would it hold water? (If there is a hole in the bottom, the answer is no).

   d. What would have improved the cooperation between *A* and *B?*

   e. What did you learn about the division of labor in a cooperative task?

  7. Each group of six shares its major conclusions and experiences with the rest of the class.

BROKEN SQUARES EXERCISE

The purpose of this exercise is to explore the results of cooperation and competition among group members in solving a group problem. The exercise is done in groups of five participants and two observers. Tables that seat five should be used. At least four groups are recommended, but two may do in a pinch. Place the tables far enough apart so that members of one group cannot observe the activities of the other groups. One set of squares is needed for each group of five. (Instructions for making a set of squares may be found in Appendix D on page 480.) Approximately one hour is needed for the exercise. The procedures for the coordinator are as follows:

  1. Introduce the exercise as one that focuses upon the way in which goals are defined by members of a group. State that it will consist of completing a group task involving a puzzle.

  2. Hand out the observation instructions to the observers. Within each group give each participant an instruction sheet and an envelope containing pieces of the puzzle (see the directions for making a set of squares). Half of the groups should receive instructions that they are to act cooperatively, and half instructions that they are to act competitively. State that the envelopes are not to be opened until the signal is given. Review the instructions with each group in such a way that cooperative groups do not hear the instructions to the competitive groups, and vice versa. Ask if the observers understand their role.

  3. Give the signal to begin. The groups are to work until all of them have solved the puzzle. Each group should be carefully timed by its observers. If a group becomes deadlocked for more than twenty-five minutes, this phase of the exercise should be ended.

  4. Collect the observation sheets and record the information in the table below. While you are doing this the groups should pair off, a cooperative group with a competitive group, and share and discuss their instructions and experiences with each other. Group observers are to participate fully in this discussion. By the end of the discussion the groups should have recorded their conclusions about the differences between working in a cooperatively oriented and a competitively oriented problem-solving group.

  5. Share the results of the discussions among all the groups. Then present the information gathered by the observers. Using the material in the following section on goal structures, define cooperation and competition and discuss the impact of goal structures on group functioning and effectiveness.

You may conduct this exercise with only one group by leaving out the instructions about cooperative and competitive orientations and the comparison between cooperative and competitive groups. The issue of goal structure can still be discussed profitably.

Data From Observation Sheets

	Cooperative	Competitive
Number of groups completing the task		
Time for task completion		
Number of times a member gave away a puzzle piece		
Number of times a member took a puzzle piece		
Number of members who cut themselves off from others		
Cooperative behaviors		
Competitive behaviors		

Broken Square Exercise:
Instructions to Each Member of the Cooperative Group

Each member of your group has an envelope containing pieces of cardboard for forming squares. When the signal is given to begin, the task of the group is to form one square in front of each member. Only parts of the pieces for forming the five squares are in each envelope. The exercise has two goals: your individual goal of forming a square in front of yourself as fast as possible and the group's goal of having squares formed in front of every member as fast as possible. The individual goal is accomplished when you have a completed square in front of you. The group goal is accomplished when all group members have completed squares in front of them.

You are to role-play a member of a group whose members are all highly cooperative. To you the group goal is far more important than the individual goal. Your job is to cooperate with the other group members as much as possible in order to accomplish the group goal in the shortest period of time possible. To you the other group members are your partners, and you are concerned with helping them put together a completed square. All members of your group have received the same instructions.

The specific rules for the exercise are as follows:

1. No talking, pointing, or any other kind of communication is allowed among the five members of your group.
2. No person may *ask* another member for a piece of the puzzle or in any way signal that another person is to give her a puzzle piece.

3. Members may *give* puzzle pieces to other members.

4. Members may not throw their pieces into the center for others to take; they have to give the pieces directly to one person.

5. Anyone may give away all the pieces of his puzzle, even if he has already formed a square.

6. Part of the role of the observers is to enforce these rules.

Broken Squares Exercise:
Instructions to Each Member of the Competitive Group

Every person in this group has an envelope that contains pieces of cardboard for forming squares. When the signal is given to begin, your task is to form a square in front of you. Only parts of the pieces for forming the five squares are in each envelope. The exercise has two goals: your individual goal of forming a square in front of you as fast as possible and the group's goal of forming squares in front of every member as fast as possible. The individual goal is accomplished when you have a completed square in front of you. The group goal is accomplished when all group members have completed squares in front of them.

You are to role-play a member of a group whose members are all highly competitive. To you the individual goal is far more important than the group goal. Your job is to compete with the other group members to see who can get a completed square in front of himself first. At the end of the exercise group members will be ranked on the basis of their speed in completing their square. The member finishing first will be labeled the "best" person in the group, the person finishing second will be labeled, "second best" person in the group, and so on, with the last person finishing being labeled the "worst" person in the group. The other group members are your competitors, and you are concerned with completing your square before they do. If you complete your square and then decide to give a piece of it away, you lose your previous rank in terms of the order of members completing their squares and must start over. All members of your group have received the same instructions.

The specific rules for the exercise are as follows:

1. No talking, pointing, or any other kind of communicating is allowed among the five members of your group.

2. No person may *ask* another member for a piece of the puzzle or in any way signal that another person is to give her a puzzle piece.

3. Members may *give* puzzle pieces to other members.

4. Members may not throw their pieces into the center for others to take; they have to give the pieces directly to one person.

5. Part of the role of the observers is to enforce these rules.

Broken Squares Exercise: Instructions for Observers

Your job is part observer, part recorder, and part rule enforcer. Do your best to strictly enforce the rules on the instruction sheet for participants. Then observe and record as accurately as possible the items listed below. The information you record will be used in a discussion of the results of the exercise.

1. Did the group complete the task?   _____ Yes _____ No

2. How long did it take the group to complete the task?   _____ minutes, _____ seconds

3.	Number of times a group member took a puzzle piece from another member:	Number of times a group member gave a puzzle piece to another member:

4. Number of members who finished their square and then divorced themselves from the struggles of the rest of the group? _____

5. Were there any critical turning points at which cooperation or competition increased? _____ _____

6. What behaviors in the group showed cooperativeness or competitiveness? _____ _____ _____ _____

COOPERATIVE, COMPETITIVE, AND INDIVIDUALISTIC GOAL STRUCTURES EXERCISE

The purposes of this exercise are (1) to provide an experiential definition of the three goal structures and (2) to direct participants' attention to the contrasting patterns of interaction created by these three structures. (The correct answers are in Appendix D on page 481.) The procedure for the coordinator is as follows:

1. Assign participants to heterogeneous groups of three.

2. Conduct a competitive task experience as follows:

    a. State that the members of each triad are to compete to see who is best in identifying how many squares are in a certain geometric figure. The criterion for winning is simply to identify more correct squares than the other two triad members. Ask the participants to turn their "square figure" right side up, and tell them to begin.

    b. At the end of four or five minutes instruct the participants to stop. Ask them to determine who is the winner of each triad, ask the winners to stand, and then have everyone applaud.

    c. Tell the participants to turn away from their triad and, working by themselves, write down (1) how they felt during the competition and (2) what they noticed during the competition. Give them another three or four minutes to do this.

3. Conduct an individualistic task experience as follows:

    a. State that participants are to work individualistically to find as many two-sided figures in a geometric figure as they can. All participants who find 95 percent of the biangles will receive an evaluation of "excellent," all those who find 90 percent will receive an evaluation of "good," and so forth. Tell the particpants to turn their "biangles figure" right side up and begin.

b. At the end of four or five minutes ask the participants to stop. Then announce the number of biangles in the figure. Ask the participants to leave their triad and, working by themselves, describe (1) how they felt and (2) what they noticed during this task. Give them another three or four minutes to do this.

4. Conduct a cooperative task experience as follows:

a. State that the participants are to reform their triads and work as a group to identify as many triangles in a geometric figure as they can, making sure that all members of the triad can correctly identify all the triangles. When they are finished, the members of each triad should sign the group's paper to indicate their agreement

Goal Structures and Interaction Among Group Members

	Goal Structures		
	cooperative	*competitive*	*individualistic*
Interaction			
Communication			
Facilitation of others' efforts			
Peer influence			
Utilization of others' resources			
Divergent thinking			
Emotional involvement in task			
Acceptance and support among members			
Trust among members			
Conflict management			
Division of labor			
Fear of failure			

In the spaces provided above, summarize your observations of the three types of task situations.

with the group's answer. All members of the groups finding 95 percent of the triangles will receive an evaluation of "excellent," all members of the groups finding 90 percent of the triangles will receive an evaluation of "good," and so forth. Tell the participants to turn their "trangles figure" right side up and begin.

b. At the end of nine or ten minutes tell the participants to stop. Inform them of the number of triangles in the figure. Then ask them to turn away from their triad and, working by themselves, write down (1) how they felt and (2) what they noticed during the cooperative task. Give the participants four minutes to do this.

5. Instruct the participants to share their reactions to the three types of task situations with the other members of their triad. Give them ten or twelve minutes to do so. Then sample the reactions of the triads in a class discussion. Ask the participants to make conclusions about the reactions of the triads to the three task experiences.

6. Instruct the triads to fill out the table below on the basis of their experiences in the three goal structures and the comments made by the other triads. In the spaces provided, they should summarize their observations of the interaction that occurred in three task situations.

7. Review with the entire class the conceptual definitions of the three goal structures and discuss their views of the impact of each of these structures on group functioning and productivity.

Goal Structures Exercise: Squares

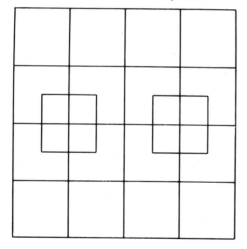

How did I feel?

What did I notice?

Goal Structures Exercise: Biangles

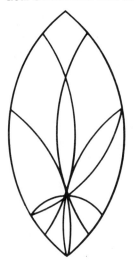

How did I feel?

What did I notice?

Goal Structures Exercise: Triangles

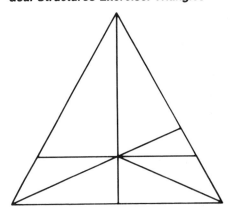

How did I feel?

What did I notice?

SUBSISTANCE EXERCISE

The purpose of this exercise is to observe the effect of unequal resources on the development of cooperation or competition within a group. The exercise simulates the effects of poverty and affluence in a life and death situation. The procedure is as follows.

1. Form groups of seven. One member should volunteer to be the recorder and another member should volunteer to be the observer. Each group should have five participants, one recorder, and one observer.

2. To play the game contained in this exercise the group needs a pack of blank 3 x 5 inch index cards to serve as food cards. The group also needs a pack of hunting and gathering cards. Each card should have one of the statements listed on page 157 written on it.

3. The basic procedure of the game is as follows:
   a. Each participant receives three food cards.
   b. The recorder shuffles the hunting and gathering cards and places them in the center of the group.
   c. Each participant draws a card in turn (going counterclockwise), reads it to the group, and receives from or gives to the recorder the required number of food cards.
   d. The day's hunting and gathering is over when every participant has drawn one card. Participants may give any number of food cards to each other. At the end of the day they must give one food card to the recorder. Failure to do so results in death by starvation and dropping out of the game.
   e. After seven rounds the week's hunting and gathering is over. Points are awarded to group members.
   f. The game is played for a minimum of two weeks.

4. The role of the observer is to record the frequency of the behaviors listed on the observation sheet. The frequencies are reported to the group during the concluding group discussion.

5. The role of the recorder is to:
   a. Read the Subsistence Instruction Sheet to the group.
   b. Review the rules with participants.
   c. Give each participant three food cards.
   d. Shuffle the hunting and gathering cards and place them in the center of the group.
   e. Distribute and collect food cards on the basis of the cards drawn.
   f. At the end of each round collect one food card from each participant.
   g. Ensure that each participant announces how many food cards they have at the end of each round.
   h. Announce how many participants starved to death and who has the most food cards at the end of each week (seven rounds).

6. When the game is over, discuss the following questions:
   a. Who survived and who died?
   b. How was a cooperative or a competitive strategy decided on?
   c. How did participants feel about the impending death by starvation?
   d. How did the dead feel when they knew others could have saved them?
   e. How did the survivors feel when others died when they had extra food cards?

f. Who organized the group to create a "just" distribution of food?

g. What real life situations parallel this exercise?

Subsistence Instruction Sheet

A severe drought has devastated your world. Because food is so scarce you have banded together into a hunting and gathering group. It is more efficient for several people to coordinate their hunting and gathering so that more territory may be covered in any one day. There are five members of your hunting and gathering group. The food cards in your hands represent all you have left of your dwindling food supply. Since you are already weakened by hunger, you must eat at the end of each day (round) or die. At that time, you must give up one food card. When you are out of cards, you will die of starvation. A member who does not have one food card at the end of a day (round) is considered to be dead and can no longer participate in the group. Members with only one food card may not talk. Only members with two or more food cards may discuss their situation and converse with each other. You may give food cards to each other whenever you wish to do so.

Rules for Subsistence Exercise

1. The game begins when the recorder gives all participants three food cards, shuffles the hunting and gathering cards, and places them in the center of the group.

2. The purpose of the game is to gain points. You receive eight points if at the end of the week of hunting and gathering (seven rounds) you have more food cards than does any other participant in your group. If no one in your group has starved at the end of the week of hunting and gathering, all participants receive five points.

3. The game is played for a minimum of two weeks. At the beginning of each week all participants begin with three food cards and with all five participants alive.

4. You draw one card during each round. You read it aloud to the group and receive from or give to the recorder the number of food cards indicated.

5. During a round you may give food cards to other participants if you wish to.

6. All participants read the hunting and gathering cards aloud. Only those with two or more food cards, however, may discuss the game with each other. Participants with one or no food cards must be silent.

7. At the end of each round participants hold up their food cards and announce to the group how many food cards they have.

8. At the end of each round participants give one food card each to the recorder. This symbolizes the food eaten during the day to stay alive.

9. If a participant cannot give a food card to the recorder at the end of a round, the participant dies of starvation and is excluded from further rounds during that week.

10. At the end of each week of hunting and gathering (seven rounds) the recorder announces who has the most food cards and how many participants starved to death. Points are then awarded.

Subsistence Record Sheet

Name	Round 1	Round 2	Round 3	Round 4	Round 5	Round 6	Round 7

Subsistence Observation Sheet

	Round 1	Round 2	Round 3	Round 4	Round 5	Round 6	Round 7
Number of cards given away							
Number of cards taken away							
Number of people starved							
Cooperative strategy suggested							
Competitive comment							
Other							
Other							

Subsistence Exercise: Hunting and Gathering Cards

You found no food today.

You made a beautiful shot at what looked like a deer, but it turned out to be a strangely shaped rock. You got no food today.

You shot a bird. You get one food card from the recorder.

Wild dogs chased you and to get away you threw them one day's food. Give the recorder one food card. If you do not have a food card, and if no one will give you one, you die of starvation.

You fell asleep and slept all day. You got no food today.

Excellent shot. You killed a deer worth two days' of food. You get two food cards from the recorder.

You met a member of another group and fell in love. To impress your new love you gave him/her one day's food. Give the recorder one food card. If you do not have a food card, and if no one will give you one, you die of starvation.

You shot a snake. You get one food card from the recorder.

Army ants chased you and to get away you threw them one day's food. Give the recorder one food card. If you do not have a food card, and if no one will give you one, you die of starvation.

You shot a lizard. You get one food card from the recorder.

While running away from a lion, you took refuge in a peach tree. You receive one food card from the recorder.

You shot at a deer but missed. You got no food today.

Lucky fluke! You shot at a deer and hit a rabbit. You get one food card from the recorder.

While you were hunting, a skunk broke into your hut and ate two days' worth of food. Give two food cards to the recorder. If you do not have two food cards, and if no one will give you one, you die of starvation.

While you were hunting, a lion ate you and all your food. Give all your food cards to the recorder and drop out of the game. Since you did not starve, your group's points are not effected. You are reborn the next week.

You found a nest of field mice and bopped them all on the head. You get one food card from the recorder.

You found no food today.

You shot a bird. You get one food card from the recorder.

You found a berry bush. Berries are in season. You get one food card from the recorder.

Lucky fluke! You shot at a wild pig and hit a rabbit. You get one food card from the recorder.

Excellent shot. You aimed at a bird you thought was standing on a rock. Your arrow hit the rock, which turned out to be a wild pig. You get two food cards from the recorder.

You found a deer, but a bear scared it away before you could shoot at it. You got no food today.

Excellent shot. Just as you shot at a deer, a wild pig ran in the way and got killed. You receive two food cards from the recorder.

You shot a rabbit. You get one food card from the recorder.

You found no food today. Probably too hot for anything to be out and around.

You found some wild carrots. You get one food card from the recorder.

You found an apple tree. Birds had eaten almost all of them. You get one food card from the recorder.

Excellent shot. You killed a wild pig. You get two food cards from the recorder.

While hunting, you accidentally stepped on a snake and killed it. You receive one food card from the recorder.

On your way home you fell into a swamp. You lost two days' worth of food to a hungry crocodile. Give two food cards to the recorder. If you do not have them, and if no one will give them to you, you die of starvation.

Excellent shot. You killed a deer. You get two food cards from the recorder.

You found some wild lettuce. You get one food card from the recorder.

You shot a rabbit. You get one food card from the recorder.

You shot a bird. You get one food card from the recorder.

You shot an ardvark. You get one food card from the recorder.

While hunting, you found a berry bush. Berries are in season. You get one food card from the recorder.

Best of luck! You found a deer with a broken leg. You killed it with your stone club. You get two food cards from the recorder.

You looked and looked and looked but found no food today.

You shot at a rabbit but it zigged instead of zagged. You got no food today.

You walked for miles and found nothing to gather or shoot at. You got no food today.

GROUP GOALS AND INTERDEPENDENCE AMONG MEMBERS

A dilemma faced by members of many groups is, should they act competitively or individualistically to maximize their immediate self-interests, or should they act cooperatively, knowing that in the long run the majority of the group members will benefit if they do. For any group to survive or be effective, the personal goals of group members must be structured cooperatively. Coordinated action, pooling of resources, division of labor, open and accurate communication, trust, cohesion, and many other aspects of effective groups depend on cooperatively oriented group members and a cooperative goal structure within the group. There is nothing more destructive in both the task and the maintenance areas of group functioning than members acting competitively or individualistically. Yet many groups are made up of highly competitive and individualistic persons and have competitive or individualistic goal structures.

Groups may be structured cooperatively, competitively, or individualistically (Deutsch, 1949, 1962; Johnson and Johnson, 1975). In other words, there may be positive, negative, or no interdependence among the goals of group members. A *cooperative* goal structure exists when there is a positive correlation among group members' goal attainments—that is, when group members perceive that they can achieve their goal if and only if the other members with whom they are cooperatively linked obtain their goal. When a team of climbers, for example, reaches the summit of a mountain, the success is experienced by all members of the team.

A *competitive* goal structure exits when there is a negative correlation among group members' goal attainments—that is, when group members perceive that they can obtain their goals if and only if the other members with whom they are competitively linked fail to obtain their goal. When one runner wins a race, for example, all the other runners in the race fail to win. An *individualistic* goal structure exists when there is no correlation among group members' goal attainments—that is, when group members perceive that obtaining their goal is unrelated to the goal achievement of other members. A person's success in swimming fifty yards, for example, is unrelated to whether others swim fifty yards or not.

The classic theoretical work on the three goal structures was done by Morton Deutsch (1949). Deutsch was born in 1920, graduated from City College of New York in 1939, and obtained a masters degree from the University of Pennsylvania in 1940. After serving in the United States Air Force from 1942 to 1945 he entered the doctoral program in social psychology at M.I.T. to study with Kurt Lewin. His dissertation, completed in 1948, developed and tested a theory of cooperation and competition based on Lewin's field theory. He has subsequently developed theories of trust, bargaining and negotiation, and justice. Since 1963 he has headed the training program for social psychologists at Teachers College, Columbia University. Deutsch has received a variety of professional rewards during his career, including the prestigious Kurt Lewin Memorial Award for contributions to the solution of social problems through theory and research and the Gordon Allport Memorial Award for contributions to constructive intergroup relations through theory and research. Following in Lewin's footsteps, Deutsch has become noted as an outstanding social psychologist due to his commitment to the development of theory about complex social issues, his ability to find ways to study these issues in a laboratory setting, and his dedication to the solution of social problems.

Considerable research based on Deutsch's classic work on cooperation and competition has been conducted during the past thirty years. The research has found that each goal structure promotes a different pattern of interaction among group members. The interaction patterns affect group productivity, morale, and effectiveness. Coopeation provides opportunities for positive interaction among group members, competition promotes cautious and defensive member interaction (except under limited conditions), and in individualistic situations group members work by themselves and do not interact with other members. There is considerable research documenting the relative effects of the three goal structures on the pattern of interaction among group members (Johnson, 1980; Johnson and Johnson, 1975, 1978). The evidence (summarized in Table 4.1) indicates that a cooperative goal structure, compared with competitive and individualistic ones, promotes more effective communication and exchange of information among members, greater facilitation of one another's work, more helping and sharing of resources among members, more peer influence toward productivity, higher utilization of other

TABLE 4.1 Interaction among group members in three types of goal structures

Cooperative	Competitive	Individualistic
High interaction	Low interaction	No interaction
Effective communication and information exchange	Misleading or threatening, communication and information exchange, or none at all	No interaction
Facilitation of others' productivity; helping and sharing	Obstruction of others' productivity	No interaction
Peer influence toward productivity	Peer influence against productivity	No interaction
High utilization of other members' resources	Low utilization of others' resources	No interaction
High divergent and risk-taking thinking	Low divergent and risk-taking thinking	No interaction
High emotional involvement in and commitment to productivity by all members	High emotional involvement in and commitment to productivity by the few members who have a chance to win	No interaction
High acceptance and support among members	Low acceptance and support among members	No interaction
High trust among members	Low trust among members	No interaction
Problem-solving conflict management	Win-or-lose conflict management	No interaction
Division of labor possible	Division of labor impossible	No interaction
Decreased fear of failure	Increased fear of failure	No interaction

members' resources, higher incidence of divergent and risk-taking thinking, higher emotional involvement in and commitment to productivity by more members, higher acceptance and support among members, more of a problem-solving orientation to conflict management, more possibility of divisions of labor, and a lower fear of failure by members.

These interaction patterns dramatically affect the productivity, morale, and effectiveness of groups (Johnson, 1980; Johnson and Johnson, 1975, 1978). Some of the major results of the research in these three areas are as follows.

Productivity

Since 1924 there have been over 122 research studies on the effects of cooperative, competitive, and individualistic goal structures on group productivity. Recently, Johnson, Maruyama, Johnson, Nelson, and Skon (1981) reviewed these studies, comparing the relative effectiveness of cooperation, cooperation with intergroup competition, interpersonal competition, and individualistic goal structures. The 122 studies reviewed contained 286 comparisons of group productivity among the four types of goal structures. Three meta-analysis procedures were used: voting method, effect-size method, and z-score method. The results of these meta-analyses appear in Table 4.2. A number of conclusions may be made from the meta-analyses results. First, from the studies directly comparing the productivity of cooperation structured with and without intergroup competition, no real difference resulted. When cooperation is compared with interpersonal competition, the voting-method indicates that cooperation promotes higher productivity than does competition by 65 to 8 (with 36 no differences). The effect size of .78 favoring cooperation indicates that the average person in the cooperative condition performed .75 standard deviations above the average person in the competition, or at the 78th percentile of the competitive condition. The z-score of 16.00 favoring cooperation indicates that the probability that the difference between cooperation and competition is due to chance is less than one in a million. It would take 7,859 additional studies finding exactly no difference between cooperation and competition on productivity to produce a z-score that is statistically nonsignificant.

When cooperation is compared with individualistic efforts, the voting-method indicates that cooperation promotes higher productivity by a score

TABLE 4.2 Meta-Analyses Comparing Relative Productivity of Four Different Goal Structures

	Method								
	voting			effect size			z score		
conditions	N	ND	P	M	SD	N	z	N	fail-safe n
Cooperative vs. group competitive	3	6	4	.00	.63	9	.16	13	
Cooperative vs. competitive	8	36	65	.78	.99	70	16.00	84	7,859
Group competitive vs. competitive	3	22	19	.37	.78	16	6.39	31	430
Cooperative vs. individualistic	6	42	108	.78	.91	104	24.01	132	27,998
Group competitive vs. individualistic	1	10	20	.50	.37	20	11.37	29	1,356
Competitive vs. individualistic	12	38	9	.03	1.02	48	4.82	50	380

N = negative; ND = no difference; P = positive.

Johnson, D. W., Maruyama, G., Johnson, R., Nelson, D., & Skon, L., Effects of Cooperative, Competitive, and Individualistic Goal Structures on Achievement: A Meta-analysis. *Psychological Bulletin*, 1981, *89*, 47–62. Reprinted by permission.

of 108 to 6 (with 42 no differences). The effect size of .78 favoring cooperation indicates that the average person in the cooperative condition performed at the 78th percentile of the individualistic condition. The z-score of 24.01 favoring cooperation indicates that the probability that the difference is due to change is less than one in a million. It would take 27,998 additional studies finding exactly no difference between cooperative and individualistic efforts on productivity to produce a z-score that is statistically nonsignificant.

Not all the research supporting the use of a cooperative goal structure has been experimental. Balderston (1930) conducted a study of group-incentive plans by collecting written descriptions of such plans from a number of companies. In each instance, the pay of all members depended on the achievement of the group as a whole. Balderston found that this method of work doubled the efficiency of the workers, increased their pay about 25 percent, and reduced their costs a good amount compared to the flat rate previously paid to each individual. The users of group incentive stated that their plans were valuable because they increased cooperation and team spirit among members, reduced monotony on the job, and caused workers to focus on a common goal.

Morale

Numerous studies have compared the impact of cooperative, competitive, and individualistic goal structures on the attitudes of group members toward each other, themselves, their superiors, the task, and the group itself (Johnson, 1980; Johnson and Johnson, 1975, 1978, 1980). There is considerable evidence that cooperative experiences, compared with competitive and individualistic ones, result in more positive relationships among members, relationships characterized by mutual liking, positive attitudes toward each other, mutual concern, friendliness, attentiveness, feelings of obligation to each other, and a desire to win each other's respect. These results hold even when group members are from different ethnic groups, social classes, and ability levels.

Cooperative experiences, compared with competitive and individualistic ones, also promote more positive attitudes toward supervisors and organizational superiors. Superiors are viewed as being more supportive and accepting in cooperative situations. Such positive perceptions by group members of their relationship with superiors are important for many reasons, not the least of which is that the more positive the relationship between a group member and an organizational superior, the less the superior has to rely on direct power and coercion to motivate group members to comply with organizational norms and role definitions.

There is also evidence that cooperative groups are more cohesive than groups dominated by competitive or individualistic relations and that the members of cooperative groups like the group better, like their tasks better, and like the organization within which the group is embedded better. The self-esteem and overall psychological health of group members is higher when the group is dominated by cooperative rather than competitive or individualistic relations. Group members feel better about themselves and base their appraisals of their self-worth on basic self-acceptance when the group is dominated by cooperation.

Group Effectiveness

A cooperative goal structure, compared with competitive and individualistic ones, affects members' motivation, social skills, and mutual influence, all of which in turn influence overall group effectiveness (Johnson, 1980; Johnson and Johnson, 1975, 1978). Motivation is most commonly viewed as a combination of the perceived likelihood of success and the perceived incentive for success. The greater the likelihood of success and the more important it is to succeed, the higher the motivation. Success that is intrinsically rewarding is usually seen by researchers as being more desirable for productivity than having members believe that only extrinsic rewards are worthwhile. In a cooperative situation there is a greater perceived likelihood of success and success is considered more important than in a competitive or individualistic situation. The more cooperative group members are, furthermore, the more they are intrinsically motivated to complete the group's tasks.

Members of groups dominated by cooperation are more willing to be influenced by other group members and are more able to influence their fellow members than is the case in groups dominated by competitive and individualistic goal structures. The influence, furthermore, tends to be based on persuasion and reason rather than coercion. Cooperation also promotes greater increases in social skills such as communication, leadership, conflict management, and social perspective-taking.

It should also be noted that the effectiveness of a group can easily be damaged when a competitive member is added. Kelley and Stahelski (1970) found that several things happen in such a situation. First, the cooperative members begin behaving in competitive ways, violating trust, hiding information, and cutting off communication. Second, the competitive person sees the formerly cooperative members as having *always* been competitive. Third, the cooperative members are aware that their behavior is being determined by the other's competitive behavior, but the competitive person is not aware of his or her impact on the cooperators. Effective patterns of interaction among members are usually far easier to destroy than to build.

It should be noted that in most groups all three goals structures exist simultaneously. Group members may be committed to group goals and work to maximize joint outcomes and at the same time seek to outperform a peer and to meet personal needs unrelated to the concerns of other members. What matters is which goal structure dominates group life, not whether any one goal structure is present or absent.

Other Ways to Achieve Cooperative Interdependence

Cooperation may be structured among group members in a number of ways other than through the group's goal structure. Through a division of labor group members can be cooperatively interdependent. The resources or information the group needs to complete the task can be divided among group members, thereby creating cooperative interdependence. The role assignments of group members can be such that a positive interdependence results. Finally, rewards can be distributed in ways that promote positive or negative interdependence among group members. Through task, resource, role, and reward interdependence as well as through goal interdependence cooperation may be structured within a group. The way in which the distribution of rewards affects the productiveness and morale of groups, however, has been of special interest to social psychologists concerned with cooperation.

GOAL STRUCTURES AND THE ALLOCATION OF REWARDS AMONG GROUP MEMBERS

It is inherent in our species that we engage in joint endeavors that benefit all who participate. We join together and combine our efforts to achieve mutual goals. Individuals join groups because in the long run they are better off being part of the group than not. The better the group functions, the better off the individual members are; the better off the individual members are, the more they can contribute to the group's efforts, and therefore the better the group functions. Part of the process whereby effective cooperation among members is promoted in order to ensure their individual well-being is the distribution of rewards. The way in which rewards are distributed among group members can have a marked effect on how members behave toward one another in the future and how effective the group is (Deutsch, 1975, 1979). Depending on the circumstances, rewards may be distributed according to merit, equality, or need.

The *merit* view of distributing rewards has been presented by Homans (1961) as a basic rule of distributive justice and equity theory: in a just distribution, rewards will be distributed among individuals in proportion to their contributions. In other words, those members who contribute the most to the group's success should receive the greatest benefits. There are a number of problems with the merit approach to distributing rewards within a group. One is that the economic values upon which equity theory is based can have unfortunate effects on group members' views of themselves and each other as well as on the relationships among members. From a utilitarian, economic point of view group members are of value only to the extent that they contribute to the group's success. Rewards are valuable because they are scarce commodity that one competes with others to obtain.

The view that people are of value only to the extent that they are useful results in a depersonalization of both oneself and others, and the attitude that different members have different value undermines the basis for mutual respect and self-respect. Members may view their self-worth as being related to the rewards they receive, which in turn are related to the contributions they make to group goal accomplishment. Other members are viewed in the same way. Thus, if a member contributes little to group success and receives disproportionately small rewards, he or she is viewed as having little personal worth. Diesing (1962) describes such a situation as being alienated from oneself and others.

A utilitarian view of rewards may cloud their intrinsic value by making it dependent on the extent to which others want them. The utilitarian value of a reward increases with the number of persons who want the reward; the reward becomes a scarce commodity when its supply is far less than the demand for it. The symbolic meaning of the reward may become far more important than the intrinsic value of the reward: children fight over being first in line not because of the intrinsic value of the position but rather because it symbolizes that they are a winner, superior to those who are positioned behind them. Diesing (1962) describes such a situation as being alienated from one's possessions and creations. Thus, the competition among group members that is fostered by rewards being proportionate to members' contributions may seriously reduce the cohesiveness of the group, cause morale problems, and undermine group effectiveness as trust and communication among members deteriorate.

Group members who are successful under a merit system often misattribute their success to their efforts rather than to their talents. Certain group members will have more resource attractors than others. A *resource attractor* is an attribute that tends to attract other resources because it gives the possessor an advantage in a competition for these other resources. Examples of resource attractors are ability, training, previous experience, drive, and character. Group members with a high number of resource attractors often get higher rewards than members with few resource attractors and may attribute their success to their worthiness and effort (implying that those who have fewer resource attractors are less worthy and more lazy).

Finally, a merit system often results in a situation in which the group members who are rewarded the most are given the power to distribute future rewards on the basis of their assessment of how much each member is contributing to the group effort. Deutsch (1975, 1979) notes that this allows those who are in power to bias the system of allocation to perpetuate their disproportionate rewards and power even when they are no longer making relatively large contributions to the group's well-being.

An *equality* system of distributive justice rewards all group members equally. If a football team wins the Super Bowl, all members receive a Super Bowl ring. If a learning group completes an assignment at an *A* level, all members of the group receive an *A*. Deutsch (1975, 1979) notes that a consequence of an equality system of distributive justice is mutual esteem, equal status, and mutual respect among members. He states that the principle of equality is more congenial to the fostering of enjoyable, personal relationships, group loyalty, and cooperativeness.

The distribution of rewards according to *need* results in a situation in which the group members who are most in need of the rewards receive a disproportionate amount of them. The member who has the largest family may receive the highest monetary bonus, the member who is grieving for the death of her parents may be asked to do the least work, or the member who has the least ability will be given the most support and assistance for completing his assigned tasks. A student who has never received an *A* might be given the highest grade in the group. Rawls (1971) pointed out that one of the natural duties of members of a group is to help another member who is in need or in jeopardy, providing one can do so without excessive loss or risk to oneself. The gain to the member who needs help is seen as far outweighing the loss of those required to assist him. Such a system of distributive justice emphasizes the confidence and trust members may have in their colleagues' good intentions. Deutsch (1975, 1979) notes that a caring-oriented group will stress responsibility for each other, permissiveness toward members expressing their needs, heightened sensitivity to each other's needs, and support and nurturance of each other's legitimate needs.

Whatever system of distributing rewards a group uses, it has to be perceived as "just" by group members. When rewards are distributed unjustly the group may be characterized by low morale and high conflict among its members, which in turn may decrease productivity.

QUIZ

Check your reading of this section by answering the following questions. Answers are on page 177. Match the following group descriptors with the correct goal structure.

_____ 1. In order for a person to reach his goals, no one else must reach his goals.

_____ 2. In order for a person to reach her goals, the group must reach its goals.

_____ 3. The goals of the members are independent of each other.

_____ 4. Positive interaction.

a. Cooperation
b. Competition
c. Individualistic

_____ **5.** No interaction.

_____ **6.** Cautious and defensive interaction.

_____ **7.** Effective communication.

_____ **8.** Misleading communication.

_____ **9.** Helping, sharing.

_____ **10.** Low divergent thinking.

_____ **11.** Higher group productivity.

_____ **12.** More positive attitudes.

13. Keith is a very competitive person. What is likely to happen when he joins a cooperative group? (check three)

a. Keith starts acting cooperatively.

b. The cooperative people start acting competitively.

c. Keith sees the cooperative people as being competitive.

d. Keith sees the cooperative people as being cooperative.

e. The cooperative people see that their behavior is being changed by Keith.

f. Keith sees that he is changing the behavior of the cooperative people.

g. Keith gets thrown out of the group.

True False   **14.** It is not possible for group members to be cooperative, competitive, and individualistic at the same time.

True False   **15.** Cooperation can be structured through the goal structure, division of labor, rewards, and/or roles.

Match the outcomes with the correct reward system:

_____ **16.** Individual rewards given in proportion to contributions.

_____ **17.** Individual rewards given as assistance.

_____ **18.** All group members rewarded the same.

_____ **19.** Members compete for rewards.

_____ **20.** Promotes mutual self-esteem, status, and respect.

a. Merit system
b. Equality system
c. Need system

CLEAR AND UNCLEAR GOAL EXERCISE

This exercise shows the contrasting behavioral consequences of having clear and unclear goals. Approximately one hour is needed to complete it. Here is the procedure for the coordinator:

1. Seat the participants in groups of six to eight, formed into circles.

2. Introduce the exercise as focusing upon clear and unclear group goals.

3. Have each group select an observer, who reports to a designated place for instructions. While the observers are being briefed, urge the group members to get acquainted with one another.

4. Give each observer a copy of the observation guide and tell them that the groups will work on two tasks. The first task will be unclear, the second clear. Their job is to make careful observations of group behavior on the two tasks. The observers then return to their groups, but sit outside the circle.

5. Brief all groups as follows: "We are going to study group behavior by working on two brief tasks. Your observer will not participate, but will report to you at the end of the second task. Your first task will take about eight minutes. I will give you a warning a minute before the time is up. The task is: list the most appropriate goals to govern the best developmental group experiences in order to maximize social development in a democratic society."

6. While the groups work on the task, the observers should take notes. After seven minutes give the warning and after eight minutes end the discussion.

7. Give Task 2: "List as many of the formally organized clubs or organizations that exist in a typical community as you can." State that the groups will have six minutes to work on the task. At the end of five minutes give a one-minute warning and after six minutes end the discussion.

8. Give a copy of the observation form to all participants. Then have each group discuss its experience, using the information obtained by the observers as its major resource. This discussion should last ten to fifteen minutes.

9. Form clusters by asking one group to pull its chairs in a circle around another group. The inner group becomes group A and the outer group becomes group B. Instruct group A to produce a list of characteristics of clear and unclear goals with one person recording them on newsprint in two columns. Allow six minutes for this task. Group B is to listen to group A, take notes, and be ready to add to the list. After six minutes instruct group B to comment on the list and have both groups jointly select the four or five most important characteristics of clear and unclear goals from the list. Give them nine minutes to do so.

10. Groups A and B then change places, with group B now in the center. Group B is told to list behavioral symptoms of each of the characteristics of clear and unclear goals listed on the newsprint, beginning with the most important characteristics. After nine minutes group A joins the discussion, which should take another six minutes.

11. Each cluster presents its work to the other group. Hold a general discussion on the nature of group goals and their consequences in feeling and behavior, using the material in the following section.

Clear and Unclear Goals Exercise: Observation Guide

During this exercise the groups will work on two tasks. The first task will be unclear, and the second will be clear. Your job as an observer is to make careful notations of group behavior on the two tasks. When you understand the form below, return to your group but sit outside the circle.

	First Task	Second Task
1. Number of times a member clarified the goal or asked that it be clarified.		
2. Assessment of "working" climate of the group: Was it cooperative, hostile, pleasant, critical, accepting, and so forth? At the beginning?		
At the middle?		
At the end?		
3. Frequency of verbal behavior not directly related to getting the job done (side conversations, jokes, comments).		
4. Frequency of nonverbal behavior not related to getting the task done (looking around the room, horseplay, bored withdrawal, hostility).		
5. How much progress did the group make in getting the task done? (Make an estimate.)		

CLEAR AND OPERATIONAL GOALS

For individual members to perform effectively within a group they must know what the group's goals are, understand what actions need to be taken to accomplish them, know the criteria by which the group can tell when they have been reached, and be aware of how their own behavior can contribute to group actions. Goal and task accomplishment depend upon members' coordinating and synchronizing their actions. The clarity of the group goal and the clarity of the actions required to achieve it are important if individual members are to accept the group goal, to experience a feeling of group belongingness, to be interested in goal-related behaviors, and to be willing to accept influence from the group. One of the most common practical problems of groups is trying to keep up with precisely where the group is in relation to its goals and what steps need to be taken by group members to reach them. The group and the group's tasks become more attractive as the goal becomes clearer and as the nature of the tasks and the responsibilities of each member within the group are made more tangible. Goals become clarified as they are made more specific, operational, workable, measurable, and observable.

How are operational and nonoperational goals distinguished? First, a goal is operational if a basis exists for relating it to possible action by the group. If it can be determined to what extent the goal will be achieved by a particular sequence of group actions, then the goal is *operational;* otherwise it is not. An example of an operational goal is "Name three qualities of a good group member"; an example of a nonoperational goal is "Make conclusions about the theoretical and empirical findings of qualities of effective actions by a group member." Second, a goal is operational if alternative courses of action for achieving it can be tested. Broad, long-range goals are often nonoperational and can be related to specific actions only through the formation of subgoals. Subgoals are often substituted for the more general goals of a group so that the group can gain operational advantages, as we will see below.

A crucial aspect of even a well-stated group goal is being able to tell when it has been accomplished. There is no sense in going somewhere if you do not know when you have arrived. An operational goal has indicators that will make it evident when it has been achieved. The goal "Name three qualities of a good group member" is operational in that when you have listed three items, and if they refer to group membership, you will know the goal has been reached. The goal "Make conclusions about the theoretical and empirical findings of qualities of effective actions by a group member" is nonoperational in that it may be difficult to tell when such a goal has been achieved. Whatever indicators are used to tell when a group has accomplished its goals, several of them are better than one, and indicators that are observable, countable, and specific are better than those that are nonobservable, noncountable, and ambiguous. Usually the goal of a problem-solving group will have indicators that reflect both the accomplishment of the goal (profit, new members gained, problems solved) and to group processes and group maintenance (group cohesion, communication effectiveness, decision-making ability, level of trust among members).

There are several advantages for a group in having operational goals. The main advantage is in helping communication among its members and between the group and other groups. A goal must be stated in such a way that it succeeds in telling what the group intends to accomplish, and this communication is successful when any knowledgeable person can look at the group's behavior or products and decide whether or not the goal has been reached. When the goal has been made sufficiently workable—in the sense that a series of behaviors for achieving it have been identified—that others can reliably agree on whether a group's performance or product fulfills the goal, then the goal is sufficiently specific.

The second advantage in having operational goals is that they help guide the group in planning and carrying out its tasks. If a group is not certain what outcomes it is trying to effect, it will have difficulty planning how it will do its work. Operational goals help a group to select and to organize the appropriate resources and methods it will need in working on its tasks. They make it easier for a member to diagnose what leadership behaviors are needed and to accept responsibility for achievement. The more group members know what they are trying to accomplish with any specific task, the better they can direct their attention and efforts. Finally, the problems of revision, modification, and change in the group are helped when the overall effort is broken down into smaller operational parts.

The third advantage of operational goals is that they help the group evaluate both the group process and the group outcome or product. By specifying its goals and the criteria by which it will know when it has reached them, the group can evaluate how well it has accomplished them. Similarly, operational goals facilitate feedback among group members about the accomplishments resulting from their behavior and the effectiveness of current procedures.

A fourth advantage is that when goals are operational, conflicts and differences about the course of group action are more likely to be decided by rational, analytic processes. When goals are not operational or when the operational subgoals are not relevant to most group members, differences are less likely to be adjusted through negotiation. If goals are operational, members can more readily see the logic of different courses of action. If goals are nonoperational, there is no logical and testable answer to such differences of judgment, and it is likely not only that a compromise result will be based upon concessions and trading but that a greater emphasis will be placed upon maintaining harmony within the group than upon accomplishing its goals.

How are clear, operational goals developed? It must be recognized that for most groups clear goals cannot always be determined in advance, especially if they are to be acceptable to all or most of the members. The first job of any group, therefore, is to modify any stated goal until all the group members understand it and a consensus exists concerning how it is to be operationalized or put into practice. Through such discussions, commitment to goals is built and the goals become acceptable to the group members. The more time a group spends establishing agreement on clear goals, the less time it needs in achieving them—and the more likely it will be that the members will work effectively for the common outcome.

How do you tell whether a group's goals are sufficiently understood and operationalized? If you have done the preceding exercise, you will have a list of both the characteristics of clear and unclear goals and the behavioral symptoms of groups with clear and unclear goals. Remember that some of the symptoms of unclear goals are a high level of group tension, joking or horseplay, distraction of the group by side issues, and the group's failure to use, support, or build on good ideas.

EFFECTIVE GROUP GOALS

Research has shown that the effectiveness of group goals depends on several variables:

1. The extent to which the goals are operationally defined, countable, and observable.
2. The extent to which group members see the goals as being meaningful, relevant, realistic, acceptable, and attainable.
3. How cooperative the goal structure is and how cooperatively oriented the group members are.
4. The degree to which both group goals and individual members' goals can be achieved by the same tasks and activities.
5. The degree to which conflict exists among the group members about the group's goals and the tasks the group must complete to achieve the goals.
6. The extent to which the goals are challenging and offer a moderate risk of failure.
7. The degree of coordination achieved among group members.
8. The availability of the resources needed for accomplishing the group's tasks and goals.
9. How specific the goals are, because specific goals indicate what needs to be done next.

10. How easily the goals can be modified and clarified.

11. How long a group has to attain its goals.

HELPING GROUPS SET EFFECTIVE GOALS

The first job of any group is to clarify and modify stated goals until they are clear and acceptable. The two methods of helping groups set effective goals are the survey-feedback method and program evaluation and review.

The survey-feedback method begins with the consultant or leader interviewing the individual members of the group about group goals and the priorities of the group as they see them. These interviews are conducted before a periodic meeting of the group (such as annually or semiannually). On the basis of the information collected, and working within organizational goals, the consultant conducts a group session in which the group sets its goals and priorities for the next six months or year. During this meeting the group plans its short-term goals, reviews its long-range goals, develops the tasks necessary for accomplishing its short-term goals, defines specific responsibilities for working on the tasks, ranks the tasks and goals in terms of priority to the group, and sets group-development goals for more effective group work. Special attention is paid to specifying the leadership and membership-role relationships necessary not only for working on the tasks, but also for developing ways in which to identify and solve group-relationship problems that might hinder goal achievement.

In program evaluation and review—or the critical path method, as it is sometimes called—groups are helped by a consultant to set effective goals by first specifying the end state they want to achieve. Working backward from this final goal, the group then details what must happen immediately *before* it is achieved, and the tasks and subgoals needed to accomplish it are all spelled out. The group decides which of the activities and subgoals are most critical for final goal accomplishment, and allocates resources accordingly. A timetable for accomplishing each subgoal is set. The whole process is then reviewed and responsibilities assigned.

QUIZ

Check your reading of this section by answering the following questions. Answers are on page 174.

1. For individual members to perform effectively within a group, they must (choose four):

a. know what the group goals are.
b. understand what actions are needed to accomplish the goals.
c. know the other members of the group.
d. know how their own behavior contributes to group actions.
e. know the criteria by which the group can tell when the goal is reached.
f. know what the other members want out of the group.

2. Characteristics of operational goals are (choose two):
   a. you can tell when you've accomplished them.
   b. you are not sure when you've accomplished them.
   c. they are related to broad and general ideas.
   d. they are related to a specific course of action.
   e. they have to do with doctors.

3. You are on a committee to upgrade the medical facilities in your town. The committee is considering the following four goals. Which one is an operational goal?
   a. to achieve better hospital care.
   b. to raise the $5 million needed for the new hospital.
   c. to upgrade the hospital services.
   d. to get more doctors and nurses in town.

4. What are four advantages of operational goals?
   a. they help communication among the group members and between other groups.
   b. they help get a variety of responses from the group members.
   c. they guide the group in planning and carrying out its task.
   d. they help get compromises based on concessions and trading.
   e. they help the group evaluate both the outcome and the group process.
   f. they put emphasis on group harmony and getting along.
   g. they offer a basis for solving differences of opinion rationally.

5. You are a teacher who wants to develop clear, operational goals for your classes. How would you best do this?
   a. talk to the principal, discussing and changing the goals until they are clear.
   b. consult with other teachers, discussing and changing the goals until they are clear.
   c. talk over the goals with the students, discussing and changing them until they are clear.
   d. sit down and write the goals yourself, remembering that they must be clear, specific, and observable.

True   False   6. The more time a group spends in discussing its goals, the more likely it is that it will use up the time needed to achieve them.

True   False   **7.** The first job of a group is to modify goals and make them clear and acceptable.

True   False   **8.** In the Survey-feedback Method of goal setting, a consultant interviews group members separately, compiles the information, and sends to the group its composite long- and short-term goals for them to act upon.

True   False   **9.** In the Program Evaluation and Review Method of goal setting, groups state their final goal. Then, working backwards to detail the critical tasks and subgoals needed, allocate resources and assign responsibilities.

True   False   **10.** If a group spends a great deal of time socializing, that must be a group goal.

YOUR GOAL–RELATED BEHAVIOR EXERCISE (II)

Describe on a separate sheet of paper how you would act if you were a member of a problem-solving group that did not have clear goals and whose members were not only not committed to them but had competing personal goals. Use all your experiences in the exercises in this chapter, the content in the chapter, and any other personal experience that is relevant. After thirty minutes meet with two other group members and discuss what each of you wrote about your behavior.

SUMMARY

In this chapter you learned about setting group goals and the importance of setting operational ones. You have practiced setting group goals and have experienced groups with both clear and unclear goals. However, in order to set clear goals and to work toward them, group members must be able to communicate and listen clearly and effectively. You will learn how to do this in the next chapter.

ANSWERS

Page 139—1. d; 2. d.

Page 142—1. a, b, c, d; 2. a, b, d, e, f, h; 3. a, c, e; 4. false; 5. false.

Page 146—1. true; 2. false; 3. false; 4. true; 5. true; 6. true; 7. false; 8. false; 9. true; 10. true.

Page 167—1. b; 2. a; 3. c; 4. a; 5. c; 6. b; 7. a; 8. b; 9. a; 10. c; 11. a; 12. a; 13. b, c, e; 14. false; 15. true; 16. a; 17. c; 18. b; 19. a; 20. b.

Page 174—1. a, b, d, e; 2. a, d; 3. b; 4. a, c, e, g; 5. c; 6. false; 7. true; 8. false; 9. true; 10. true.

5

Communication within Groups

In this chapter a number of concepts are defined and discussed. The major ones are listed below. The procedure for learning these concepts is as follows:

1. The class forms heterogeneous groups of four.
2. Each group divides into two pairs.
3. The task for each pair is to:
   a. define each concept, noting the page on which it is defined and discussed.
   b. make sure that both members of the pair understand the meaning of each concept.
4. In each group, members compare the answers of the two pairs. If there is disagreement, the members look up the concept in the chapter and clarify it until they all agree on the definition and understand it.

Concepts

1. interpersonal communication
2. effective communication
3. sender
4. receiver
5. message
6. channel
7. defensive behavior
8. one-way communication
9. two-way communication
10. communication network
11. information gatekeepers
12. leveling
13. sharpening
14. assimilation

INTRODUCTION AND DEFINITIONS

Communication is the basis for all human interaction and for all group functioning. Every group must take in and use information. The very existence of a group depends on communication, on exchanging information and transmitting meaning. All cooperative action is contingent upon effective communication, and our daily lives are filled with one communication experience after another. Through communication members of groups reach some understanding of one another, build trust, coordinate their actions, plan strategies for a goal accomplishment, agree upon a division of labor, conduct all group activity—even exchange insults. It is through communication that the members interact, and effective communication is a prerequisite for every aspect of group functioning.

One primary difficulty in discussing communication within groups is that there are so many definitions of communication and so little agreement about which definition is the most useful. Dance (1970), for example, did a content analysis of ninety-five definitions of communication that he found published in several different academic fields. Among these definitions were several distinct concepts of communication. He noted that this variety of definitions has taken different theorists and researchers in different and sometimes contradictory directions. Dance concluded that the concept of communication is overburdened and that a family of concepts needs to be developed to replace it. Despite the difficulties in defining communication, however, there are ways in which to view the process of transmitting information that are helpful in discussing interpersonal and group communication skills.

Two persons seeing each other have a continuous effect on each other's perceptions and expectations of what the other is going to do. Interpersonal communication, then, can be defined broadly as any verbal or nonverbal behavior that is perceived by another person (Johnson, 1981, 1973). Communication, in other words, is much more than just the exchange of words: all behavior conveys some message and is, therefore, a form of communication. *Interpersonal communication,* however, is more commonly defined as a message sent by a person to a receiver (or receivers) with the conscious intent of affecting the receiver's behavior. A person sends the message "How are you?" to evoke the response "Fine." A teacher shakes his head to get two students to stop throwing erasers at him. Under this more limited definition, any signal aimed at influencing the receiver's behavior in any way is communication.

This definition of communication does not mean that there is always a sequence of events in which a person thinks up a message, sends it, and someone else receives it. Communication among persons is a process in which everyone receives, sends, interprets, and infers all at the same time: there is no beginning and no end. All communication involves persons sending one another symbols to which certain meanings are attached. These symbols can be either verbal (all words are symbols) or nonverbal (all expressions and gestures are symbols). The exchange of ideas and experiences between two persons is possible only when both have adopted the same ways of relating a particular nonverbal, spoken, written, or pictorial symbol to a particular experience.

How do you tell when communication is working effectively and when it is not? What is effective communication? What is ineffective communication? *Effective communication* exists between two persons when the receiver interprets the sender's message in the same way the sender intended it. If John tries to communicate to Jane that it is a wonderful day and he is feeling great by saying "Hi" with a warm smile, and if Jane interprets John's "Hi" as meaning John thinks it is a beautiful day and he is feeling well, then effective communication has taken place. If Jane interprets John's "Hi" as meaning he wants to stop and talk with her, then ineffective communication has taken place.

The model of communication presented by Johnson (1981) is typical of the applied approaches to interpersonal communication. In this model (Figure 5.1) the communicator is referred to as the *sender* and the person at whom the message is aimed is the *receiver*. The *message* is any verbal or nonverbal symbol that one person transmits to another; it is subject matter being referred to in a symbolic way (all words are symbols). A *channel* can be defined as the means of sending a message to another person: the sound waves of the voice, the light waves that make possible the seeing of words on a printed page. Because communication is a process, sending and receiving messages often taken place simultaneously: a person can be speaking and at the same time paying close attention to the receiver's nonverbal responses.

Figure 5.1 represents a model of the process of communication between two persons. The model has seven basic elements:

1. The intentions, ideas, and feelings of the sender and the way he decides to behave lead him to send a message.
2. The sender encodes his message by translating his ideas, feelings, and intentions into a message appropriate for sending.
3. The sender sends the message to the receiver.
4. The message is sent through a channel.
5. The receiver decodes the message by interpreting its meaning. Her interpretation depends on how well she understands the content of the message and the intentions of the sender.
6. The receiver responds internally to this interpretation of the message.
7. Noise is any element that interferes with the communication process. In the sender, noise refers to such things as his attitudes and frame of reference and the appropriateness of his language or other expression of the message. In the receiver, noise refers to such things as attitudes, background, and experiences that affect the decoding process. In the channel,

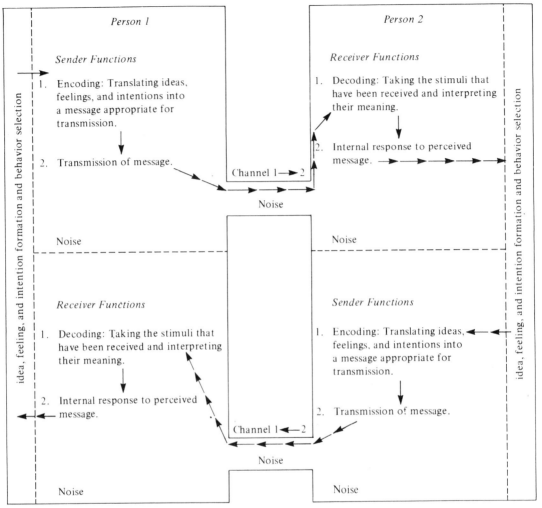

FIGURE 5.1 The interpersonal-communication process. Source: David W. Johnson, *Reaching Out,* 2nd ed. (Englewood Cliffs, N.J.: Prentice-Hall, 1981), p. 75.

noise refers to (a) environmental sounds, such as static or traffic, (b) speech problems, such as stammering, and (c) annoying or distracting mannerisms, such as a tendency to mumble. To a large extent, the success of communication is determined by the degree to which noise is overcome or controlled.

QUIZ

To check your understanding of this section, please answer the following questions (answers are on page 224):

True   False   **1.** Communication is the basis for all human interaction and all group functioning.

True   False   **2.** Interpersonal communication is any verbal or nonverbal behavior that is sent by a person.

True   False   **3.** Effective communication takes place when the receiver interprets the sender's message in the way it was intended.

True   False   **4.** Noise is any element that interferes with the communication process.

True   False   **5.** Prejudice can be a form of noise in the communication process.

                    6. Describe the communication model to someone to see if you received it correctly.

YOUR COMMUNICATION EXERCISE (I)

What is your communication behavior like in a group? How would you describe your communication actions? Begin a discussion of communication within groups by answering the following questions as honestly as possible:

1. If I as group chairperson were giving a set of instructions and the other group members sat quietly with blank faces, I would:
   ____ state the instructions clearly and precisely and then move on.
   ____ encourage members to ask questions until I was sure that everyone understood what they were supposed to do.
2. If the group chairperson gave a set of instructions to the group that I did not understand, I would:
   ____ keep silent and later ask another group member what he or she meant.
   ____ immediately ask the chairperson to repeat the instructions and answer my questions until I was sure I understood what he or she wanted me to do.
3. How often do you let other group members know when you like or approve of something they say or do?
   Never   1 : 2 : 3 : 4 : 5 : 6 : 7 : 8 : 9   Always
4. How often do you let other group members know when you are irritated or impatient with, embarrassed by, or opposed to something they say or do?
   Never   1 : 2 : 3 : 4 : 5 : 6 : 7 : 8 : 9   Always
5. How often do you check out what other group members are feeling and how they are reacting rather than assuming that you know?
   Never   1 : 2 : 3 : 4 : 5 : 6 : 7 : 8 : 9   Always
6. How often do you encourage other group members to let you know how they are reacting to your behavior and actions in the group?
   Never   1 : 2 : 3 : 4 : 5 : 6 : 7 : 8 : 9   Always
7. How often do you check to make sure you understand what other group members mean before agreeing or disagreeing?
   Never   1 : 2 : 3 : 4 : 5 : 6 : 7 : 8 : 9   Always

8. How often do you paraphrase or restate what other members have said before responding?
   Never 1 : 2 : 3 : 4 : 5 : 6 : 7 : 8 : 9 Always

9. How often do you keep your thoughts, ideas, feelings, and reactions to yourself in group sessions?
   Never 1 : 2 : 3 : 4 : 5 : 6 : 7 : 8 : 9 Always

10. How often do you make sure that all information you have about the current topic of discussion is known to the rest of the group?
    Never 1 : 2 : 3 : 4 : 5 : 6 : 7 : 8 : 9 Always

These questions deal with several aspects of communication in groups that will be discussed in this chapter. The first two questions refer to whether communication is one-way (from the chairperson to the rest of the group members) or two-way. The third and fourth questions focus on your willingness to give feedback to other group members on how you are receiving and reacting to their messages. Questions five and six refer to your willingness to ask for feedback about how other group members are receiving and reacting to your messages. Questions seven and eight focus on receiving skills, and the final two questions relate to your willingness to contribute (send) relevant messages about the group's work. Review your answers to these questions and summarize your present communication behavior in a group.

EFFECTIVE INTERPERSONAL COMMUNICATION

All communication within groups is between individuals and is, therefore, interpersonal communication. There are many discussions of the skills needed for effective interpersonal communication. One of the authors, for example, has published a training program for interpersonal-skill development that includes communication skills (Johnson, 1981). The focus in this chapter is on the unique aspects of communication among members of a problem-solving group, including the communication of task-relevant information among group members and the passage of messages through several authority levels. An example of the latter would be the passage of a chairperson's message to a vice-chairperson, who sends it to a committee chairperson, who sends it to the rest of the group.

Sending Messages Effectively

The first aspect of effective communication is the sending of a message. The three basic requirements for sending a message so that it will be understood are to phrase the message so it may be comprehended, have credibility as a sender, and ask for feedback on how the message is affecting the receiver. Research supports the following conclusions about the sending of messages (Johnson, 1974):

1. *Clearly "own" your messages by using first-person singular pronouns ("I," "my").* Personal ownership includes clearly taking responsibility for the ideas and feelings that one expresses. People disown their messages when they use phrases such as "most people," "some of our friends," and "our group." Such language makes it difficult for listeners to tell whether the individuals really think and feel what they are saying or whether they are repeating the thoughts and feelings of others.

2. *Make your messages complete and specific.* Include clear statements of all necessary information the receiver needs in order to comprehend the message. Being complete and specific seems so obvious, but often people do not communicate the frame of reference they are using, the assumptions they are making, the intentions they have in communicating, or the leaps in thinking they are making.

3. *Make your verbal and nonverbal messages congruent.* Every face-to-face communication involves both verbal and nonverbal messages. Usually these messages are congruent: the person who is saying that he appreciates your help is smiling and expressing warmth in other nonverbal ways. Communication problems arise when a person's verbal and nonverbal messages are contradictory. If a person says "Here is some information that may be of help to you" with a sneer on his face and a mocking tone of voice, the meaning you receive is confused by the two different messages being sent.

4. *Be redundant.* Sending the same message more than once and using more than one channel of communication (such as pictures and written messages as well as verbal and nonverbal cues) will help the receiver understand your messages.

5. *Ask for feedback concerning the way your messages are being received.* In order to communicate effectively you must be aware of how the receiver is interpreting and processing your messages. The only way to be sure is to continually seek feedback as to what meanings the receiver is attaching to your messages.

6. *Make the message appropriate to the receiver's frame of reference.* Explain the same information differently to an expert in the field and a novice, to a child and an adult, to your boss and a co-worker.

7. *Describe your feelings by name, action, or figure of speech.* When communicating your feelings it is especially important to be descriptive. You may describe your feelings by name ("I feel sad"), by actions ("I feel like crying"), or by figures of speech ("I feel down in the dumps"). Description will help communicate your feelings clearly and unambiguously.

8. *Describe others' behavior without evaluating or interpreting.* When reacting to the behavior of others be sure to describe their behavior ("You keep interrupting me") rather than evaluating it ("You're a rotten, self-centered egotist who won't listen to anyone else's ideas").

One of the most important elements in interpersonal communication is the credibility of the sender. *Sender credibility* refers to the attitude the receiver has toward the perceived trustworthiness of the sender's statements. Sender credibility has several dimensions:

1. The reliability of the sender as an information source—the sender's dependability, predictability, and consistency.
2. The sender's motives: the sender should be open as to the effect she wants her message to have upon the receiver.
3. The expression of warmth and friendliness.
4. The majority opinion of others concerning the trustworthiness of the sender. If most of our friends tell us the sender is trustworthy, we tend to believe it.
5. The sender's expertise on the topic under discussion.
6. The dynamism of the sender. A dynamic sender is seen as aggressive, emphatic, and forceful and tends to be viewed as more credible than a passive sender.

There is little evidence from the studies on sender credibility to suggest which of these dimensions is the most important. It seems that a highly credible sender is one who is perceived in a favorable light in *all* of these dimensions. A sender low in credibility, on the other hand, is one who is perceived in a negative light in *any one* of the dimensions. Unless we appear credible to a receiver, he will discount our message and we will not be able to communicate effectively with him. Sender credibility, in short, might be defined as the perceived trustworthiness of the sender.

Effective message-sending skills are prerequisite to the skills covered in this chapter. Sending skills are examined in detail in Johnson (1981), which discusses the basic theory behind sending effective verbal and nonverbal messages and includes specific exercises for developing these skills. You should learn and review these skills before (or in combination with) the skills presented in this chapter.

Receiving Messages Effectively

Developing sending skills meets only half the requirements for communicating effectively; you must also have receiving skills. The skills involved in receiving messages are based on giving feedback about the reception of the message in ways that clarify and aid continued discussion. Receiving skills have two basic parts: (1) communicating the *intention* of wanting to understand the ideas and feelings of the sender, and (2) understanding and interpreting the sender's ideas and feelings. Of the two, many theorists consider the first—communicating the intention to understand correctly, but not evaluate, a message—to be the more important. The principal barrier to building effective communication is the tendency of most persons to judge or evaluate the message they are receiving: the sender makes a statement and the receiver responds inwardly or openly with "I think you're wrong," "I don't like what you said," "I think you're right," or "That is the greatest (or worst) idea I have ever heard!" Such evaluative receiving will make the sender defensive and cautious, and thereby decrease the openness of the communication. Though the tendency to give evaluative responses is common in almost all conversations, it is accentuated in situations where emotions are deeply involved. The stronger the feelings, the more likely two group members will evaluate each other's statements from their own point of view only. Thus it is highly important for the receiver to indicate that he wants to fully understand the sender before he makes an evaluation.

The specific receiving skills are paraphrasing, checking one's perception of the sender's feelings, and negotiating for meaning. Let's look at each of these skills in turn.

1. *Paraphrase accurately and nonevaluatively the content of the message and the feelings of the sender.* The most basic and important skill in receiving messages is paraphrasing—restating the words of the sender. Paraphasing should be done in a way that indicates an understanding of the sender's frame of reference. The basic rule to follow in paraphrasing is this: *Speak for yourself only after you have first restated the ideas and feelings of the sender accurately and to the sender's satisfaction.* When paraphrasing it is helpful to restate the sender's expressed ideas and feelings in your own words rather than repeating her words exactly, avoid any indication of approval or disapproval, neither add nor subtract from her message, and try to place yourself in her shoes to understand what she is feeling and what her message means.

2. *Describe what you perceive to be the sender's feelings.* Sometimes it is difficult to paraphrase the feelings of the sender if they are not described in words in the message. Thus a second receiving skill is to check your perception of the sender's feelings simply by describing that perception. This description should tentatively identify those feelings without expressing approval or disapproval and without attempting to interpret them or explain their causes. It is simply saying, "Here is what I understand your feelings to be; am I accurate?"

3. *State your interpretation of the sender's message and negotiate with the sender until there is agreement as to the message's meaning.* Often the words contained in a message do not carry the actual meaning. A person may ask "Do you always shout like this?" and mean "Please quiet down." Sometimes, therefore, paraphrasing the content of a message will do little to communicate your understanding of it. In such a case, you must negotiate the meaning of the message. You may wish to preface your negotiation for meaning with "What I think you mean is . . ." If you are accurate, you then make your reply; if you are inaccurate, the sender restates the message until you can state what its

essential meaning is. Keep in mind that it is the process that is important in negotiating meaning, not the actual phrasing you use. After the process becomes natural a variety of introductory phrases will be used. Be tolerant of others who are using the same phrases over and over as they are developing this skill.

A complete treatment of these basic receiving skills, so important to effective communication, can be found in Johnson (1981), which also contains exercises for developing verbal and nonverbal competence in them. These skills should also be learned and reviewed as a prerequisite for the skills discussed in this chapter.

One of the major influences upon the reception of a message is the usefulness of its content in accomplishing the receiver's goals and tasks. All messages may be evaluated in terms of whether they help or hinder the receiver's task performance within the group, and messages that are seen as helping goal and task accomplishment are comprehended most accurately and easily. Of course, it is quite common for group members to misunderstand the usefulness of certain messages. Opposition and disagreement, for example, are often seen as short-term obstructions instead of the long-term aids they might be by generating new and better ways of accomplishing tasks and goals.

QUIZ

To check your understanding of this section, please answer the following questions (answers are on page 224):

1. It is a good communication practice when sending messages to (choose three):
   a. use more than one way of getting the message across.
   b. ask the receiver to give feedback on the content and intentions of the message.
   c. make evaluations and inferences when listening to other group members.
   d. describe your feelings.
   e. speak for others in the group who are too shy to speak for themselves.
2. The two basic parts of communication-receiving skills are (choose two):
   a. understanding that the sender wants to communicate.
   b. communicating the message.
   c. understanding the message.
   d. communicating that you want to understand the message.
3. The major barrier to effective communication is the tendency most people have to:
   a. talk too much.
   b. talk too little.
   c. judge and evaluate.
   d. not listen.

4. Paraphrasing is the receiving skill of:
  a. changing the phrasing of a message.
  b. checking on the sender's feelings and negotiating for their meaning.
  c. being able to reply to the message to the sender's satisfaction.
  d. being able to restate the message and feelings, without evaluation, to the sender's satisfaction.

BEWISE COLLEGE EXERCISE

The purpose of this exercise is to examine the communication patterns within a task-oriented group. Our objectives are to see how task-relevant information is shared within a work group and to explore the effects of collaboration and competition in group problem solving. The materials to be used in the exercise are a briefing sheet, a series of data sheets, a candidate summary sheet, and an observer frequency chart. The exercise takes about two hours. Participants are organized into groups of five role players and two observers. An unlimited number of groups may be directed at the same time. The procedure for the coordinator is as follows:

1. Introduce the exercise as focusing upon communication within a problem-solving situation. Set the stage for the role playing by reviewing the briefing sheet in a realistic manner.

2. Divide the class intro groups of seven—five participants plus two observers. Instruct the groups to choose the correct president based upon the data they will receive. Suggest that there is one correct solution to their problem and caution them that they must reach their solution independent of the other groups. Then distribute a briefing sheet, a candidate summary sheet, and one data sheet to each participant. Ensure that the five differently coded data sheets are distributed to different members in each group. Each sheet is coded by the number of dots, ranging from one to five, following the second sentence in the first paragraph. Part of each sheet contains data unique to that sheet. Tell the participants not to let other group members read their sheets.

3. While the five role players are studying their sheets, meet with the observers. Distribute copies of the frequency chart and brief observers on how they are used. A copy of the chart appears below. Each observer will need several copies of the chart, so time should be given for them to make their extra copies.

4. Give the signal to begin the group meeting. You may introduce an element of competition by posting groups' solutions in order of completion and by posting the number of minutes used by each group in solving the problem.

5. After all the groups have submitted their solution to the problem, review the answers and compare them with the correct answer, which appears on page 481 in Appendix D. Then ask the group to discuss their experience, using the observations of the observers. Here are some relevant questions for discussion:
  a. What were the patterns of communication within the group? Who spoke to whom? Who talked, how often did they talk, and for how long? Who triggered whom in what ways? How did members feel about the amount of their participation? What could have been done to gain wider participation?
  b. Was the needed information easily obtained by all the group members? Did group

members share their information appropriately, request each other's information, and create the conditions under which the information could be shared?

c. Were the resources of all group members used? Was everyone listened to?

d. How cooperative or competitive were the group members?

e. How did the group make decisions?

f. What problems did the group have in working together?

g. What conclusions about communication can be made from the group's experience?

6. Have all the groups share their conclusions with one another. Review the observation sheets and discuss the nature of communication within goal-oriented groups.

Observer Frequency Chart: Patterns of Communication

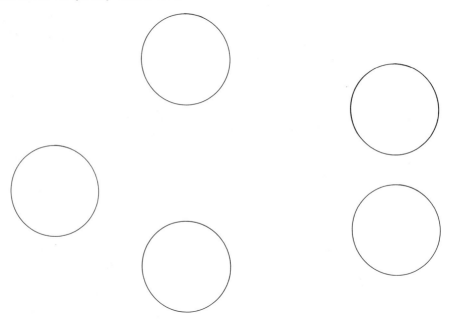

Interval _____ (Use one sheet for each five-minute interval.) Label the circles with the names of the group members. Indicate a message from a sender to a receiver with an arrow; when someone sends a message to the entire group, indicate this with an arrow to the center. Indicate frequency of message sending with tally marks (卌 II). Place an "x" in the member's circle every time he or she interrupts or overrides another group member; place a check "√" in the member's circle every time he or she encourages another member to participate. Here is an example:

Bewise College Briefing Sheet

1. This is the first meeting of your group.

2. Basically, the data you bring with you are in your head.

3. Assume there is one solution.

4. Assume that all information in your data sheet is correct.

5. There must be substantial agreement within the group when the problem has been solved.

6. You must work on the problem as a group.

Bewise College Data Sheet

You are a member of a committee consisting of board members, administrators, faculty, and students of Bewise College. Your group has been authorized by the board of regents to select a new president of the college from the list of candidates.

Each of the represented groups (board of regents, administrators, faculty, and students) has its own list of requirements for the new president. Your group is pledged to select a candidate who meets these requirements.

Bewise College was established in 1969. It is located in the heart of an industrial city with a population of about 100,000. In addition to a standard liberal-arts curriculum, Bewise College offers a curriculum in which students can receive college credit for work and learning experiences outside the college. Bewise College was established to provide higher education for persons such as minority-group members, working-class, and lower-class students, the elderly, and dropouts from other colleges and universities.

The new president faces a series of challenges. The board of regents is most concerned about the ability of the president to act in a public-relations capacity for the college and raise money. The college has been losing money for the past two years and is in financial trouble. Students and teachers are concerned with the quality of teaching at Bewise College and want a president who is qualified to judge the teaching ability of faculty members. The latter are having a very difficult time in the classroom and want to make sure the new president has had experience in working with the types of students attending Bewise College.

Bewise College Data Sheet

You are a member of a committee consisting of board members, administrators, faculty, and students of Bewise College. Your group has been authorized by the board of regents to select a new president of the college from the list of candidates. .

Each of the represented groups (board of regents, administrators, faculty, and students) has its own list of requirements for the new president. Your group is pledged to select a candidate who meets these requirements.

Bewise College was established in 1969. It is located in the heart of an industrial city with a population of about 100,000. In addition to a standard liberal-arts curriculum, Bewise College offers a curriculum in which students can receive college credit for work and learning experiences outside the college. The faculty of Bewise College is made up primarily of young and dedicated but not highly experienced teachers.

The new president faces a series of challenges. The Board of Regents is most concerned about the ability of the president to be a public-relations person for the college and raise money. The college has been in the "red" for the past two years and may have to close if it cannot balance its budget. The new president will be expected to make many public speeches in order to raise money in the community. The students are angry about the quality of teaching and want a president who can judge the teaching ability of faculty members. Members of the college administration have nightmares about getting a president who is an incompetent administrator.

Bewise College Data Sheet

You are a member of a committee consisting of board members, administrators, faculty, and students of Bewise College. Your group has been authorized by the board of regents to select a new president of the college from the list of candidates.

Each of the represented groups (board of regents, administrators, faculty, and students) has its own list of requirements for the new president. Your group is pledged to select a candidate who meets these requirements.

Bewise College was established in 1969. It is located in the heart of an industrial city with a population of about 100,000. In addition to offering a standard liberal-arts curriculum, Bewise College also provides a curriculum in which students can receive college credit for work and learning experiences outside the college. Since universities are always larger than colleges, Bewise is smaller than the state university, but it is growing rapidly.

The new president faces a series of challenges. The students are dissatisfied with the faculty's teaching, and the only qualification they recogize as a valid basis for judging faculty teaching ability is for the president to have an education degree. The faculty, on the other hand, demands that the new president have experience in working with the types of students attending Bewise. The board of regents sees the need for a president who can raise money for the college.

Bewise College Data Sheet

You are a member of a committee consisting of board members, administrators, faculty, and students of Bewise College. Your group has been authorized by the board of regents to select a new president of the college from the list of candidates. . . .

Each of the represented groups (board of regents, administrators, faculty, and students) has its own list of requirements for the new president. Your group is pledged to select a candidate who meets these requirements.

Bewise College was established in 1969. It is located in the heart of an industrial city with a population of about 100,000. In addition to offering a standard liberal-arts curriculum, Bewise College also provides a curriculum in which students can receive college credit for work and learning experiences outside the college. Within the state, only Brown College, Samuels College, and Mulholland College are larger, which makes Bewise one of the largest colleges in the state; Andrews College is the smallest.

The new president faces a series of challenges. The board of regents wants a president who can raise money for the college. The college administration will not accept a new president who does not have administrative experience. The faculty is upset about the difficulty of teaching the students and therefore wants a president with experience in teaching the types of students who attend Bewise. Teaching experience is also considered crucial because it would make the president sympathetic to the problems of the faculty.

Bewise College Data Sheet

You are a member of a committee consisting of board members, administrators, faculty, and students of Bewise College. Your group has been authorized by the board of regents to select a new president of the college from the list of candidates. . . .

Each of the represented groups (board of regents, administrators, faculty, and students) has its own list of requirements for the new president. Your group is pledged to select a candidate who meets these requirements.

Bewise College was established in 1969. It is located in the heart of an industrial city with a population of about 100,000. In addition to offering a standard liberal-arts curriculum, Bewise College also provides a curriculum in which students can receive college credit for work and learning experiences outside the college. There is only one other college in the same city; it is the smallest college in the state, and until 1954 all students attending it were black Americans.

The new president faces a series of challenges. The board of regents wants a president who can raise money for the college, which is now in a desperate financial position. The college administration is very much afraid of a president who will not be a competent administrator. Students are dissatisfied with faculty teaching, and faculty members are dissatisfied with student unresponsiveness to their teaching. Both students and faculty see the necessity of having a president with a background that would provide him or her with insights into the types of students attending Bewise.

Bewise College Candidate Summary Sheet

Name: David Wolcott

Education: Graduated from Andrews College in liberal arts in 1957; Master of Education from Winfield University in English in 1959; doctorate in political science from Winfield University in 1968.

Employment: Instructor in English at Windfield University, 1959–1963; taught political science at James University, 1963–1972; representative in state legislative, 1965–1967; chairman of the department of political science at James University, 1972–1977; dean of students at James University, 1972 to the present.

Other: Is well known for his scholarship and intelligence.

Name: Roger Thornton

Education: Graduated from Samuels College in industrial arts in 1950; Master of

Education in chemistry from Smith University in 1957; doctorate in administration from Smith University in 1971.

Employment: High-school chemistry teacher, 1957–1964; high-school principal, 1964–1971; school superintendent, 1971 to the present.

Other: Very innovative and efficient administrator; very successful political speaker (the superintendent of schools is elected in his district); his father is vice-president of a large bank.

Name: Edythe Holubec

Education: Graduated from Brown College in liberal arts in 1960; Master's in accounting from Smith University in 1965; doctorate in administration in 1973 from Smith University.

Employment: Insurance agent, 1960–1965; certified public accountant, 1965–1973; vice-president of finance, Williams College, 1973 to the present.

Other: Taught accounting in night school for eight years; volunteer director of a community center in a lower-class neighborhood for four years; has a competing job offer from a public-relations firm for which she has worked part time for two years.

Name: Frank Pierce

Education: Graduated from Smith University in liberal arts in 1963; Master of Education in mathematics in 1966 from Smith University; doctorate in administration from Johnson Institute in 1972.

Employment: Neighborhood worker, 1963–1966; coordinator of parent-volunteer program for school system, 1966–1970; assistant superintendent for community relations, 1970 to the present.

Other: Has written a training program for industrial education.

Name: Helen Johnson

Education: Graduated from Brown College in social-studies education in 1961; Master of Education in social studies in 1965 from Brown College.

Employment: Teacher of basic skills in a neighborhood center run by school system, 1961–1965; chairwoman of student teaching program, Smith University, 1965–1969; dean of students, Smith University, 1969–1975; vice-president for community relations and scholarship fund development, Smith University, 1975 to the present.

Other: Grew up in one of the worst slums in the state; has written one book and several scholarly articles. Given award for fund-raising effectiveness.

Name: Keith Clement

Education: Graduated in biology education from Mulholland College in 1962; Master's in administration from Mulholland College in 1964.

Employment: Biology teacher in a high school, 1962–1967; consultant in fund raising, public-relations firm, 1967 to the present.

Other: Is recognized as one of the best fund raisers in the state; has written a book on teaching working-class students; extensive volunteer work in adult education.

SOLSTICE-SHENANIGANS MYSTERY EXERCISE

The purpose of this exercise is to study the way in which information is communicated in problem-solving groups. A mystery situation is used. Each of the accompanying clues should be written on a separate card. (The answers appear on page 481 in Appendix D.) The procedure is as follows:

1. The class forms heterogeneous groups of six. One member should volunteer to be an observer. The observer's task is to record the communication patterns of the group, using the observation chart from the previous exercise.
2. The task of each group is to work cooperatively to solve a mystery. Each group is to decide:
   a. what was stolen.
   b. how it was stolen.
   c. who the thief was.
   d. what the thief's motive was.
   e. what time the crime took place.
3. Each group receives a deck of cards. On each card is written a clue to the mystery. Keeping the cards face down so that the clues cannot be read, one member deals them all out so that each member has several clues.
4. Each group member is to read aloud the clues on his or her cards, but not show them to anyone else. Members may take notes, but may not show them to other members. All communication in the group is to be verbal.
5. When a group has answered the five questions above, it may wish to answer the following two questions if the other groups are not yet done:
   a. What happened to the other items?
   b. Who was present at the party?
6. Each group is to discuss the communication patterns they used in solving the mystery. Members may use the following questions to structure the discussion.
   a. What were the patterns of communication within the group? Who spoke to whom? Who talked, how often did they talk, and for how long? Who triggered whom in what ways? How did members feel about the amount of their participation? What could have been done to gain wider participation?
   b. Was the needed information easily obtained by all the group members? Did group members share their information appropriately, request each other's information, and create the conditions under which the information could be shared?
   c. Were the resources of all group members used? Was everyone listened to?
   d. How did the group make decisions?
   e. What problems did the group have in working together?
   f. What conclusions about communication can be made from the group's experience?
7. Each group share its conclusions with the rest of the class.

Solstice Shenanigans Mystery Clues

Mr. Purloin showed great interest in Mrs. Klutz's expensive diamond ring.

Mr. Purloin danced all evening with Ms. Beautiful.

Mrs. Klutz was always losing things.

Mrs. Klutz could not find her diamond ring after leaving the party.

The Hosts had a big party to celebrate the summer solstice.

The Hosts had a painting by Artisimisso.

Artisimisso was a sixteenth-century Italian artist.

Paintings by sixteenth-century Italian artists are quite valuable.

Mr. Avarice was heard to say that he would do anything for a valuable painting.

Mr. Klutz is a dealer in fine art.

Mr. Klutz needed money badly to keep his business from failing.

Mr. Klutz always carried his briefcase with him.

Mr. Avarice is known to be very rich.

All of Artisimisso's paintings are small.

Mrs. Klutz spent most of the evening in a dark corner of the patio with Mr. Handsome.

Ms. Perceptive saw something glitter in a corner of the patio as she was getting ready to leave the party.

Ms. Perceptive admired a painting by Artisimisso when she arrived at the party.

Ms. Perceptive noticed that the picture she admired was not there when she left the party.

Ms. Perceptive left the party at 10:00.

Ms. Wealthy brought her dog to the party.

Ms. Wealthy could not find what she had brought to the party.

The Neighbors owned three dogs.

The Neighbors found four dogs in their back yard after the party.

Mrs. Klutz admired the painting by Artisimisso when she left the party.

Mrs. Klutz left about 9:30.

Mr. Handsome was a kleptomaniac.

Mr. Handsome left the party twenty minutes after Mrs. Klutz.

Mr. and Mrs. Klutz left the party together.

Mr. Purloin was a jewel thief.

Ms. Beautiful noticed the painting when she left the party at 9:45.

Ms. Beautiful left the party with Mr. Purloin.

Ms. Wealthy and Mr. Avarice left the party together.

Ms. Wealthy left the party about the time Mr. Klutz did.

LIEPZ AND BOUNZ EXERCISE

The following exercise is based on the same principle as the two mystery exercises. It may be conducted in 45 minutes. Use the same procedures, observation tasks, and discussion tasks as used in the mystery exercises. Use six group members (including one observer). The solution is on page 482 in Appendix D.

The instructions for the exercises are as follows:

Pretend that liepz and bounz are new ways of measuring distance and that hobz, skibz, and jumpz represent a new way of measuring time. David jogs from Farmland through Parker and Selma to Muncie. The task of your group is to determine how many jumpz the entire trip took. You will be given cards containing information related to the task of the group. You may share this information orally, but do not show your cards to anyone. You have twenty minutes for the task. The information for individual group members is as follows:

Each of the following pieces of information is to be placed on a card. The cards are randomly distributed among the five group members.

It is 5 liepz from Farmland to Parker.

It is 8 liepz from Parker to Selma.

It is 9 liepz from Selma to Muncie.

A liepz is 10 bounz.

A liepz is a way of measuring distance.

There are 4 bounzes in a mile.

A hobz is 10 skibz.

A skibz is 10 jumpz.

A jumpz is a way of measuring time.

There are 4 jumpz in an hour.

A hobz is a way of measuring time.

A skibz is a way of measuring time.

David jogs from Farmland to Parker at the rate of 25 liepz per jumpz.

David jogs from Parker to Selma at the rate of 20 liepz per jumpz.

David jogs from Selma to Muncie at the rate of 15 liepz per jumpz.

COMMUNICATING INFORMATION IN A PROBLEM–SOLVING GROUP

For any problem-solving group to be effective, the members have to obtain the information they need to solve the problem and they have to put it together in such a way that an accurate or creative solution results. The previous exercises focused on the communication of information within a group. The situation in each exercise can be seen in Figure 5.2.

In most problem-solving groups, some information is shared by everyone, some information is known only to a few members, and each member has information that no one else in the group knows. Each member is responsible for communicating what he knows to the other members of the group. Each member is also responsible for seeking out the information known by the other members but not by him. Thus, effective sending and receiving skills are both essential for all group members. What makes the exchange

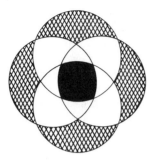

FIGURE 5.2 Communication of information: the shaded area represents information known to all group members; the crosshatched area represents information known to only one group member; the unmarked but enclosed area represents information known to two or more members of the group.

of information problematic is the "noise" that is usually present in problem-solving groups. Noise is defined as anything that gets in the way of effective communication. Determinants of noise include how a group member is perceived, how much information a group member thinks each of the others has, how trustworthy a member has been in the past, how the messages are formulated and sent, what receiving skills are used, how cooperative the group is, and whether the member believes his information will contribute to the group's efforts.

The coordination of information, ideas, experiences, and opinions is an essential part of problem solving in a group. How successful a group is with such coordination depends on the skills of the group members in sending and receiving messages and on the group norms about and procedures for communicating.

PATTERNS OF COMMUNICATION AMONG GROUP MEMBERS

The patterns of communication among group members are an important aspect of group process to observe and discuss. There are several patterns of communication within a group that are often helpful to observe. (The frequency chart in the Bewise College exercise is one means of distinguishing them.) One of these patterns is the relative frequency and length of communication acts—who talked, how often he or she talked, and how much of the total available time that person used. A second pattern to figure out is who communicates to whom. Some persons speak to those they are trying to impress, others to those from whom they want support, and still others to those from whom they expect opposition. Information on this pattern of communication among group members is often helpful in pinpointing conflicts that must be resolved and increasing the group members' understanding of how they are relating to one another.

A third pattern of communication to observe is who "triggers" whom and in what ways. There are clear patterns of triggering. For example, whenever one member speaks another may always speak next, even if the remarks are not initially directed to her. This kind of triggering may reflect either support ("Attaboy") or a desire to undo the point ("Yeahbut") that has just been made. Schein (1969) quotes a businessman as saying that in group discussions in his company it takes at least three attaboys to undo the damage of one yeahbut. Another type of triggering is when one member of a group interrupts other members. Knowing who interrupts whom gives the observer clues as to how members see their own status or power in the group relative to that of other members. Generally, high-authority members feel freer to interrupt low-authority members and vice versa. Interrupting others is one of the more common and more destructive kinds of communication behavior, and observing the patterns of interruption often reveals a great deal about relationships among members.

EFFECTS OF COMPETITION ON COMMUNICATION

A considerable body of research shows that when a situation within a group is cooperatively structured, relevant information is communicated openly, accurately, and honestly; in a competitively structured situation, communication is either lacking or misleading. With a cooperative structure each group member is interested in informing as well as being informed by others. Competition, on the other hand, gives rise to (1) espionage or other techniques for getting information another group member is unwilling to communicate, and (2) tactics for misleading other group members about oneself. The more intense the competition, the more likely communication will be blocked or, if group members have to communicate with one another, the more likely they will communicate only lies and threats. The very nature of competition, in which one works to gain an edge toward winning and fears the possibility of losing, promotes a great deal of defensiveness among group members.

Defensive behavior in a group is behavior that occurs when a person feels threatened or anticipates a threat. Competition is inevitably accompanied by defensive behavior, and defensive individuals, even if they work on the group's tasks, devote a lot of energy just to defending themselves. They think about how they look to others, how they may win over or dominate their peers, how they may impress their superiors, how they may keep from losing, and how they may protect themselves from anticipated attacks. As a person becomes more and more defensive, furthermore, he becomes less and less able to see correctly the motives, values, emotions, and content involved in messages of other group members. Gibb (1961) demonstrated that defensive behavior is correlated positively with losses in efficiency and effectiveness of communication. Thus as people become less defensive their communication behavior becomes more efficient and effective. Competitiveness in one group member breeds competition in all group members, and defensiveness will continue to spiral as long as competition thrives among members.

The arousal of defensiveness makes it difficult, if not impossible to communicate ideas clearly and move purposefully toward accomplishing the group's goals. In an eight-year study of communication behavior in groups, Gibb (1961) found several behaviors that prompt defensiveness among group members as well as other behaviors that lessen defensiveness. For example, if one group member sends messages that she is evaluating or judging other group members, they will become defensive. Descriptive messages, on the contrary, tend to arouse little uneasiness. Messages that try to control other group members increase their defensiveness, especially if the control attempts are subtle and denied. Yet if the sender is oriented toward the group problem, communicates a desire to help in defining and solving it, and implies that she has no predetermined solution, attitude, or method to impose upon the other group members, the same problem orientation tends to be created in the receivers. When the sender is seen as being engaged in a strategy involving many ambiguous motives, the receivers again tend to become defensive: no one likes to be the victim of some hidden motivation, and most groups dislike deceit. Behavior that seems to be spontaneous and free of deception reduces defensiveness in the receivers.

Gibb also found that when neutrality in communication appears to the receiver to evidence lack of concern for her welfare, she becomes defensive. Communications that are particularly persuasive in reducing defensiveness are those that show empathy with the feelings of the receiver and respect for her worth. When a person communicates that he feels superior in some way to the receiver, defensiveness is aroused. When the sender communicates a willingness to enter into participative planning with others in mutual trust and respect, on the other hand, defensiveness is lessened. Finally, those who seem to know the answers, who need no additional information, and who see themselves as teachers rather than co-workers tend to arouse defensiveness in others. A person minimizes that defensiveness of receivers by communicating that he is willing to experiment with his own behavior, attitudes, and ideas. These behaviors, which are characteristic of either a competitive or a cooperative orientation in a group, are summarized below.

Competitive Orientation	*Cooperative Orientation*
evaluation	description
control	problem orientation
strategy	spontaneity
neutrality	empathy
superiority	equality
certainty	provisionalism

Groups that display a high cooperative orientation, groups whose members are good listeners, more accepting of the ideas of others, and less possessive of their own, generally demonstrate greater sending and receiving skills. Achievement will be higher in a cooperative group than in a competitive one, more attentiveness will be paid to members' ideas, and a friendlier climate will prevail. A cooperative orientation leads to increased cohesiveness and greater group productivity. One sound means of improving the communication among group members is to increase their cooperativeness and decrease their competitiveness.

PHYSICAL BARRIERS TO COMMUNICATION

Physical factors can also block effective communication within a group. Group members should pay attention to the acoustics of the room in which they are meeting; how members are seated; the duration of the meeting; the ventilation, temperature, and lighting in the room; and what time of day it is. All of these are potential physical barriers to effective communication among members. Once noted, of course, they can usually be changed or compensated for.

QUIZ

Check your reading of this section by answering the following questions. Answers are on page 224.

True   False   **1.** If you do not seek information from other group members, you are not communicating effectively within the group.

True   False   **2.** An example of noise within a group could be how trustworthy a member is seen.

True   False   **3.** Since most people in a group are guilty of interrupting, watching who interrupts who is not a useful source of interaction information.

True   False   **4.** A triggering pattern to look for is who speaks after who.

True   False   **5.** Defensive behavior takes place when one person disagrees with the group.

True   False   **6.** Defensive behavior in just one group member will not really interfere with the group's communications.

7. Patterns of communication helpful to observe in a group are (choose three):
   a. who talks, how often, and how long.
   b. who shows the most hostility and anger.
   c. who talks to who.

    d. who has the best way with words.

    e. who triggers who and in what ways.

8. Behaviors which lead to defensiveness on the part of group members are (choose four):

    a. evaluating or judging messages.

    b. descriptive messages.

    c. control messages.

    d. problem-solving messages.

    e. hidden or ambiguous motive messages.

    f. superiority or Know-All-The-Answers messages.

Match the following behaviors with the kind of group in which they are found:

__ **9.** Certainty	**a.** Cooperative
__ **10.** Control	**b.** Competitive
__ **11.** Description	
__ **12.** Empathy	
__ **13.** Evaluation	
__ **14.** Problem orientation	
__ **15.** Spontaneity	
__ **16.** Strategy	

TRANSMISSION OF INFORMATION EXERCISE

The objective of this exercise is to show the effects of using one-way and two-way communication to pass information through a series of group members. At least ten persons and two observers are required. The time needed to complete the exercise is approximately one hour, and the procedure for the coordinator is as follows:

1. Introduce the exercise as an example of information being passed from member to member within a group.

2. Ask ten persons to leave the room. They are to constitute two groups of five members each. The first group is to demonstrate *one-way communication.* Entering the room one by one, each is to listen to a brief story and repeat it to the next person in his own way without help from other participants or his group's observer. The receiver cannot ask questions or comment: he must simply listen to the story and then repeat it to the next person. The second group is to demonstrate *two-way communication.* Entering the room one by one, each is to listen to the story and ask questions about it to clarify its meaning and to make sure that she knows what the story is about. She then repeats the story to the next person in her group in her own way without help from other participants or her group's observer; the receiver can ask as many questions as she wants. You may wish to record the whole experience so that it can be played back for the participants' benefit.

3. After the ten participants have left the room, pass out copies of the accompanying observation sheets and a copy of "The Story" to the observers. Discuss the use of the observation sheet and read the story aloud. Explain the basic concepts of leveling, sharpening, and assimilation (these are discussed in the section on the effects of one-way communication on a message).

4. Begin the demonstration of one-way communication. Ask the first person to enter the room, read the story once, ask the second person to enter, have the first person repeat the story to the second person, and so on until the fifth person repeats the story to the observers.

5. Begin the demonstration of two-way communication. Ask the first person to enter the room, read the story once, answer all questions he has about the story, ask the second person to enter, have the first person repeat the story to the second person and answer all of the second person's questions, and so on until the fifth person repeats the story to the observers.

6. Reread the original story out loud. Using the results recorded by the observers and the following summary tables and summary graph, chart the percentages of original details retained correctly in the successive reproductions and compare the one-way and two-way communications. Discuss the results, incorporating the material in the sections on the characteristics of communication within an authority hierarchy and the effects of one-way communication on a message. Ask the group for further evidence that leveling, sharpening, and assimilation occurred. Then ask what conclusions about one-way and two-way communication can be made on the basis of the results of the demonstration. Finally, ask the group what conclusions can be made about communication in authority hierarchies.

Other stories can be used in this exercise. Often, the more the cultural background of the story differs from the listener's culture the more the story is taken in. A story from the Eskimo culture that might be used in this exercise appears below "The Story."

Summary Table: One-Way Communication

Person	Details Correct		Details Incorrect		Details Left Out		Total Details
	Number	Percentage	Number	Percentage	Number	Percentage	
1							20
2							20
3							20
4							20
5							20

Summary Table: Two-Way Communication

Person	Details Correct		Details Incorrect		Details Left Out		Total Details
	Number	*Percentage*	*Number*	*Percentage*	*Number*	*Percentage*	
1							20
2							20
3							20
4							20
5							20

Summary Graph

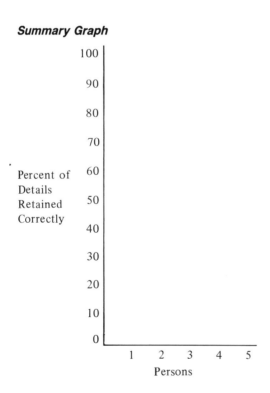

On this graph plot the percentages of original details retained correctly in one-way and two-way communication. Connect the one-way results with a solid line and the two-way results with a broken line.

The Story*

A *farmer* in *western Kansas* put a *tin roof on his barn.* Then a *small tornado blew* the roof off, and when the farmer found it *two counties away,* it was *twisted and mangled* beyond repair.

A *friend and a lawyer* advised him that the *Ford Motor Company* would pay him a *good price* for the scrap tin, and the farmer decided he would *ship the roof* up to the company to see *how much he could get for it.* He crated it up in a *very big wooden box* and sent it off to *Dearborn, Michigan,* marking it plainly with his *return address* so that the Ford Company would know where to *send the check.*

Twelve weeks passed, and the farmer didn't hear from the Ford Company. Finally he was just on the *verge of writing them* to find out what was the matter, when he *received an envelope* from them. It said, "We don't know *what hit your car,* mister, but we'll have it fixed for you by the *fifteenth of next month."*

The War of the Ghosts

One night two young men from Egulac went down to the river to hunt seals, and while they were there it became foggy and calm. Then they heard war cries, and they thought: "Maybe this is a war party." They escaped to the shore, and hid behind a log. Now canoes came up, and they heard the noise of paddles, and they saw one canoe coming up to them. There were five men in the canoe and they said:

"What do you think? We wish to take you along. We are going up the river to make war on the people."

One of the young men said: "I have no arrows."

"Arrows are in the canoe," they said.

"I will not go along. I might be killed. My relatives do not know where I have gone. But you," he said, turning to the other, "may go with them."

So one of the young men went, but the other returned home.

And the warriors went on up the river to a town on the other side of Kalama. The people came down to the water and they began to fight, and many were killed. And presently the young man heard one of the warriors say: "Quick, let us go home. That Indian has been hit." Now he thought, "Oh, they are ghosts." He did not feel sick, but they said he had been shot.

So the canoes went back to Egulac, and the young man went ashore to his house and made a fire. And he told everybody: "Behold I accompanied ghosts, and we went to fight. Many of our fellows were killed, and many of those who attacked us were killed. They said I was hit, but I did not feel sick."

He told it all, and then he became quiet. When the sun rose he fell down. Something black came out of his mouth. His face became contorted. The people jumped up and cried.

He was dead.

---

*This story by Samuel J. Sackett, whose actual title is "Tin Lizzie," is included in Botkin (1957). This title should not be mentioned until the end of the exercise.

Observation Sheet: One-way Communication

List in the first column the twenty specific details of the story (these appear in italics in the story). Verify the list when the coordinator reads the story to the first person. As person 1 repeats the story to person 2, note the mistakes in person 1's version by writing the wrong words or phrases in the proper row and column. To help in scoring, use a check mark for details correctly reported and a zero for details left out. Repeat this procedure for the rest of the participants.

Detail	Original Story	Version 1	Version 2	Version 3	Version 4	Version 5
1						
2						
3						
4						
5						
6						
7						
8						
9						
10						
11						
12						
13						
14						
15						
16						
17						
18						
19						
20						

Observation Sheet: Two-way Communication

List in the first column the twenty specific details of the story (these appear in italics in the story). Verify the list when the coordinator reads the story to the first person. As person 1 repeats the story to person 2, note the mistakes in person 1's version by writing the wrong words or phrases in the proper row and column. To help in scoring, use a check mark for details correctly reported and a zero for details left out. Repeat this procedure for the rest of the participants.

Detail	Original Story	Version 1	Version 2	Version 3	Version 4	Version 5
1						
2						
3						
4						
5						
6						
7						
8						
9						
10						
11						
12						
13						
14						
15						
16						
17						
18						
19						
20						

ONE- AND TWO-WAY COMMUNICATION EXERCISE

This is another exercise that contrasts the impact of one-way and two-way communication on communication effectiveness. For this exercise each participant needs two sheets of paper and a pencil. The coordinator needs copies of the accompanying square arrangements which are given on pages 482–483 in Appendix D. The coordinator may wish to copy the three summary tables below onto a blackboard or a large sheet of paper. The procedure for the coordinator is as follows:

TABLE A: MEDIANS FOR TRIALS I AND II

Medians	I	II
Time elapsed:	_____	_____
Guess accuracy:	_____	_____
Actual accuracy	_____	_____

TABLE B: FIRST TRIAL

Number correct	Guess	Actual
5	_____	_____
4	_____	_____
3	_____	_____
2	_____	_____
1	_____	_____
0	_____	_____

TABLE C: SECOND TRIAL

Number correct	Guess	Actual
5	_____	_____
4	_____	_____
3	_____	_____
2	_____	_____
1	_____	_____
0	_____	_____

1. Select a sender and two observers (if the group has less than seven members, select only one observer). The sender should be a person who communicates well and who speaks clearly and loudly enough to be heard.
2. Have the sender sit either with her back to the group of receivers or behind a screen. Give her the first square arrangement being careful that the group members

do not see it. Tell her to study the arrangement of squares carefully for two minutes in order to be prepared to instruct the group members on how to draw a similar set of squares on their paper.

3. Ask the first observer to note the behavior and reactions of the sender during the exercise and to make notes for later comments. Ask the second observer to make notes on the behavior and reactions of the group members. Facial reactions, gestures, posture, and other nonverbal behaviors may be observed.

4. Give the group these instructions: "The sender is going to describe a drawing to you. You are to listen carefully to her instructions and draw what she describes as accurately as you can. You will be timed, but there is no time limit. *You may ask no questions of the sender and give no audible response.* You are asked to work independently."

5. Display the three summary tables in the front of the room. Then tell the sender to proceed to give the instructions for drawing the first arrangement of squares as quickly and accurately as she can. Make sure that there are no questions or audible reactions from the group members.

6. When the sender has completed giving the instructions for the first square arrangement, record the time it took her to do so in the proper space in the first table. Ask each member of the group to write down on his paper the number of squares he thinks he has drawn correctly in relation to the preceding square.

7. Instruct the sender to face the group members. Give her the second square arrangement and tell her to study the relationship of the squares in this new diagram for two minutes in preparation for instructing the group members on how to draw it.

8. Give the group these instructions: "The sender is going to describe another drawing to you. This time she will be in full view of you and you may ask as many questions as you wish. She is free to reply to your questions or amplify her statements as she sees fit. She is not, however, allowed to make any hand signals while describing the drawing. You will be timed, but there is no time limit. Work as accurately and rapidly as you can."

9. Tell the sender to proceed.

10. When the sender has completed giving instructions for the second figure, record the time in the appropriate space in Table A. Ask the group members to guess the number of squares they have drawn correctly and to record the number on their papers.

11. Obtain a median for guessed accuracy on the first drawing by recording the number of group members who guessed zero, the number who guessed one, and so on in Table B. Find the median guessed number by counting from zero the number of group members guessing each number until you reach half the members of the group. Then record the median in Table A.

12. Repeat this method to get the median of accurate guesses for the second drawing.

13. Show the group members the master drawing for the first set of squares, and point out the relationship of each square to the preceding one. Each square must be in the exact relationship to the preceding one as it appears on the master drawing in order to be counted as correct. When this step has been completed ask the members to count and record the actual number right. Have them make a similar count for the second square arrangement.

14. Obtain the median for accuracy for the first and second arrangements and place them in Table A.

15. Discuss the following questions with the class:

   a. What may be concluded from the results in terms of time, accuracy, and level of confidence?

   b. What did the observers record during the exercise? How did the behavior of the sender and the group members vary from one situation to the other? What were the group members and the sender feeling during the two situations?

   c. How does this exercise compare with situations you find yourself in at work, school, or at home? How might you change your behavior in relating to your friends and acquaintances as a result of what you have experienced during this exercise?

COMMUNICATION WITHIN AN AUTHORITY HIERARCHY

Within every organization and in many groups there is an authority hierarchy. An authority hierarchy exists when role requirements are established in such a way that different members perform different roles and members performing particular roles supervise the other members to make sure they fulfill their role requirements. If a group, for example, is divided into several committees, each responsible for a different aspect of the group's work, its role structure would look like Figure 5.3. The members are supervised by the committee chairpersons and the committee chairpersons are supervised by the group chairperson. Within an authority hierarchy a system of rewards and punishments is usually established so that a supervisor will have some power over the persons he is supervising. Although authority hierarchies are established to facilitate the effectiveness of the group, they can often interfere with its effectiveness by undermining necessary processes such as distributed participation and leadership, equalization of power, controversy procedures, and communication. In this chapter we will focus on the effect of authority hierar-

FIGURE 5.3 A group and its internal authority hierarchy.

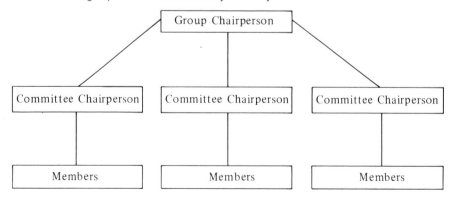

chies upon communication within a group and thus elaborate on the conclusions resulting from the previous exercises.

In order to organize itself to accomplish its goals, maintain itself in good working order, and adapt to a changing world, a group must structure its communication. Meetings will be scheduled; reports from group members will be requested; conferences among members will be set up; summaries of group progress may be written and sent to all members. All of these activities are structured communication opportunities. The *communication network* thus created determines the amount and type of information a group member will receive from the other members. The very nature of a group implies that communication is selective, that a communication network exists, that incentives to use it properly are present, and that members must use certain procedures for communicating with each other. Thus, a college seminar will schedule meetings and teacher–student conferences as the communication network, be selective in the material upon which communication will be based, use learning and grades as incentives for participating in the network, and encourage certain procedures (for example, when the teacher talks students listen). The formal network, incentives, and procedures are established to coordinate members' efforts to accomplish goals. In addition to the formal communication network, in many groups there is an informal network, which include patterns of friendship and social contact among group members.

The procedures used within a formal communication network of a group can be examined in several different ways; the approach most relevant to a discussion of authority hierarchies focuses on three types: one-way, one-way-with-feedback, and two-way. In an authority hierarchy a one-way communication procedure is characterized by a group chairperson giving instructions or making announcements to the other group members, who are not allowed to communicate with her. The listeners, then, are entirely passive, and communication effectiveness is determined by how the messages are created and presented. Usually there is someone higher in the authority hierarchy who communicates messages to the chairperson, who then communicates them to the group members. One-way communication takes little time compared with the other two procedures, but it is less effective. And though it is less frustrating for the sender, it is far more unsatisfactory for the receivers.

One-way-with-feedback communication is often called directive or coercive communication (McGregor, 1967). In this communication procedure within an authority hierarchy, the chairperson presents the message and the group members give feedback on how well they understand it. The exchange is completed when the group members indicate to the chairperson that they have received the message correctly. This procedure is called coercive because no provision exists for mutual influence or exchange: communication begins with the belief that the chairperson's position is correct, and that the only information he needs from the group members is that they correctly understand and accept the message. The chairperson influences while the group members merely understand. This second procedure is, in the short run, faster than two-way communication and less frustrating for the chairperson, but also less accurate and more frustrating for the group members.

When one-way and one-way-with-feedback communication procedures are used in groups, communication can be so poor that informal communication among group members is necessary in order for them to complete the group's tasks adequately. This reduces the long-term effectiveness of these procedures. The original messages can become distorted as they pass through the informal network, and this can hinder the coordination of member behavior. Such distortion and misunderstanding are most frequent when the most influential members of the informal network disagree with the decisions and points of view of the chairperson and her superiors (if she has them), or when distrust and competition exist among group members or between the chairperson and the group members. Unless group members have the opportunity to communicate freely with the chairperson, the informal network may become more influential, powerful, important, and effective than the group's formal network.

Two-way communication is a reciprocal process in which each member starts messages and tries to understand the other members' messages. In a two-way communication procedure the chairperson and the other group members freely exchange ideas and information in a productive discussion. Both sending and receiving skills are needed. All members are able to participate at will, and minority opinions are encouraged and more apt to be expressed. Feelings of resistance or doubt can be discussed and resolved at the time they are experienced so that they are not potential barriers to commitment. Two-way communication encourages open and candid member interaction, distributed participation and leadership, consensual decision making, and other elements of group effectiveness. Although two-way communication is much more time-consuming than the one-way procedures and more frustrating for the chairperson, it is less frustrating for the group members and much more effective in the long run. Any goal-directed, problem-solving group that hopes to be effective must use two-way communication procedures.

Even when a two-way communication procedure is encouraged, the authority hierarchy will influence communication among group members. High-authority group members usually do most of the talking, and most of the messages are directed at them. Low-authority members often do not communicate very much with each other during a group meeting, preferring to address their remarks to high-authority members. Because they generally fear evaluation by those with power, members without power can be expected to take few risks, speak inconsequentially, and avoid frankness in their remarks. High-authority members often hesitate to reveal any of their own limitations or vulnerability, a tendency that also decreases open and effective communication among group members. Thus, several influences push the group's use of communication procedures toward practices that thwart the kind of discussion and problem solving needed for it to function effectively.

How can these tendencies be avoided so that communication within a group is effective? There are two answers to this question. The first is to establish a cooperative group climate that encourages the equal participation of all members. The second is to promote group norms that foster the feeling that a member's ideas and views, no matter what his authority level, are of real interest to other group members. If a group is to function effectively, it must adopt a two-way communication procedure and develop a cooperative group climate and group norms that facilitate interaction among members. Since communication is an interpersonal phenomenon, furthermore, anything that interferes with the relationships among group members interferes with their communication. Much attention, therefore, must be paid to the interpersonal relationships of group members.

INFORMAL COMMUNICATION NETWORKS AND OPINION LEADERS

When one-way communication procedures are used in a group, comprehension of messages is often so poor that group members turn to the informal communication network to clarify what has been communicated. Often certain group members will be better able to interpret messages from higher-ups. In such cases other members will seek them out and ask them what the higher-ups meant by the latest communication. Such members are called opinion leaders or gatekeepers because they have more influence over members' comprehension of messages than do the persons in higher-authority positions who originated the messages. There are two common types of opinion leaders: *information gatekeepers,* who receive messages from superiors and outside sources or who read, listen, and reflect upon written reports and verbal messages to a greater extent than other group members, and *technological gatekeepers,* who read more of the theory and research literature in their field and consult more with outside sources than do the other group members.

Opinion leaders frequently serve as *translators* by taking messages from superiors and rephrasing them into more understandable form and into the specific meanings they have for different group members. When one-way communication procedures are being used, the original source is often not available for questioning and clarification of messages; group members, therefore, must rely on the opinion leaders to clarify the messages and what meanings they have for the specific group members. Group members, furthermore, may remember an opinion leader's interpretation of a message they themselves heard, better than the original message! Research on testimony in court cases indicates that people remember initial reports of events they witnessed better than the events themselves (Jones and Gerard, 1967). If the opinion leader misconstrues the message, errors in understanding are amplified as interpretations are passed from member to member. Even within a two-way communication procedure group members will at times be unable to clarify a message and will use opinion leaders to help them do so.

EFFECTS ON THE MESSAGE OF A ONE–WAY COMMUNICATION PROCEDURE

Some basic research has been conducted on what happens to information when it is passed through several persons with little or no clarification. The more the message is passed from person to person, the more distorted and changed it will become. Three psychological processes characterize the communication between persons who are unable to communicate directly with the original source of a message (Allport and Postman, 1945; Bartlett, 1932). These three processes are attempts to reduce the message to a simple one that has significance for the receiver in terms of her own interests, experience, frame of reference, and tasks. The three processes are as follows:

Leveling. The receiver tends to reduce the amount of information he receives by remembering much less of the message than was presented by the sender. The message tends to grow shorter, more concise, and more easily grasped and told. In successive versions, fewer words are used and fewer details are mentioned.

Sharpening. The receiver sharpens certain parts of the information so that a few high points are readily remembered while most of the message is forgotten. Sharpening then, is the selective retaining, perceiving, and reporting of a limited number of details from a larger context. It is the reciprocal of leveling: one cannot exist without the other. Certain points become dominant, and all the others are grouped about them.

Assimilation. The receiver takes much of the message into her own frame of reference and personality. Thus, her interpretations and memories of what she heard are affected by her own thoughts and feelings. This process involves not only changing the unfamiliar to some known context, but leaving out material that seems irrelevant and substituting material that gives meaning in the person's own frame of reference.

Because these three processes are at work whenever one-way procedures are being used, inefficient and ineffective communication usually results. This is true even when opinion leaders supplement the procedure.

QUIZ

Check your reading of this section by answering the following questions. Answers are on page 225.

True   False   **1.** An authority hierarchy is a system of role definitions that gives supervisors power over subordinate roles.

True   False   **2.** Personal relationships have little influence on communication within a hierarchical organization.

True   False   **3.** Opinion leaders or gatekeepers have more influence over the understanding of messages than do the higher authorities who originated them.

4. A communication network consists of (choose three):
   a. several people yelling at each other.
   b. the way interaction is structured among group members.
   c. the incentives to communicate in prescribed ways.
   d. the seating arrangement of group members.
   e. procedures for communicating when members interact.

5. Four characteristics of the two-way communication procedure is that it:
   a. takes less time than other methods.
   b. takes more time than other methods.
   c. is less frustrating for group members.
   d. is more frustrating for group members.
   e. is less frustrating for the chairperson.
   f. is more frustrating for the chairperson.
   g. is less effective.
   h. is more effective.

6. When some group members have more authority than other group members:
   a. low authority members talk mainly to other low authority members.
   b. low authority members talk mainly to high authority members.
   c. low authority members talk to both low and high authority members.

Match the following procedures for communicating with their definitions:

____   **7.** Leader gives instructions; members clarify meaning.   **a.** One-way

____   **8.** Leader gives instructions; members listen.   **b.** One-way with feedback

____   **9.** Leader and members have free exchange of ideas.   **c.** Two-way

Match the following processes with their definitions:

____ **10.** Certain points become dominant and the others are grouped around them.   **a.** Leveling

                                                                                         b. Sharpening

____ **11.** The material is affected by the receiver's own frame of reference.   **c.** Assimilation

_____ **12.** The message is shortened and made more concise.

GROUP OBSERVATION EXERCISE

Review the material in the last three sections by taking the frequency chart used in the Bewise College exercise and observing at least two groups of which you are a member—one group in which there is a chairperson (such as a teacher) who dominates the meeting and another group in which free and open discussions are held among members. Observe the communication patterns in both groups and compare them. Write a description of the communication patterns in each group and discuss them with other members of your class.

NORMS AND COMMUNICATION EXERCISE

This exercise should develop participants' awareness of how group norms affect communication among group members. The participating groups must be groups that have worked together for several hours. Observation sheets similar to the frequency chart used in the Bewise College exercise are needed; participants can construct their own. The exercise will take approximately one hour to complete. The procedure for the coordinator is as follows:

1. Introduce the exercise as a structured experience in learning how group norms affect communication among group members.
2. Have each group select two observers. The observers need to construct six observation sheets, making the number of circles on the sheets equal to the number of members in the group they are observing. Explain the use of these sheets.
3. Give each group a copy of the accompanying discussion sheet and state that the groups have thirty minutes to discuss the topic. Give the signal to begin.
4. At the end of thirty minutes ask the observers to report to their groups. Groups are to discuss the communication pattern among their members and how it relates to the group norms they have been listing. Each group should also discuss how its members feel about the amount of their participation and how it could change group norms so as to gain more widespread participation and more effective communication among members. Each group should then revise its list of group norms in light of the discussion. Allow twenty minutes for this discussion.
5. Have the groups share their conclusions in a general discussion.

Discussion Sheet: What Is a Norm

Norms develop in groups so that members will know how they are expected to behave and what is appropriate member behavior. They are common rules or customs followed by group members. In some groups, for example, members address each other by their last names; in other groups first names are used. All groups have norms, and usually these norms are eventually followed without conscious thought. Norms can develop so that every member does the same thing (dressing formally for a group meeting) or something different (dressing differently for a group meeting).

Norms are not built from scratch, but develop from the values, expectations, and learned habits that the members bring with them when the group is first formed. "Don't interrupt the chairperson," an expression of respect for authority, is a norm that most persons bring with them into new groups. Norms can also be implied by the setting in which the group meets. Most persons do not sit on the floor in a room that appears to be arranged formally. Most persons do not remain standing when their group is meeting at a beach.

Norms have a powerful influence upon communiation within a group. Such influences are seldom examined. It is even rarer that a group attempts to change its norms so as to facilitate goal accomplishment. Usually group members simply follow norms without question. This does not mean that norms do not change. Norms do change as expectations of appropriate member behavior change, but this is commonly an unobtrusive process.

What norms have developed in your group? Do you all sense where you are supposed to sit? Do you all sense who should be listened to and who should be ignored? Do you interrupt each other, or is politeness a group norm? Are jokes allowed, or is the tone of the group serious? How do discussions usually start? How are boredom and frustration generally expressed, if at all? Are certain topics permissible to talk about and others avoided? Is the emotional involvement of members supposed to be high or low? In answering these questions you will become more conscious of the norms that are present in your group.

Spend the next thirty minutes discussing your group norms and making a list of what they are.

SITTING IN A CIRCLE EXERCISE

How a group sits has a great deal of influence on how its members communicate. This exercise focuses upon the effects of sitting in a circle. The procedure for each group is to engage in three five-minute discussions. After each one each member writes down several adjectives to describe his reactions to the discussion. A different position is to be used for each discussion: (1) a circle in which everyone's back is to the center, (2) a circle with members face to face and a large rectangular table between them, and (3) a circle with members face to face and nothing between them.

After the fifteen minutes of discussion members compare their reactions to the three positions. What were the differences in feelings? Was there any difference in how productive the discussion was? What effects did the different positions have upon the discussion? How was communication affected? The advantage of sitting close together in a circle with nothing between members is that their unobstructed view of one another increases their opportunities to receive and send nonverbal messages. This type of circular seating arrangement also encourages more equal participation because there is no podium or seat at the head of a table to suggest that a particular member should assume leadership.

COMMUNICATION NETWORKS EXERCISE

The purpose of this exercise is to compare the impact of four different communication patterns on productivity and morale. The procedure is as follows:

1. The class forms heterogeneous groups of six. One member needs to volunteer to be an observer. The task of the observer is to time how long it takes the group to complete its task and to make notes about the behavior and apparent feelings of the participants.

2. The five participants in each group place themselves in a straight line with everyone facing the same way. Each member receives five cards from a regular deck of playing cards. No verbal communication is allowed, but members may write notes to the person in front of or behind them. Members may pass cards to the person in front of or behind them. The *group task* is to select one card from each member's hand in order to make the highest-ranking poker hand possible. After the group has decided on a poker hand each member should write an answer to the following questions:
   a. How satisfied are you with the group and its work?
   b. How did you feel?
   c. What did you observe?

3. The same task with the same rules is repeated, but this time the group members arrange themselves in a circle. Members may pass notes and cards only to the person on their left or right. No verbal communication is allowed. After the group has completed the task each member writes answers to the same three questions.

4. The same task with the same rules is repeated, but this time the group members arrange themselves in a wheel, as in Figure 5.4. Members on the outside may pass notes and cards only to the person in the middle; the member in the middle may pass notes and cards to anyone. No verbal communication is allowed. After the group has decided on a poker hand each member answers the same three questions.

5. The same task is repeated, this time with the members sitting in a circle. Any member may communicate with anyone else in the group. Members may pass cards and notes, and *may* speak to whomever they wish in the group. After the group has decided on a poker hand each member answers the same three questions.

6. Using the reactions of the group members and the observer's impressions, the group should discuss the advantages and disadvantages of each communication pattern. Here are some questions the group may wish to talk about:
   a. What were the feelings of the members in the middle of a communication pattern? What were the feelings of those on the fringe?

FIGURE 5.4 Communication networks.

Circle   Chain   Y   Wheel   Open

    b. In what communication pattern was the shortest amount of time needed to arrive at a group poker hand?

    c. If you were in charge of a company, which communication pattern would you try to use?

    d. How many messages were sent in each type of communication pattern?

    e. Did each pattern have a leader? For those patterns that did, what position did the leader occupy?

7. Each group shares its conclusions with the rest of the class.

COMMUNICATION STRUCTURES AND NETWORKS

If a group is to function effectively, its members must be able to communicate easily and efficiently. Communication within the group needs to be arranged so that ideas, knowledge, and other information may flow freely among group members. To this end a number of studies have been conducted on the physical arrangement of communication networks—that is, who can communication with whom and whether the communication is direct or via another group member. Typically these studies imposed various communication networks on groups in order to determine their effects on group process. Some of the networks that have been investigated are diagramed in Figure 5.4. The circles represent individual group members and the lines represent links in the communication network. The most common procedure for imposing communication networks was first formulated by Alex Bavelas (1948). He suggested placing group members in cubicles connected by slots in their walls, through which written messages could be passed. When all slots are open every group member can communicate directly with every other member. Other patterns are formed merely by selection of the appropriate slots.

Communication networks have been found to influence the emergence of leadership, the development of organization, the morale of group members, and the efficiency of problem solving (Leavitte, 1951; Shaw, 1964). The group member who occupies a central physical position in a communication network usually emerges as the leader of the group. Because the central member has more information she can coordinate group activities.

A group becomes organized when it follows a consistent pattern of information exchange during the course of problem solution. Research has found two basic patterns of organization in communication networks: centralized and each-to-all. In the centralized pattern all information is funneled to one person, who solves the problem and distributes the answer to the other group members. In the each-to-all pattern all available information is communicated to all group members, each of whom solves the problem independently. When a centralized communication network is imposed on a group, the group adopts a centralized organization. When a decentralized communication network is imposed on a group, each-to-all organization tends to develop.

TABLE 5.1 Differences between centralized (wheel, chain, Y) and decentralized (circle, comcon) networks as a function of task complexity.

	Simple problems*	Complex problems†	Total
Time			
Centralized faster	14	0	14
Decentralized faster	4	18	22
Messages			
Centralized sent more	0	1	1
Decentralized sent more	18	17	35
Errors			
Centralized made more	0	6	6
Decentralized made more	9	1	10
No difference	1	3	4
Satisfaction			
Centralized higher	1	1	2
Decentralized higher	7	10	17

* Simple problems: symbol-, letter-, number-, and color-identification tasks.

† Complex problems: arithmetic, word arrangement, sentence construction, and discussion problems.

Source: M. E. Shaw (1964). Reprinted with permission.

Members who occupy a central position in a communication network are usually more satisfied with the group's work than members who occupy fringe positions. Typically, the morale of a group is higher in decentralized (circle, open) communication networks than in centralized ones (chain, Y, wheel).

Finally, when a task is simple and requires only the collection of information, a centralized network is more efficient in terms of speed and lack of errors. But when the task is complex and requires the analysis of information, the decentralized networks are more efficient, as we can see in Table 5.1. The problem with centralized communication networks is that the members in the centralized positions may easily receive more messages than they can handle. Any extra demands, furthermore, that must be addressed by a member in a centralized position are likely to interfere with the efficiency of the network.

SEATING ARRANGEMENTS

The way in which group members seat themselves in relation to each other exerts significant influences on their perceptions of status, patterns of participation, leadership activities, and affective reactions (Gardin, Kaplan, Firestone, and Cowan, 1973; Howells and Becker, 1962; Myers, 1969; Steinzor, 1950; Strodtbeck and Hook, 1961). Members who perceive themselves to have relatively high status in the group select positions (such as the head of the table) that are in accord with this perception. Members sitting at the end positions of a rectangular arrangement participate more in the group and are seen as having more influence on the group decision than members seated at the sides. There is a strong tendency for members to communicate with members facing them rather than with members adjacent to them. Easy eye contact among members enhances frequency of interaction, friendliness, cooperativeness, and liking for the group and its work. The more formal a seating arrangement, the more anxious members may feel. The group's formal leader usually sits at the head of the table, and the member setting at the head of the table is usually perceived to be the leader.

TAKING A SURVEY

Group effectiveness is always improved when members have clear expectations of the kinds of behaviors are expected of them as group members. One way to clarify such expectations is the survey method. In this method any member may ask for the opinion of all the others at any time. Each member then states in two or three sentences his current position on the topic under discussion. A survey is not a vote, and it does not bind the group members to a fixed position; it is a device to help communication and problem solving within a group.

IMPROVING COMMUNICATION AMONG GROUP MEMBERS

To improve communication among group members, one must observe their communication behavior in order to diagnose possible sources of difficulty. Once a diagnosis has been made and enough data have been gathered to confirm existing problems, both communication skills and the group's awareness of its present behavior need to be examined. If certain members—or all of them—lack some basic skills, this situation can be easily corrected by a training program. If members have the skills but are not fully aware that they are not using them, an analysis of the communication behavior in the group can be a great help. After examining member self-awareness and skills one may analyze the effect of group norms and traditional practices to find out if they are suppressing effective communication behaviors and promoting ineffective ones. Group norms can then be adjusted so that communication effectiveness among members will increase.

Because communication is interpersonal, whatever interferes with the relationships among group members interferes with their communication. Changes in the relationships in a group can result in basic improvements in communication. And as we have noted before, perhaps the most powerful influence on the relationships among members and on communication in a group is the members' orientation toward participation in the group and toward its goal structure. Cooperativeness helps a group's effectiveness. Competitiveness, either in goal structure or member orientation, is highly destructive of communication and relationships.

QUIZ

Check your reading of this section by answering the following questions. Answers are on page 225.

1. As organization president, Buddy is very careful about the development of the communication networks because they have influence on (choose four):
   a. the emergence of leadership.
   b. the morale of group members.
   c. the carefulness of work accomplishment.
   d. the development of organization.
   e. the demands for pay increments.
   f. the efficiency of problem-solving.

2. Edye has a central position in a communication network group which means that she (choose four):
   a. can communicate well.
   b. will emerge as group leader.
   c. coordinates group activities.
   d. will be more satisfied with the group's work.
   e. can manipulate the group to her liking.
   f. can be overwhelmed with information.

3. Dale wants to sit where he can have the most influence on the decision making and has the most contact with his boss, who always sits at the head of a rectangular table. Where should he sit?
   a. At the end of the table.
   b. At the side of the table next to the boss.
   c. At the side of the table far from the boss.

4. What are the characteristics of a group survey? (choose three)
   a. Getting a binding vote on the topic under discussion.
   b. Improving group effectiveness.

    c. Getting current opinion on the topic under discussion.

    d. A device to help communication and problem solving.

    e. Going door to door as a group to solicit opinions.

5. Several ways of improving communication among group members are (choose five):

    a. have a training program to teach communication skills.

    b. have a training program to train the group leaders.

    c. analyze the communication patterns in the group.

    d. examine the norms and traditional practices of the group.

    e. change the goals of the group.

    f. change the members of the group.

    g. change the relationships in the group.

    h. structure the group cooperatively rather than competitively.

Match the following characteristics with the communication network they describe:

    ____ **6.** All information is communicated to all members.

    ____ **7.** Emerges from a decentralized communication network

    ____ **8.** Higher group morale

    ____ **9.** Most efficient for simple tasks

    ___ **10.** Most efficient for complex tasks

    ___ **11.** Can cause overload of information for central position person.

a. Centralized

b. Each-to-all

Match the following characteristics with the appropriate group size they describe:

    ___ **12.** Energy is needed to coordinate members' contributions

    ___ **13.** More liking, supporting, and valuing of members

    ___ **14.** More absenteeism and dissatisfaction

    ___ **15.** More conflict and formality

a. Large group

b. Small group

___ **16.** Adding a new member adds resources

___ **17.** More opportunity for rewards

___ **18.** More feelings of threat

___ **19.** More inhibition to participate

___ **20.** More domination by a few members

YOUR COMMUNICATION BEHAVIOR EXERCISE (II)

How would you now describe your communication behavior in a problem-solving group? What are your strengths in communicating, and in what areas do you still wish to build skills? After completing the exercises in this chapter take twenty minutes or so to write a description of how you see your communication behavior in problem-solving groups. Include a description of the way you formulate and send messages, the receiving skills you use, the way in which you contribute your information and ideas to the group, the way in which you receive information about group meetings and group business, and so on.

After you have written your description, meet with two persons who know you well and discuss it with them. Is it accurate? Can they add anything? Do they have other ideas that might help clarify your communication behavior?

SUMMARY

Now you are aware of the problems of communicating within a group and have had an opportunity to diagnose and practice effective and ineffective communication patterns. As groups become more developed, they must learn to deal with controversy and maximize their opportunities for creativity. This will be discussed in the next chapter.

ANSWERS

Page 182—1. true; 2. false; 3. true; 4. true; 5. true.

Page 188—1. a, b, d; 2. c, d; 3. c; 4. d.

Page 201—1. true; 2. true; 3. false; 4. true; 5. false; 6. false; 7. a, c, e; 8. a, c, e, f; 9. b; 10. b; 11. a; 12. a; 13. b; 14. a; 15. a; 16. b.

Page 214—1. true; 2. false; 3. true; 4. b, c, d; 5. b, c, f, h; 6. b; 7. b; 8. a; 9. c; 10. b; 11. c; 12. a.

Page 222—1. a, b, d, f; 2. b, c, d, f; 3. a; 4. b, c, d; 5. a, c, d, g, h; 6. b; 7. b; 8. b; 9. a; 10. b; 11. a; 12. a; 13. b; 14. a; 15. a; 16. b; 17. b; 18. a; 19. a; 20. a.

6

CONTROVERSY AND CREATIVITY

In this chapter a number of concepts are defined and discussed. The major ones are listed below. The procedure for learning these concepts is as follows:

1. The class forms heterogeneous groups of four.
2. Each group divides into two paris.
3. The task for each pair is to:
   a. define each concept, noting the page on which it is defined and discussed.
   b. make sure that both members of the pair understand the meaning of each concept.
4. In each group, members compare the answers of the two pairs. If there is disagreement, the members look up the concept in the chapter and clarify it until they all agree on the definition and understand it.

Concepts

1. conflict
2. controversy
3. constructive conflict
4. destructive conflict
5. conceptual conflict
6. epistemic curiosity
7. perspective taking
8. cognitive perspective
9. win-lose orientation
10. problem-solving orientation
11. differentiation of positions
12. integration of positions
13. creativity
14. open-mindedness
15. dogmatism
16. brainstorming

THE NATURE OF CONFLICT

> People . . . are trying to either shun conflict or crush it. Neither strategy is working. Avoidance and force only raise the level of conflict. . . . They have become parts of the problem rather than the solution.
>
> DeCecco and Richards, 1975

Conflicts among group members are inevitable. They will occur no matter what group members do. The issue is not whether conflicts can be prevented, but rather how they can be managed. A conflict among group members is a moment of truth in group effectiveness, a test of the group's health, a crisis that can weaken or strengthen the group, a critical event that may bring creative insight and closer relationships among members or lasting resentment, smoldering hostility, and psychological scars. Conflicts can push members away from one another or pull them into closer and more cooperative relationships. Conflicts may contain the seeds of group destruction or the fuel for increased group unity and cooperation. Conflicts may bring aggression or mutual understanding. They can have both highly constructive and highly destructive effects on group functioning. Being able to promote conflicts and capitalize on their constructive outcomes is an essential group skill.

Most persons can easily recognize when they or others are in a conflict. Yet the concept has not been an easy one for psychologists to define. Some psychologists have focused on frustration, others have focused on decisions among attractive and unattractive alternatives, and still others have concentrated on the feelings of the persons involved, such as rage, anger, distrust, fear, and rejection. Probably the most influential definition of conflict is that of Deutsch (1969), who stated that a *conflict* exists whenever incompatible activities occur. An activity that is incompatible with another activity is one that prevents, blocks, interferes with, injures, or in some way makes the second activity less likely or less effective. Incompatible activities may originate in one person, between two or more persons, or between two or more groups. If, for example, you wish to spend Saturday afternoon both sleeping and reading, you are in conflict with yourself. If you wish to cross the street and someone decides to prevent, block, or interfere with your doing so, you are involved in an interpersonal conflict. If your group decides to win a football game and the other group decides it also wants to win, your group is in a conflict with the other group.

There are at least four important types of conflicts: controversies, conflicts of interest, developmental conflicts, and conceptual conflicts. The first and the most important in effective group decision making and problem solving is *controversy*, the situation that exists when one person's ideas, information, conclusions, theories, and opinions are incompatible with those of another. The second and the most important in settling rivalries and disputes among incompatible needs and values is *conflict of interest,* the situation that exists when incompatible activities are based on differences in needs, values, and goals; scarcities of certain resources, such as power, time, space, popularity, money, and position; and competition for rewards and privileges. *Developmental conflicts* exist when incompatible activities are based on the opposing forces of stability and change within a person. *Conceptual conflicts* arise when incompatible ideas exist simultaneously in a person's mind. Developmental and conceptual conflicts are discussed at length in Johnson (1979). Controversies are discussed in this chapter and conflicts of interest in the following chapter; they are discussed separately because they have different effects on group functioning and are resolved and managed in different ways.

THE AVOIDANCE OF CONFLICTS

Despite the inevitability of conflicts, there seems to be a general feeling in our society that conflicts are bad and should be avoided. Many persons believe that a good group is one in which there are no conflicts among members. Many discussions of conflict cast it in the role of causing divorces, separations, psychological distress, social disorder, violence, and even war. The disintegration of many groups has been blamed on conflict. Yet a lack of conflict may signal apathy and noninvolvement, not a healthy group. There is a growing recognition that it is the failure to handle conflicts in constructive ways that leads to the destruction of groups and relationships, not the mere occurrence of conflicts.

Many persons in our society fear conflicts and avoid them. DeCecco and Richards (1974) conducted a seven-year study in which they interviewed more that 8,500 persons in schools, 8,000 of them students, in more than sixty junior and senior high schools in the New York City, Philadelphia, and San Francisco areas. They found that both school personnel and students avoided verbal expression of anger and open negotiation of conflicts. But ignoring the conflicts did not make them go away. The avoidance and denial of conflicts seemed to make the schools angry places in which students questioned every rule and committed acts of defiance astonishing in their destructiveness. School personnel would then react with strict punishments, armed hallway guards, and other forms of repression. The outcomes of 61 percent of the conflicts reported by students were perceived by them as bad. In only 9 percent of the conflicts did students believe the good outcomes resulted. In 91 percent of the conflicts students reported that their tension level was *not* lowered by the way in which the conflict was managed. Conflicts that are not openly expressed and constructively resolved will be expressed indirectly at great cost to the group or organization, and the indirect expression of conflicts will persist far longer than would open confrontation and settlement of the conflicts (Walton, 1969).

Schools are not the only organizations in which conflicts are ignored. Avoidance of conflicts has been found to be characteristic of hospitals, mental-health centers, government agencies, churches, businesses, industrial organizations, and social-work agencies (Argyris, 1970; Beckhard, 1969; Blake and Mouton, 1969; Deutsch, 1973; Johnson, 1973; Robbins, 1974; Walton, 1969). Many married couples go to great lengths to avoid open discussion of conflicts (Bach and Wyden, 1969).

Some of the avoidance of conflict in our society is perhaps based on a lack of the skills needed for effective conflict management and insufficient knowledge of the procedures involved. Deutsch (1973), Blake and Mouton (1970), and Johnson (1970, 1979) have all stated that there is little formal training in the procedures and skills of constructive conflict resolution in or outside our school systems. They believe that a considerable educational effort is needed to socialize the current generation of citizens into conflict-management skills. Most educators, furthermore, seem inadequately trained to deal effectively with conflicts, let alone teach constructive conflict-management skills.

Although many persons fear and avoid the open expression of conflict, it is not the presence of conflict but rather the destructive and ineffective management of conflict that causes psychological distress, violence, termination of relationships, social disorder, and group disintegration. Conflicts are a natural and desirable part of any relationship and group; when managed constructively they are extremely valuable. Conflicts are absolutely necessary if a group is to maintain its viability and effectiveness. Yet too few group members accept conflict, and almost none attempt to stimulate it. Most groups need more conflict—constructive conflict—not less. More groups are dying from complacency and apathy than from too much conflict. Conflicts do have many potential constructive outcomes for groups.

THE CONSTRUCTIVE OUTCOMES OF CONFLICTS

Conflicts, when skillfully managed, can be of great value to a group. Here are several of the potentially constructive outcomes of conflict:

1. Conflicts make us more aware of problems in our relationships that need to be solved. Conflicts increase our awareness of what the problems are, who is involved and how they can be solved.

2. Conflicts encourage change. There are times when things need to change, when new skills need to be learned, when old habits need to be modified.

3. Conflicts energize and increase one's motivation to deal with problems. Awareness of conflict can trigger a great deal of physical energy and an intensity of psychological focus, which in turn result in a strong motivation to resolve the conflict and put one's plans into action.

4. Conflicts make life more interesting. Being in a conflict often sparks curiosity and stimulates interest. Arguments about politics, sports, work, and societal problems make interpersonal interaction more intriguing and less boring. The disagreement of others with your ideas may inspire you to find out more about the issue.

5. Better decisions are generally made when there is disagreement about what the decision should be among the persons responsible for making it. Disagreement often causes the decision to be thought through more carefully.

6. Conflicts reduce the day-to-day irritations of relating to someone. A good argument may do a lot to resolve the small tensions of interacting with others.

7. Conflicts help you understand what you are like as a person. What makes you angry, what frightens you, what is important to you, and how you tend to manage conflicts are all highlighted when you are in conflict with someone. Being aware of what you are willing to argue about and how you act in conflicts can help you learn a great deal about yourself.

8. Conflicts can be fun when they are not taken too seriously. Many persons seek out conflicts through such activities as competitive sports and games, movies, plays, books, and teasing. They do so because they enjoy being involved in such conflict situations.

9. Conflicts can deepen and enrich a relationship, strengthening each person's conviction that the relationship can hold up under stress, communicating the commitments and values of each person that the other must take into account, and generally keeping the relationship clear of irritations and resentments so that positive feelings can be experienced fully.

10. Conflicts can stimulate creativity by promoting an awareness of different ways of viewing problems and situations. The reorientation gained from viewing a problem from several different perspectives generates insights into the problem and fosters the formation of creative solutions.

11. When a group enters into conflict with another group its cohesiveness increases and its sense of identity becomes clearer.

12. Conflicts promote the social development of group members by reducing their cognitive egocentrism and promoting higher levels of cognitive and moral reasoning.

HOW TO TELL WHETHER CONFLICTS ARE CONSTRUCTIVE

There are four things to look for in deciding whether a conflict has been constructive:

1. If the relationships among group members are stronger, and the members are better able to interact and work with each other, the conflict has been constructive.

2. If the group members like and trust each other more, the conflict has been constructive.

3. If *all* the members of the group are satisfied with the results of the conflict, the conflict has been constructive.

4. If the members of the group have improved their ability to resolve future conflicts with one another, the conflict has been constructive.

Conflicts are a pervasive and inevitable part of any group, and can lead to growth and development of the group as well as of each individual member. Because of this it is important to learn the skills involved in handling conflicts constructively. If a group puts emphasis on avoiding conflicts, resolving them prematurely, or stifling any discussion of differences, serious difficulties will arise within the relationships among group members and the group's effectiveness and productivity will suffer. Unless a group is able to withstand the stress of a conflict among members, it is not likely to last very long. The objectives of this chapter and the following one, therefore, are (1) to communicate how conflicts may be managed in constructive ways and (2) to provide some practice in managing conflicts constructively.

QUIZ

Check your reading of this section by answering the following questions. Answers are on page 277.
Match the following types of conflict with their definitions:

___ 1. There are opposing forces toward stability and change within a person.

___ 2. One person's ideas, information, conclusions, or opinions are incompatible with another's.

___ 3. Incompatible ideas exist simultaneously within a person's mind.

___ 4. Incompatible activities are based on differences in needs, scarcities of resources, or competition for rewards.

a. Controversy
b. Conflict of interest
c. Developmental conflicts
d. Conceptual conflicts

True   False   **5.** Conflict can and should be avoided whenever possible.

True   False   **6.** Conflicts are usually destructive to a group.

True   False   **7.** A conflict exists whenever incompatible activities occur.

True   False   **8.** Lack of conflict is a sign of a healthy group.

True   False   **9.** Ignoring conflicts usually causes them to dissipate and go away.

True   False   **10.** Conflicts that are not openly expressed and constructively resolved will be expressed indirectly and persist.

True   False   **11.** It is not possible to teach people how to deal with conflicts effectively.

True   False   **12.** Conflicts are valuable and even necessary to a group.

True   False   **13.** A conflict uses up energy and thus decreases a group's ability to work effectively.

True   False   **14.** Conflicts can bring about better decision-making.

True   False   **15.** Conflicts are destructive to relationships.

True   False   **16.** Conflicts promote higher levels of cognitive and moral reasoning.

True   False   **17.** Conflicts help you understand what you are like as a person.

18. Conflict has been constructive if (choose four):
    a. Relationships are stronger.
    b. The group has dissolved.
    c. Group members like and trust each other more.
    d. Most group members are satisfied with the results.
    e. All group members are satisfied with the results.
    f. Future conflict resolution ability is improved.

YOUR BEHAVIOR IN CONTROVERSIES EXERCISE (I)

This exercise has two purposes: (1) to make you more aware of your typical actions when you are involved in a controversy and (2) to make your group more aware of the patterns of behavior of its members when they are involved in a controversy. The procedure is as follows:

1. Working by yourself, complete the following questionnaire.

2. Using the scoring table that follows the questionnaire, determine your score and then the group average for each of the controversy-managing strategies.

3. Discuss with the other members what strategies are used most frequently in your group and how controversies among members can be managed more constructively. Then write a description of the pattern your group exhibits in managing controversies among members. Finally, write a description of how this controversy pattern may be improved.

Understanding My Controversy Behavior

Each of the following questions describes an action taken during a controversy. On a sheet of paper write down the numbers 1 through 30 in a column at the left-hand side of the page. For each question put a *5* if you *always* behave that way, *4* if you *frequently* behave that way, *3* if you *occasionally behave that way, 2* if you *seldom* behave that way, and *1* if you *never* behave that way.

1. When I disagree with other group members, I insist that they change their opinions to match mine.
2. If someone disagrees with my ideas and opinions, I feel hurt and rejected.
3. I often infer that persons who disagree with me are incompetent and ignorant.
4. When others disagree with me, I try to view the issue from all points of view.
5. I try to avoid individuals who argue with me.
6. When others disagree with me, I view it as an interesting opportunity to learn and to impove the quality of my ideas and reasoning.
7. When I get involved in an argument with others, I become more and more certain that I am correct and argue more and more strongly for my own point of view.
8. When others disagree with my ideas, I get hostile and angry at them.
9. When I disagree with others, I am careful to communicate respect for them as persons while I criticize their ideas.
10. I am careful to always paraphrase thinking and feelings of others when they present ideas and opinions that are different from mine.
11. When others disagree with me, I generally keep my ideas and opinions to myself.
12. When others disagree with me, I encourage them to express their ideas and opinions fully, and seek to clarify the differences between their position and perspective and mine.
13. I view my disagreements with others as opportunities to see who ''wins'' and who ''loses.''
14. I often insult those who criticize my ideas and opinions.
15. When another person and I disagree, I carefully communicate, ''I appreciate you, I am interested in your ideas, but I disagree with your current position.''
16. When others disagree with me, I keep thinking of my ideas and opinions so that I do not forget them or get confused.
17. I am careful not to share my ideas and opinions when I think others may disagree with them.
18. When I disagree with others, I listen carefully to their ideas and opinions and change my mind when doing so is warranted by their information and reasoning.
19. When others and I disagree, I try to overpower them with my facts and reasoning.
20. I tend to dislike those who disagree with my ideas and opinions.

21. When I am disagreeing with and criticizing others' ideas and opinions, I let them know that I like them as persons.

22. I try to view the situation and issue from my opponent's shoes when involved in a disagreement about ideas and opinions.

23. I refuse to get into an argument with anyone.

24. When others disagree with me, I try to clarify the differences among our ideas and opinions, clarify the points of agreement, and seek a creative integration of all our ideas and information.

25. When others and I disagree, I have to convince them that I am right and they are wrong.

26. When others disagree with my ideas and opinions, it means that they are angry with me and dislike me.

27. While I am disagreeing with others I let them know that I appreciate their ability to present a challenging and thought-provoking position.

28. When I am involved in an argument, I restate and summarize the opposing positions.

29. When others disagree with me I stay very quiet and try to avoid them in the future.

30. When I am involved in an argument, I never forget that we are trying to make the best decision possible by combining the best of all our facts and reasoning.

Scoring

Write your answer for each question in the space provided and total your answers for each controversy-managing strategy. The higher the total score for each controversy strategy, the more frequently you tend to use that strategy; the lower the total score for each controversy strategy, the less frequently you tend to use it. Add the scores of all group members for each strategy and divide by the number of members in the group. This will give your group average for each strategy.

Win-Lose	Rejection	Confirmation	Perspective-Taking	Withdrawal	Problem-Solving
___ 1.	___ 2.	___ 3.*	___ 4.	___ 5.	___ 6.
___ 7.	___ 8.	___ 9.	___ 10.	___ 11.	___ 12.
___ 13.	___ 14.	___ 15.	___ 16.*	___ 17.	___ 18.
___ 19.	___ 20.	___ 21.	___ 22.	___ 23.	___ 24.
___ 25.	___ 26.	___ 27.	___ 28.	___ 29.	___ 30.
___ Total	___ Total	___ Total	___ Total	___ Total	___ Total

* Reverse the scoring on this question by substituting 1 for 5, 2 for 4, and so on.

THE NATURE OF CONTROVERSY

Participation, involvement, controversy, and creative problem solving are all closely related. To define clear, cooperative goals to which members are committed, to make effective decisions, to communicate effectively, to develop distributed leadership—all require the active participation of every member in the group. Involved participation results in the full use of the group's resources and in member commitment to the implementing of decisions. Widespread participation means that different ideas, opinions, beliefs, and information will surface, which in turn means that controversies among group members will occur. Within any group conflicts among the ideas and opinions of group members are inevitable. Such controversies are a necessary condition for creative insights and high-quality decisions.

Controversy is a form of conflict among group members. In most conflicts both substantive issues and personal emotions are involved. In a group the sources of conflict over substantive issues are differences in information, beliefs, opinions, assumptions, and ideas. Such conflicts are labeled controversies because they involve disagreement within a problem-solving framework in which members of a group are trying to define, diagnose, and solve a problem. A *controversy* exists when one group member's ideas, information, conclusions, theories, and opinions are incompatible with those of another and the two then seek to reach an agreement. The conflict resides in the two members' attempts to reach a common position. Decisions are by their very nature controversies, as alternative solutions are suggested and debated

in most decision making. Basically, a decision represents the ending of a controversy by a particular course of action.

Controversy among group members is essential, as it is primarily through controversy that involvement, creativity, commitment to task accomplishment and group maintenance, and high-quality decisions evolve. In this chapter we concentrate on the productive management of controversies among group members, a process that increases a group's effectiveness in making creative, high-quality decisions that members will commit themselves to implementing and that will improve the problem-solving effectiveness of the group.

STRANDED IN THE DESERT EXERCISE

There is nothing quite as beautiful as a desert night. And there are few places more dangerous to be stranded than the desert during the night or day. In such a situation effective decision making is a matter of life or death, and since the emotional content of the arguments over what a stranded group should do will be high, skills in managing controversies constructively are essential. The purpose of this exercise is to examine the dynamics of controversy and its effects on the decision making of a group caught in a survival dilemma. The materials needed for the exercise are a description of the situation, a group decision form, a postdecision questionnaire, a summary table, a controversy-observation form, and a constructive-controversy checklist. Approximately one and a half hours are needed for the exercise. The procedure for the coordinator is as follows:

1. Introduce the exercise by stating its objective and reviewing the overall procedure and tasks.
2. Form groups of six. Ideally, the total number of groups should be divisible by five. One member from each group should volunteer to be an observer. The observer's role is to record the nature of each member's participation in the group, using the accompanying observation form. Each observer needs two copies of this form.
3. Introduce the situation, have the groups read the description of the situation, and assign each group one of these five basic positions:
   a. Your position is that the group members have to walk to the nearest ranch if they are to survive. Plan carefully the best procedure for doing so. Select the five or six possessions of the group that are most important for implementing your plan and rank them from *1* (the most important) to *5* or *6* (the least important).
   b. Your position is that the group members have to gather food and water if they are to survive. Plan carefully the best procedure for doing so. Select the five or six possessions of the group that are most important for implementing your plan and rank them from *1* (the most important) to *5* or *6* (the least important).
   c. Your position is that the group members have to signal search planes and vehicles if they are to survive. Plan carefully the best procedure for doing so. Select the five or six possessions of the group that are most important for implementing your plan and rank them from *1* (the most important) to *5* or *6* (the least important).

d. Your position is that the group members have to protect themselves from the heat of the day and the cold of the night if they are to survive. Plan carefully the best procedure for doing so. Select the five or six possessions of the group that are most important for implementing your plan and rank them from *1* (the most important) to *5* or *6* (the least important).

e. Your position is that the group members must stay by the wreck and keep physical movement to a minimum if they are to survive. Plan carefully the best procedure for doing so. Select the five or six possessions of the group that are most important for implementing your plan and rank them from *1* (the most important) to *5* or *6* (the least important).

4. Instruct the groups to build as good a rationale for their position as possible. Give them twenty minutes to do so.

5. Form new groups of five by taking one participant from each of the previous groups and placing them together in a new group. All participants should now be in a new group, and each member in a group should be representing a different position. Assign a group to each observer. The observer's role is to record the nature of each member's participation on a copy of the controversy-observation form.

6. Instruct the new groups to read the situation description and then rank the twelve possessions of the group from *1* (the most important possession for the survival of the group members) to *12* (the least important possession). The group is to derive one ranking to which every member agrees. Moreover, every member should be able to explain why each item is ranked where it is. There is a correct ranking in Appendix D according to which the group's ranking will be evaluated. Give the groups thirty minutes to decide on their ranking. After twenty-five minutes announce that they have five minutes left.

7. Instruct participants to complete the postdecision questionnaire. Then have the observers determine the group mean for each question in the questionnaire while you inform the class of the correct ranking of the twelve items (see page 484 in Appendix D).

8. In front of the whole class compile the results for each group the summary table.

9. Instruct each group to discuss its experiences, using:
   a. the decision and questionnaire results.
   b. the information collected by the observers.
   c. the impressions of the group members.
   d. the constructive-controversy checklist.

The following questions may help the groups discuss how they managed the controversy:

   a. How did the group manage disagreements among its members? (Use the checklist for constructive controversy as a guide.)
   b. From its experience, what conclusions can the group make about the constructive handling of controversies?
   c. Did the opinions of group members change as a result of the group's discussion during the ranking task? Did members gain insight into other points of view? Did they learn new things about survival in the desert?
   d. What did members learn about themselves and other group members? How did each member react to the controversy?

10. Have each group share its conclusions about the constructive management of controversy with the rest of the class.

Stranded in the Desert Situation

You are one of the members of a geology club that is on a field trip to study unusual formations in the New Mexico desert. It is the last week in July. You have been driving over old trails, far from any road, in order to see out-of-the-way formations. At about 10:30 A.M. the specially equipped minibus in which your club is riding overturns, rolls into a twenty-foot ravine, and burns. The driver and professional adviser to the club are killed. The rest of you are relatively uninjured.

You know that the nearest ranch is approximately forty-five miles east of where you are. There is no closer habitation. When your club does not report to its motel that evening you will be missed. Several persons know generally where you are, but because of the nature of your outing they will not be able to pinpoint your whereabouts.

The area around you is rather rugged and very dry. There is a shallow water hole nearby, but the water is contaminated by worms, animal feces and urine, and several dead mice. You heard from a weather report before you left that the temperature would reach 108 degrees, making the surface temperature 128 degrees. You are all dressed in lightweight summer clothing and you all have hats and sunglasses.

While escaping from the minibus each member of your group salvaged a couple of items; there are twelve in all. Your group's task is to rank these twelve items according to their importance to your survival, starting with *1* for the most important and proceeding to *12* for the least important.

You may assume that the number of club members is the same as the number of persons in your group and that the group has agreed to stick together.

Stranded in the Desert Decision Form

Rank the following items according to their importance to your survival, starting with ''1'' for the most important and proceeding to ''12'' for the least important:

_____ Magnetic compass
_____ 20 ft. by 20 ft. piece of heavy-duty, light-blue canvas
_____ Book, *Plants of the Desert*
_____ Rearview mirror
_____ Large knife
_____ Flashlight (four battery size)
_____ One jacket per person
_____ One transparent, plastic ground cloth (6 ft. by 4 ft.) per person
_____ .38-caliber loaded pistol
_____ One two-quart plastic canteen per person, full of water
_____ Accurate map of the area
_____ Large box of kitchen matches

Stranded in the Desert Postdecision Questionnaire

1. To what extent did other members of the group listen to, and understand your ideas?
    Not at all   1 : 2 : 3 : 4 : 5 : 6 : 7 : 8 : 9   Completely

2. How much influence do you feel you had on the group's decision?
    None at all   1 : 2 : 3 : 4 : 5 : 6 : 7 : 8 : 9   Complete

3. To what extent do you feel committed to, and responsible for the group's decision?
    Not at all   1 : 2 : 3 : 4 : 5 : 6 : 7 : 8 : 9   Completely

4. To what extent are you satisfied with your group's performance?
    Very dissatisfied   1 : 2 : 3 : 4 : 5 : 6 : 7 : 8 : 9   Very satisfied

5. How much did you learn about the issue under discussion?
    Nothing at all   1 : 2 : 3 : 4 : 5 : 6 : 7 : 8 : 9   A great deal

6. Write two adjectives describing the way you now feel.   _____

Constructive-Controversy Checklist

____ **1.** There was no winner or loser, only a successful, creative, and productive solution. The cooperativeness of group members should outweigh by far their competitiveness.

____ **2.** Disagreements among members' positions were initiated.

____ **3.** All members actively participated in the group discussions, sharing their information, conclusions, and perspectives.

____ **4.** Every member's contributions were listened to, respected, and taken seriously.

____ **5.** Effective communication skills were used, including paraphrasing and other listening skills and "I" messages and other sending skills.

____ **6.** Issues and problems were viewed from all available perspectives.

____ **7.** Group members criticized ideas and positions, not individuals. Members disagreed with each other while confirming each other's competence.

____ **8.** Group members viewed disagreement as an interesting situation from which something could be learned, not as personal rejection or a sign that they were being perceived as incompetent or ignorant.

____ **9.** There was appropriate pacing of differentiation and integration of member's positions. Differentiation took place first, followed by integration.

____ **10.** Emotions were allowed and members were encouraged to express them.

____ **11.** The rules of rational argument were followed. Members presented organized information to support their positions, reasoned logically, and changed their minds when others presented persuasive and convincing arguments and proof.

____ **12.** The arguments of all members were given equal consideration, regardless of how much formal power a member had.

Summary Table: Response to Postdecision Questionnaire

Group	Group Score	Understanding	Influence	Commitment	Satisfaction	Learning	Feelings
1							
2							
3							
4							

Determine the group means from the questionnaire responses and record them in the appropriate column, except for the first and the last columns. In the "Feelings" column put representative adjectives from the questionnaires.

Controversy-Observation Form

Behaviors	Participants					
Contributes ideas and opinions						
Asks others for their ideas and opinions						
Emphasizes mutual goals						
Emphasizes win-lose competition						
Asks others for proof, facts, and rationale						
Paraphrases, summarizes						
Criticizes and disagrees with others' ideas						
Criticizes other members as persons						
Differentiates positions						
Integrates positions						
Other						

Insert the name of each group member above the columns. Then record the frequency with which each member engages in each behavior.

WHO SHOULD GET THE PENICILLIN EXERCISE

The purpose of this exercise is to examine the dynamics of controversy within the context of a social-studies lesson. The materials needed for the exercise are a description of the situation, a briefing sheet for the military point of view, a briefing sheet for the medical point of view, a postdecision questionnaire, a summary table, a controversy-observation form, and a constructive-controversy checklist. (The last four items are the same as in the previous exercise, and are also used in the following three exercises.) Approximately one and a half hours are needed for the exercise. The procedure for the coordinator is as follows:

1. Introduce the exercise by stating its objective and reviewing the overall procedure.
2. Form groups of five members. One member from each group should volunteer to be an observer. The observer's role is to record the nature of each member's participation in the group, using the controversy-observation form.
3. Divide the remaining four members of each group into two pairs. Give one pair a copy of the medical viewpoint and the other pair a copy of the military viewpoint.
4. Introduce the situation. Instruct the pairs to build as good a rationale for their assigned position as they can in fifteen or twenty minutes, using the information on the briefing sheet as a guide.
5. Instruct the pairs to meet together as a group of four. The group is to come to a decision that all four members can agree to. The decision should reflect the best reasoning of the entire group. The group discussion should follow these steps:
   a. Each pair presents its position as forcefully and persuasively as it can while the opposing pair takes notes and clarifies anything the two members do not fully understand.
   b. Have an open discussion in which members of each pair: (1) argue forcefully and persuasively for their position, presenting as many facts as they can to support it; (2) listen critically to members of the opposing pair, asking them for the facts that support their point of view.
   This is a complex issue and members need to know both sides in order to come to a thoughtful decision.
6. Instruct the pairs to reverse their perspectives by switching sides and arguing for the opposite point of view as forcefully and persuasively as possible. Members should see if they can think of any new facts that the opposing pair did not present in support of its position, and should elaborate on that position.
7. Instruct the groups to come to a joint decision by:
   a. summarizing the best arguments for both points of view.
   b. detailing the facts they know about World War II and the African campaign.
   c. achieving consensus among the members.
   d. organizing the rationale supporting the decision that they will present to the rest of the class. They should be ready to defend the validity of their decision to groups who may have come to the opposite decision.
8. Instruct participants to complete the postdecision questionnaire. Then have the observers determine the group mean for each question.

9. Summarize the decision of each group in front of the entire class. Then summarize the results of the postdecision questionnaire, using the summary table.

10. Instruct each group to discuss their experience, using:

    a. the decision and questionnaire results.

    b. the information collected by the observers.

    c. the impressions of the group members.

    d. the constructive-controversy checklist.

The following questions may help the groups discuss how they managed the controversy:

    a. How did the group manage disagreements among its members? (Use the checklist for constructive controversy as a guide.)

    b. From its experience, what conclusions can the group make about the constructive handling of controversies?

    c. Did the opinions of the group members change as a result of the group's discussion? Did members gain insight into the other point of view through the perspective-reversal procedure? Did members learn anything new about World War II?

    d. What did members learn about themselves and other group members? How did each member react to the controversy?

11. Have each group share its conclusions about the constructive management of controversy with the rest of the class.

Who Should Get the Penicillin Exercise Situation

In 1943 penicillin, which is used for the prevention of infection, was in short supply among the U.S. armed forces in North Africa. Decisions had to be made whether to use this meager supply for the thousands of hospitalized victims of veneral disease or for the thousands of victims of battle wounds at the front. If you were a member of a team of medical and military personnel, whom would you use the penicillin for?

____ victims of veneral disease

____ victims of battle wounds

Share your position and rationale with your group. Stick to your guns unless logically persuaded otherwise. At the same time, help your group achieve consensus on this issue.

Briefing Sheet: The Medical Viewpoint: Who Should Get the Penicillin Exercise

Your position is to give the penicillin to the battle-wounded. Whether or not you agree with this position, argue for it as strongly and as honestly as you can, using arguments that make sense and are rational. Be creative and invent new supporting arguments. Seek out information; ask members of other groups who may know the answers to your questions. Remember to learn the rationale for both your position and the military position. Challenge the military position; think of loopholes in its logic; demand facts and information that back up its arguments.

1. Our responsibility is to treat the wounded and save as many lives as possible. Without the penicillin many of the wounded will die needlessly. Minor wounds will get infected and become major, life-threatening wounds.

2. Our strategies must be based on the premise that human life is sacred. If one person dies needlessly, we have failed in our responsibility. The soldiers who have sacrificed so much to help us win the war must be treated with all the care, concern, and resources we can muster. Our soldiers must be able to fight harder than the German soldiers.

3. Troop morale is vital. Nothing raises troop morale as much as the men's knowledge that if they are wounded they will receive top-notch medical treatment.

4. Morale at home is vital. People must make sacrifices to produce the goods and materials we need to win the war. Nothing raises morale at home more than knowing that sons and brothers are receiving the most effective medical care that is humanly possible. It would be devastating for word to reach the United States that we were needlessly letting soldiers die for lack of medical care.

5. Even though we are at war, we must not lose our humanity. It will do no good to defeat Germany if we become Nazis in the process.

6. At this point the war is going badly in North Africa. Rommel and the German army are cutting through our lines like butter. We are on the verge of being pushed out of Africa, in which case we will lose the war. Rommel must be stopped.

7. Fresh troops and supplies are unavailable. The German submarines control the Atlantic, and we cannot get troop ships or supply ships into African ports. We have to make due with what we have.

8. Penicillin is a wonder drug that will save countless lives if it is used to treat the wounded.

Briefing Sheet: The Military Viewpoint:
Who Should Get the Penicillin Exercise

Your position is to give the penicillin to the VD patients. Whether or not you agree with this position, argue for it as strongly and as honestly as you can, using arguments that make sense and are rational. Be creative and invent new supporting arguments. Seek out information that supports your position. If you do not have needed information, ask members of other groups who may. Remember to learn the rationale for both your position and the medical position. Challenge the medical position; think of loopholes in its logic; demand facts and information that back up its arguments.

1. Our responsibility is to win the war for our country at all costs. If we lose Africa, we will lose Europe to Hitler, and eventually we will be fighting in the United States.

2. Our strategies to win must be based on the premise of "the greatest good for the greatest number." We may have to sacrifice soldiers in order to win the war, save our democracy, and free Europe.

3. Troop morale is vital. Our soldiers must be able to fight harder than the German soldiers. Nothing raises troop morale like seeing fresh troops arrive at the front.

4. Morale at home is vital. People must make sacrifices to produce the goods and materials we need to fight the war. Nothing raises morale at home like hearing of

battles won and progress being made in winning the war. Victories give our people at home more dedication.

5. At this point, the war is going badly in North Africa. Rommel and the German army are cutting through our lines like butter. We are on the verge of being pushed out of Africa, in which case we will lose the war. Rommel must be stopped at all costs!

6. Penicillin is a wonder drug that will send VD into remission, and within twenty-four hours the VD patients will be free from pain and able to function effectively on the battlefield.

FALLOUT SHELTER EXERCISE

The purpose of this exercise is to provide a decision-making situation in which controversy will occur. The procedure for the exercise is as follows:

1. Form groups of six. One member should volunteer to be an observer. The observer should use the Conflict Observation Form on page 242.

2. Each group member individually completes the Fallout Shelter Ranking Task.

3. The group decides by consensus on the best ranking possible on the Fallout Shelter items. There should be one ranking for the group, every member should agree with the ranking, and be able to explain the rationale behind the ranking of each item.

4. Members complete the Post-Decision Questionnaire. Compute the group means for each question and place them in the summary table.

5. Score the accuracy of the group's ranking by comparing it with the experts' ranking on page 486 in Appendix D. Find the absolute difference between the group's ranking and the experts' ranking for each item and add them together. The lower the score the more accurate the group's ranking.

6. Using the observer's information, the post-decision questionnaire results, the members' impressions, and the accuracy score for the ranking, discuss the way in which controversy was managed in the group. The constructive controversy checklist and the discussion questions given on page 240 may be helpful. The group should write down its conclusions about the constructive management of controversy.

7. Groups should share their conclusions with the entire class.

Fallout Shelter Exercise: Ranking Task

The possibility of a nuclear war has been announced and the alert signal has been sounded. You and the members of your group have access to a small basement fallout shelter. When the attack warning signal is announced, you must immediately go to the shelter. In the meantime, you must decide what to take with you to help you survive during and after the attack. You are outside the immediate blast areas. The greatest danger facing you is from radioactive fallout. In order to help in your decision making, rank the following items in order of their importance to your survival in the shelter:

____ one large and one small garbage can with lids
____ broom

_____ containers of water

_____ blankets

_____ canned heat stove

_____ matches and candles

_____ canned and dried foods

_____ liquid chlorine bleach

_____ vaporizing liquid fire extinguisher

_____ flashlight and batteries

_____ battery powered radio

_____ soap and towels

_____ first-aid kit with iodine and medicines

_____ cooking and eating utensils

_____ geiger counter

CONTROVERSY: PROCESS AND OUTCOMES

> Have You Learned Lessons Only Of
>   Those Who Admired You, And
>   Were Tender With You, And
>   Stood Aside For You?
> Have You Not Learned Great
>   Lessons From Those Who
>   Braced Themselves Against
>   You, And Disputed The
>   Passage With You?
>
> Walt Whitman, 1860

Effective problem solving and decision making cannot take place without conflicts over ideas and opinions. For any group to work productively toward goal accomplishment and group maintenance its members must correct, resist, differ from, and oppose one another. Most groups waste the benefits of disputes, but every effective group thrives on what controversy has to offer.

If managed effectively, controversies can increase the motivation of group members, facilitate perspective taking, promote higher levels of cognitive reasoning, increase the mastery and retention of relevant information, spark creativity, increase the quality of problem solving, and promote higher morale and satisfaction among group members. There have been a number of recent reviews of the research on controversy and a couple of new studies with important findings (Johnson, 1979, 1980; Johnson and Johnson, 1979; Lowrey and Johnson, 1981; Smith, Johnson, and Johnson, 1981). For the specific references attesting to these benefits of controversy, see those reviews and articles.

The process by which controversy sparks the above outcomes is outlined in Figure 6.1. During a constructive controversy group members move from

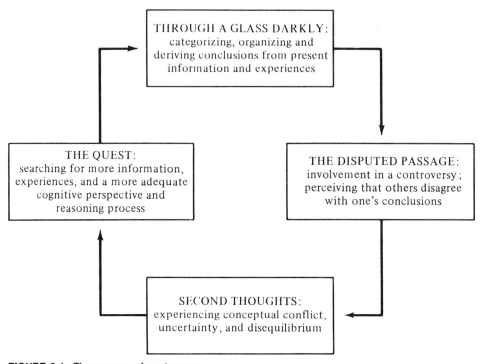

FIGURE 6.1 The process of controversy.

their original partial, incomplete understanding (the problem seen through a glass darkly), to the disputed passage, to second thoughts, to the quest, and back again to a conclusion based on seeing the problem through a glass somewhat less darkly. More specifically, the group members will move:

1. from an initial conclusion based on current experiences and information,
2. to having that conclusion challenged by other group members as they present opposing viewpoints and positions,
3. to experiencing a state of internal conceptual conflict, uncertainty, and disequilibrium.
4. to actively seeking more information, new experiences, and a more adequate cognitive perspective and process of reasoning about the problem in hopes of resolving their uncertainty,
5. to reaching a new or reorganized conclusion that takes into account the reasoning and perspectives of others.

This process promotes a number of important outcomes for groups, as long as certain conditions are met that keep the discussion of the controversy constructive.

FIGURE 6.2 The process of controversy.

Outcomes of Controversy

1. motivation. Two aspects of motivation are affected by the occurrence of controversy among group members: the immediate search for more information about the problem being discussed and the long-term search for such information. The immediate search for more information is prompted by conceptual conflict and epistemic curiosity. Controversy among group members creates conceptual conflict, which in turn leads to epistemic curiosity. *Conceptual conflict* exists when two ideas do not seem compatible or when information being received does not seem to fit with what one already knows (Berlyne, 1957, 1966). Disagreement with another person can be a source of conceptual conflict that provokes attempts to explore the other person's ideas and perspective. The greater the disagreement among group members, the greater the conceptual conflict, uncertainty, and *epistemic curiosity*—an active search for more information, new experiences, and a more adequate cognitive perspective and process of reasoning in hopes of resolving the uncertainty.

The long-term search for more information is reflected in the continuing motivation of group members to learn more about the issue being discussed. Thus, even after the group makes a decision members will be interested in learning more about the issues discussed.

2. perspective taking. In resolving controversies group members need to be able to both comprehend the information being presented by their opposition and understand the cognitive perspective their opposition is using to organize and interpret the information. A *cognitive perspective* consists of (a) the cognitive organization being used to give meaning to a member's knowledge and (b) the structure of the member's reasoning. A number of studies have found that engaging in a controversy increases the accuracy of the participants' understanding of each other's perspectives. As we will see in the next chapter, perspective taking is an important aspect of resolving conflicts constructively.

3. cognitive reasoning. Cognitive-development theorists have posited that repeated interpersonal controversies in which group members are forced again and again to take cognizance of the perspectives of others, promotes cognitive and moral development, the ability to think logically, and the reduction of egocentric reasoning. In reaching decisions that effectively solve important problems, group members need to reason in the most effective and sophisticated manner possible. There is considerable evidence that controversy promotes the transition to higher stages of cognitive and moral reasoning.

4. mastery and retention of material. Effective problem solving requires that group members retain considerable information about the problem and the history and current influences on various possible solutions. There is evidence that controversies among group members result in greater mastery and retention of the information relevant to the problem solving. For one thing, group members engage in considerable verbal rehearsal of what they know and listen carefully to what their opposition knows. Furthermore, group members who have engaged in a controversy are better able to generalize the principles they learn to a wider variety of situations.

5. creativity. Controversy is an important aspect of gaining creative insight: by seeing a problem from a different perspective one can reformulate it in a way that lets new orientations to a solution emerge. Controversy in problem solving increases the number of ideas, quality of ideas, feelings of stimulation and enjoyment, and originality of expression. Controversy also results in more creative problem solutions. It encourages group members to dig into a problem, raise issues, and settle them in ways that show the benefits of using a wide range of ideas. At the same time, controversy results in a high degree of emotional involvement in and commitment to solving the problems the group is working on.

6. high quality of problem solving. Not only does controversy result in a higher-quality problem solution and decision, but disagreements within a group have been found to provide a greater amount of information and variety of facts, and a change in the salience of known information that in turn results in shifts in judgment. In other words, open-minded and high-quality problem solving seems to result from controversy within a group.

7. cohesion. Members of groups that engage in controversy, in comparison with members of groups that avoid controversy, generally are more satisfied with their group, like being in the group better, and like the other group members more. Group members feel more accepted and supported by group-mates when controversy is emphasized within their group. They like controversy and find it increases their interest in and liking for the problem solving engaged in by the group.

Conditions Determining the Constructiveness of Controversy

Although disputes among group members concerning their ideas, information, conclusions, theories, and opinions can operate in a benefial way, they will not do so under all conditions. As with all forms of conflict, the potential for either constructive or destructive outcomes is present in a controversy. Whether there are positive or negative consequences depends on the conditions under which the controversy occurs and the way in which it is managed. These conditions and procedures include: (1) the goal structure within which the controversy occurs, (2) the heterogeneity of group members, (3) the amount of relevant information distributed among group members, (4) the ability of members to disagree with each other without creating defensiveness, and (5) the perspective-taking skills of the members.

1. goal structure. Deutsch (1973) emphasizes that the context in which conflicts occur has important effects on whether the conflict turns out to be constructive or destructive. There are two possible contexts for controversy: cooperation and competition. There are several ways in which a cooperative context facilitates constructive controversy and a competitive context promotes destructive controversy (see Chapter 4 and Johnson and Johnson, 1975, 1978):

a. In order for controversy to be constructive, information must be accurately communicated. Communication of information is far more complete, accurate, encouraged, and utilized in a cooperative context than in a competitive context.

b. Constructive controversy requires a supportive climate in which group members feel safe enough to challenge each other's ideas. Cooperation provides a far more supportive climate than competition.

c. In order for controversy to be constructive, it must be valued. Cooperative experiences promote stronger beliefs that controversy is constructive.

d. Constructive controversy requires dealing with feelings as well as with ideas and information. There is evidence that cooperativeness is positively related and competitiveness is negatively related to the ability to understand what others are feeling and why they are feeling that way—the ability known as affective perspective taking.

e. How controversies are defined has a great impact on how constructively they are managed. Within a cooperative context controversies tend to be defined as problems to be solved jointly, whereas within a competitive context controversies tend to be defined as "win-lose" situations.

f. Constructive controversy requires a recognition of similarities between positions as well as differences. Group members participating in a controversy within a cooperative context identify more of the similarities between their positions than do members participating in a controversy within a competitive context.

2. heterogeneity among members. Differences among group members in personality, sex, attitudes, background, social class, reasoning strategies, cognitive perspectives, information, and skills lead to diverse organization and processing of present information and experiences, which in turn begins the cycle of controversy. More controversy occurs in heterogeneous than in homogeneous groups.

3. distribution of information. If controversy is to lead to effective group problem solving, group members must possess information that is relevant to the solution of the problem on which they are working. The more information a group has about a problem, the better their solutions tend to be. Having relevant information available, however, does not mean that it will be utilized. Members need the interpersonal and group skills necessary to ensure that all members contribute their relevant information and that the information is synthesized effectively.

4. skilled disagreement. In order for controversies to be managed constructively, group members need to be able to disagree with each other's ideas while confirming each other's personal competence. Disagreeing with others, while imputing that they are incompetent tends to increase their commitment to their own ideas and their rejection of one's ideas. Confirmation of opponents' competence, however, results in being better liked and in the opponents being less critical of one's ideas and more open-minded about them, more interested in learning more of one's ideas, and more willing to incorporate one's information and reasoning into their own analysis of the problem.

5. perspective-taking skills.   Perhaps the most important set of skills for exchanging information and opinions within a controversy are those of perspective taking. More information, both personal and impersonal, is disclosed when one is interacting with a person engaging in perspective-taking behaviors. Perspective-taking ability increases one's capacity to phrase messages so that they are easily understood by others, and to comprehend accurately the messages of others. Engaging in perspective-taking behaviors in conflicts results in increased understanding and retention of the opponent's information and perspective. Perspective taking facilitates the achievement of creative, high-quality solutions. Finally, perspective taking promotes more positive perceptions of the information-exchange process, fellow group members, and the group's work. To obtain a creative synthesis of all positions in a controversy, group members must obtain a clear understanding of all sides of the issues and an accurate assessment of their validity and relative merits. In order to do this fully, they must accurately perceive the frame of reference from which a person is viewing and analyzing the situation and problem.

THE "WIN–LOSE" VERSUS THE PROBLEM–SOLVING ORIENTATION

Competing with and defeating an opponent is one of the most widely recognized aspects of interpersonal interaction in our society. The language of business, politics, and even education is filled with "win-lose" terms. One "wins" a promotion or a raise, "beats" the opposition, "outsmarts" a teacher, puts competitors "in their place." In an environment that stresses winning it is no wonder that competitive behavior persists where it is not appropriate. It is not unusual in a group meeting for members to interrupt each other to voice their own ideas without listening to what the other members are saying, and to form power blocs in support of their position and in opposition to those of others. The original purpose of the group becomes overshadowed by the struggle to win.

Destructive controversies are characterized by an orientation on the part of the persons involved to "win" at the expense of the other group members, whose ideas are defeated and who therefore "lose." In a win-lose situation every action of other group members is seen in terms of one person dominating the others. The outcomes of a win-lose situation are predictable. Members tend to deny the legitimacy of the other members' interests and to consider only their own needs. They try to force the other members to give in while trying to augment their own power and undermine that of the others. The loser in a win-lose situation has little motivation to carry out the actions agreed upon, resents the winner, and has no chance to contribute his resources to the problem-solving process. The winner finds it hard to enforce the implementation of her ideas. Cohesion decreases and the group has severe maintenance problems. Distrust is rampant, communication limited and inaccurate, and group members are hostile toward one another.

If any group is to function effectively, cooperation among its members must be maintained at a high level. Without strong cooperation among the members, there is no coordination of behavior, no communication, no prolonged interaction. Cooperation is the most important and basic form of human interaction, and by far the most important aspect of effective groups. The competitive, win-lose way of dealing with controversy sabotages all aspects of group effectiveness by undercutting the cooperation needed among group members. The cooperative way of dealing with controversy, however, helps all aspects of group effectiveness. When controversy is approached from a problem-solving point of view, members tend to recognize the legitimacy of one another's interests and search for a solution accommodating the needs of all. They try to influence one another through persuasion, working to build up *mutual* power, not personal power.

Group members should always be concerned with finding a mutually satisfying course of action. This orientation is constructive because it (1) increases every member's motivation to implement the decisions of the group (through the principle of participation), (2) strengthens the chances of finding a high-quality solution, (3) develops critical-thinking skills, (4) lessens hostility while increasing amiability among group members, (5) requires no enforcement of group decisions, (6) cuts out the need for power to be exercised, (7) extends trust and promotes full and accurate communication, (8) aids group cohesion, and (9) results in everyone treating everyone else with respect. Nothing is more essential to a group than making sure that differences in opinions, ideas, values, beliefs, goals, and so on are all approached from a cooperative, problem-solving orientation, not a competitive, win-lose orientation.

VALUES AND BELIEFS

The constructive management of controversy within a group requires that members share a common set of values and beliefs about controversy. As we saw earlier, most persons in our society have a negative conception of controversy. They regard conflicts as something undesirable, as a sign of sickness in group functioning. Groups that fight together, however, not only stay together but function creatively and productively. Thus, group members must have a positive value system about fighting: they must see it as a productive way of handling conflicts. Verbal controversies are highly constructive and highly desirable. When group members fight according to a proper set of rules and norms they are able to improve their relationship with the group while enhancing group productivity and creativity. The positive values of controversies are four.

First, controversies are a natural and desirable part of any problem-solving situation. They should *not* be avoided or repressed. Controversies are inevitable if members are involved in the group's work and committed to high-quality task accomplishment and group maintenance. If differences in opinions, interests, and values are not dealt with directly, group task accomplishment and maintenance will deteriorate. Controversial discussion is a cooperative skill that requires at least two persons, and when it is handled successfully group members will be increasingly involved and committed to one another. Group discussion with a high rate of controversy is more productive than individual thinking. Since the goal is for the group (not the individual) to come up with creative, productive ideas, controversy is a highly desirable means for doing so. Working through differences of opinion may lead to more creative solutions to problems than could be achieved by any single person. All group members profit from effective controversies, in terms of both group goal accomplishment and better relationships among members.

Second, controversies can greatly reduce the natural tension and frustration that arises when individuals work together. Group members can interact with fewer inhibitions and avoidances. Fighting can provide a system for programming individual aggression. Almost everyone has aggressive feelings about other group members at one time or another, and fighting allows a person to express this aggression directly and constructively. Expressing hostile feelings is a good way to keep from withdrawing and to become emotionally involved in group work and in one's relationships with other members. Controversies allow for the expression of emotions such as anger and indignation that would interfere with group work if repressed. Feelings that are unresolved and are not dealt with make for biased, nonobjective judgments and actions. It is quite common for a person to refuse to accept a good idea because he dislikes the person who suggests it. Feelings that are unresolved affect a person's perception of events and information: such a person often denies, ignores, or distorts facts that are threatening or otherwise unpleasant and develops blind spots that end in misinterpretation of others' ideas and actions. Suppression of feelings can lead to personal barriers, irreversible conflicts, and a deterioration of relationships.

Third, controversies keep arguments up to date and help group members avoid being bothered by the past, which they cannot change. Group members who fight regularly and constructively need not carry gunnysacks full of grievances. All past conflicts have been dealt with so that they do not constrain working together and appreciating one another in the present.

Last, controversies bring information to group members about where they are, what is important to each of them, how group work can be bettered, and how their relationships can be improved. Opposition leads to greater understanding and closer relationships, not rejection and dislike.

NORMS AND RULES FOR CONSTRUCTIVE CONTROVERSY

Constructive controversy requires that a group agrees on norms and rules for managing disagreements among members' ideas, information, conclusions, theories, and opinions. There are no cookbook rules for making controversies productive, but the following guidelines can help group members argue more constructively and transform disagreement among themselves into a positive experience.

1. The context within which the controversy takes place should be cooperative, not competitive. There should be no winner and no loser, only a successful, creative, and productive solution to a problem. The emphasis should be on achieving the group's goals, not on dominating the group. Members should not argue over who is "right" and who is "wrong." The issue is not to establish who has the best answer but to make the best group decision possible by exploring different perspectives and integrating different information. All members should benefit equally from a constructive controversy. Statements such as "We are all in this together" and "Let's make the best possible decision" should dominate the group, not "I am right and you are wrong." When members begin to compete, the nature of the group's goals, the feeling of mutuality shared by members, and the complementary use of members' resources to ensure a collaborative and productive group should be highlighted.

2. Controversies among members should be initiated through such strategies as highlighting contrasting viewpoints, pointing out disagreements, trying to discover inadequacies in proposed solutions and reasoning, and promoting challenging tasks. Look for and initiate disagreements among members' ideas, information, theories, and conclusions.

3. Every member should take an active part in group discussions. Every members' ideas and feelings should be expressed openly and honestly without defensiveness. Every member should share her position and ideas in order to get comments and reactions from other members that will help improve the quality of group work. Members should follow up their ideas, spin creative fantasies about the issues under discussion, state their hunches about appropriate group action, insist on exploring the implications of their ideas, collect data that support their contentions, and plan arguments that will show the soundness of their ideas.

4. The response to one another's ideas and feelings should be such that everyone's contribution is valued, respected, and taken seriously. An enthusiastic hearing should be granted to all ideas. A warm, intense interest in all contributions should be communicated.

5. Open, honest, accurate, complete, and effective communication should be worked for continually. Good sending and receiving skills should be emphasized. Members should assume ownership of their ideas and feelings,

describe them clearly, phrase them in ways that other members can readily understand, ask for feedback by other members on their understanding of messages sent, make their nonverbal and verbal messages congruent, paraphrase other members' ideas and feelings accurately without making value judgments about them, view the messages of other members from their perspective, and negotiate the meaning of other members' messages. (See Johnson, 1981, for a full discussion of these skills and for skill-building exercises.)

6. Members who disagree with each other should achieve an understanding of both the position and the frame of reference of each other. Emphasis should be placed on viewing the issue under discussion from a variety of perspectives. Understanding the statements of another member is not enough; the frame of reference from which the member is speaking must also be clearly understood. The use of good listening skills such as paraphrasing and negotiating for meaning are helpful in gaining insight into other members' perspectives.

7. Group members should be critical of ideas, not of persons. Arguments should concern ideas, not personality traits. There should be nothing personal in disagreement. Members should be highly critical of each other's ideas while affirming each other's competence. When disagreeing with another member, group members should criticize ideas while communicating respect and appreciation for the member as a person. Any inference of incompetence or weakness and any hint of rejecting another member should be avoided. "I appreciate you, I am interested in your ideas, but I disagree with your current position" should be communicated rather than, "You are stupid and ignorant and I do not like you."

8. Members should not take personally other members' disagreements and rejection of their ideas. That other members disagree with one's ideas and conclusions should be taken as an interesting situation from which something can be learned, not as a personal attack. One should not say "Other members think I am stupid and do not like me," when one means to say "Other members see my ideas as incorrect and disagree with me." Members should never take disagreement with their ideas, information, theories, conclusions, and opinions as a personal rejection or a sign that other members view them as incompetent or ignorant. One must not confuse rejection of one's ideas and opinions with personal rejection. Members should separate the validity of one's thinking from one's competence and worth as a person.

9. Members should ensure that there are several cycles of differentiation (bringing out differences in positions) and integration (combining several positions into one new, creative position). Differentiation must come before integration is attempted:

a. *Differentiation* involves seeking out and clarifying differences among members' ideas, information, conclusions, theories, and opinions. It involves highlighting the differences among members' reasoning and seeking to understand fully what the different positions and perspectives are. All different points of view must be presented and explored thoroughly before new, creative solutions are sought.

b. *Integration* involves combining the information, reasoning, theories, and conclusions of the various group members so that all of them are satisfied. After it has differentiated positions the group needs to seek a new, creative position that synthesizes the thinking of all the members.

The group should never try to integrate members' positions before adequate differentiation has taken place. The potential for integration is never greater than the adequacy of the differentiation already achieved. Most controversies go through a series of differentiations and integrations.

10. Members should encourage one another to express their emotions during the debate, whether or not the emotions are positive or negative. Members should follow the guidelines for the effective communication of emotions detailed in Johnson (1981).

11. Members should follow the canon of rational argument. They should generate ideas, collect and organize relevant information, reason logically, and make tentative conclusions based on current understanding. Each member should present her perspective and the rationale for her position as well as her conclusions. At the same time, she should ask other members for proof that their analyses and conclusions are accurate. Members should keep an open mind, changing their conclusions and positions when other members are persuasive and convincing in their presentation of rationale, proof, and logical reasoning. The abilities to gather, organize, and present information, to debate, and to engage in rational argument are essential for the constructive management of controversies.

12. The group should balance the situational power of all members. Each member should have only one vote in determining what decision the group should make. Any inclination by group members to tell their boss what he wants to hear or to keep silent rather than openly disagree with a formal leader must be avoided. Contributions need to be evaluated on their soundness, not on the basis of who proposed them. Members who have relevant information and interesting ideas should be listened to, regardless of the amount of formal power they possess. Make sure that the formal leader is *not* saying "Everyone in favor say 'aye,' and everyone opposed say 'I quit.'" Situational power must be equalized in order for members to feel free to argue strongly for their point of view and position.

QUIZ

Check your reading of this section by answering the following questions. Answers are on page 277.

1. Name the seven outcomes which can result from constructive controversy within a group. Refer back to the chapter to check your answers.

   a. _____

   b. _____

   c. _____

   d. _____

   e. _____

   f. _____

   g. _____

True   False   **2.** Effective problem solving and decision making cannot take place without conflicts over ideas and opinions.

True   False   **3.** When a group makes a decision, any epistemic curiosity aroused by a controversy is usually cut off.

True   False   **4.** There is considerable evidence that controversy inhibits the transition to higher stages of cognitive and moral reasoning.

True   False   **5.** Group members who have engaged in controversy remember the information better and generalize the principles they learn to a wide variety of situations.

True   False   **6.** Controversy stifles creativity by discouraging different approaches to a problem.

True   False   **7.** Members of groups that engage in controversy generally dislike their group more than members of groups that avoid controversy.

True   False   **8.** If the goal structure of the group is cooperative, controversy will be more constructive than if the members are competitive.

True   False   **9.** Controversy occurs less in heterogenous than in homogenous groups.

True   False   **10.** Group members must have interpersonal skills needed to make all group members contribute relevant information if controversy is to lead to effective problem solving.

True   False   **11.** Disagreeing with people and putting them down tends to get them to give up their ideas.

True   False   **12.** In order to fully communicate in a conflict, both sides must correctly understand the point of view of the other.

True   False   **13.** In a win-lose situation, every action of the other group members is seen in terms of one person dominating the others.

True   False   **14.** In a win-lose situation, the loser has high motivation to carry out the group decision.

True   False   **15.** Cooperation is the most important aspect of effective groups.

True   False   **16.** Controversies are a natural and desirable part of any problem situation and should not be repressed.

True   False   **17.** Working through differences of opinion can lead to a more creative solution.

True   False   **18.** Controversies can better the relationships between group members.

True   False   **19.** The natural tension and frustration of working together can be greatly reduced through controversy.

True   False   **20.** Telling about hostile feelings is a way of withdrawing from the group.

True   False   **21.** Unresolved feelings affect a person's perceptions of what is going on in the group.

True   False   **22.** Controversy keeps the past from interfering with the present.

True   False   **23.** Controversy keeps group members informed on what can be improved in the group.

True   False   **24.** Group members who insist on exploring the implications of their ideas interfere with constructive resolution of controversy.

True   False   **25.** Never try to integrate members' positions before adequate differentiation has taken place.

True   False   **26.** Most controversies go through a series of differentiations and integrations.

Match the following terms with their definitions:

____ **27.** Active search for more information in order to resolve uncertainty.

____ **28.** Understanding the other person's point of view on an issue.

____ **29.** Incompatible ideas, information, conclusions, or opinions.

____ **30.** Information received does not fit information one already has.

a. Controversy
b. Conceptual conflict
c. Epistemic curiosity
d. Cognitive perspective-taking

31. Which of the following characteristics of a cooperative group encourage positive outcomes from controversy (choose six)?
   a. accurate communication
   b. prolonged communication
   c. supportive climate
   d. high valuing of controversy
   e. perspective on others' feelings
   f. win-lose definition
   g. problem solving definition
   h. identification of position similarities
   i. identification of position differences

32. When controversy is approached in a problem-solving way (choose three):
   a. group decisions must be enforced.
   b. members try to persuade each other.
   c. power needs to be used.
   d. the group tries to build up mutual power.
   e. hostility is decreased and liking is increased.
   f. trust and communication are decreased.

33. Pick out the guidelines for constructive controversy (choose seven):
   a. There can be no winner or loser.
   b. People who disagree should understand the position and frame of reference of the other.
   c. Putting ideas together should start as soon as differences appear.
   d. Everyone's contributions are valued and encouraged.
   e. Be critical of people, not of ideas.
   f. Work on using effective communication skills.
   g. Take disagreements as personal rejection.
   h. Power should be balanced among members.
   i. Stick to ideas; don't discuss emotions.
   j. People who disagree should be left alone to work it out.
   k. Context of controversy should be cooperative.
   l. Initiate and encourage disagreements among ideas.

AVOIDING CONTROVERSIES EXERCISE

People often find ingenious methods to keep from having to deal directly with controversies. How do you behave when you want to avoid a dispute? How do the other members of your group behave?

The following exercise is designed to produce feedback about how other group members see your behavior when you want to avoid a controversy. Its objective is for participants to examine their own behavior in controversies and disagreements. Understanding avoidance behavior, or how people avoid responding, can be as helpful as increasing their awareness of constructive behaviors. The procedure for the coordinator is as follows:

1. Introduce the exercise as a chance for each group member to get feedback from other group members on his behavior.
2. Tell each group member to place a sheet of newsprint on the wall with his name clearly written at the top.
3. Have group members walk around the room writing down their impressions on the newsprint of how each of the others behaves when he wants to avoid a controversy. You may wish to use the checklist below to start ideas.
4. Each member should classify himself according to the checklist below and then read the remarks other group members have written on his sheet.
5. Divide the participants into groups of three and have them discuss the content of the remarks written on their sheets, their own perceptions of their behavior, and the feelings generated by the exercise. Note that although the defenses against directly facing controversy are not helpful to the group and will promote destructive outcomes, they are at times very helpful and of constructive value to the individual. Participants should ask themselves whether there are ways to protect themselves without being harmful to the group.

Defenses Against Controversy

1. *Ostrich:* deny the controversy exists; refuse to see the potential or actual disagreement.
2. *Turtle:* withdraw from the issue and the persons disagreeing with you.
3. *Lemming:* give in and accept the other person's point of view or ideas.
4. *Weasel:* rationalize by stating that the issue is not important, that you really don't hold an opposing opinion, that the issue is one on which you have no expertise, and so on.
5. *Gorilla:* overpower the other members by forcing them to accept your ideas and point of view.
6. *Owl:* intellectualize about the issue and ideas so that all feelings and emotions are hidden.
7. *Sheep:* formulate, support, and conform to group norms forbidding the expression of opposition and disagreement in the group.

BELIEFS ABOUT CREATIVITY EXERCISE

The purpose of this exercise is to provoke a discussion concerning the nature of creativity. The procedure is as follows:

1. Working by yourself, answer the following questions about creativity.
   a. Creativity and intelligence are: (1) unrelated. (2) highly related to each other in the sense that creativity promotes cognitive development.

    b. Creativity is a: (1) stable trait that some persons are born with and others lack. (2) a process of problem solving characterized by an interaction between group members and the challenges of their environment.

    c. Creativity: (1) is at the same level across situations—a creative person is creative in every situation (2) varies a great deal from situation to situation, depending on the problem-solving process being used.

    d. Creativity is something that: (1) cannot be taught because it is an inborn trait. (2) can be taught because it is a problem-solving process.

    e. The role of the school is to: (1) discover or identify creative students and place them in accelerated programs so that their creativity is utilized. (2) develop creative competencies in all students by providing the needed challenges and teaching them the problem-solving skills necessary for a creative response.

2. Form heterogenous groups of six and arrive at a group consensus for each question.

3. Compare your group's answers with those of the other groups in the class.

CREATIVITY

Creativity is a *process* of bringing something new into existence. Group creativity results from productive controversy during the problem-solving process. The creative process consists of a sequence of overlapping phases:

1. Recognizing and experiencing a problem challenging enough to motivate members of a group to solve it.

2. Gathering the necessary knowledge and resources within the group and planning an intense, long-term effort to solve the problem.

3. Experiencing an incubation period during which group members feel frustration, tension, and discomfort due to their failure to produce an adequate solution to the problem and temporarily withdraw from the issue.

4. Seeing the problem from different perspectives and reformulating it in a way that lets new orientations to a solution emerge. This phase usually results from controversy among diverse points of view. The controversy produces a moment of insight or inspiration by one or more group members. The insight is often accompanied by intense emotional experiences of illumination and excitement and leads to the formulation of a tentative solution.

5. Elaborating, detailing, and testing the solution against reality.

6. Giving the validated solution to relevant audiences.

    There are several key elements in such a process of creative problem solving: motivation to persist in trying to solve a challenging problem, the availability of diverse information and viewpoints, controversy among persons with diverging ideas and perspectives, and open-mindedness in viewing the problem from diverse perspectives.

For the possibility of creativity to exist, group members need to be aroused to a level of motivation sufficient to sustain problem-solving efforts despite frustrations and dead ends (Deutsch, 1969). This level of motivation, however, cannot be so intense that it overwhelms members or keeps them too close to the problem. The motivation to persist is increased by both controversy and a group tradition supporting the view that with time and effort constructive solutions can be discovered or invented for seemingly insoluble problems. The more varied the members of a group, the more likely the group will arrive at a creative solution. Both male and female, lower-class and middle-class, white and minority, high-achieving and low-achieving persons should be placed in the same cooperative problem-solving groups so as to maximize the possibility of creative solutions being found.

Once diverse ideas and perspectives are available, they need to be presented so that they can be put together into new and varied patterns. As the differences among group member's perspectives and ideas are understood, the range of available solutions will broaden. The debate among group members in and of itself will tend to spark new ideas and approaches. As with all productive controversies, each group member needs the freedom, support, and self-confidence to express herself without being afraid of censure. The exchange of ideas has to be encouraged. And controversy has to be an exciting and accepted procedure for the group.

Disagreements, arguments, debates, and diverse information and ideas are all important aspects of gaining creative insight. There is evidence that such interpersonal interaction increases the number and quality of ideas, feelings of stimulation and enjoyment, and originality of expression in creative problem solving (Bahn, 1964; Bolen and Torrance, 1976; Dunnette, Campbell, and Jaastad, 1963; Triandis, Bass, Ewen, and Mikesele, 1963). And there is evidence that controversies result in more creative solutions and more member satisfaction, compared with group efforts that do not include controversies (Glidewell, 1953; Hoffman, Harburg, and Maier, 1962; Maier and Hoffman, 1964; Rogers, 1970). Controversies have been shown to encourage group members to dig into a problem, raise issues, and settle them in ways that show the benefits of a wide range of ideas being used. Controversies also result in a high degree of emotional involvement in and commitment to solving the problems the group is working on.

In order for group members to derive creative answers to problems they are working on, they must be allowed time to reflect. Instant answers should not be demanded. Creative thinking "is commonly typified by periods of intense application and periods of inactivity" (Treffinger et al., 1974, p. 21). After all sides of a controversy have been presented, group members should be allowed to think about solutions for a day or so before trying to put things together in new and varied patterns.

For controversy to result in creativity, group members must be open-minded about different beliefs, opinions, information, ideas, perspectives, and assumptions. Group discussion must be such that members do not feel threatened or under too much pressure (Deutsch, 1969; Rokeach, 1960; Stein, 1968). Feeling threatened prompts defensiveness and reduces both tolerance of ambiguity and receptiveness to the new and the unfamiliar. Too much tension leads to stereotyping of thought processes. Feeling threatened and under pressure prevents group members from becoming sufficiently detached from their original viewpoint to be able to see the problem from new perspectives.

Group members must seek out different perspectives and different ways of viewing the problem when analyzing it. The extent to which a member can receive, evaluate, and act on relevant information on its *own* merits (as opposed to viewing it only from his own perspective) defines the extent to which the student is *open-minded* (as opposed to being closed-minded) (Rokeach, 1960). Without seeing the problem from several perspectives, members will not be able to analyze it and synthesize various ideas so as to produce creative solutions. Controversy is an essential ingredient in discovering new perspectives on the problem being solved.

How do you tell if a group is open- or closed-minded? Closed-minded groups are characterized by: (1) emphasis on the differences between what they believe and what they do not believe; (2) denial of information that is contrary to what they believe; (3) the existence of contradictory beliefs that go unquestioned; (4) the discarding as irrelevant of similarities between what they believe and what they reject; and (5) avoidance of exploring differences in beliefs and distortion of information that does not fit their beliefs. Open-minded groups are characterized by (1) the seeking out of opposing and differing beliefs; (2) the discovery of new beliefs; (3) the remembering of information that disagrees with currently held beliefs; and (4) the organization of new beliefs that lead to the solution of the problem. Open-mindedness is an important aspect of controversy, creativity, and problem solving.

DEVELOPING AND FOSTERING CREATIVITY

From the process perspective, leaders are given the responsibility for developing creative skills and attitudes in group members and fostering creative problem-solving. Here is a set of procedures that can be used to promote creativity:

1. Using a cooperative goal structure, give members problems to be solved through the use of inquiry procedures.
2. Structure the cooperative groups as heterogenously as possible.
3. Promote controversy among ideas, opinions, information, theories, and perspectives.
4. Model curiosity and inquiry, the ability to shift perspectives, the recombin-

ing of already known facts into new combinations and relationships, and general open-mindedness.

5. Allow members time to reflect on their ideas after periods of intense work.

6. Encourage persistence in the face of failure to solve problems: do not take members off the hook by giving them answers. Let them struggle, and support such struggling. Communicate to them that creative individuals such as Einstein and Picasso experienced great difficulties before achieving insight.

7. Be enthusiastic about originality in thinking and problem solving. Reinforce it whenever you see it.

8. Introduce members to provocative ideas, books, persons, things, and procedures.

9. Encourage manipulation of objects and ideas.

10. Encourage members to immerse themselves in a specific area of interest if they become excited about it.

11. Communicate that creative insights are valuable by such procedures as having members keep a personal notebook of their new and important ideas.

David and Houtman (1968) are the authors of a book intended to teach creativity. They suggest four methods of generating novel ideas that can be taught: part changing, using a checkerboard figure, using a checklist, and finding something similar. The *part-changing method* involves group members in identifying the parts or attributes of something that might be changed. The following is an example:

> Four qualities of a chair are color, shape, size, and hardness. Invent a new kind of chair by listing fifteen different colors, ten different shapes, five sizes, and five grades of hardness. Try to think of different ideas, and do not worry about whether or not they are any good. Think of different ways to change each part of the chair. Use your imagination.

The *checkerboard method* involves making a checkerboard figure with spaces for entering words or phrases on the vertical and horizontal axes. Different sets of properties or attributes are listed on the axes. Then group members examine the interaction or combination of each pair of things or attributes. For example:

> Your group is to invent a new sport. Place materials and equipment along the top, horizontal axis and place the things the players do (such as running, batting, kicking, hanging from their knees) down the side or vertical axis. Then examine the combination of each item on each axis with all the other items on the other axis.

The *checklist method* involves developing and using checklists to make sure that something is not left out or forgotten. David and Houtman suggest a checklist that includes these procedures:

1. Change color.
2. Change size.
3. Change shape.
4. Use new or different material.
5. Add or subtract something.
6. Rearrange things.
7. Identify a new design.

A group can apply this checklist to any object or problem.

The *find-something-similar method* involves encouraging group members to come up with new ideas by thinking of other persons, animals, or social units in the world that perform the same acts the group wants to perform. Here is an example:

> Imagine your city has a parking problem. Find ideas for solving this problem by thinking of how bees, squirrels, ants, shoe stores, clothing stores, and so on store things.

Another technique designed to enhance the creativity of students is *synectics,* developed by William J. Gordon (1961). Gordon stresses the importance of psychological states in achieving creativity and the use of metaphor in achieving the proper psychological state. He suggests using three interrelated techniques for making the strange appear familiar and the familiar strange:

1. Personal analogy in which persons imagine how it feels to be part of the phenomenon they are studying. Asking them how they would feel if they were an incomplete sentence or if they were Paul Revere's horse are examples.
2. Direct analogy, in which group members are asked to think about a parallel situation in order to gain insight into what they are studying. Asking them to describe how a book is like a lightbulb or how a beaver chewing on a log resembles a typewriter are examples.
3. Compressed conflict, in which group members are forced to perceive an object or concept from two frames of reference. Asking them to give examples of "repulsive attraction" or "cooperative competition" are illustrations.

Check your reading of this section by answering the following questions. Answers are on page 277.

1. Identify five key elements in creative problem solving:
   a. motivation to persist
   b. emphasis on differences
   c. diverse information and viewpoints
   d. large group size
   e. acceptance of controversy
   f. open-mindedness in perspective-taking
   g. time to reflect

Match the characteristic with the correct group type:

_____ 2. Emphasizing differences between what is and what is not believed.

_____ 3. Discovery of new beliefs.

_____ 4. Contradictory beliefs are unquestioned.

_____ 5. Seeking out opposing and differing beliefs.

_____ 6. Exploration of differences in beliefs avoided.

_____ 7. Remembering information that disagrees with currently held beliefs.

_____ 8. Denying information contrary to beliefs.

a. Closed-minded
b. Open-minded

Match the method of generating ideas with its name:

_____ 9. Janice lists different sets of attributes on vertical and horizontal axes and examines the combinations.

_____ 10. Michael thinks of another entity that does what the problem entity does.

a. Part-changing
b. Checkerboard
c. Checklist
d. Find-something-similar

——— **11.** Melba identifies the attributes of something that might be changed.

——— **12.** Sammie makes a systematic way of determining whether something is left out of his thinking.

CREATIVITY EXERCISE

This problem requires creativity on the part of the group that is attempting to solve it. The class should divide into groups of three. Each group's assignment is to connect all nine dots with only four straight and connected lines. (Answer A on page 487 in Appendix D).

JOE DOODLEBUG EXERCISE

This problem also requires group creativity to solve. It is taken from Rokeach (1960). The procedure for the coordinator is as follows:

1. Have the class divide into groups of three.

2. Hand out copies of the problem sheet and state that it contains all the necessary information. The problem is *why* Joe *has* to take *four* jumps to reach the food, which is only three feet away. The groups have thirty minutes to come up with an answer. Explain that you will give hints after fifteen, twenty, and twenty-five minutes if the groups have not solved the problem.

3. After fifteen minutes give the first hint, after twenty minutes the second, and after twenty-five minutes the third (see page 487 in Appendix D).

4. At the end of thirty minutes stop the groups and give them the answer (it appears on page 488 in Appendix D). After clarifying the answer, conduct a discussion of moving outside one's belief system to solve a problem. Then ask the group to discuss how they worked together, listened to each other, handled controversies, and so on.

The Problem

Joe Doodlebug has been jumping all over the place getting some exercise when his master places a pile of food three feet directly west of him. Joe notices that the pile of food is a little larger than he. As soon as Joe sees all this food he stops dead in his tracks facing north. After all his exercise Joe is hungry and he wants to get the food as quickly as possible. Joe examines the situation and then says, "I'll have to jump four times to get the food." Why does Joe have to take four jumps to get to the food?

Joe Doodlebug, a strange sort of imaginary bug, can and cannot do the following things: (1) he can jump only in four different directions: north, south, east, and west (he cannot jump diagonally, such as southwest); (2) once he starts in any direction he *must* jump four times in that direction before he can change direction; (3) he can only jump, not crawl, fly, or walk; (4) he cannot jump less than one inch per jump or more than ten feet per jump; (5) Joe cannot turn around.

OPEN VERSUS CLOSED BELIEF SYSTEMS

For controversy to be constructive, group members must be receptive to information, ideas, perspectives, assumptions, beliefs, conclusions, and opinions different from their own. They must be willing to modify their cognitive structures so that they will be able to incorporate this new information. The systematic personality differences that exist among people that affect their openness to new information that may modify their attitudes and cognitive structures. These personality differences may also affect the extent to which constructive consequences result from controversy.

Rokeach (1954, 1960) has developed the concept of *dogmatism* to categorize persons in terms of the openness or closedness of their belief system. He defines dogmatism as "(a) a relatively closed cognitive organization of beliefs and disbeliefs about reality, (b) organized around a central set of beliefs about absolute authority which, in turn, (c) provides a framework for patterns of intolerance toward others." In discussing dogmatism Rokeach (1960, p.57) states that

> every person must be able to evaluate adequately both the relevant and irrelevant information he receives from every situation. This leads us to suggest a basic characteristic that defines the extent to which a person's system is open or closed, namely, the extent to which the person can receive, evaluate, and act on relevant information received from the outside on its own intrinsic merits, unencumbered by irrelevant factors in the situation, within the person, or from the outside.

When a group member is willing to attend to, comprehend, and gain insight into information, ideas, perspectives, assumptions, beliefs, conclusions, and opinions discrepant from her own, she is open-minded. When she resists such opportunities, she is closed-minded and dogmatic. Numerous studies on dogmatism have been reviewed by Ehrlich and Lee (1969) and by Vacchiano, Strauss, and Hochman (1969). This research indicates that closed-minded persons, compared with open-minded individuals:

1. are less able to learn new beliefs and to change old beliefs.
2. are less able to organize new beliefs and integrate them into their existing cognitive systems during problem-solving, and thus take longer to solve problems involving new beliefs.
3. are less accepting of belief-discrepant information.
4. are more resistant to changing their beliefs.
5. more frequently reject information that is potentially threatening to their perceptual and attitudinal organization.
6. have less recall of information that is inconsistent with their beliefs.
7. evaluate information that is consistent with their beliefs more positively.
8. have more difficulty in discriminating between the information received and its source, so that the status of an authority is confused with the validity of what the authority is stating; in other words, dogmatic persons tend to accept what authorities say as the truth and discount what low-status individuals say as invalid.
9. resolve fewer issues in conflict situations, are more resistant to compromise, and are more likely to view compromise as defeat.

The solution of the Joe Doodlebug problem requires open-mindedness in that group members must give up a series of beliefs about the situation and replace them with a set of new beliefs. They must then synthesize the new beliefs in order to solve the problem.

In solving the problem group members must first overcome three beliefs, one by one, and replace them with three new beliefs. The first is the *facing belief.* In everyday life we have to face the food we are to eat. But Joe does not have to face the food in order to eat it—he can land on top of it. The second is the *direction belief.* In everyday life we can change direction at will. But Joe is not able to do this because he must forever face north. The only way Joe can change direction is by jumping sideways and backward. The third belief that must be replaced is the *movement belief.* When we wish to change direction in everyday life, there is nothing to stop us from doing so immediately. But Joe's freedom of movement is restricted by the fact that once he moves in a particular direction (north, south, east, or west) he has to continue four times in that direction before he can change it. Many group members assume that Joe is at the end rather than possibly in the middle of a jumping sequence.

The replacement of old beliefs with new beliefs is called the *analytic phase* of the problem-solving process. Once new beliefs have superseded the old ones, group members must organize them in a way that leads them to the solution. This organizational step is called the *synthesizing phase* of the problem-solving process. In creative problem solving, controversies and open-mindedness help a group obtain different perspectives and develop appropriate beliefs that members can synthesize in order to help solve the problem. Controversy, replacement of old beliefs with new ones, and the synthesis of new beliefs are all essential.

BRAINSTORMING

Within the problem-solving process there are times when divergent thinking is necessary, when it is incumbent upon members to produce many diverse ideas. There are other times, of course, when convergent thinking is necessary, when the group needs to agree about its course of action. Brainstorming is a procedure that encourages divergent thinking and the production of many different ideas in a short period of time. It is a method of generating ideas in quantity and gaining the full participation of all group members in doing so. In essence, all evaluation is suspended and ideas are allowed to develop freely on a particular issue. Brainstorming is a time for free association of ideas and for the opening of new avenues of thought. Some of the reasons why brainstorming helps problem-solving groups become more creative are as follows:

1. It increases member participation and involvement.
2. It is a means of getting the most ideas in a relatively short period of time.
3. It reduces the need to look for the "right" idea in order to impress authority figures in the group.
4. It makes problem solving more fun and stimulating.
5. It reduces the possibility of negative subgrouping, competition, and one-upmanship during the problem-solving process.

To assure that the brainstorming session will be a success, group members should be familiar with a number of ground rules:

1. All criticism or evaluation of ideas is ruled out. Ideas are simply placed before the group.
2. Wild ideas are expected in the spontaneity that evolves when the group suspends judgment. Practical considerations are not important at this point. The session is to be freewheeling.
3. The quantity of ideas counts, not their quality. All ideas should be expressed, and none should be screened out by any individual. A great num-

ber of ideas will increase the likelihood of the group discovering good ones.

4. Build on the ideas of other group members when possible. Pool your creativity. Everyone should be free to build onto ideas and to make interesting combinations from the various suggestions.

5. Focus on a *single* problem or issue. Don't skip around to various problems or try to brainstorm a complex, multiple problem.

6. Promote a congenial, relaxed, cooperative atmosphere.

7. Make sure that all members, no matter how shy and reluctant to contribute, get their ideas heard.

8. Record *all* ideas.

After the period of brainstorming all the ideas should be categorized and the group should critically evaluate them for possible use or application. The best critical judgment of the group members should be applied to the ideas, though members should seek clues to something sound in even the wildest idea. Priorities should be selected and the best ideas applied.

For new groups unfamiliar with brainstorming a warm-up session in which the rationale and rules are explained might be helpful. If groups are being formed for brainstorming, it is important that some diversity of opinion and background be present in each group.

Brainstorming is useful because many of the reasons that ideas are never born—or, once born, are quickly stifled—have nothing to do with their value. Domineering members, stereotypes of each other's expertise and intelligence, interpersonal conflicts, habitual patterns of uninvolvement and silence, fear of ridicule or evaluation—all can smother the majority of members in a group. It is like a vice-president in charge of a group of managers saying "Those opposed will signify by clearing out their desks, putting on their hats, and saying 'I resign.'"

It is a common saying among social psychologists that there is no such thing as a creative person, only creative groups. The thinking of all of us is highly influenced by the thinking of those with whom we talk and otherwise interact. It is almost always possible to be part of a group process that encourages, supports, and rewards our potential for creativity. The ideas of others spark our own. The theory of one group member may help build a much more creative theory by touching off all sorts of new ideas among the rest of the members. When controversy is encouraged and diversity sought and used, a group can engage in untold amounts of creative problem solving.

QUIZ

Check your reading of the previous section by answering the following questions. Answers are on page 277.

1. Research indicates that closed-minded people (choose four):
   a. are short.
   b. are more able to learn new beliefs.
   c. accept what authorities say as truth.
   d. resolve fewer issues in conflict situations.
   e. positively evaluate information consistent with their beliefs.
   f. reject information inconsistent with their beliefs.
   g. are authors of books on group theory.

True   False   2. The replacement of old beliefs with new beliefs is essential for creativity.

True   False   3. The synthesizing phase involves organizing new beliefs in a way that leads to solutions.

True   False   4 In brainstorming, the quality of ideas counts, not the quantity.

True   False   5. Practical rather than wild ideas should be expressed in brainstorming.

True   False   6. Brainstorming helps groups become more creative.

True   False   7. Brainstorming decreases member involvement and participation.

True   False   8. Brainstorming decreases attempts to impress authority figures during the process.

True   False   9. Brainstorming is best used for solving complex, multiple problems.

True   False   10. After brainstorming, ideas are categorized and evaluated.

BRAINSTORMING EXERCISE

The objective of this exercise is to come up with a large number of ideas or solutions to a problem by temporarily suspending criticism and evaluation—in other words, to experience the process of brainstorming. The procedure is as follows:

1. The ground rules for brainstorming are reviewed by the group.
2. The group is presented with a problem: one of the authors of this book has been cast ashore nude on a desert island with nothing but a glass peace symbol on a leather thong.
3. The group has fifteen minutes to generate ideas as to what can be done with this object.
4. The group has another fifteen minutes to critically select their best ideas.
5. The group discusses how well it applied the rules of brainstorming and what its results were. Was creativity enhanced? Did it help the group to discover interesting ways of using the object?

After initial exposure to brainstorming a group should pick a specific problem it is working on and apply brainstorming to it to see if new, creative perspectives can be gained. If, however, a second practice session is desired, the following story can be used:

> A small wholesaler in the hinterland of New Mexico called his buyer in Santa Fe and asked him to obtain a large order of pipe cleaners from Mexico. The buyer agreed. He also agreed to advance the wholesaler the money to finance the deal. A month later, just as the shipment of pipe cleaners was arriving, the buyer received a disastrous phone call from the wholesaler: his warehouse and outlet store had burned down and there simply was no more business. The buyer was suddenly faced with the prospect of trying to sell 20,000 pipe cleaners.

In one minute group members should generate as many ideas as possible (with a recorder counting the number of different ideas) for selling pipe cleaners. (A relatively spontaneous group will create approximately twenty-five ideas in a little more than a minute. If the group creates fifteen ideas or less, it should be given more training in brainstorming.)

In brainstorming a group problem it is important that the problem be well defined and specific. It must also be a problem that the group has the power to do something about. If possible, the group members should be notified in advance about the issue to be explored so that they will have given some thought to it.

CREATIVITY WARM-UP EXERCISES

Have you ever felt in a rut? Have you ever felt embarrassed about sharing new or wild ideas? Have you ever ignored your thinking because you felt it was too far out? Do you ever enjoy letting your imagination and thoughts run wild? Have you ever been so critical of your own thoughts that you could not get started?

Here are six short, fun exercises to loosen up group thinking and warm up group creativity:

1. The group sits in a circle (group size should be limited to eight members or so). The person nearest the window says the first thing that comes to his mind. The statement should be short, not over a sentence or two. Without pause the person to his left says what comes to her mind. Her statement must be relevant to something the first person said. The relevance may be of any kind—an association, a contrast, an alternative, a continuation, and so on. The process continues at high speed until at least three rounds have been completed. Members critique the process by discussing the feelings they had during the exercise.

2. The group sits in a circle and identifies a problem or issue. The person nearest the door states his solution. Each subsequent group member (to his left) states his, using as many ideas of previous speakers as he can. The process is continued until a plan generally acceptable to all the group members is arrived at. When a member cannot add anything new, he passes. Finally, members' reactions to and feelings about the experience are discussed.

3. The group sits in a circle and a group problem or issue is identified. The first person

states her solution to the problem. The next person immediately states what her opposition to the first person's solution is. The third person immediately states her opposition to the second person's opposition. The process is continued until everyone in the group has spoken at least three times. The emphasis is upon generating creative ideas in arguments. Members' reactions to and feelings about the experience are discussed.

4. The group lies on the floor, members' heads toward the center of the room. The first person begins with a fantasy about what the group could be like. After no more than two or three minutes the fantasy is passed on to the next group member, who continues it, adding his own associations and fantasies. The process continues until everyone has spoken at least three times. Members' reactions to and feelings about the exercise are examined.

5. The group has before it a number of assorted materials, such as clay, water paints, Tinker Toys, magazines, newspapers, and so on. It then creates something out of the materials—a mural, a collage, a design. If more than one group participates, they end the exercise by discussing one another's creations.

6. The group acts out a walk through the woods. Each member takes the leadership role for a while and directs the walk, indicating what she is experiencing and seeing. What the members learn about one another, the group, and walking through the woods should be discussed.

YOUR BEHAVIOR IN CONTROVERSIES EXERCISE (II)

How do you behave in controversies? Has your behavior changed as a result of your experiences connected with this chapter? How would you now describe your behavior?

1. When I find myself disagreeing with other members of my group, I:

____ stand by my ideas and continue to defend my position, actively trying to get it accepted by the group and incorporated into any decisions made for as long as it takes to do so.

____ try to explore the points of agreement and disagreement and the feelings that other group members have about these points and why; I press a search for alternatives that take everyone's views into account.

2. Controversies are:

____ valuable to clear the air and enhance involvement and commitment and, when productively handled, result in increased creativity.

____ destructive because opposition leads to dislike, and disagreement over ideas means personal rejection of other group members.

3. When I am involved in a controversy, I:

____ feel rather fearful and concerned about how other members like me and whether I really like them.

____ feel angry at their ignorance and rather annoyed that I have to be around such stupid people.

____ am stimulated and feel full of excitement and fun as I think about the issues being discussed.

4. Which of the following is more typical of your behavior?

_____ When I find myself in disagreement with other group members, I always state my position and feelings so that everything is out in the open.

_____ When I find myself in disagreement with other group members I keep quiet and "sit the discussion out."

5. When I get involved in a good argument, I:

_____ find my ideas becoming more and more creative as I incorporate other members' ideas and notions and begin to see the issue from different perspectives.

_____ become more and more certain that I am correct and argue more and more strongly for my own point of view.

Compare your answers with the answers you gave to the questionnaire at the beginning of the chapter. Have you changed? How would you now describe your behavior in controversy situations? Write a description of your controversy behavior, and share it with two persons who know you well and who have participated in some of the controversy exercises with you. Ask them to add to and modify your self-description.

SUMMARY

The materials in this chapter concentrated on the productive management of controversies among group members in order to increase a group's effectiveness in making creative, high-quality decisions. You have practiced dealing with controversies and making creative decisions. The next chapter will continue along this same theme by showing you how to negotiate in dealing with conflicts of interest.

ANSWERS

Page 232—1. c; 2. a; 3. d; 4. b; 5. false; 6. false; 7. true; 8. false; 9. false 10. true; 11. false; 12. true; 13. false; 14. true; 15. false; 16. true; 17. true; 18. a, c, e, f.

Page 258—2. true; 3. false; 4. false; 5. true; 6. false; 7. false; 8. true; 9. false; 10. true; 11. false; 12. true; 13. true; 14. false; 15. true; 16. true; 17. true; 18. true; 19. true; 20. false; 21. true; 22. true; 23. true; 24. false; 25. true; 26. true; 27. c; 28. d; 29. a; 30. b; 31. a, c, d, e, g, h; 32. b, d, e; 33. a, b, d, f, h, k, l.

Page 268—1. a, c, e, f, g; 2. a; 3. b; 4. a; 5. b; 6. a; 7. b; 8. a; 9. b; 10. d; 11. a; 12. c.

Page 273—1. c, d, e, f; 2. true; 3. true; 4. false; 5. false; 6. true; 7. false; 8. true; 9. false; 10. true.

7

Conflicts of Interest

BASIC CONCEPTS TO BE COVERED IN THIS CHAPTER

In this chapter a number of concepts are defined and discussed. The major ones are listed below. The procedure for learning these concepts is as follows:

1. The class forms heterogeneous groups of four.
2. Each group divides into two pairs.
3. The task for each pair is to:
   a. define each concept, noting the page on which it is defined and discussed.
   b. make sure that both members of the pair understand the meaning of each concept.
4. In each group, members compare the answers of the two pairs. If there is disagreement, the members look up the concept in the chapter and clarify it until they all agree on the definition and understand it.

Concepts

1. conflict of interest
2. negotiation
3. primary gain from negotiations
4. secondary gain from negotiations
5. avoiding conflicts of interest
6. resolving conflicts of interest
7. confrontation
8. information dependence
9. norm of reciprocity
10. norm of equity
11. dilemma of trust
12. dilemma of honesty and openness
13. threat
14. win-lose dynamic
15. psychodynamic fallacy
16. self-fulfilling prophecy
17. triggering event
18. outcome dependence

WHAT ARE CONFLICTS OF INTEREST?

Imagine you are part of a group that has just been given five thousand dollars to spend in any way it wishes over the next two weeks. Your group has six members: Jane, Mary, Joe, John, Edythe, and yourself. Jane and Mary want to donate the money to the women's-liberation movement. Edythe, John, and Joe want to give a series of parties for all their friends. You want the group to use the money for a college scholarship for your younger brother. Your group is in conflict, and it is more than just a matter of opposing opinions. There is a scarce resource (money) that the group must decide to allocate among the competing needs of the members. Since different members have vested interests in spending the money in different ways, your group has a conflict of interest.

Conflicts of interest exist when the actions of one person attempting to maximize his advantages or benefits prevent, block, interfere with, injure, or in some other way make less effective the actions of another person attempting to maximize her advantages or benefits. The term *interest* is used with the meaning of benefit, profit, advantage, concern, right, or claim. Conflicts among interests can be based on: (1) differences in needs, values, and goals; (2) scarcities of certain resources, such as power, influence, money, time, space, popularity, and position; or (3) rivalry. Within any group different persons will have different interests, and at times they will be in conflict with each other. The management of conflicts of interest is an important aspect of maintaining the cooperation among group members that is needed for group effectiveness.

All the potential values of conflict discussed at the beginning of Chapter 6 are applicable to conflicts of interest. Though not helpful in producing a creative, high-quality decision, a conflict of interest, if managed properly, can help ensure that all group members are committed to implementing the group's decisions and that the group's problem-solving ability does not deteriorate during the decision-making process. In this chapter we shall focus on the use of negotiation to resolve conflicts of interest among group members and among groups.*

You may check your understanding of this section by answering the following question (answer at the end of the chapter):

---

* In his book *Reaching Out* (1981), Johnson has devised a program for helping persons improve their skills in handling interpersonal conflicts constructively. The book offers a combination of theory and structured exercises to this end, and its chapters on conflict, confrontation, and problem definition provide a foundation for the material covered in this chapter. *Reaching Out* focuses on increasing one's awareness of one's past and present styles of conflict management, confronting others constructively, defining a conflict constructively, getting an accurate perception of the other's position and feelings, making sure there is correct and effective communication in a conflict, developing a climate of trust, structuring cooperative interdependence in resolving the conflict, and managing stress and anger constructively.

What are conflicts of interest?

a. conflicts in which everyone is interested in participating.

b. conflicts that come from scarcity, rivalry, or differences in needs, values, or goals.

c. conflicts that indicate differences of opinions or ideas.

d. conflicts caused by misunderstanding and mistakes.

YOUR CONFLICT STRATEGIES EXERCISE

Different persons learn different ways of managing conflicts. The strategies you use to manage conflicts may be quite different from those used by your friends and acquaintances. This exercise gives you an opportunity to increase your awareness of what conflict strategies you use and how they compare with the strategies used by others. The procedure is as follows:

1. With your classmates, form groups of six. Make sure you know the other members of the group. Do not join a group of strangers.

2. Working by yourself, complete the following questionnaire.

3. Working by yourself, read the accompanying discussion of conflict strategies. Then make five slips of paper. Write the names of the other five members of your group on the slips of paper, one name to a slip.

4. On each slip of paper write the conflict strategy that best fits the actions of the person named.

5. After all group members are finished, pass out your slips of paper to the persons whose names are on them. In turn you should end up with five slips of paper, each containing a description of your conflict style as seen by another group member. Likewise, each member of your group should end up with five slips of paper describing her conflict strategy.

6. Score your questionnaire, using the table that follows the discussion of conflict strategies. Rank the five conflict strategies from the one you use the most to the one you use the least. This will give you an indication of how you see your own conflict strategy. The second most frequently used strategy is your backup strategy, the one you use if your first one fails.

7. After drawing names to see who goes first, one member describes the results of his questionnaire. This is his view of his own conflict strategies. He then reads each of the five slips of paper on which are written the views of the group members about his conflict strategy. Next he asks the group to give specific examples of how they have seen him act in conflicts. The group members should use the rules for constructive feedback. The person to the left of the first member repeats this procedure, and so on around the group.

8. Each group discusses the strengths and weaknesses of each of the conflict strategies.

How You Act in Conflicts

The proverbs listed below can be thought of as descriptions of some of the different strategies for resolving conflicts. Proverbs state traditional wisdom, and these proverbs reflect traditional wisdom for resolving conflicts. Read each of the proverbs carefully. Using the following scale, indicate how typical each proverb is of your actions in a conflict.

5 = very typical of the way I act in a conflict
4 = frequently typical of the way I act in a conflict
3 = sometimes typical of the way I act in a conflict
2 = seldom typical of the way I act in a conflict
1 = never typical of the way I act in a conflict

_____ **1.** It is easier to refrain than to retreat from a quarrel.

_____ **2.** If you cannot make a person think as you do, make him or her do as you think.

_____ **3.** Soft words win hard hearts.

_____ **4.** You scratch my back, I'll scratch yours.

_____ **5.** Come now and let us reason together.

_____ **6.** When two quarrel, the person who keeps silent first is the most praiseworthy.

_____ **7.** Might overcomes right.

_____ **8.** Smooth words make smooth ways.

_____ **9.** Better half a loaf than no bread at all.

_____ **10.** Truth lies in knowledge, not in majority opinion.

_____ **11.** He who fights and runs away lives to fight another day.

_____ **12.** He hath conquered well that hath made his enemies flee.

_____ **13.** Kill your enemies with kindness.

_____ **14.** A fair exchange brings no quarrel.

_____ **15.** No person has the final answer but every person has a piece to contribute.

_____ **16.** Stay away from people who disagree with you.

_____ **17.** Fields are won by those who believe in winning.

_____ **18.** Kind words are worth much and cost little.

_____ **19.** Tit for tat is fair play.

_____ **20.** Only the person who is willing to give up his or her monopoly on truth can ever profit from the truths that others hold.

_____ **21.** Avoid quarrelsome people as they will only make your life miserable.

_____ **22.** A person who will not flee will make others flee.

_____ **23.** Soft words ensure harmony.

_____ **24.** One gift for another makes good friends.

_____ **25.** Bring your conflicts into the open and face them directly; only then will the best solution be discovered.

_____ **26.** The best way of handling conflicts is to avoid them.

_____ **27.** Put your foot down where you mean to stand.

_____ **28.** Gentleness will triumph over anger.

_____ **29.** Getting part of what you want is better than not getting anything at all.

_____ **30.** Frankness, honesty, and trust will move mountains.

_____ **31.** There is nothing so important you have to fight for it.

_____ **32.** There are two kinds of people in the world, the winners and the losers.

_____ **33.** When one hits you with a stone, hit him or her with a piece of cotton.

_____ **34.** When both give in halfway, a fair settlement is achieved.

_____ **35.** By digging and digging, the truth is discovered.

Conflict Strategies: What Are You Like?

Different people use different strategies for managing conflicts. These strategies are learned, usually in childhood, and they seem to function automatically. Usually we are not aware of how we act in conflict situations. We just do whatever seems to come naturally. But we do have a personal strategy; and because it was learned, we can always change it by learning new and more effective ways of managing conflicts.

When you become engaged in a conflict, there are two major concerns you have to take into account:

1. Achieving your personal goals—you are in conflict because you have a goal that conflicts with another person's goal. Your goal may be highly important to you, or it may be of little importance.
2. Keeping a good relationship with the other person—you may need to be able to interact effectively with the other person in the future. The relationship may be very important to you, or it may be of little importance.

How important your personal goals are to you and how important the relationship is to you affect how you act in a conflict. Given these two concerns, it is possible to identify five styles of managing conflicts:

the turtle (withdrawing). Turtles withdraw into their shells to avoid conflicts. They give up their personal goals and relationships. They stay away from the issues over which the conflict is taking place and from the persons they are in conflict with. Turtles believe it is hopeless to try to resolve conflicts. They feel helpless. They believe it is easier to withdraw (physically and psychologically) from a conflict than to face it.

the shark (forcing). Sharks try to overpower opponents by forcing them to accept their solution to the conflict. Their goals are highly important to them, and relationships are of minor importance. They seek to achieve their goals at all costs. They are not concerned with the needs of others. They

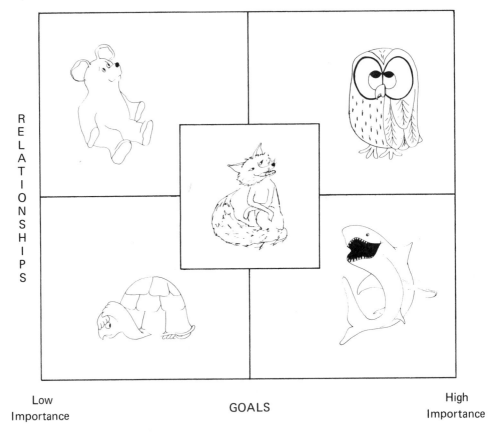

High
Importance

R
E
L
A
T
I
O
N
S
H
I
P
S

Low
Importance

GOALS

High
Importance

do not care if others like or accept them. Sharks assume that conflicts are settled by one person winning and one person losing. They want to be the winner. Winning gives sharks a sense of pride and achievement. Losing gives them a sense of weakness, inadequacy, and failure. They try to win by attacking, overpowering, overwhelming, and intimidating others.

the teddy bear (smoothing). To teddy bears the relationship is of great importance while their own goals are of little importance. Teddy bears want to be accepted and liked by others. They think that conflict should be avoided in favor of harmony and that people cannot discuss conflicts without damaging relationships. They are afraid that if the conflict continues, someone will get hurt, and that would ruin the relationship. They give up their goals to preserve the relationship. Teddy bears say "I'll give up my goals and let you have what you want, in order for you to like me." Teddy bears try to smooth over the conflict out of fear of harming the relationship.

the fox (compromising). Foxes are moderately concerned with their own goals and their relationships with others. Foxes seek a compromise: they give up part of their goals and persuade the other person in a conflict to give up part of his goals. They seek a conflict solution in which both sides gain something—the middle ground between two extreme positions. They are willing to sacrifice part of their goals and relationships in order to find agreement for the common good.

the owl (confronting). Owls highly value their own goals and relationships. They view conflicts as problems to be solved and seek a solution that achieves both their own goals and the goals of the other person. Owls see conflicts as a means of improving relationships by reducing tension between two persons. They try to begin a discussion that identifies the conflict as a problem. By seeking solutions that satisfy both themselves and the other person, owls maintain the relationship. Owls are not satisfied until a solution is found that achieves their own goals and the other person's goals. And they are not satisfied until the tensions and negative feelings have been fully resolved.

Scoring

Withdrawing	Forcing	Smoothing	Compromising	Confronting
____ 1.	____ 2.	____ 3.	____ 4.	____ 5.
____ 6.	____ 7.	____ 8.	____ 9.	____ 10.
____ 11.	____ 12.	____ 13.	____ 14.	____ 15.
____ 16.	____ 17.	____ 18.	____ 19.	____ 20.
____ 21.	____ 22.	____ 23.	____ 24.	____ 25.
____ 26.	____ 27.	____ 28.	____ 29.	____ 30.
____ 31.	____ 32.	____ 33.	____ 34.	____ 35.
____ Total	____ Total	____ Total	____ Total	____ Total

The higher the total score for each conflict strategy, the more frequently you tend to use that strategy. The lower the total score for each conflict strategy, the less frequently you tend to use that strategy.

QUIZ

Check your reading of this section by answering the following questions. Answers are on page 333.

1. What are conflicts of interest?
   a. Conflicts in which everyone is interested in participating.
   b. Conflicts caused by scarcity, rivalry, or differences in needs.

    c. Conflicts caused by differences of opinions or ideas.

    d. Conflicts caused by misunderstandings and mistakes.

2. What two major concerns should you take into account when engaged in a conflict?

    a. Where and when to fight.

    b. The importance of your goals.

    c. The importance of your relationship.

    d. The importance of winning.

Match the following styles of conflict management with their characteristics:

____ **3.** The goals are important; the people are not.	**a.** Withdrawing
____ **4.** The people are important; the goals are not.	**b.** Forcing
	c. Smoothing
____ **5.** Neither the goals nor the people are important.	**d.** Compromising
	e. Confronting
____ **6.** Both the goals and the people are important.	
____ **7.** The goals and the people are moderately important.	
____ **8.** Stay away from the issues and people in a conflict.	
____ **9.** Conflicts are seen as problems to be solved.	
____ **10.** Conflict should be avoided in favor of harmony.	
____ **11.** Sacrifice in part to find a common agreement.	
____ **12.** Win by attacking and overpowering.	

GROUP-MEMBER EXCELLENCE EXERCISE

The objective of this exercise is to look at the dynamics of interpersonal negotiation in a group. The exercise can be conducted in less than one hour. The procedure for the coordinator is as follows:

1. Introduce the exercise as a chance to study the dynamics of negotiation among members of the same group. Divide the class into groups of fourteen: twelve participants and two observers. You need at least two groups. Distribute one copy of the accompanying instruction sheet to all members and observers and one copy of the observers' instructions to the observers. Without letting the groups know that they are getting different instructions, give half of them copies of the accompanying win-lose-negotiation instructions and the other half copies of the problem-solving-negotiation instructions.

2. Meet with the observers to make sure they understand what they are expected to do.

3. Distribute a bag of marbles to each group member, using the accompanying table as a guide. Answer any questions members have about the exercise. Do *not*, however, tell them anything about the number of marbles or arrangement of colors in the bags or how to collect fifteen marbles of the same color. Collect twenty-five cents from each participant, to be awarded to the members who finish the task. Announce that participants have fifteen minutes to finish the task. Give the signal to begin.

4. At the end of fifteen minutes announce that the time is up and the negotiations must end. Ask each participant to write two adjectives on her negotiation instruction sheet that describe her feelings during the negotiations. Gather the sheets and record how many participants completed the task and which type of negotiation instructions they had. Then divide the money among the members who completed the task.

5. Have each group meet separately with its observers to discuss the experience. The focus of the discussion should be upon the negotiation strategies used, how members reacted to one another's strategies, and how successful the different strategies were. Then, on a sheet of newsprint summarize the strategies, their success, how members reacted to them, and any conclusions that can be drawn about their effectiveness.

6. Have the groups share their instructions for negotiation and the strategies members used, and ask them what conclusions they can make about the effectiveness of the different strategies. Announce how many persons with win-lose instructions completed the task and how many with problem-solving instructions completed it. The adjectives win-lose participants wrote down should be compared with the adjectives problem-solving participants used. An interesting subject to explore is how often coalitions formed in which two or more members pooled their marbles and negotiated with other members as a bloc. Sometimes a member will collect two colors of marbles in order to be flexible until the last few minutes. Summarize the major points of the discussion.

7. Have the participants read the subsequent sections on negotiation and compare their conclusions about the exercise with the material in those sections

General Instructions

Systems for evaluating the performance of group members have many shortcomings. Different members behave in different ways to accomplish their objectives. These variations make most comparisons difficult and unfair. To overcome this problem, we have developed a simulation that all members will participate in. From your behavior in this exercise we will be able to tell if you are a poor, average, good, or excellent group member. The exercise provides an impartial and equal measure of a participant's performance.

Here is how the exercise works: You are being issued a bag containing ten marbles of four different colors—red, green, blue, and rainbow. Different members have different proportions of the colors, but each person has ten marbles. Your objective is to collect fifteen marbles of the same color and turn them in to the coordinator of the exercise. You will have fifteen minutes to do so. Extra points will be awarded for more than fifteen marbles: you will receive a 10-percent bonus for each marble over the fifteen that you collect. Thus, if you turn in eighteen green marbles, you will receive the regular award for fifteen marbles *plus* 30 percent more.

Observers' Instructions

As an observer your task is to obtain as much information about what is taking place as possible. There are three areas on which you should concentrate: what strategies of negotiation are being used in the group, how members are reacting to each other's strategies, and how successful the strategies are. Observations of any other aspect of negotiating behavior will also be helpful. Write down your observations and make as many as possible.

Distribution of Marbles to the Twelve Participants

Member	Red	Blue	Green	Rainbow
1	4	3	2	1
2	1	4	3	2
3	2	1	4	3
4	3	2	1	4
5	3	3	2	2
6	3	2	3	2
7	2	3	2	3
8	2	2	3	3
9	2	2	2	4
10	2	2	4	2
11	2	4	2	2
12	4	2	2	2

Instructions for Problem-solving Negotiation

In this exercise your group is to adopt a problem-solving negotiation strategy in which members try to define the task and find creative solutions to it that are satisfying to as many members as possible. In negotiating with other group members, try to make the problem solving as creative as possible. Communicate openly and honestly about your needs and try to find ways in which to help both your own and the other group members' success. Avoid all threats and deception, which might destroy trust among group members. The problem is to figure out how as many group members as possible can complete the task.

Instructions for Win-Lose Negotiation

In this exercise your group is to adopt a win-lose negotiation strategy in which each member will try to obtain more marbles of the same color than anyone else. Obviously, some of the members of your group are going to win and some are going to lose. You want to be a winner. The use of deceit, threats, and force may be helpful in negotiating with the other members. During the negotiations try to achieve the best outcome for yourself, and use your power and skill in any way that helps you do so. Remember, if you keep the other group members from winning, you will increase your own chances of winning.

NEGOTIATION EXERCISE

This exercise consists of three situations in which members of the same organization or group have to negotiate a conflict of interest. In each situation the basic procedure for the coordinator is the same. The exercise takes less than one hour to complete.

1. Introduce the exercise as one in which the dynamics of negotiation among members of a group become apparent. Divide the class into groups of three (two participants and one observer) for case studies 1 and 2 and groups of four (three participants and one observer). You need at least two groups. Distribute the accompanying background sheets and role-playing sheets to the participants and observers. Give each observer one copy of the observers' instructions used in the previous exercise. Without letting the groups know that they are getting different instructions, give half of them copies of the accompanying bargaining instructions and the other half copies of the role-reversal instructions.

2. Meet with the observers to make sure they understand what they are expected to do.

3. Give the signal to begin. Groups have up to twenty-five minutes to negotiate an agreement. If they finish before their time is up, note how long it took them to negotiate an agreement and what type of negotiation instructions they had.

4. At the end of twenty-five minutes announce that the time is up and the negotiations must end. Ask each participant to write on a sheet of paper two adjectives describing his feelings during the negotiations and hand it to you. Record how many groups negotiated an agreement and which type of instructions (bargaining or role-reversal) they had.

5. Ask each group to discuss its experience with its observer. The main topics of the discussion should be the negotiation strategies used, how members reacted to one another's strategies, and how successful the different strategies were. Then, on a sheet of newsprint have each group summarize its strategies, how successful they

were, how member reacted to them, and any conclusions members can make about their effectiveness.

6. In a general session have each group share its instructions for negotiation, the strategies its members used, and its conclusions about their effectiveness. You can then reveal how participants with bargaining instructions reacted to the negotiations compared with participants with role-reversal instructions, how many groups with each type of instructions completed the negotiations successfully, and how long it took these groups to do so. Summarize the main points of the discussion.

7. Have the participants read the subsequent sections on negotiation and compare their conclusions with the material in those sections.

Negotiation Exercise: Case Study 1

background. Jim and Chris (a female) both work for a research firm but in different divisions. Chris has been assigned project leader of a study, and Jim has been assigned from the other division to work on it. This does not necessarily imply that Chris is Jim's boss. This arrangement has been in effect for about a year, and it is relatively unsatisfactory to Chris, who would like to have Jim taken off the project.

Meetings of the project team are often dominated by arguments between Chris and Jim. As a result Chris has often held meetings without notifying Jim.

Jim and Chris are meeting to see if the conflict between them can be resolved.

Chris. Jim is a know-it-all who is always trying to tell you how to run your project. You do not agree with his approach. What he wants to study is not the subject of the research.

You cannot stand Jim's voice. He has an extremely grating voice that he uses with imperious overtones. He is generally obnoxious.

He comes into meetings, slumps down in a chair, and demands that everyone pay attention to him, even if he is late and they have already started.

He doesn't give others a chance to talk, and always interrupts if they do get a chance.

He does not care about the project. If he finds something else to do that he likes better, he simply ignores his responsibilities for completing work on the project. The group had to miss one deadline because he chose to do something else, and in the report before, you had to rewrite one whole section because what he turned in was not adequate. He was busy working on something for the director of the organization just to make a name for himself. Meanwhile, he sacrificed your reputation by causing your project to be late and your group to produce inferior work.

Jim. Chris thinks she is better than anyone else around here. She thinks she is some kind or prima donna and that only the research she is doing is any good. She thinks all the other work in the organization is "trash" except for hers.

You feel that what you were working on for the director was more important for the organization. But she is not willing to agree that anyone except herself can do anything well.

You do not agree with her approach to the project. Her main emphasis is on something that is not relevant to the problem. We need answers in order to make decisions today, not five years from now.

You do not really feel involved in the project. Chris accepts what everyone else on the project is doing, but she chooses your area to criticize.

Negotiation Exercise: Case Study 2

background. Pat (a female) and Rich both work for a research organization. Originally the director of the organization was the leader of a project. Rich was interviewed for a position on that project and hired by the director. Pat also interviewed Rich, and strongly opposed his being hired for the project. Pat thought Rich wasn't competent to do the job.

Five or six months after work on the project began, the director decided she wanted to be relieved and proposed that Rich and Pat conduct it jointly. Pat agreed only reluctantly—with the stipulation that it be made clear she was not working for Rich. The director consented. They were to have a shared directorship.

Within a month Pat was angry because Rich was acting toward others as though he were the director of the entire project and she was working for him.

Pat and Rich are meeting to see if the conflict between them can be resolved.

Pat. Right after the joint-leadership arrangement was reached with the director, Rich called a meeting of the project team without even consulting you about the time or content. He just told you when it was being held and said you should be there.

At the meeting Rich reviewed everyone's paper line by line—including yours, thus treating you as just another team member working for him.

He sends out letters and signs himself as project director, which obviously implies to others that you are working for him.

Rich. You think Pat is all hung up with feelings of power and titles. Just because you are project director, or sign yourself that way, doesn't mean that she is working for you. You do not see anything to get excited about. What difference does it make?

She is too sensitive about everything. You call a meeting and right away she thinks you are trying to run everything.

Pat has other things to do—other projects to run—so she does not pay too much attention to this one. She mostly lets things slide. But when you take the initiative to set up a meeting, she starts jumping up and down about how you are trying to make her work for you.

Negotiation Exercise: Bargaining Instructions

Bargaining is a process by which a person attempts to reach an agreement as favorable to herself as possible. It is aimed at producing an agreement with another person that settles what each is to give and receive in a transaction between them. Usually in a bargaining situation one person "wins" and the other person "loses." A variety of strategies can be used to influence the other bargainer in such a way as to reach an agreement as favorable to oneself as possible:

1. presenting an opening offer very favorable to oneself and refusing to modify that position

2. gathering information about what the other considers a "reasonable" agreement from the other's opening offer and proposals

3. continually pointing out the validity of one's own position and the incorrectness of the other person's

4. using a combination of threats and promises to convince the other person that he has to accept one's offer

5. committing oneself to a position in such a way that if an agreement is to be reached, the other person has to agree to one's terms

In this exercise you are to bargain as toughly as you can to arrive at the best settlement possible for yourself.

Negotiation Exercise: Role-Reversal Instructions

Role reversal is defined as a negotiating action in which one person accurately and completely paraphrases, in a warm and involved way, the feelings and position of another. It is the expression of a sincere interest in understanding in other person's position and feelings. The basic rule for role reversal is this: Each person speaks up for himself only after he has first restated the ideas and feelings of the other person accurately and to the other's satisfaction. In other words, before one person presents his point of view it is necessary for him to achieve the other person's perspective or frame of reference and to understand her position and feelings so well that he can paraphrase them accurately and completely. General guidelines for role reversal are as follows:

1. Restate the other person's expressed ideas and feelings in one's own words rather than parroting the words of the other person.

2. Preface your reflected remarks with "You think . . . ," "Your position is . . . ," You feel . . . ," "It seems to you that . . . ," and so on.

3. Avoid any indication of approval or disapproval in paraphrasing the other person's statements. It is important to refrain from interpreting, blaming, persuading, or advising.

4. Make your nonverbal messages congruent with your verbal paraphrasing. Look attentive, be interested in and open to the other's ideas and feelings, and appear to be concentrating on what the other person is trying to communicate.

In this exercise you are to engage in role reversal during the entire negotiating session and use it to arrive at the solution to the problems you and the other person(s) are facing.

CONFLICTS OF INTEREST EXERCISE

The purpose of this exercise is to stimulate a discussion how conflicts of interest should be managed. The procedure is as follows:

1. Brief descriptions of four conflicts of interest appear below. Read each one. Then, working by yourself, write a description of how you would handle each conflict if you were the teacher in the classroom. Assume the students are in high school.

2. With your classmates, form heterogeneous groups of four. Working as a group, discuss each conflict and come to a consensus how it should be managed. Write out the group's plan for handling each conflict.

3. Each group shares its solutions with the rest of the class.

Conflict Descriptions

1. My friend doesn't like to lose. But the teacher keeps giving tests and he comes out last. She posts the scores so everyone in the class knows my friend is dumb. So one day she was giving a test and he tossed a lighted firecracker under her seat. She fainted. The principal came up to the class and said, "Who put that firecracker under Ms. Waterton's seat?" Several students started laughing, so the principal took them down to his office and called their parents. They got in trouble. But the look on the teacher's face when the firecracker went off was worth it. And you should have seen her face when she walked into the classroom the next day!

2. Two students begin to argue about who owns a pen. Both students claim it. The argument leads to a small fistfight. Both students end up feeling angry and rejected.

3. In your class you assigned each student a collage on a serious social problem, such as pollution, discrimination, drugs, or crime. The idea of the project was to get the students to express themselves and their ideas in a visual manner and to increase their awareness of how art can be an impressive and persuasive tool. A student raised his hand and said he didn't see the importance of this sort of thing. He said he wasn't going to do it because it sounded like a stupid waste of his time, and why couldn't you assign something more interesting and valuable.

4. Mary and George are members of a cooperative group. Yet they constantly put each other down, criticize each other, and even make fun of each other's contributions. They both want to be the group leader and spend most of their energy undermining each other's efforts to direct and control the group's activities.

MAKING A PROFIT EXERCISE

The purpose of this exercise is to give participants an opportunity to negotiate a profit-loss situation so that they may examine the dynamics of bargaining. The exercise can be conducted in less than half an hour. The procedure for the coordinator is as follows:

1. Introduce the exercise as an opportunity to study the dynamics of negotiation between two persons with different interests. The negotiation is between a buyer and a seller in a wholesale market.

2. Divide the class into heterogeneous groups of six. There needs to be an even number of members in each group (i.e., 2, 4, 6, 8, 10). Then divide each group into two subgroups of three members each. Assign one subgroup the role of buyers and the other subgroup the role of sellers. Instruct the subgroups that each member must prepare to negotiate with a member of the opposite subgroup. The purpose of the negotiation is to maximize the profits of the subgroup. The members of each subgroup will not be allowed to show their profit schedule to the negotiators from the other subgroup, and therefore must understand what possible agreements are advantageous for them. The profit schedules may be found on page 488 in Appendix D.

3. Make three pairs from each group of six, each pair comprising one person from each subgroup. Have the negotiators meet face to face. Their task is to negotiate an agreement on the price for each commodity. They can say anything they want to each other, but they may *not* show each other their profit schedule.

4. After all pairs have finished negotiating, ask all participants to write down on a sheet of paper:
   a. which commodity was most important to the opponent.
   b. which commodity was least important to the opponent.

5. Instruct participants to reform their groups of six and discuss the following questions:
   a. What were the agreements reached by the members of the group?
   b. What was the total joint outcome achieved by each buyer-and-seller pair? (The joint outcome is the sum of the profits of the buyer and the profits of the seller.) Which pair had the highest joint outcome?
   c. What negotiation strategies were used? Were they win-lose or problem-solving strategies?
   d. How did negotiators communicate information about their profit schedule, and how did they learn about the profit schedule of their opponent? Were their perceptions of what commodities were most and least important to their opponent correct? Was information exchange direct? (Did buyer and seller accurately tell each other their profit schedules?) Or was it indirect? (Did they deduce each other's profit schedule by comparing each other's responses to different package offers?)
   e. Did the negotiators make package deals or did they negotiate the commodities one at a time?
   f. What conclusions can the group make about negotiations on the basis of their experience and discussion?

6. Have each group share its conclusions with the rest of the class.

CONFLICTS OF INTEREST: AVOID OR RESOLVE?

When a conflict of interest arises, you will be faced with the decision of whether to try the control and avoid; or face it directly and try to resolve it. In order to make such a decision you will need to understand what events trigger the expression of the conflict and what barriers hinder the beginning negotiations (Walton, 1969). To *avoid* the conflict, you remove the triggering events and build up the barriers to negotiations. To *resolve* the conflict, you increase the frequency of the triggering events and decrease the barriers to negotiations. A triggering event may be as simple as two group members being physically near each other or as complex as two members being in competition. Negative remarks, sarcasm, and criticism on sensitive points are common triggering events, as is the feeling of being deprived, neglected, or ignored.

Within many conflicts of interest there are barriers to expressing the conflict and seeking its resolution. These barriers may be internal, such as attitudes, values, fears, anxieties, and habitual patterns of avoiding conflict. Or they may be external, such as time constraints, group norms disapproving of the open expression of conflict, pressure to maintain a congenial public image, and faulty perceptions of one's own vulnerability and the other's strength. Physical separation is a frequently used barrier to the expression of conflicts of interest. Placing members in different locations, avoiding being in the same room with certain other members, and removing a member from the group, can all suppress a conflict of interest.

To understand a conflict, then, you have to determine what types of barriers are customarily operating and what triggers the expression of the conflict. Since an important aspect of conflict management is choosing the right time and place for negotiations, an understanding of the barriers and triggering events allows you to suppress the expression of the conflict until the time and place is more appropriate, or to precipitate the expression when the time and place *is* appropriate. Some events, furthermore, may trigger a malevolent expression of the conflict; other triggering events may lead to a constructive confrontation. Being teased, for example, may begin a physical fight between two students; competing on a spelling drill may result only in name-calling.

Not every conflict of interest is negotiable. Your opponent or the persons involved may be too anxious, defensive, or psychologically unstable to negotiate effectively, or their motivation to change may be very low. It is a mistake to assume that you can *always* openly negotiate the resolution of a conflict; there are times when conflicts are better avoided. But *usually* conflicts of interest can be settled constructively. The vast majority of conflicts of interest within groups can be negotiated if the participants attempt to do so.

PROMOTING NEGOTIATIONS

Once you have decided to resolve a conflict of interest, you will find many procedures available—legal action, third-party roles (such as therapists, counselors, arbitrators, mediators, ombudsmen, and advocates), violence, and negotiation, among others. Negotiation is by far the most effective procedure for constructively resolving conflicts within a group. *Negotiating* is a process by which persons who want to come to an agreement try to work out a settlement. Negotiations are aimed at achieving an agreement that specifies what each group member gives and receives in a transaction between them. In a negotiation process there are concrete issues, such as competitive bids for the same resources, and emotional issues that involve negative feelings between the members, such as anger, distrust, scorn, resentment, fear, and rejection. The process of negotiation focuses almost entirely on the concrete issues. The emotional issues, however, also need to be dealt with productively if agreement is to be reached.

The discussion of negotiations in this chapter focuses on situations in which two or more members of the same group, or two or more groups, have a conflict of interest. There are two basic goals in negotiating a conflict of interest: (1) reaching an agreement and (2) not damaging the basic cooperation among the individuals involved. Participants have to be concerned about both primary and secondary gains achieved through negotiations. The *primary gain* is determined by the nature of the agreement: the more favorable the agreement is to a member's short-term goals, the greater the primary gain for her. The *secondary gain* is determined by the group: the more effective the group, the more the member's long-term goals will be met, and therefore the greater the long-term gain for her. Consequently, in negotiating a resolution to a conflict a group member has to be concerned not only with what is more desirable for her in the short term but also with what is most desirable for improving the effectiveness of the group.

There are, of course, negotiation situations in which the persons in conflict have no future relationship. Buying a new car is a situation where negotiation over price is usually not affected by the need for future cooperation between the buyer and the salesman. Such one-time interactions are different from conflicts in a goal-oriented goal (where members have a continuing relationship).

THE NEGOTIATION RELATIONSHIP

Within any group, conflicts of interest will arise such that members will need to negotiate agreements with each other. Yet not every group discussion involves negotiation: negotiating is just one of many types of activity that take place within a group. So how do you recognize negotiations when you see them? You can tell whether or not you are negotiating by using the following checklist:

_____ **1.** Is there another member involved?

_____ **2.** Are both cooperative elements (we both wish to reach an agreement) and competitive elements (we both wish the agreement to be as favorable to ourselves as possible) present in the situation?

_____ **3.** Does getting what you want depend upon the agreement of another member?

_____ **4.** Are you in the dilemma of wanting to propose an agreement that is highly favorable to yourself but not wanting to risk making the other member so mad that she refuses to negotiate?

_____ **5.** Are you dependent upon the other member to give you information about what is a reasonable agreement from her point of view?

_____ **6.** Are there contractual norms on how negotiation should be conducted?

_____ **7.** Do the negotiations have a beginning, a middle, and an end?

Let's look more closely at each of these characteristics.

You cannot negotiate by yourself. It takes two to negotiate, whether it is two group members, two groups, two organizations, or two nations. Within any negotiations, furthermore, there are both cooperative and competitive elements. A cooperative element exists when both members believe they will gain more by negotiating than by not negotiating; a competitive element exists when both members have conflicting preferences among or contending interests in the different possible agreements. In any negotiation a range of possible agreements can be made; it is the push for one particular agreement rather than another that signifies the competitive elements in the negotiation relationship.

Because both members must commit themselves to an agreement, each is dependent upon the other for the outcome. All negotiating is aimed at achieving certain outcomes for oneself, but those outcomes are possible only if the other negotiator agrees to them. This situation is called *outcome dependence*.

A fourth characteristic of negotiations is the dilemma that participants face: each wants an agreement as favorable to himself as possible, but for one to attempt to maximize his outcome might result in such an unsatisfactory agreement for the other member that she would refuse to settle and would leave the negotiation relationship. For one negotiator not to attempt to maximize his outcome, however, would provide the other with too good an agreement; one would then be settling for less than necessary. In resolving the *goal dilemma* participants must decide on a "reasonable" settlement, one that will not only get the most for one participant but have a good chance of being acceptable to the other. Each participant seeks an agreement that is the best he can do in the face of the other's opposition. Inasmuch as there is rarely any obvious "correct" agreement that is accepted immediately by both members, each must decide during the negotiations what is a reasonable outcome for him-

self and for the other negotiator. The problem is always that the more favorable the agreement to oneself the less favorable it is to the other person.

The fifth characteristic of a negotiation relationship is that the negotiators are dependent upon each other not only for their outcomes but also for information about a possible agreement. This information can be secured in one of two ways: each negotiator can openly and honestly share what her preferences, needs, and expectations are, or each can attempt to hide her preferences, needs, and expectations in hopes of making an agreement as favorable to herself as possible. This is a complicated issue because a negotiator often does not know what her expectations should be until she learns what the other negotiator's expectations are. To the point that negotiators know both what the other wants and what is the least the other will accept, they will be able to develop an effective negotiating position. This *information dependence* sets up two more dilemmas, the dilemma of trust and the dilemma of honesty and openness. The *dilemma of trust* involves how much a negotiator can believe of the other's communications. To trust the other negotiator is to risk potential exploitation: by telling lies one participant can reduce the outcome for the other if her lies are believed. To distrust the other negotiator means that there is no possibility of any agreement being reached. The *dilemma of honesty and openness* involves the risk of either being exploited for disclosing too much too quickly or seriously damaging the negotiating relationship by seeming to be deceitful or distrusting.

The sixth characteristic of the negotiation relationship is the development of *contractual norms* that spell out acceptable behavior. Such norms specify the rules to be observed and the penalties for violating them. Thus, if violations occur the penalty can be assessed without destroying the possibility of further negotiations. Two norms quite common in negotiation situations are reciprocity and equity. The *norm of reciprocity* means that a negotiator should return the same benefit or harm given him by the other negotiator; "an eye for an eye and a kiss for a kiss" is an example of a norm of reciprocity. The *norm of equity* means that the benefits received or the costs assessed by the negotiators should be equal. Contractual norms provide clear ground rules for conducting the negotiations and managing the difficulties involved in reaching an agreement.

Finally, the negotiation relationship has important time dimensions. It has a beginning, a middle, and an end. Negotiation begins when the parties acknowledge that a conflict of interest exists and either formally or informally make initial moves in the direction of its resolution. Negotiation ends when one or more of the parties chooses to leave the negotiating relationship. This may occur because an agreement has been reached and the parties conclude by mutual consent, or because one or more of the parties believes no satisfactory agreement is possible. Though ending a negotiating relationship, the parties may continue other relationships. For example, after they have negotiated an agreement, the two parties can work cooperatively toward a mutual goal. In conducting negotiations, therefore, the parties must always consider future relationships between them: it will do no good to negotiate an agreement highly favorable to one member if future cooperation is jeopardized or if the other member becomes so resentful that the agreement cannot be implemented.

QUIZ

Check your reading of this section by answering the following questions. Answers are on page 333.

True   False   **1.** When faced with a conflict, you should either try to put up with it or avoid it.

True   False   **2.** To avoid the conflict, increase the frequency of the triggering event and decrease the barriers to negotiations.

True   False   **3.** Some barriers to expressing a conflict are attitudes, fears, time constraints, and disapproval.

True   False   **4.** To understand a conflict, you have to determine what types of barriers usually operate and what triggers its expression.

True   False   **5.** Every conflict of interest can be negotiated.

True   False   **6.** Cooperation exists when both members believe they will gain more by negotiating than not negotiating.

True   False   **7.** Competition exists when both members have conflicting preferences or interests in particular agreements.

  8. Negotiation is a process by which:
    a. people who disagree work out points of disagreement.
    b. people who agree work out a settlement.
    c. people who disagree but want to agree work out a settlement.
    d. Edye gets Buddy to ask her out to dinner.

  9. In negotiation, what is a primary gain?
    a. A favorable agreement to a person's short-term goals.
    b. A favorable gain to group effectiveness.
    c. A favorable resolution to both parties.
    d. When Edye pays the bill.

10. In negotiation, what is a secondary gain?
    a. A favorable agreement to a person's short-term goals.
    b. A favorable gain to group effectiveness.
    c. A favorable resolution to both parties.
    d. When Buddy pays the tip.

Match the following terms in the negotiation process with their definitions.

_____ 11. Specify the rules to be observed and what will happen if they are violated.

_____ 12. Each party should come out of the negotiations with equal settlements.

_____ 13. Each party depends on the other for the knowledge needed to structure his proposals.

_____ 14. Negotiators should return the same benefit or harm given to them by the other party.

_____ 15. The most and least that a person can believe of the other's information.

_____ 16. The least a person can tell without seeming deceitful in order to avoid exploitation.

_____ 17. The outcomes are possible only if the other agrees to them.

_____ 18. The settlement must not only get the most benefit for oneself but must also have a good chance of being acceptable.

a. Outcome dependence
b. Information dependence
c. Dilemma of goals
d. Dilemma of trust
e. Dilemma of honesty and openness
f. Contractual norms
g. Norm of reciprocity
h. Norm of equity

STEPS IN NEGOTIATING RESOLUTIONS OF CONFLICTS OF INTEREST

There are a few especially appropriate steps that individuals can take to negotiate constructive settlements. We will look at seven of them, beginning with confrontation. The purpose of a confrontation is to initiate negotiations in which the conflict is jointly defined; the issues, feelings, and perspectives of all participants are clarified; cooperative intentions are communicated; positions are differentiated and integrated; motivation to resolve the conflict is coordinated; and an agreement satisfactory to both sides is reached.

Step 1: Confronting the Opposition

The first step in negotiating a constructive settlement is to confront the opposition (Argyris, 1970; Beckhard, 1969; Bach and Wyden, 1969; Walton, 1969). A *confrontation* is the direct expression of one's view of the conflict and one's feelings about it and at the same time an invitation to the opposition to do the same. Confrontations involve clarifying and exploring the issues, the nature and strength of the underlying needs of the participants, and their current feelings. It is a deliberate attempt to begin a direct and problem-solving discussion about the conflict with the opposition.

A series of studies have compared confrontations with other strategies for dealing with conflicts of interest. Burke (1969) found that problem-solving confrontations were strongly associated with constructive resolution of conflicts, whereas forcing the other person to accept one's position was strongly associated with ineffective conflict management. Lawrence and Lorsch (1967) examined the use of confrontation, forcing the other person to accept one's position, and smoothing over conflict in six organizations. They found that high organizational performance was associated with the use of confrontation in dealing with conflicts. Burke (1970) asked seventy-four managers to describe the way they and their immediate superiors dealt with conflicts. Although both effective and ineffective managers reported the use of confrontation, ineffective managers reported much higher use of forcing the other person to accept one's position.

Several guidelines may be helpful in confronting a fellow group member:

Do not "hit and run": confront only when there is time to jointly define the conflict and schedule a negotiating session. A confrontation is the beginning of a negotiating process, not an end in itself. Thus, confrontations are not to be confused with "hit and run" events in which one person gives his views and feelings about a conflict and then disappears before the other person can respond. Hit-and-run tactics tend to escalate conflicts in negative directions and build resentment and anger in the victims. An important aspect of confrontation is timing: five minutes before the beginning or ending of a group meeting is not a good time to confront another person, nor is a telephone call during dinner a good way to do so.

Openly communicate your feelings about and perceptions of the issues involved in the conflict, and try to do so in minimally threatening ways. Make sure not to define the conflict as being caused by the other person's personality or psychological flaws. And do not reject the other person. The more defensive the other person is, the harder it will be to negotiate effectively.

Perhaps the most difficult aspect of confrontation is the open expression of feelings. Yet it is usually necessary: if emotions are not directly expressed verbally, they will be expressed in deeds or misdeeds later. Feelings such as anger and resentment are especially difficult for many persons to express constructively during confrontations. Unexpressed anger can be turned inward and become apathy, depression, and guilt, or it can be displaced onto other persons and situations. DeCecco and Richards (1974) found that when students or school personnel did not express the anger they felt it did not vanish but was expressed nonverbally in the sudden eruption of physical violence and assaults on both persons and property. When one person expressed anger and the other did not, anger seemed to build to even higher levels. Failure to express anger verbally was found to result in violence, intimidation, coercion, and the displacement of anger onto issues, personal differences, and actions that could not be negotiated. When anger was skillfully expressed by both participants in the conflict, it had such positive functions as communicating what issues needed to be resolved and where commitments were. The verbal expression of anger also seemed to generate motivation to resolve conflicts and to abide by the agreements made. An important factor in the skillful expression of anger was focusing on issues and conditions that could be changed with reasonable amounts of effort and time. DeCecco and Richards concluded that the expression of anger must be focused on issues. Anger focused on persons often took the form of verbal threats and was more often a prelude to violence than to negotiation. Feshbach (1970) also found that the verbal expression of anger can be a substitute for physical aggression. And Levi-Strauss (1969) states that structured ways of expressing anger and other "raw" feelings, such as verbalizing them in negotiations, transforms them into more "cooked" civilized feelings. Johnson (1971d) found that the expression of anger in ways that communicate rejection of the opponent as a person decreases the likelihood that the opponent will change her attitudes about the conflict being negotiated. The person expressing the anger, furthermore, tends to underestimate the alienating effect of anger in the opponent.

Besides anger, negotiators should also express warmth. Johnson (1971b, 1971d) found that the expression of warmth (compared with coldness and rejecting anger) results in more agreements being reached in negotiations, being better liked by opponents, opponents developing positive attitudes toward the negotiations, and opponents feeling accepted.

Accurately and fully comprehend opponent's views of and feelings about the conflict. If opponents believe they are not understood, or if you respond to only a fraction of their views and feelings, they will become more defensive and hostile. The listening skills described in Chapter 5 and in Johnson (1981, 1978) are vital in this aspect of confrontation.

Step 2: Jointly Defining the Conflict

It takes two or more persons to create a conflict of interest, and two or more persons to resolve a conflict of interest. In order to reach an agreement how the conflict is to be resolved, one must define it in a way that both sides can accept. Here are some helpful guidelines for defining the conflict constructively.

Do not label, accuse, or insult an opponent—describe the opponent's actions! Focus on behavior, not on psychological states and personality characteristics. There is a tendency in defining conflicts to attribute the causes of the conflict to inner psychological states of the opponent (Blake and Mouton, 1962; Chesler and Franklin, 1968; Sherif and Sherif, 1969). Defining a conflict as the actions of a sick, perverted, and vicious troublemaker is less constructive than defining a conflict as a specific set of actions by an opponent. Like everyone else, opponents want to appear strong and capable to others, and if they believe you are trying to label them as sick, weak, incompetent, or ineffective they will refuse to compromise or negotiate flexibly (Brown, 1968; Pruitt and Johnson, 1970; Tjosvold, 1974, 1977).

Define the conflict as a mutual problem to be solved, not as a win-lose struggle. A conflict defined as a problem to be solved is much easier to resolve constructively than a conflict defined as a win-lose situation (Blake and Mouton, 1962; Deutsch and Lewicki, 1970). The total benefits for all sides in negotiations are higher than when problem-solving strategies are used (Lewis and Pruitt, 1971). Defining a conflict as a win-lose situation leads to adopting strategies such as making an opening proposal highly favorable to oneself, refusing to modify it, trying to persuade the opponent that one's position is reasonable, using threats and promises to coerce and entice the opponent to accept one's proposal, and ignoring all the opponent's arguments concerning the validity of his position (Chertkoff and Esser, 1976; Johnson, 1974; Rubin and Brown, 1974; Walton and McKersie, 1965). Although win-lose strategies often pay off in the short-run, the damage they cause significantly reduces their secondary gains. Win-lose strategies commonly impose the position of the negotiator with the most power upon the other participants. They undermine trust, inhibit dialogue and communication, and generally diminish the likelihood that the conflict will be resolved constructively. In a win-lose negotiation every action of all participants is viewed as an attempt to dominate. Negotiators tend to deny the legitimacy of opponent's interests and consider only their own needs. They try to force the opponent to give in by augmenting their own power and undermine that of the opponent. Losers have little motivation to carry out the actions agreed upon, resent the winner, and often try to sabotage the agreement. The winner finds it hard to enforce the agreement. Severe damage to interpersonal relationships results: winner and losers will generally be hostile toward each other in the future.

Despite their high probability of secondary losses, win-lose strategies are often used in schools. Both Gump (1964) and Flanders (1964) have observed that teachers try to dominate students by coercing them into doing what the teacher wants. Such negotiation strategies tend to provoke student resistance (Flanders, 1964). Rafalides and Hoy (1971), in a study of forty-five high schools involving 3,000 teachers and administrators, concluded that when a school emphasizes authoritarian control and expects students to accept teacher decisions without question, students become alienated. DeCecco and Richards (1974) noted that 55 percent of the conflicts they studied were resolved by the imposing of decisions on students by school personnel. They concluded that coercion and threats of punishment by school personnel frequently escalated conflict and prevented negotiations.

Define the conflict in the smallest and most precise way possible. The smaller and more precise the definition of a conflict, the easier it will be to resolve (Deutsch, Canavan, and Rubin, 1971). It is easier, for example, to resolve a conflict over a small rule infraction than one involving disrespect for adult authority. The more general and ambiguous the definition of the conflict, the harder it is to resolve constructively.

Step 3: Communicating Positions and Feelings

Throughout negotiations, positions on the issues being negotiated and feelings may change. Thus, the communication skills for presenting and listening to information and feelings will continually be necessary. Conflicts cannot be resolved if negotiators do not understand what they are disagreeing about. Only if you understand the differences between your position and your opponent's will you be able to propose potential agreements that may be acceptable to both parties. The general rule for negotiating conflicts of interest is to differentiate, then try to integrate your position and your opponent's. The quality of your proposed integrations and compromises will never be better than your understanding of how your opponent's position, feelings, perspective, and needs differ from yours.

Step 4: Communicating Cooperative Intentions

Numerous studies indicate that the unambiguous expression of cooperative intentions in negotiations and conflicts of interest results in agreements being reached in shorter periods of time. There is also a reduction of opponents' defensiveness and egocentrism; increased attitude change; reduction of the felt importance of having the "right" ideas about the issues being negotiated; greater comprehension and retention by an opponent of one's position and arguments; and increased perceptions by the opponent that one accurately understands the opponent's position, is an understanding and accepting person, and is a person the opponent would like to confide in (Johnson, 1971b, 1974; Johnson, McCarty, and Allen, 1976). It is a good idea, therefore, to communicate clearly one's motivations and intentions to cooperate.

Step 5: Taking the Opponent's Perspective

It is common to misunderstand the motivations behind an opponent's actions. A member's resistance to the activities you wish the group to pursue may be a complete mystery to you. And the reasons why you are trying to modify the group's activities may be a complete mystery to members. In order to understand an opponent's actions and position, you will have to see the conflict from his perspective. And this will require that you be sufficiently detached from your position to see the conflict issues from new perspectives. Negotiation requires a realistic assessment of common and opposed interests. It requires the sacrifice of some of the opposed interests so that the parties can build on common benefits, concerns, advantages, and needs. In order to settle a conflict, it is necessary to have a clear understanding of all sides of the issues and an accurate assessment of their validity and relative merits.

In their study of conflict within schools, DeCecco and Richards (1974) found that the inability to take the perspectives of others seriously impeded negotiations as a means of conflict resolution. The failure of teachers and administrators to correctly perceive the interests of students results in destructive procedures for managing conflicts. Without perspective taking, the common interests of school personnel and students were not recognized and sought after by either staff or students. Within negotiations, therefore, you will want to take the perspective of your opponents in viewing the conflict, communicate that you are doing so to them (through the use of paraphrasing—see Chapter 5), and induce them to take your perspective. One procedure for doing so is to switch chairs with the opponent and spend a period of time presenting her position as if you were she, and have the opponent spend a period of time presenting your position as if she were you. A great deal of research has been conducted on such a perspective-reversal procedure (see Johnson, 1971a). Temporarily arguing your opponent's position does result in insight into your opponent's perspective and changes your attitudes about the issues being negotiated.

Step 6: Coordinating Motivation to Negotiate in Good Faith

There are often differences in motivation to resolve a conflict. You may wish to resolve a conflict, but a fellow group member may not. Or the reverse may be true. In order for a conflict of interest to be negotiated constructively, all parties need to be motivated to resolve it. Such motivation is based on the costs and gains of continuing the conflict. The *costs* of continuing a conflict may be the loss of a friendship, less enjoyment from group membership, constant disruption in the group, lower productiveness by group members, and harassment. The *gains* for continuing a conflict may be the satisfaction of protecting the status quo or frustrating persons you dislike. To increase the motivation of a fellow group member to negotiate, you need to increase his costs of continuing the conflict and reduce the gains. To decrease the motivation of another person to negotiate, decrease his costs and increase the gains for continuing the conflict.

Step 7: Reaching an Agreement

The conflict of interest is resolved when the participants reach an agreement. All participants need to be satisfied with the agreement and committed to abiding by it. The agreement should specify the joint position on the issues being adopted, the ways in which each participant will act differently in the future, and the ways cooperation will be restored if one of the participants slips and acts inappropriately. It should also include some provision for future meetings at which the participants can check how well the agreement is working and how cooperation can be improved.

Negotiating Conflicts of Interest: A Checklist for a Problem-Solving Strategy

___ 1. Identify triggering events and barriers to negotiations. Then trigger the conflict at a moment when there is time to discuss it thoroughly.

___ 2. Clarify your goals and the degree to which you want to maintain the relationship in good working order. This helps in planning the most appropriate negotiating strategy.

___ 3. Given that you wish to achieve your goals and maintain the relationship so that future cooperation is facilitated, confront the other person, making sure you (a) do not "hit and run"; (b) openly communicate your perceptions of and feelings about the issues, focusing on the issues and not on the other person; and (c) accurately and fully comprehend the opponent's views of and feelings about the conflict.

___ 4. Negotiate a joint definition of the conflict, making sure you (a) describe the opponent's actions without labeling, accusing, or insulting the person; (b) define the conflict as a mutual problem to be solved, not as a win-lose struggle; and (c) define the conflict in the smallest and most precise way possible.

___ 5. Communicate any changes in position and feelings.

___ 6. Communicate cooperative intentions.

___ 7. Take the other person's perspective accurately and fully, making sure you understand it and that the other person knows you understand it.

___ 8. Coordinate motivation to negotiate in "good faith" by highlighting the costs of continuing the conflict and the gains for resolving it.

___ 9. Make sure the agreement is satisfactory to both parties and that it clearly specifies (a) the agreement, (b) the ways in which each person will act differently in the future, (c) the ways cooperation will be restored if one of the persons slips and acts inappropriately, and (d) when future meetings will be held so that the parties can check how well the agreement is working.

THE WIN-LOSE NEGOTIATING STRATEGY

In the win-lose strategy the goal of negotiations is to make an agreement more favorable to oneself than to the other negotiator. In all negotiations a sequence of behavior occurs in which one party presents a proposal, the other evaluates it and presents a counterproposal, the first party replies with a modified proposal, and so on until a settlement is reached. The negotiators use this sequence of behaviors to obtain information that helps resolve the dilemma of goals. On the basis of the other party's opening offer, the proposals he receives, and the counterproposals he offers, a negotiator can obtain an idea as to what sort of settlement the person will agree to. A common win-lose negotiating pattern is for both negotiators to set a relatively high but tentative goal at first; they can then change it on the basis of the other person's reactions and counterproposals. This sequence of behaviors, which allows one negotiator to assess the second negotiator's points of potential settlement, can also be used to influence the second negotiator's assessment of the first's points of potential settlement. Through her opening offer and her counterproposals a negotiator can influence the other's expectations of what he considers a "reasonable" agreement. The more one negotiator can convince the other that she will not make an agreement unless it is highly favorable to her, the more likely it is that she will obtain a profitable agreement. Thus, an opening offer by a negotiator that is extremely favorable to her, combined with her refusal to budge from that offer, may convince the other negotiator that if an agreement is to be reached he will have to modify considerably what he orignally believed was a "reasonable" agreement. Ideally, a win-lose negotiator would like to obtain the maximal information about the other's preferences while disclosing the minimal, or misleading, information about her own preferences.

Other win-lose strategies include changing the other's evaluation of one's position, using threats and promises, and sticking doggedly to a committed position. When a win-lose negotiator makes an extreme opening offer and refuses to modify it very quickly, he must simultaneously try to convince the other negotiator of the correctness of his position. He does so by pointing out not only the validity of his own position but the wrongness or incorrectness of the other's. He must present, in other words, convincing rebuttals to the other's statements in order to try to *change* her evaluation of her position. In a *threat* a negotiator states that if the other negotiator performs an undesired act (such as refusing to agree to his proposed settlement) he will make sure the other is harmed. A negotiator may threaten that unless the other person agrees to accept a certain settlement he will not make an agreement at all. In a *promise* a negotiator states that if the other negotiator performs a desired act he will make sure the other receives benefits. A negotiator may promise that if the other person makes a certain compromise he will also compromise. Through the use of threats and promises win-lose negotiators attempt to persuade each other to make certain agreements. Another win-lose tactic for influencing the other negotiator to accept a certain agreement is for a negotiator to *commit* himself to a proposal that makes it clear that it is the other negotiator's last chance of avoiding "no agreement." Thus, he may make a proposal and plug up his ears until the other negotiator says yes.

For a goal-oriented group a win-lose strategy of negotiation has some fundamental shortcomings. Although it will often result in more favorable primary gains, the damage it can cause to future cooperation among group members significantly reduces its secondary gains. Because a win-lose strategy emphasizes power inequalities, it undermines trust, inhibits dialogue and communication, and diminishes the likelihood that the conflict will be resolved constructively. Attempts to create cooperative relations between negotiators are more effective if their power is equal. Walton (1969) notes that when power is unequally distributed the low-power person will automatically distrust the high-power person because she knows that those with power have a tendency to use it for their own interests. Usually, the greater the difference in power, the more negative the attitudes toward the high-power person. The high-power person, on the other hand, tends to underestimate the low-power person's positive intent. A negotiator's power advantage may make him more likely to interpret cooperative behavior by the other as compliant rather than volitional. The result is that the other's cooperative behavior has an effect on the high-power person that is less positive than it should be. Unequal power can also inhibit the weaker negotiator, and sometimes the stronger, from giving her views in a clear and forceful way. Finally, whenever one negotiator believes the other is trying to reduce his power, he is likely to react with competition and hostility.

Negotiating Conflicts of Interest: A Checklist for a Win-Lose Strategy

____ **1.** Identify triggering events and barriers to negotiations. Now, trigger the conflict at a moment when it is most advantageous to you and least advantageous to your opponent.

____ **2.** Clarify your goals, but publicly disguise or misrepresent them.

____ **3.** Begin a strategy to force the opponent into submission by presenting an extreme opening offer and indicating that you will rigidly adhere to it. Hit and run, mislead the opponent as to your position and feelings, and deliberately misunderstand the opponent's position and feelings when it helps you force the opponent into the agreement you want. Pursue your goals, ignoring goals held in common by you and the opponent.

____ **4.** Impose your definition of the conflict on the opponent. Label, accuse, and insult the opponent, define the conflict as a win-lose situation, and define the conflict in general and large ways when it is to your advantage to do so.

____ **5.** Concede and change slowly to force concessions from the opponent. Emphasize the superiority of your position, reasoning, and perspective. Use deceitful, inaccurate, and misleading communication of your goals, needs, position, and proposals. Use cooperative actions to grab a chance to exploit the opponent's cooperativeness.

____ **6.** Communicate competitive intentions. Use threats and hostility to obtain submission. Behave unpredictably to take advantage of the element of surprise. Increase ambiguity and uncertainty in an attempt to use deception and confusion to your advantage. Adopt a posture that allows you to exploit the opponent whenever possible.

____ **7.** Avoid all empathy and understanding of the opponent's position, needs, goals, feelings, and perspective.

____ **8.** Increase your opponent's willingness to concede by highlighting the costs of holding out and the gains for conceding. Try to arrange contact in which your power is greater. Try to increase your power over your opponent by emphasizing your independence from the opponent and the opponent's dependence on you. Isolate your opponent to reduce the possibility of his forming a coalition with third parties.

____ **9.** Make sure the agreement is as favorable to you and as unfavorable to your opponent as possible.

THE USE OF ROLE REVERSAL

Many conflicts are viewed as conflicts of interests when in fact they are not. Many persons use win-lose strategies in conflicts that would be resolved more productively through the use of problem-solving strategies. One of the major problems in our society is the difficulty in establishing the skillful use of effective conflict-management procedures. The use of role reversal is often helpful in changing a win-lose-oriented negotiator to a problem-solving-oriented negotiator, in helping two problem-solving-oriented negotiators understand each other, and in helping negotiators find creative integrations of their interests. Role reversal is also helpful in managing controversies.

Johnson (1971a) has conducted a long series of research studies on the use of role reversal in conflict situations. He found that skillful role reversal increases cooperative behavior between negotiators, clarifies misunderstanding of the other's position, increases understanding of the other's position, and aids one's ability to perceive the issue from the other's frame of reference. He also found the role reversal skillfully used can result not only in a reevaluation of the issue and a change of attitude toward it, but also in the role reverser being perceived as a person who tries to understand the other's position, as an understanding person in general, a person as willing to compromise, and as a cooperative and trustworthy person. Thus, there is considerable evidence that the use of role reversal facilitates the constructive management of conflicts.

Check your reading of this section by answering the following questions. Answers are on page 333.

1. Confrontation is:
   a. directly expressing one's view of and feelings about the conflict while inviting the other to do the same.
   b. standing up to the opposition and making them back down.
   c. letting other people know how you feel in no uncertain terms.

2. The guidelines for confrontation are (choose three):
   a. confront when the other person is vulnerable.
   b. confront when there is time to define the conflict.
   c. openly communicate your feelings and perceptions.
   d. openly communicate the faults of the other person.
   e. understand your opponent's views and feelings about the conflict.

3. In confrontation, anger should be (choose two):
   a. expressed.
   b. suppressed.
   c. focused on people.
   d. focused on issues.

4. Expressions of warmth result in:
   a. greater likelihood of reaching an agreement.
   b. being better liked by opponents.
   c. negotiations being better liked by opponents.
   d. all of the above.

5. Guidelines for defining the conflict include (choose three):
   a. describing the opponent's actions.
   b. labeling the opponent's actions.
   c. defining the conflict as a win-lose struggle.
   d. defining the conflict as a problem to be solved.
   e. defining the conflict in the smallest and most precise way possible.
   f. defining the conflict in the largest and most general way possible.

True	False	6. Effective managers use confrontation and forcing strategies the most.
True	False	7. Confrontation is an attempt to begin win-lose negotiations.
True	False	8. Communicating positions and feelings help enable conflict resolution.
True	False	9. Communicating cooperative intentions encourages your opponent to take advantage of you.

True False **10.** Understanding the perspective of your opponent will weaken your position.

True False **11.** To increase motivation to negotiate, increase the gains and decrease the costs for continuing.

True False **12.** An agreement should include ways cooperation will be restored if one of the participants breaks it.

True False **13.** A win-lose negotiation strategy is a strategy to resolve the conflict cooperatively.

True False **14.** A problem-solving negotiation strategy is a strategy where the problem is approached as a test of who is stronger.

True False **15.** People who use a problem-solving strategy when their opponent is using a power-based strategy will have the advantage.

True False **16.** A power-based strategy will get more secondary gains for the user.

True False **17.** A low-power person will automatically distrust a high power person.

True False **18.** A high-power person will automatically trust a low-power person.

True False **19.** The use of role reversal is helpful in changing a win-lose negotiator into a problem solving negotiator.

True False **20.** There is no substantial evidence to indicate that role reversal helps resolve conflicts.

BREAKING BALLOONS EXERCISE

This exercise seeks to demonstrate a nonverbal conflict—which is a complete change from the previous highly verbal activities. The procedure is as follows: Each participant is to blow up a balloon and tie it to his ankle with a string. Then, when the coordinator gives the signal the participants are to try to break one another's balloons by stepping on it. The person whose balloon is broken is "out," and must sit and watch from the sidelines; the last person to have an unbroken balloon is the winner. The participants can then discuss their feelings of aggression, defense, defeat, and victory. Strategies for protecting one's balloon while attacking others should be noted. A variation on the exercise is to have teams with different colored balloons competing against each other.

INTERGROUP CONFLICT EXERCISE

This exercise studies the dynamics of intergroup conflict and negotiation among groups with conflicting positions. It takes two hours. The procedure for the coordinator is as follows:

1. Introduce the exercise as an experience in intergroup conflict and negotiation. Divide the participants into four groups of not less than six members each, and distribute a copy of one of the accompanying instruction sheets to each group. Emphasize that the exercise will determine which group is best.

2. Have each group meet separately to select a negotiator and to develop their proposals on the issue. They have half an hour to do this. At the end of this period give them the accompanying reaction form and ask them to answer only questions 1, 2, and 5 and to write the name of their group at the top.

3. Have the negotiators meet in the center of the room, each with her group sitting behind her. Give each group representative five minutes to present her group's proposals. After each representative has completed her presentation have all participants complete the reaction form, answering all questions.

4. Tell the groups to reconvene separately and brief their negotiator on the best way to proceed in a second presentation of their position. The groups have fifteen minutes to confer. At the end of this period they again answer questions 1, 3, and 5 on the reaction form.

5. Have the negotiators again meet in the center of the room with their groups seated behind them. They have up to half an hour to reach an agreement. Group members can communicate with their negotiator through written notes. At the end of fifteen minutes stop the negotiations and have everyone again complete the questionnaire. Negotiations then resume, and at the end of the thirty-minute period everyone answers the reaction form for the last time.

6. Conduct a general session in which the results of the questionnaire are presented and discussed. Ask group members how they feel about the experience and then focus upon the experience of the negotiators.

7. Have the groups meet separately to discuss how well they worked together and what the experience was like for them. Develop a list of conclusions about intergroup conflict and place it on newsprint.

8. Again conduct a general session, this time to discuss the conclusions reached by each group.

Instructions to Coordinator for Use of the Reaction Forms

1. Pick one person in each group—as many assistants as you need—to hand out and collect the reaction forms and to compute the group mean for each question each time the forms are used.

2. Copy the four accompanying charts on a blackboard or large sheets of newsprint. After each use of the reaction forms, calculate the group means and place them on the charts, using a different color for each group. The response to question 5 should be listed for use in the discussion sessions. Do not let the participants see the results until the general session in which the results are discussed.

3. In discussing the results of each question, look for certain trends. The response to question 1 should be somewhat high in the beginning, increase after comparison with other group's proposals, and drop off if agreement is reached. If no agreement

is reached it should not drop off. For question 2, look for the "hero-traitor" dynamic: satisfaction goes up if the negotiator convinces other groups that her proposals are best, and goes down if she compromises the group's position. It is often helpful to look at the notes passed to the negotiator to see how the group is reacting. The responses to question 3 should be the reverse of the responses to question 1 (if satisfaction with one's own group's proposal is high, satisfaction with the other groups' proposals is low and vice versa). This usually amounts to devaluating the other groups' proposals and a loss of objectivity in evaluation. Question 4 usually demonstrates overconfidence in one's own group's proposal, though this sense of superiority gradually slips from an initial high as negotiations progress.

Intergroup Conflict Exercise: Instructions
Teachers Group

You are residents of Engleston, a medium-sized but quickly growing suburban community that is within commuting distance of a large city. Engleston has recently been torn by a number of civil-rights demonstrations centering on the issue of school integration. Two of the public schools in Engleston contain approximately 90 percent of the underprivileged, culturally different white and black children in the community. Moreover, the high-school dropout rate (60 percent) has shown the inadequacy of the educational program for these youngsters. Acts of vandalism and other forms of juvenile delinquency have been pronounced, and costly to the town, and most of those responsible are among the dropouts.

Four opposing groups in the community, yours among them, have suggested various solutions to some of these problems. The school board has asked the four groups to get together and settle on a single set of four to six proposals, which it will then implement.

As a member of the teachers group, you are essentially opposed to breaking up the schools in any way. You are interested in creating better schools and are generally in favor of expanding the educational program.

Your group is to submit four to six recommendations for dealing with the problems at a meeting at which your representative and one from each of the other three groups will be present. You and your groupmates may prepare a simple chart of the *main* points you wish to emphasize.

Try to make your recommendations original and creative, because it will be to your advantage if the other groups accept your proposals. After the representatives have presented their group's proposals, they will negotiate a *composite proposal* of four to six points to be presented to the school board.

Parents Group

You are residents of Engleston, a medium-sized but quickly growing suburban community that is within commuting distance of a large city. Engleston has recently been torn by a number of civil-rights demonstrations centering on the issue of school integration. Two of the public schools in Engelston contain approximately 90 percent of the underprivileged, culturally different white and black children in the community. Moreover, the high-school dropout rate (60 percent) has increasingly shown the inadequacy of the educational program for these youngsters. Acts of vandalism and other forms of juvenile delinquency have become pronounced, and costly to the town, and most of those responsible are among the dropouts.

Four opposing groups in the community, yours among them, have suggested various solutions to some of these problems. The school board has asked the four groups to get together and settle on a single set of four to six proposals, which it will then implement.

You are a member of the parents group. Because the tax rate is already one of the highest in the state, you favor solutions that will *not* increase your taxes. You feel that teachers and administrators have been lax, and that what is needed is more efficient and immediate use of the present resources. You are absolutely against any busing of students, and want all students to attend the school closest to their home.

Your group is to submit four to six recommendations for dealing with the problems at a meeting at which your representative and one from each of the other three groups will be present. You and your groupmates may prepare a simple chart of the *main* points you wish to emphasize.

Try to make your recommendations original and creative, because it will be to your advantage if the other groups accept your proposals. After the representatives have presented their group's proposals, they will negotiate a composite proposal of four to six points to be presented to the school board.

Civil-Rights Group

You are residents of Engleston, a medium-sized but quickly growing suburban community that is within commuting distance of a large city. Engleston has recently been torn by a number of civil-rights demonstrations centering on the issue of school integration. Two of the public schools in Engleston contain approximately 90 percent of the underprivileged, culturally different white and black children in the community. Moreover, the high-school dropout rate (60 percent) has increasingly shown the inadequacy of the education program for these youngsters. Acts of vandalism and other forms of juvenile delinquency have become pronounced, and costly to the town, and most of those responsible are among the dropouts.

Four opposing groups in the community, yours among them, have suggested various solutions to some of these problems. The school board has asked the four groups to get together and settle on a single set of four to six proposals, which it will then implement.

As a member of the civil-rights group, you are totally committed to immediate integration. You believe the schools have to be integrated through immediate busing of students. You feel that reforms generally take place too slowly, and you are extremely dissatisfied with the present situation.

Your group is to submit four to six recommendations for dealing with the problems at a meeting which your representative and one from each of the other three groups will be present. You and your groupmates may prepare a simple chart of the *main* points you wish to emphasize.

Try to make your recommendations original and creative, because it will be to your advantage if the other groups accept your proposals. After the representatives have presented their group's proposals, they will negotiate a *composite proposal* of four to six points to be presented to the school board.

School-Administrators Group

You are residents of Engleston, a medium-sized but quickly growing surburban community that is within commuting distance of a large city. Engleston has recently been torn by a number of civil-rights demonstrations centering on the issue of school integration. Two of the public schools in Engleston contain approximately 90 percent of the underprivileged, culturally deprived white and black children in the community. Moreover, the high-school dropout rate (60 percent) has increasingly shown the inadequacy of the educational program for these youngsters. Acts of vandalism and other forms of juvenile delinquency have become pronounced, and costly to the town, and most of those responsible are among the dropouts.

Four opposing groups in the community, yours among them, have suggested various solutions to some of these problems. The school board has asked the four groups to get together and settle on a single set of four to six proposals, which it will then implement.

As a member of the school-administrators group, you are generally satisfied with the way things are and believe that anything but gradual and carefully planned change would lead to chaos. Moreover, you believe that the complaining has been done chiefly by extremist groups at work in the community. In your opinion all school-policy decisions should be made by your group—and parents, teachers, and community groups should not butt it.

Your group is to submit four to six recommendations for dealing with the problems at a meeting at which your representative and one from each of the other three groups will be present. You and your groupmates may prepare a simple chart of the *main* points you wish to present.

Try to make your recommendations original and creative, because it will be to your advantage if the other groups accept your proposals. After the representatives have presented their group's proposals, they will negotiate a *composite proposal* of four to six points to be presented to the school board.

Reaction Form

Group: _____

1. How satisfied are you with your own group's proposals?
   Very dissatisfied   1 : 2 : 3 : 4 : 5 : 6 : 7 : 8 : 9   Very satisfied
2. How satisfied are you with the negotiator your group has selected?
   Very dissatisfied   1 : 2 : 3 : 4 : 5 : 6 : 7 : 8 : 9   Very satisfied
3. How satisfied are you with the proposals of the other groups?
   Very dissatisfied   1 : 2 : 3 : 4 : 5 : 6 : 7 : 8 : 9   Very satisfied

4. How do you think the final composite proposal will compare with your group's proposals?

Very inferior 1 : 2 : 3 : 4 : 5 : 6 : 7 : 8 : 9 Very superior

5. Write one adjective describing the way you now feel about what is taking place:

Chart A: Satisfaction with Own Group's Proposals

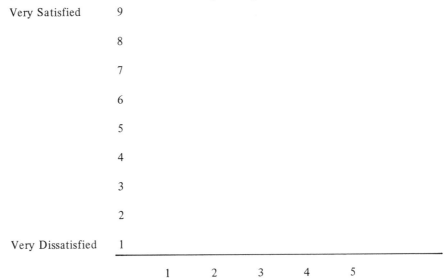

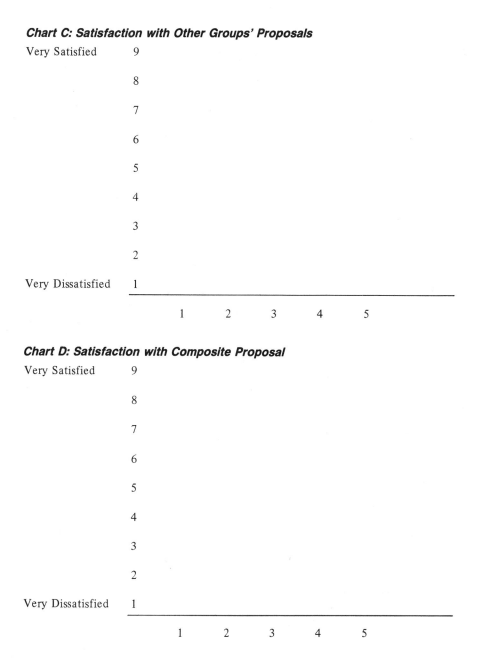

Chart C: Satisfaction with Other Groups' Proposals

Very Satisfied	9
	8
	7
	6
	5
	4
	3
	2
Very Dissatisfied	1

1   2   3   4   5

Chart D: Satisfaction with Composite Proposal

Very Satisfied	9
	8
	7
	6
	5
	4
	3
	2
Very Dissatisfied	1

1   2   3   4   5

BATTLESHIP EXERCISE

This exercise is designed to increase participants' understanding of a group's decision-making process during an intergroup conflict and to further their understanding of the dynamics of intergroup conflict. Here is the procedure for the coordinator:

1. Divide the class into groups of eight—six members and two observers. Introduce the exercise as an experience in group decision making during an intergroup conflict. State that each group will have the same task, the same instructions, and the same time limit. Performance on the task will be scored objectively. Each group member is to contribute fifty cents to a pool; the group with the highest score will collect 70 percent of the pool and the group with the next highest score will collect 30 percent. After the scores of the groups have been tabulated and the pool money distributed, the two winning groups must decide how to allocate their treasure by some rule other than dividing the money equally among group members. In other words, each member of the winning groups must receive a different amount of money. Each group will have twenty minutes to plan its organization prior to performing the task; each will have thirty minutes to complete the task, including reading the instructions.

2. While the groups begin organizing, brief the observers. They are to observe the task and maintenance behaviors of the group members (they will need copies of the task-behavior and maintenance behavior forms in Chapter 2 for this), note the dynamics of the decision making within the groups, and record the effects of intergroup competition on intragroup functioning. These subjects are covered in this chapter and in Chapters 2 and 3. As soon as the briefing is over, the observers return to their groups.

3. At the end of twenty minutes distribute copies of the accompanying instruction sheet and the grid sheet. Then take a grid sheet and draw the target mass anywhere on it, using the model on page 489 as an example. Record the salvos fired by each group and give the groups their total score for each salvo. Deal only with the official representatives of the groups. Do not accept more than four salvos from any one group.

4. At the end of thirty minutes stop all action. Announce the winning groups and distribute the money between them. While the winning groups are parceling out the money among their members, ask the other groups to (a) describe the process by which they made decisions and (b) classify each person in the group in terms of the task and maintenance behaviors in which he engaged.

5. Give each group twenty minutes to analyze its effectiveness. Groups should use the information gathered by their observers as a beginning point of the discussion. Conclusions about the impact of intergroup competition on intragroup functioning should be written on newsprint and shared with the other groups during the last few minutes of the exercise.

Battleship Exercise Instructions

1. The object of the exercise is to get the highest possible score from shooting sixteen times at a target.

2. The shots have to be fired in four salvos of four shots each. Any salvo may be fired at any time prior to the expiration of the thirty minutes. The coordinator will give a score of zero for any shots not fired before time expires.

3. On the ten-by-ten-square grid there is a target mass consisting of between six and fifteen adjacent squares. *Adjacent* means horizontally or vertically, not diagonally.

4. The squares in which the target is located differ in point value: some are worth one point, some three points, and some five.

5. A salvo is "fired" by being announced to the coordinator in terms of the coordinates of its targets (for example, A3, E5, C10, F2). The coordinator will then announce the *total* score obtained by the group for that salvo. He will *not* report the point value of an individual shot, only the *total salvo score.*

6. Shots may continue to be fired at the same squares. For example, if a group fires a four-shot salvo and gets a score of six points, it may continue to fire its remaining salvos at these same squares and obtain a score of six points for each salvo.

7. Your group must select a representative who will announce the coordinates of all salvos to the coordinator. Only that person's "shots" will be accepted. If the representative announces a shot not on the grid—for example, P5—the coordinator will give a score of zero.

8. Your group may mark its grid sheet in any way it chooses.

9. Your group may not ask any questions of the coordinator. All the necessary instructions are contained on this sheet.

10. Remember, the thirty-minute period began with the distribution of these instructions.

GRID SHEET

	A	B	C	D	E	F	G	H	I	J
1										
2										
3										
4										
5										
6										
7										
8										
9										
10										

OTHER EXERCISES IN INTERGROUP CONFLICT

Other intergroup-conflict exercises can easily be created around the general procedure given on pages 311–317. The task can be to state the five most important principles of leadership, the qualities of an effective supervisor, the five most important things for a teacher to know, and so on. The dynamics of intergroup conflict are so predictable that if people are divided into groups and told to compete, develop their position, and represent that position in negotiations, they are bound to be present.

WIN–LOSE INTERGROUP CONFLICT

How groups relate to one another within organizations has considerable bearing on the effectiveness of the organization. Groups are often in conflict, and just as cooperation is needed between different members of the same group, when two groups are part of the same organization or goal-directed effort a high degree of cooperation between them is essential. The dynamics of intergroup conflict are about as destructive as they are predictable. And the more the intergroup conflict is defined as a win-lose situation, the more predictable are the effects of the conflict on the relationships of members within the group, on relationships between the groups, on negotiations between the groups, on the group that wins, and on the group that loses (Sherif, 1966; Blake and Mouton, 1962; Watson and Johnson, 1972).

A group in the throes of an intergroup conflict experiences a strong upward shift in cohesion as the members join together to defend their group against defeat. The group becomes more closely knit and gleans greater loyalty from its members; members close ranks and "table," or put aside, some of their conflicts with one another. There is a sharpening and banding together of the ingroup power structure as militant leaders take control and group members become more willing to accept autocratic leadership. Maintenance needs become secondary to task needs, and the group becomes more tightly structured and organized. Satisfaction among the members runs high, along with their sense of identification with the group and with its position on the issues in the conflict. At the same time the opposing group and its positions are belittled and devalued. Conformity is demanded; "a solid front" must be presented.

Between the groups, an attitude of hostility develops. Each sees the other as the enemy. Inaccurate and uncomplimentary stereotypes form. Distortions in perception (see Johnson, 1981) increase: each group sees only the best parts of itself and the worst parts of the other group. Interaction and communication decrease between members of the conflicting groups. Doubt is cast upon the validity of the position of the other group; its position is seen as distinctly inferior to that of one's own group. Group members tend to listen only to what supports their own position and stereotypes. They misperceive and fail to lisen carefully to the other group's position. All of these dynamics only intensify the conflict and deepen distrust.

In negotiations, there are distortions of judgment about the merits of the conflicting positions, with one's own position recognized as "good" and the other group's position assessed as "bad." Negotiators are relatively blind to points of agreement between their own and the other side's proposals, and they tend to emphasize the differences. The orientation of the negotiators for the two sides is to win for their group, not to reach an agreement that satisfies everyone. This stance inevitably results in the hero-traitor dynamic: the negotiator who "wins" is seen as a "hero" and the one who "loses" as a "traitor." When a neutral third party decides who is "right" and who is "wrong," the winner considers the third party to be impartial and objective; the loser views the third party as biased and thoughtless. Each side sees itself as objective and rational and the other side as unjust and irrational—thereby excluding from the negotiations any elements of genuine objectivity. With the only loyalty being to one's own group's position, the common result of win-lose negotiations is a deadlock. The win-lose strategy can result, of course, in the representative being caught in a conflict between his own beliefs and perceptions and the mandate given him by his group.

The group that "wins" becomes even more cohesive. It also tends to release tension, lose its fighting spirit, and become self-satisfied, casual, even playful. The leadership that was responsible for the victory is consolidated. Though there is a high concern for maintenance, there is little tendency to work. Members believe that winning has confirmed their positive stereotype of their group and the negative stereotype of the other group, and that as a result there is little need to reevaluate perceptions or reexamine group operations to learn how to improve them.

The group that "loses" frequently splinters, seeks the reasons for its defeat, and then reorganizes. Members bring to the surface unresolved conflicts among themselves in an effort to find the reasons for the defeat. Tension increases and the group begins to work even harder. Maintenance concerns abate as task concerns rise in a group effort to recover from defeat. The group often seeks someone to blame for the defeat—the leader, the judges, those who made the rules of the conflict situation, the least conforming members, and so on—and replaces the leadership responsible for the loss. If future victories seem impossible, members may become completely demoralized and assume a defeatist, apathetic attitude toward the group. The losing group tends to learn a great deal about itself because its positive stereotype of itself and its negative stereotype of the other group have been upset by the loss; it has therefore had to reevaluate its perceptions. Consequently, the losing group is likely to reorganize and become more cohesive and effective once it has accepted the loss realistically.

The most important point about intergroup conflict on a win-lose basis is that it should be prevented if at all possible. It is a lot easier to do this by making sure that the groups share a cooperative goal structure and that problem-solving methods are at work between them than it is to undo the conflict once the groups have gotten into a win-lose situation.

Though intergroup conflict has been discussed above from the point of view of the need to resolve it in a way that enhances cooperation among groups, it should be noted that intergroup competition can have many benefits. It often increases the involvement, fun, commitment, interest, and motivation of group members working on tasks. For a discussion of the use of such intergroup competition in schools, see Johnson (1970) and Johnson and Johnson (1975).

QUIZ

Check your reading of this section by answering the following questions. Answers are on page 333.

True   False   **1.** In a win-lose situation between groups, members become more closely knit and loyal to the group.

True   False   **2.** In a win-lose situation, groups see only their best and the other group's worst.

True   False   **3.** In a win-lose situation, when a third party decides the winner, both sides are satisfied.

True   False   **4.** The group likely to become more cohesive and casual after a decision is the winning group.

True   False   **5.** The best way to solve a win-lose situation is to prevent it.

Match the following terms with their definitions:

_____ **6.** The other group's behavior is seen in terms of personality.

_____ **7.** Assumptions about the other group's behavior lead to actions which evoke that behavior.

_____ **8.** Every action of the other group is seen as an attempt to dominate.

a. Win-lose dynamic

b. Psychodynamic fallacy

c. Self-fulfilling prophecy

INTERGROUP CONFRONTATION EXERCISE I

This procedure was developed by Blake and Mouton (1962), and has since been used quite successfully in conflicts in a variety of organizations. It has probably been applied to every type of intergroup conflict one can imagine. Its purpose is to change the win-lose orientation to intergroup conflict to the cooperative, problem-solving orientation. The exercise takes at least two or three hours to conduct (Blake and Mouton usually spend about nineteen hours on it in actual union–management conflicts). The procedure for the coordinator is as follows:

1. Introduce the exercise as an experience in resolving conflicts between two or more groups. State that the objective is to change win-lose orientations to problem-solving orientations. You might discuss the previous success Blake and Mouton have had with the exercise in difficult union–management conflicts. Use the accompanying description of a union–management conflict to set up a role-play that participants can use in the exercise.

2. Have each group meet separately and develop on newsprint how it sees itself as a group and how it sees the other group. Allow the groups at least one hour to complete this task.

3. Have the two groups come together and share their viewpoints. Have them compare, with your help, how each side sees itself with how the other side sees it. It is rather common for each group to see the other as unreasonable, unethical, and unwilling to cooperate while seeing itself as extraordinarily reasonable, ethical, and cooperative. The differences in the perception of how each group sees the other group are then clarified.

4. Ask the two groups to meet separately for at least one hour to diagnose their present relationship. They should answer such questions as, What problems exist? Why aren't they being constructively handled? What does the other group contribute to conflict? What does one's own group contribute to the conflict? The groups should place this material on newsprint.

5. Have the groups meet together to share their diagnoses. Help them to summarize the key issues causing the conflicts between them and the main sources of friction. Keeping the material on constructive conflicts in mind, the two groups should plan the next stages of their cooperative solution of their conflict.

6. Ask the two groups to assess their reactions to the exercise and summarize what they have learned about resolving intergroup conflict. Conclusions about preventing intergroup conflict should also be presented and discussed.

Union–Management Conflict

The teacher's union of a large city has asked the local board of education for certain across-the-board increases in pay and fringe benefits. The board has refused to meet these "excessive demands," and has made an offer that the union leadership considers unacceptable. Still without a contract agreement at midnight of the day school is to open, the union has voted to go on strike—and to remain on strike until a satisfactory agreement is reached. Divide into union and management groups and carry out the above procedures.

THREE BASIC TRAPS

Blake and Mouton emphasize that those who use this procedure must avoid three basic traps that lead to increased, rather than decreased, conflict.

The first to avoid is the *win-lose dynamic*—seeing every action of the other group as a move to dominate. The participants must learn to recognize win-lose attitudes and behaviors and be able to set norms that stress their avoidance. The second trap to avoid is the *psychodynamic fallacy*—seeing the motivation for the other group's behavior in terms of personality factors rather than the dynamics of intergroup conflict. It is much easier to blame the conflict on sick, vicious, power-hungry persons than to view the other group's behavior as a predictable result of intense intergroup conflict. The final trap to avoid is the use of *self-fulfilling prophecies*. For example, one group assumes that the other is belligerent and proceeds to engage in hostile behavior in an attempt to defend itself by mounting a good offense—thereby provoking belligerence on the part of the other group, which confirms the original assumption.

INTERGROUP CONFRONTATION EXERCISE II

A procedure has been established by Beckhard (1969) for determining the relevant cooperative goals toward which all groups can take committed action. Because he recommends that the exercise be used when groups are in conflict and the members are experiencing stress, the procedure is one of conflict management. The objective of the exercise is to get the groups moving toward a plan of action and a set of priorities for change and improvement that will resolve existing conflicts and establish cooperative goal accomplishment. Beckhard conducts the exercise as a one-day activity, but it can be shortened to a couple of hours when used strictly for learning. The procedure for the coordinator is as follows:

1. Introduce the exercise as an experience in setting cooperative goals among groups presently experiencing intergroup conflict. Stress that the exercise is an opportunity for the participants to influence the actions of their groups, and urge them to be open and honest with their feelings and ideas. The union–management situation used in the previous exercise can be applied here for role-playing purposes.

2. Divide the participants into groups of five or six and have them meet separately. the task of these conflicting groups is to think of ways in which life would be better for their members and for their relationship with other groups. Ask each group to make a list of its ideas and place them on newsprint. This phase takes between thirty and forty-five minutes.

3. You or the participants should categorize the ideas listed.

4. Have the groups complete the following tasks:
   a. Go through the entire list and select three or four items that most affect you and your group. Determine what action your group will take on them, and establish a timetable for beginning work on those problems. Prepare to report your decisions in a general session.

b. Go through the list again and select those items to which you think all groups should give highest priority. These items should be problems that your group cannot deal with alone.

5. In a general session have the groups share the results of their meetings. Combine the lists. The groups should then outline plans of action for implementing their decisions and determine the necessary follow-up procedures. In doing this they should emphasize intergroup cooperation.

6. Ask the groups to assess their reactions to the exercise and summarize what they have learned about resolving intergroup conflicts. Conclusions about preventing intergroup conflict should also be presented and discussed.

INTERGROUP CONFLICT AND SUPERORDINATE GOALS

Perhaps the most interesting and best known studies of intergroup conflict were performed under the direction of Muzafer Sherif (1966). Sherif was born in 1906 in Izmir, Turkey. After attending Izmir International College, he studied at the University of Istanbul, receiving a master's degree in 1928. Awarded a fellowship in national competition for study abroad, he went to Harvard University in 1929, received another master's degree in 1932, and then traveled to Germany where he attended Kohler's lectures and the University of Berlin. He then taught in Turkey, returned to Harvard to conduct research, and then studied at Columbia University (1934–1936), where he received the Ph.D. degree in 1935. His dissertation was published as a book, *The psychology of group norms,* (discussed in Chapter 9). He studied in Paris, taught in Turkey until January 1945 when he returned to the United States. After a time at both Princeton and Yale, he became Director of the Institute of Group Relations at the University of Oklahoma, a position he held from 1949 to 1966. In 1966 he moved to the Pennsylvania State University. It was during the years he spent at Oklahoma that he encountered his famous research on superordinate goals.

To study intergroup conflict and its resolution, Sherif, his students, and his colleagues ran a summer camp for twelve-year-old boys in the early 1950s. All the boys were strangers to one another prior to attending the camp, so there were no established relationships among them. The camp setting, isolated from outside influences, afforded the experimenters a unique opportunity to manipulate the conditions and circumstances of interaction among the camp members. The investigators were interested in studying intergroup relations, and especially the effectiveness of various techniques for reducing hostility between groups. To create intergroup conflict, the experimenters divided up the campers into groups and instilled in each group an esprit de corps by such procedures as assigning names like Bull Dogs and Red Devils to the groups and structuring their daily activities so that interdependent, coordinated activity among the group members was necessary for achieving desired goals (the food, for example, needed to be cooked over a campfire and distributed among the group members).

Following the successful development in the camp of two ingroups characterized by mutual good feeling between their members, the experimenters attempted to induce conflict between the two groups by requiring them to participate in competitive activities in which the winning group was rewarded and the losing group was not. For a time the two groups displayed good sportsmanship, but in the course of the competitive activities they became increasingly hostile toward each other. Eventually the two groups were having garbage fights—throwing mashed potatoes, leftovers, bottle caps, and the like—in the dining hall.

Sherif (1966) and his associates next tested several different methods of reducing the conflict between the groups. To find out the effects of social contact between groups on intergroup conflict, Sherif devised several pleasant situations in which members of the rival groups could engage in such contact. These situations included eating together in the same dining room, watching a movie together, and shooting firecrackers in the same area. These contact situations had no effect in reducing intergroup conflict. If anything, they were utilized by members of both groups as opportunities for further name-calling and other forms of conflict. Sherif concluded that contact between groups in pleasant situations does not in itself decrease existing intergroup tension.

The next strategy researched by Sherif (1966) and his associates was the establishment of a common enemy. Sherif did demonstrate that it is possible to reduce the hostility between two groups by presenting them with a common enemy against whom they are banded together. He arranged a softball game in which the two groups in conflict were combined to play against a group of boys from a nearby town. The common enemy did bring the two groups of campers together and reduced some of the hostility between them. This approach, however, has little promise for conflict resolution, as it fails to resolve the conflict but only transfers it from two small groups to two larger groups. Bringing some groups together against other means larger and more devastating conflicts in the long run.

Sherif (1966) hypothesized that contact between the rival groups would resolve the conflict only when the groups came together to work cooperatively toward goals that were more important to the groups than the continuation of their conflict. Since cooperation toward common goals had been effective in forming the two ingroups, Sherif reasoned, it would be effective in reducing the conflict between the groups. Sherif therefore arranged a series of superordinate-goal situations for the two antagonistic groups of campers to engage in. He defined *superordinate goals* as goals that cannot be easily ignored by members of two antagonistic groups, but whose attainment is beyond the resources and efforts of either group alone; the two groups, therefore, must join in a cooperative effort in order to attain the goals. One such goal was to repair the water-supply system, which the experimenters had earlier sabotaged. Another was to obtain money to rent a movie that both groups wanted to see. Still another was to push a truck to get it started after it had suddenly broken down on its way to a camp-out with food. After the campers had participated in a series of such activities their attitude toward members of the outgroup changed; several friendships among members of different groups were formed, members of the rival group were no longer disliked, and the friction between the groups disappeared.

The characteristics of the superordinate goals introduced by Sherif and his associates in their studies were as follows:

1. They were introduced by a more powerful third party (the experimenters).
2. They were perceived by campers to be natural events in no way identified with the third party.
3. They were not perceived by the two groups of campers as being aimed at resolving the conflict.
4. They transcended the conflict situation and restructured the competitive relationship between the groups into a cooperative one.

In most conflict situations such superordinate goals are not feasible alternatives. A third party, for example, rarely had the power to initiate goals with the above characteristics. Nor could a participant in a conflict easily initiate such a goal in an attempt to resolve the conflict.

Johnson and Lewicki (1969) compared the effectiveness of a superordinate goal having all of the characteristics of the superordinate goals used by Sherif with the effectiveness of a superordinate goal that was initiated by one of the groups in the conflict, was identified with the initiating group, and was perceived as being aimed at resolving the conflict. The subjects were a group of thirty-six college students who were participating in a four-day leadership-training program. An intergroup-competition exercise similar to ones used in the experiments of Blake and Mouton (1962) was used. Johnson and Lewicki found that although the Sherif-type superordinate goal was effective in reducing competition and hostility between groups, it tended to lead to a premature cooperation that left the basic conflict between the groups unresolved. They hypothesized that after the superordinate goals were accomplished the groups would still be faced with a basic conflict that might subsequently be reactivated. The second type of superordinate goal, on the other hand, became caught up in the competitiveness of the situation and increased, rather than decreased, the conflict. The group initiating the superordinate goal used it as a key argument in an attempt to reach an agreement with the opposing group. Believing that they had the best interests of both groups at heart and that initiating the superordinate goal was an initial concession on their part, they felt that the opposing group would be quite accommodating to their wishes. The opposing group, however, tended to view the superordinate goal as part of a competitive strategy aimed at furthering the initiating group's vested interests, and refused to accept it. The result was an intensification of the conflict, increased misunderstanding, and a refusal by both groups to compromise. From the Johnson and Lewicki study it may be concluded that introducing superordinate goals to resolve a conflict between groups is a complex process that needs to include activities that resolve the differences between the groups and that needs to dissociate the superordinate goals from the negotiating ploys and strategies of the groups involved in the conflict.

Sherif's notion of resolving conflicts through the use of superordinate goals in an elaboration of the principle that groups that cooperate with one another toward the accomplishment of common goals will have harmonious and friendly relations. Deutsch's (1949, 1962) theory of cooperation and competition states such a principle, and a number of research studies support the principle's validity (Johnson and Johnson, 1975). Deutsch's theory predicts that even when there is intense hostility between two groups, cooperative action to accomplish goals that are of vital importance to both will result in mutual liking and continued cooperation.

CONSTRUCTIVE MANAGEMENT OF CONFLICTS OF INTEREST

If any group is to function effectively, a high level of cooperation among its members must prevail. Whatever the method used to either control or resolve conflicts, it must establish as much cooperation as possible among group members to be effective. The management of conflicts of interests in ways that maximize member cooperation depends on the group having a common set of values and norms about the management of conflict and an agreed-upon vocabulary for discussing conflicts among members.

As with controversies, group members in a conflict of interest must have a system of positive beliefs about fighting: they must view it as a productive way of handling differences. Members must believe that conflicts of interest are natural and should not be avoided or repressed; that the natural tension and frustration of working together can be greatly reduced through conflicts; that conflicts help group members avoid stockpiling anger and resentment and being bothered by the past; and that conflicts bring information to group members about how they are progressing, what is important to each member, and how group work and members' relationships can be improved. In addition to the points on negotiating covered in this chapter, some additional norms and procedures conducive to constructive conflict management are as follows.

1. The circumstances that brought about the conflict should be understood by group members. Such circumstances involve both barriers to the beginning of negotiations and events that trigger expressions of the conflict (Walton, 1969). Internal barriers include negative attitudes, values, fears, anxieties, and habitual patterns of avoiding conflict. External barriers may include task requirements, group norms for avoiding conflict, and faulty perceptions of one's vulnerability and others' strength. Despite these potential barriers, however, particular circumstances called *triggering events* may be capable of bringing about open negotiations. The diagnosis of a conflict involves discovering (a) the barriers to negotiation and (b) what triggers open expression of the conflict. From such knowledge group members can help choose the time and place for negotiations. If an appropriate time is not immediately available, the barriers to expressing the conflict can be increased and the triggering events can be decreased in order to avoid the conflict temporarily. Some events may trigger a destructive cycle of conflict and others may trigger problem solving; group members will want to maximize the latter type of triggering event. An analysis of events that surround or precede a conflict often provides clues to the basic issues of the conflict.

2. The entry state of the participants should be assessed by the group. The *entry state* of a group member is that person's ability to deal constructively with the conflict. Members' level of self-awareness, their ability to control their behavior, their skills in communicating and in other ways being interpersonally effective (see Johnson, 1981), their ability to withstand stress, and their ability to incorporate their strengths in constructive conflict behavior are all important aspects of their entry state. Group support and consultation can raise the entry state of each participant.

3. Standards should be set on what "weapons" are to be allowed and when "beltlines" are to be established for each member. The intensity and area of attack should be kept within each member's revealed capacity to deal with the hurt.

4. The situational power of all participants should be balanced. Power can involve being more verbal, having a louder voice, or having more authority. The group should help minimize such differences so that negotiations can be conducted among equals.

5. Intermissions should take place during which participants can reflect on the conflict and what they are learning from it.

6. An optimal tension level should be maintained by each throughout the negotiations. A period of high tension that generates motivation to negotiate in good faith, followed by a reduction to a moderate level of tension that does not interfere with a person's ability to integrate and use information, is often the best way to manage conflicts of interest.

7. The consequences of the conflict of interest should be clearly understood. Consequences can be either costs or gains. When a group is involved

in negotiations among its members, an appreciation of the costs and gains of the conflict for each member is essential. Both the primary and the secondary costs and gains for the negotiators and for the group as a whole need to be correctly assessed, especially when members begin using win-lose negotiation strategies. An analysis of the consequences of a conflict may yield an understanding of why the conflict is tending to intensify, subside, or stay at the same pitch. An understanding of the consequences of a conflict permits group members to identify the desirable and realistic ones and plan strategies accordingly. In examining the consequences of a conflict members should never ignore the positive outcomes; it is all too easy to focus only on the costs and not on the benefits.

8. The constructive management of conflict often requires a common language about conflicts. The group language might include such terms as *win-lose, problem-solve, confront, beltline,* and *gunnysack.* To *gunnysack* is to store up grievances for a long time and then unload them all on an offending group member. A common language about conflicts facilitates the identification of constructive and destructive strategies of negotation. Every group may develop its own vocabulary for describing conflict behaviors and procedures.

9. In negotiations, many participants wish to appear hard to influence. The toughness of negotiators in fighting for their interests is especially important when they are following win-lose strategies and attempting to dominate the opposition. Under such circumstances negotiators may rather not reach a constructive agreement in order to maintain their *bargaining reputation.* Groups may wish to find ways of minimizing the concern of their members that the reputation of the negotiators will be affected if they reach constructive agreements.

10. Besides being aimed at resolving a conflict, negotiations can have important side effects, such as maintaining contact with an adversary, substituting negotiations for violent action, gathering intelligence, practicing deception, issuing propaganda, and having an impact on third parties (Ikle, 1964). It may be in the interests of the whole group to encourage continued negotiation between two members in order to obtain desired side effects as well as a resolution of the conflict.

11. The most important aspect of negotiating conflicts among group members is to ensure that they focus on the long-term joint outcomes of an agreement, not on short-term individual outcomes. Many conflicts of interest can be resolved in ways that maximize the long-term benefit of the members and the group as a whole. Members who become locked into a win-lose negotiating strategy often focus on short-term self-interests in a way that blinds them to the longer-term mutual benefits to themselves and the entire group. The group should ensure that conflicts of members are resolved so as to maximize secondary rather than primary gains.

NEGOTIATION STRATEGIES: CONSTRUCTIVE AND DESTRUCTIVE

In the research and theorizing on negotiations, numerous strategies have been suggested. Those in the partial list below were taken from studies of union–management and international negotiations. Since most such negotiations are treated as win-lose situations, the strategies listed are not necessarily recommended by the authors. Readers interested in further study of negotiation strategies, however, are referred to Douglas (1962), Ikle (1964), Schelling (1960), and Stevens (1963).

Every negotiator is continually faced with a threefold choice: (1) accept the available terms for agreement, (2) try to improve the available terms through further negotiation, and (3) discontinue negotiations without agreement and with no intention of resuming them. If the choice is to continue negotiations, a variety of strategies can be used to influence: (1) the opponent's expectations as to what a reasonable outcome is for her, (2) the opponent's perceptions of what one's expectations of a reasonable agreement is, and (3) the opponent's perceptions of how influenceable one is. Among these strategies are the following:

1. Establish the negotiating range or the boundaries of negotiation by adopting an extreme opening offer and refusing to compromise in order to build a reputation of toughness and to influence the opponent's notion of what an acceptable agreement is.

2. Search for possible points of agreement beneath the surface of the current disagreement. Obtaining accurate information about potential agreements that would be acceptable to the opponent is a vital element of their strategy.

3. Precipitate a decision-making crisis in which you try to force the opponent into making a decision favorable to yourself. This is done by gaining control over the opponent's perception of the situation, limiting the opponent's perceived alternatives, luring the opponent's attention in the desired direction, and using pressure to speed the opponent along toward an end to the negotiations.

4. Compromise.

5. Add new demands until the other negotiator agrees to terms less favorable than those originally proposed.

6. Propose a package deal in which several issues that are considered part of the agreement are settled.

7. Introduce an issue considered extraneous by your opponent—a *tie-in*—and offer to accept a certain settlement provided this issue is also settled to your satisfaction.

8. Carve an issue out of a larger context, settle it, and leave the related issues unsettled.

9. Coercion: make a threat that you will carry out if the opponent does not agree to your terms.

10. Commit yourself to an action that leaves the last clear chance of avoiding disaster or nonagreement to the other negotiator, thereby limiting her alternatives.

11. Create an impression of being uncertain about what you will do, being out of control, or being irrational, so that the opponent will want to settle quickly before you do serious harm to everyone involved.

QUIZ

Check your reading of this section by answering the following questions. Answers are on page 333.

Match the following terms with their definitions:

_____ 1. The present ability of the participants to deal constructively with the conflict.

_____ 2. Storing up grievances for a long time and unloading them all at once.

_____ 3. Attitudes, values, fears, needs, and habitual patterns of avoiding conflicts.

_____ 4. Perceptions of one's own and the other's vulnerability, task requirements, and group norms.

_____ 5. Something that brings about an open conflict, despite potential barriers.

_____ 6. Two competing groups must work together to accomplish something which must be done.

a. Superordinate goals
b. Gunnysacking
c. Internal barriers
d. External barriers
e. Triggering events
f. Entry state

True False   7. A superordinate goal will resolve the conflict between two groups.

True False   8. A superordinate goal imposed by one of the competing groups will reduce the conflict.

True False   9. A superordinate goal can induce cooperation and liking between competing groups.

True False   10. The most important aspect of negotiating conflicts is to focus on long-term, joint outcomes rather than on short-term, individual outcomes.

YOUR CONFLICT BEHAVIOR

Having completed this chapter on conflict, you may find it helpful to focus again on your behavior in conflict situations. To do so, form a group with two persons who know you well and who have participated with you in some of the exercises in this book. Then complete the following tasks, taking at least two hours to do so.

1. Give one another feedback about the animal, song, or book that each person reminds the others of on the basis of how he deals with conflict. Each person explains why he chose the animal, song, or book that he did.

2. Write down your individual strengths in handling conflicts constructively. Share your lists and see what you can add to the other members' lists.

3. Write down the individual skills you need to develop in order to handle conflict more constructively. Then share your lists and see what you can add to the other members' lists.

4. Discuss the feelings each of you have in conflict situations and why you react the way you do. Help each other think of alternative ways of feeling or reacting to conflict situations.

5. From magazine pictures and any other available materials build a collage about the way in which you behave in conflict situations. Share the collage with the others. Add ideas to their collages.

SUMMARY

Now that you are acquainted with the dynamics involved in resolving conflicts of interest and have practiced resolving them, you are ready to encounter power. You will do so in the next chapter.

ANSWERS

Page 285—1. b; 2. b, c; 3. b; 4. c; 5. a; 6. e; 7. d; 8. a; 9. e; 10. c; 11. d; 12. b.

Page 299—1. false; 2. false; 3. true; 4. true; 5. false; 6. true; 7. true; 8. c; 9. a; 10. b; 11. f; 12. h; 13. b; 14. g; 15. d; 16. e; 17. a; 18. c.

Page 310—1. a; 2. b, c, e; 3. a, d; 4. d; 5. a, d, e; 6. false; 7. false; 8. true; 9. false; 10. false; 11. false; 12. true; 13. false; 14. false; 15. false; 16. false; 17. true; 18. false; 19. true; 20. false.

Page 322—1. true; 2. true; 3. false; 4. true; 5. true; 6. b; 7. c; 8. a.

Page 332—1. f; 2. b; 3. c; 4. d; 5. e; 6. a; 7. false; 8. false; 9. true; 10. true.

8

THE USE OF POWER

BASIC CONCEPTS TO BE COVERED IN THIS CHAPTER

In this chapter a number of concepts are defined and discussed. The major ones are listed below. The procedure for learning these concepts is as follows:

1. The class forms heterogeneous groups of four.
2. Each group divides into two pairs.
3. The task for each pair is to:
   a. define each concept, noting the page on which it is defined and discussed.
   b. make sure that both members of the pair understand the meaning of each concept.
4. In each group, members compare the answers of the two pairs. If there is disagreement, they look up the concept in the chapter and clarify it until they all agree on the definition and understand it.

Concepts

1. trait-factor view of power
2. dynamic-interdependence view of power
3. credibility
4. attractiveness
5. forewarning
6. inoculation
7. power
8. outcome dependence
9. information dependence
10. resistance
11. manipulation
12. rule of self-direction
13. strength
14. reward power
15. legitimate power
16. referent power
17. information power
18. expert power
19. coercion power

POWER ORIGIN EXERCISE: IS POWER A PERSONAL ATTRIBUTE OR AN ASPECT OF A RELATIONSHIP?

There has been some controversy over whether power is an attribute of a person or an aspect of a relationship between two or more persons. The purpose of this exercise is to structure a critical discussion of the issue. The procedure is as follows:

1. The class forms groups of four.

2. Each group is ultimately to write a report summarizing its position on whether power is a personal attribute or an aspect of a relationship. The report is to contain the group's overall conclusions and the facts and rationale supporting its position. The supporting facts and rationale may be obtained from this chapter, the entire book, and outside reading.

3. Each group divides into pairs. One pair is assigned the position that power is a personal attribute and the other pair the position that power is an aspect of a relationship between two or more persons. Each pair reviews the supporting sections of this chapter, the procedure for the exercise, and the rules for constructive controversy (p. 31).

4. The pairs meet separately to prepare as forceful a three-minute presentation of their position as possible. They are to make sure that both members have contributed to building a persuasive case for their position and that it includes as many facts and research findings as possible. Both members need to master all the rationale supporting their position. Ten minutes are allowed for this phase.

5. The group of four meets. Each pair presents its position, being as forceful and persuasive as possible, while the other pair takes notes and asks for clarification of anything that is not fully understood. Each pair is allowed about three minutes to present its position.

6. The group of four has an open discussion of whether power is a personal attribute or an aspect of a relationship. Each side presents as many facts and research findings as it can to support its point of view. Members listen critically to the opposing position and ask for supporting facts for any conclusions made by the opposing pair. Participants should ensure that all the facts supporting both sides are brought out and discussed. The rules for constructive controversy should be followed. About ten minutes are allowed for this phase.

7. The perspectives in each group are now reversed, each pair arguing the opposing pair's position. Members should be as forceful and persuasive as they can in arguing for the opposing pair's position. They should elaborate on the opposing position, seeing if they can think of any new arguments or facts that the opposing pair did not present. Each pair has about three minutes for its presentation.

8. Each group of four should derive a position that all members can agree on. The members should summarize the best arguments for each position, detailing as many facts as they can on whether power is a personal attribute or an aspect of a relationship. When they have consensus in their group, they should organize their arguments for presentation to the rest of the class. Since other groups will have other conclusions, each group may need to explain the validity of its position to the class. About ten minutes are allowed for this phase.

9. The coordinator samples the decisions made by the groups of four by having several of them present their position to the class. The class then discusses similarities and differences among the positions and the coordinator summarizes what the participants have learned about power and influence.

INTRODUCTION

All human interaction involves power and influence. Yet many persons are unaware of the influence they exert on others, and many are unaware of how necessary and constructive mutual influence is in building effective groups and collaborative relationships among members. Being skillful in influencing other group members and taking responsibility for such influence are important parts of being a group member. In this chapter, power and influence (the two terms can be considered synonymous, and they are used interchangeably in this chapter) are defined from two points of view: the trait-factor perspective and the dynamic-interdependence perspective. The chapter begins with an explanation of these two views. The remainder of the the chapter focuses on several topic concerning the use of power in a group in ways that increase the group's effectiveness and clarify conflicts that can then be resolved productively: personal power and personal-goal accomplishment, the bases of power, power and problem solving, interaction between high- and low-power members, and power and conflict.

THE TRAIT–FACTOR APPROACH TO INFLUENCE

One night long, long ago a princess lay down to sleep on a bed that contained thirteen mattresses. At the bottom of the pile of mattresses had been placed a tiny pea. The princess tossed and turned all night, unable to sleep. This fairy-tale princess was unable to sleep because it is part of the nature of princesses to be disturbed by provocations that those of us with mundane natures do not even notice. Winston Churchill could offer the people of England "blood, sweat, and tears" and inspire them to great effort and sacrifice during World War II because it is part of the nature of great leaders to influence others in ways that those of us with mundane natures cannot. The princess and Winston Churchill illustrate the trait-factor approach to power and influence. They are credited with having innately supernatural, religious, or instinctual dispositions. Who can deny their divine spark or conscience?

The trait-factor approach to power and influence may be traced to Aristotle, whose rhetoric dealt at some length with the characteristics of an effective influencer and gave detailed advice on the techniques of persuasion. From the trait-factor point of view, influence is a function of the characteristics of (1) the person exerting the influence, (2) the person receiving the influence, and (3) the influence attempt itself. The general approach of a trait-factor theory is to identify the factors that explain why an individual is as she is and how she became so, and to determine how these factors maintain her so, despite circumstances, fortune, and opportunities. The trait-factor approach is *static,* in that it focuses more on continuity than on change; *atomistic,* in that it assumes that complex phenomena can be analyzed into their component parts; *historical,* in that it assumes that causation of present behavior is a function of genetic and experiential factors acting cumulatively over relatively long periods of time; and *inductive,* in that it stresses accounting for empirically observed phenomena more than seeking empirical validation for general theoretical statements. According to the trait-factor approach, certain individuals are somehow born with a self-contained capacity to influence others.

The major post-World War II application of the trait-factor approach to power and influence was the Yale Attitude Change Program, which was headed by Carl Hovland immediately after World World II (Hovland, Lumsdaine, and Sheffield, 1949). Most of the research in this program focused on the area in which the trait-factor view is strongest—the effects of a single attempt to influence delivered through the mass media. In situations where a politician is giving a speech to an audience, an announcer is delivering a television commercial, or a health official is warning the public about a health danger, the findings from the Yale Program are quite useful. In each of these situations the contact between the communicator and the receiver of the communication is brief and not repeated. Moreover, the communication is one-way; there is no interaction between the two parties. Because single instances of one-way communication are essentially static, a trait-oriented theory is quite helpful in analyzing them.

Much of the post–World War II research on social influence stemmed from Hovland's wartime studies of propaganda and was organized around the theme question "Who says what to whom with what effect?" Investigators have usually broken this question down into variables relating to the source (the characteristics of the communicator), the message (the characteristics of the communication), and the receiver (the characteristics of the person receiving the message). The exercise of power may thus be seen as a credible and attractive communicator's delivery of an effectively organized message to a vulnerable or influenceable audience. Trait-factor researchers assume that people are rational in the way they process information and are motivated to attend to a message, learn its contents, and incorporate it into their attitudes.

The Effects of the Source

credibility. Aristotle noted that an effective communicator must be a person of good sense, good will, and good moral character. Following this notion, most of the research on the personal characteristics of the communicator has focused on the dimension of credibility. The *credibility* of a communicator is his perceived ability to know valid information and his perceived motivation to communicate this knowledge without bias. More specifically, credibility depends on the following factors (Giffin, 1967; Johnson, 1973):

1. Objective indicators of *expertise* relevant to the topic under discussion (for example, a Ph.D. or an affiliation with a prestigious organization).
2. *Reliability* as an information source (for example, of communicator, or perceived character such as his dependability, predictability, and consistency).
3. The *motives and intentions* of the communicator. (Communicators who argue against their own self-interest or who appear not to be attempting to influence a receiver tend to be regarded as more trustworthy than communicators who overtly attempt to influence on the basis of self-interest).
4. The expression of *warmth and friendliness.*
5. The *dynamism* of the communicator. (A confident, forceful, and active communicator tends to be regarded as more credible than a self-conscious, listless communicator.)
6. The *majority opinion* of others concerning the expertness and trustworthiness of the communicator.

attractiveness. The attractiveness of the communicator is also an important influence on her power to influence an audience. The following factors have been found to be determinants of how attractive one person appears to another:

1. *Cooperativeness and goal facilitation* (Johnson and Johnson, 1975). A person likes others who are cooperating with him and facilitating his goal achievement.
2. *Physical appearance* (Berscheid and Walster, 1974). Other personal attributes being equal, physically attractive persons tend to be liked better than homely persons.
3. *Liking* (Byrne, 1969). If one person knows that she is liked by another, she is apt to reciprocate that liking.
4. *Similarity* (Byrne, 1969). Although the point is controversial, considerable evidence suggests that individuals who perceive themselves to be similar in basic values and other characteristics tend to like each other.
5. *Competence* (Blanchard, Weigel, and Cook, 1975). Persons who are perceived to be competent in important areas tend to be liked.
6. *Warmth* (Johnson, 1971). Warm, friendly persons tend to be liked.
7. *Familiarity and propinquity* (Berscheid and Walster, 1969; Watson and Johnson, 1972). Although the point is equivocal, some findings suggest that

a person likes others with whom he is familiar. "To know them is to love them."

The Effects of the Message

Without a message there can be no influence exerted on another person. Like Aristotle, the Yale researchers were deeply concerned with the nature of arguments, their logical coherence and emotional appeal, and the language used by the communicator to convey these aspects of the message. Here are the basic findings from the research on message variables (Aronson, 1972; McGuire, 1969; Watson and Johnson, 1972):

1. In general, messages that inspire fear tend to be persuasive with receivers who have high self-esteem but not with those who have low self-esteem. High-fear appeals with specific instructions for action tend to be more persuasive than high-fear appeals without these instructions.
2. With intelligent receivers, messages that acknowledge opposing viewpoints (two-sided messages) are most persuasive than one-sided messages. With less intelligent receivers, one-sided messages tend to be more effective.
3. When a communicator is credible, the greater the discrepancy between the position she advocates and the receiver's initial position, the greater the change. If a communicator is not credible, she will be most effective with mildly discrepant positions.

The Effects of the Receiver

Social psychologists have examined a multitude of personality characteristics and other differences among the receivers of persuasive communications for their effect on the acceptance of persuasion. Among the variety of findings, the most salient and consistent variables are these:

1. *Self-esteem* (McGuire, 1969; Watson and Johnson, 1972). When self-esteem is varied experimentally, the most frequent result is that receivers with low self-esteem are more persuasible than receivers with high self-esteem. When long-term self-esteem is measured and correlated with persuasion, this clearly negative relationship is less frequent and less pronounced.
2. *The receiver's present attitudes* (Watson and Johnson, 1972). Receivers may refuse to listen to messages that disagree with their present attitudes, or they may misinterpret what the communicator is stating. Attitudes that are integral to the individual's self-conception appear to be more difficult to change than less integral attitudes (Rokeach, 1968).
3. *Forewarning* (Watson and Johnson, 1972). Forewarning receivers of the communicator's intention of converting them to his point of view creates resistance to his message.

4. *Role playing* (Watson and Johnson, 1972). Actively role-playing a previously unacceptable position increases its acceptability to the receiver.

5. *Inoculation* (McGuire, 1964). Having receivers practice defending their position and then giving them additional arguments to support it decreases their susceptibility to attempt to influence them.

6. *Distraction* (Baron, Baron, and Miller, 1973). Receivers are generally more susceptible to influence when they are distracted during the communicator's statement of her message.

7. *Intelligence* (McGuire, 1969). Intelligence and influence are negatively related in the middle and upper portions of the IQ distribution and positively related in the lower portion.

Summary

Attempts to exert power over other group members are enhanced if one is credible and attractive; if one phrases one's messages so that they are two-sided, action-oriented, and discrepant with members' current beliefs; and if the other group members have low self-esteem, see their attitudes under modification as peripheral to them, have no forewarning of the influence attempt, role-play positions that agree with one's own, have not been inoculated, are distracted while one is presenting the message, and are not very intelligent. The trait-factor approach to influence, however, is weak both logically and empirically in situations where two or more individuals are constantly interacting. We thus turn next to the dynamic-interdependence approach to influence.

THE DYNAMIC-INTERDEPENDENCE VIEW OF INFLUENCE

Group members adjust in many ways to one another. They take turns talking, they put aside individual interests to discuss mutual interests, they adjust their expression of their attitudes and beliefs to take into account the reactions of other members, they speed up or slow down their activity to stay coordinated with one another. Group members constantly modify their behavior to make it fit the group in which they are participating. When you are a member of a group you constantly influence and are influenced by the other group members. In fact, any two persons who interact constantly influence and are influenced by each other.

In the dynamic-interdependence view of influence, power is viewed as an aspect of a relationship between two or more persons. Relationships, and the exertion of influence within them, according to this view, are constantly changing as the group members modify and adjust their behavior to stay coordinated with one another. The relationships among group members are dynamic because the members are dependent on each other for the achievement of their joint goals. The basis of influence within a relationship is the mutual dependence of group members as they strive to achieve their mutual goals. Group members are interdependent and influence each other to the extent that they mediate or contribute to the attainment of important goals for each other. The degree of influence is dynamic: it is constantly changing as the group members make progress in obtaining their goals, as their costs (in energy, emotion, time, and so forth) of working collaboratively vary, and as other relationships and groups become available in which the goals of group members might be better achieved (Cartwright, 1959; Thibaut and Kelley, 1959). If the group members make progress toward achieving their goals and the costs of working together go down so that no other group would be as rewarding, the ability of members to influence each other increases. If, on the other hand, the group is not making progress toward goal accomplishment, if the costs to group members in terms of emotion and energy are high, and if other groups are available that are more effective and less demanding, the ability of group members to influence each other decreases. In the latter case, members may even terminate their membership and join other groups, thereby reducing to zero the capacity of the original group members to influence and be influenced by them.

From the dynamic-interdependence viewpoint, power is an attribute of a relationship, not of a person. It takes two persons for power to exist. A person cannot be an influencer if there is no influencee. The exertion of power requires a relationship and some mutuality or goal interdependence. The dynamic-interdependence approach to power is *dynamic,* in that it focuses more on the changing nature of influence within a relationship as the members strive to achieve their mutual goals than on who possesses power; *holistic,* in that it assumes that power is a complex phenomenon that has to be studied as a whole and that cannot be meaningfully broken into components; *phenomenological,* in that it stresses the immediate experience of group members and the ways they influence each other in the present rather than focusing on their history and genetic makeup; and *deductive,* in that it attempts to apply and validate theoretical principles concerning the nature and use of power.

Within a group, mutual power exists to the extent that one member can affect the goal accomplishment of other members. The more cooperative the group, the greater the goal interdependence of group members and the more influence members exert on each other. Through mutual influence the coordination of member behavior necessary for goal accomplishment is achieved. Leadership has been defined as the use of power to promote the goal accomplishment and maintenance of the group. Decisions cannot be made without members influencing one another. Controversies and conflicts of interest cannot be managed or resolved without the use of influence. Even communication cannot take place without mutual influence. Thus, the use of power is essential to all aspects of group functioning. Power cannot be ignored, abdicated, or denied. Every group member should be aware of her power, accept it, and take responsibility for its use. The possession of power within a group is inevitable, and it is through the exercise of mutual influence that cooperation takes place and the group effectively achieves its goals.

A DEFINITION OF POWER AND INFLUENCE

The terms *power, influence,* and *control* are sometimes defined differently and sometimes synonymously by social psychologists. *Power* has been defined variously as the actual control of another's behavior, the capacity to influence another's behavior, the capacity to affect another person's rewards and costs, the ability of one person to get others to behave in a particular way or to carry out certain actions, and the capacity to affect another's goal accomplishment. *Influence* has been defined as an attempt to use power to change another person in a desired direction. *Control* has been defined as having the influence behaving as the influencer intended.

For the purposes of this chapter, however, *power* and *influence* will be defined as one person's control over resources valued by another. More specifically, individual A has power with respect to individual B when B perceives that A controls resources that B values. In turn, B's valuing of these resources depends on (1) the availability of alternative sources of these or similar resources at the same or a lower cost, and (2) the importance B attaches to the goals whose attainment is mediated by A's resources. Group member A influences group member B to the extent that A furnishes resources needed by B for the accomplishment of highly valued goals and to the extent that B cannot obtain these resources at a lower cost from other members or other groups. Social power and influence, then, depend on a need–resource correspondence among group members. When Helen and Frank, for example, are studying this chapter with Edythe and wish to understand the above definition of power, they are dependent on Edythe to the extent that she understands and can explain that definition; Edythe is thereby able to influence Helen and Frank's thinking about power. But if Helen and Frank are able to get a clearer explanation from Roger with less trouble, then Edythe's ability to influence their thinking is reduced.

In a group, members depend on one another for help in accomplishing their goals (outcome dependence) and for information about how to achieve their goals (information dependence). *Outcome dependence* is a function of the ability of others to affect one's costs of engaging in goal-directed behavior (that is, one's expenditure of energy, feelings of anxiety, and fear of displeasing important persons) and the benefits of that behavior. *Information dependence* is a function of the ability of others to supply one with the information one needs for determining which strategies to use in attempting to achieve one's goals, the costs of each strategy, and one's ability to implement the strategies. When other group members have the information one needs to make a decision about which strategy for achieving one's goals to adopt, a state of information dependence exists.

When group members are taking part in cooperative activities, and when their goals are compatible, they assert power in the same direction and there is little or no resistance to accepting the influence of another member. When group members have incompatible goals, however, or are in competition with one another, then their power assertions will conflict and there will be resistance to accepting another member's influence. *Resistance* is the psychological force aroused in a person that keeps him from accepting influence. Its magnitude is determined by the way in which power is exerted. Resistance can also be generated if the behavior desired of the members by the person exerting the power fails to help them achieve their goals.

A final point to be made about mutual dependence and power is that it is the *perception* of a group member's resources that affect the behavior of other members, not her actual resources. A member can have large resources that are unknown or ignored by other group members and therefore have little power over the others. On the other hand, a group member can have few vital resources but be seen as having many resources and thereby have a great deal of influence over the other group members.

AVERSION TO THE USE OF DIRECT INFLUENCE

Although influence pervades all human relationships and although it has played a significant role in the lives of all members of succeeding civilizations, from antiquity to the present, some persons are averse to the planned use of direct influence. Our behavior is influenced by many forces—education, government, law, interpersonal expectations, religion, social norms, organizational-role requirements, and even advertising. But a group member consciously planning how best to influence other members may seem to some of us to be violating their freedom of choice and self-direction. London (1969) states that in our society there are at least three rules that oppose the influencing of others' behavior:

1. The rule of noncoercion: people should not be forced to do what others want but should be free to refuse them.
2. The rule of explication: people should not be seduced into compliance but should be told what is wanted of them.
3. The rule of self-direction: people should be free to decide for themselves how they want to guide their lives.

For some persons words like *power* and *influence* seem to violate these rules; such persons frequently say they do not wish to have power over others.

Those who are averse to the exerting of power may actually be confusing the use of influence with manipulation. All human interaction involves mutual influence; manipulation is a certain type of influence. *Manipulation* is the managing or controlling of others by a shrewd use of influence, especially in an unfair or dishonest way, and for one's own purposes and profit. It is the influencing of others in ways they do not fully understand and with consequences that are undesirable for them but highly desirable for oneself. It is the use of power for one's own benefit at the expense of others. People characteristically react with anger, resentment, and retaliation if they find they have been manipulated. In proceeding through this chapter keep in mind that we are focusing on the constructive use of influence to increase cooperation among group members and group effectiveness; the use of manipulation is destructive in that it eventually decreases cooperation among members and causes severe maintenance problems for the group. The procedure for constructively influencing other group members without violating the three rules listed above is presented in the following section.

QUIZ

Check your reading of this section by answering the following questions. Answers are on page 369.

_____ **1.** Power is an aspect of a relationship between two or more people.

_____ **2.** Focuses on continuity and who possesses power.

_____ **3.** Focuses on the changing nature of influence.

_____ **4.** Focuses on credibility and attractiveness of communicator.

_____ **5.** Assumes that complex phenomena can be analyzed into component parts.

_____ **6.** Assumes that complex phenomena have to be studied as a whole.

a. Trait-factor

b. Dynamic-interdependence

_____ 7. Accounts for observed phenomena rather than empirical validation.

_____ 8. Attempts to apply and validate theoretical principles.

_____ 9. One-way communication with no interaction.

_____ 10. Two-way communication with interaction.

True False 11. The credibility of a communicator depends on her perceived expertise and reliability.

True False 12. Communicators who openly argue for their interests and to influence others are trusted more than those who hide their motives.

True False 13. Less attractive people are liked and trusted more than more attractive people.

True False 14. People who are perceived as warm, friendly, and competent will be influencers.

True False 15. Messages that inspire fear will influence people with low esteem but not those with high esteem.

True False 16. Messages that acknowledge opposing viewpoints influence high intelligence receivers more than they do low intelligence ones.

True False 17. If a communicator is credible, she should stick to only mildly discrepant positions to be most effective.

True False 18. People with low self-esteem are more easily influenced than people with high self-esteem.

True False 19. Forewarning receivers of an intention to convert them decreases their resistance to the message.

True False 20. Receivers are less susceptible to influence when they are distracted during the message.

True False 21. Basically, power is bad and should not be used.

True False 22. Power is defined as one person's power over resources valued by another.

True False 23. If members have compatible goals, they assert power in the same direction and there is little resistance to influence.

True False 24. It is the perception of a group member's resources rather than his actual resources that cause him to have influence.

True False 25. The use of manipulation is a necessary aspect of power.

PERSONAL POWER AND PERSONAL–GOAL ACCOMPLISHMENT EXERCISE*

A basic need of every group member is some influence over what takes place in the group. A person joins a group to accomplish goals he cannot achieve, or cannot achieve as easily, without group membership. The power a person needs within a group is the power that will ensure that his goals are accomplished.

There is a definite process by which a person mobilizes her power in order to accomplish her goals. The process consists of (1) determining one's goals, (2) assessing one's resources and information level, (3) determining what coalitions will obtain the needed information and resources for accomplishing the goals, (4) contracting a coalition committed to accomplishing the goals, and (5) carrying out the activities necessary for the accomplishment of the goal. This exercise is an opportunity for you to acquire experience with this process, step by step.

Step 1: Determining Your Goals

The first step in using your power within a group is to clarify your personal goals. Goals are based upon your needs, wants, and self-interests. The term *goal* is used here in the broadest possible sense to refer to the rewards consciously sought as well as the rewards obtained unconsciously through relationships with other group members. In order to plan to attain your goals you must be *aware* of them and accept them as valuable and worthwhile. Because many persons work for power they do not need and for goals they do not really want, it is essential that you first be clear about what you want. Group members have to deal realistically with what each of them wants; an effective group is one in which most members have their goals met. So, it is essential that a group member be clear about his goals, accept them as worthwhile, and be willing to enlist aid of other group members to accomplish them. And in order to build and keep trust, a group member must be honest and accurate in his statements about his personal goals and be willing to work openly for their accomplishment.

At this point, with your classmates divide into groups of four. Each person should first state all the desires, needs, wants, goals, and so on that he might work toward in this group. After everyone has had his say, each member should state which three goals he would like the group to accomplish first. Write these on newsprint, and include your name. Then go on to the next step.

Step 2: Determining Your Resources

The second step in the process of mobilizing your power is to affirm the resources you bring to the group. You must be aware of and accept your resources in order to tell others about them. Moreover, awareness and acceptance of your resources are basic to an understanding by others of what you can contribute toward the accomplishment of your goals and the goals of other group members. Using the resources of

---

* This exercise was inspired by the work of George Peabody in this area.

members is a key issue for effective groups. Not only should the group take an inventory of its resources before beginning work, but the individual members should take a personal inventory to determine their ability to accomplish their own goals.

All of us have *many* different strengths upon which we base our interactions with others. All group members have solid strengths that are often unidentified and unused, both by the group and by themselves. The word *strength* refers to any skill, talent, ability, or personal trait that helps one function more productively. The objective of this part of the exercise is to increase your awareness of your strengths. The procedure for each group is as follows:

1. Individually, think of all the things you do well, all the things you are proud of having done, all the things for which you feel a sense of accomplishment. List all your positive accomplishments and your successes.

2. Share your lists with one another. Then, with the help of the other three members, examine your past successes and identify the personal strengths you used to achieve them. Make a list of these strengths.

3. After you have all made your list of strengths, give one another feedback about additional strengths. Add to each person's list the qualities, skills, and characteristics she has overlooked or undervalued.

4. Each member should then discuss the question "What might be keeping me from using all my strengths?" The group helps each person explore the ways in which she can free herself from constraints on the use of her strengths.

5. If possible, review the material on self-acceptance and the acceptance of others in Johnson (1981).

Step 3: Determining Your Needed Coalitions

The third step in the process of mobilizing your power in a group is to assess what coalitions with other members are necessary for securing the information and resources you need in order to accomplish your goals. The question to ask yourself is "Who has the information and resources I need, and how can I ally myself with them in order to help my goal accomplishment?" After identifying such persons ask yourself "What are their goals, and how might I contribute resources and information they need for their goal accomplishment?" Then ask yourself "What coalitions can I make with members who have compatible, similar, or complementary goals?"

To begin this step, take out the personal-goal sheets you composed in step 1. Review your goals and change them in any way you believe appropriate. Then, as a group of four, look for similarities among your goals. Decide as a group upon the three goals that are most in accord with the personal goals of each member. List them on newsprint. Then review the strengths listed in step 2. Try to determine what resources are needed for the accomplishment of each of the three goals, and who has them. In determining these resources, you may find it helpful to read the following section on the bases of power and apply it to the strengths of your group's members. What are your bases of power? What are your resources? In what ways can you influence the goal achievement of the other group members? In what ways can they influence your goal achievement? How can you use your power to guarantee that your goals are met? In deciding which coalitions will help your goal accomplishment you should consider all of these questions.

In participating in this exercise you may experience either the frustration of finding little or no compatibility between your own goals and those of the other group members or the rejection of having your resources overlooked, undervalued, or underused. You may also experience the disappointment of finding that other members are more skillful in making coalitions. It is possible that two members will find themselves in basic disagreement with the other two group members. It is from such situations that conflicts are born. In the previous chapter we discussed at length the nature of such conflicts and how they can be managed productively. At this point the group should bring such conflicts out in the open, make them explicit, and be very clear about how they are to be dealt with.

Do not at this point make any formal coalitions with other group members. Limit yourself to determining what coalitions are needed. Then go on to the next step.

Step 4: Contracting Help with Your Goals

The interdependence among group members should now be obvious. In contributing resources to the achievement of the group's three top goals, different members have different levels of motivation and different levels of energy in working toward goal accomplishment. The degree to which your personal goals are reflected in the group's goals and the degree to which your resources are recognized and used will usually determine the amount of energy you contribute to the accomplishment of the goals. In planning how resources will be utilized to help achieve a goal, group members often develop formal or informal contracts with one another. The forming of a contract is step 4 in the mobilization of one's power in a group. The contract usually includes at least three items: (1) what I want from the group members; (2) what the other group members want from me; (3) what we exchange so that everyone can accomplish his goals.

In the previous three steps you set group goals, surveyed resources, and made judgments about what coalitions needed to be formed in order for you to help your goal accomplishment. Now, in step 4, consciously work out formal contracts with other group members and form open coalitions. In doing so, focus specifically on the three items involved in a contract. Write your contracts on newsprint so that all members can see and read them. In essence, these contracts are a plan for group members to cooperatively apply their resources in certain ways toward the achievement of the group's goals.

Step 5, implementing the contracts, will not be discussed.

Discussion

After completing the five steps the groups should discuss their experiences. The following questions may be used to stimulate discussion:

1. How was power developed in the group?

2. How did members use power to form the group's goals and identify needed resources?

3. What was the outcome of the five steps? To what extent were everyone's goals integrated in the group's goals, and to what extent were everyone's resources committed to the accomplishment of the group's goals?

4. What are the present reactions and feelings of each group member to the five steps?

5. With the help of the other group members, each member should answer the following questions:

    a. What are my goals?

    b. What are my sources of power in the group?

    c. How did I apply my power in order to make sure my goals were accomplished?

    d. How successful was I?

    e. How can I do better for myself next time?

6. On the basis of the group's experiences, what conclusions can be made about the use of power in a group? Groups should write the answers to question 6 on newsprint. When all groups have finished their discussion, the conclusions should be shared.

THE BASES OF POWER

In discussing how power is developed and used, many behavioral scientists have given particular attention to its sources (French and Raven, 1959; Raven and Kruglanski, 1970). According to them, there are six possible bases of a person's power: his ability to *reward* and to *coerce,* his *legal* position, his capacity as a *referent,* his *expertise,* and his *information.*

A person has *reward* power over other group members if she has the ability to deliver positive consequences or remove negative consequences in response to their behavior. Her power will be greater the more the group members value the reward, the more they believe that she can dispense the reward, and the less their chances appear of getting the reward from someone else. The successful use of reward power will generally produce a "moving toward" the person. Group members will comply with the person's requests, seek her out, increase their liking for her, and communicate effectively with her. Under certain conditions, however, the reward power can backfire. Too many rewards of the development of suspicion on the part of the group members that they are being bribed or conned into going along can lead to a "moving away" or "moving against" the person.

A person has *coercive* power over other group members if he can mete out negative consequences or remove positive consequences in response to the behavior of group members. Punishment for a member who fails to get the group to go along with his wishes often increases the pressure on group members to engage in the desired behavior. Coercive power frequently causes the group to avoid the person and to like him less. Group members may do what he wants, but they tend to avoid interacting with him in the future. Only when the use of coercive power brings a conflict out into the open to be resolved can it have many positive effects.

When a person has *legitimate* power group members believe she ought to have influence over them because of her position in the group or organization (such as an employer) or because of her special role responsibilities (such as those of a policewoman). Group members invariably believe it their duty to follow the commands of a person with legitimate power, even when it means restricting themselves to a limited set of behaviors. Legitimate power is often used to reduce conflict—when the person with it plays the role of an arbitrator or mediator or when those with less power simply conform to her wishes.

When a person has *referent* power group members identify with or want to be like him and therefore do what he wants out of respect, liking, and wanting to be liked. Generally, the more the person is liked, the more the group members will identify with him.

When a person has *expert* power group members see her as having some special knowledge or skill and as being trustworthy. They believe she is not trying to deceive them for selfish purposes. The successful use of expert power results in "movement toward" the person, for the group members are convinced of the correctness of her request. Only if her expertise fosters feelings of inadequacy in the group members will it have negative effects.

When a person has *informational* power group members believe that he has resources of information that will be useful in accomplishing the goal and that are not available anywhere else. The power is based upon the logic of a person's arguments or the superiority of his demonstrated knowledge; it has effects similar to those that result from the use of expert power.

At this point, review the sources of power used in the previous exercise and classify them according to the bases of power discussed in this section. What power bases do you usually rely upon?

Match the following bases of power with their definitions (answers at the end of the chapter):

____ **1.** Reward
____ **2.** Coercive
____ **3.** Legitimate
____ **4.** Reference
____ **5.** Expert
____ **6.** Informational

a. Group members believe the person has useful knowledge not available elsewhere.

b. Group members believe the person ought to have power because of her position or responsibilities.

c. A person can deliver positive consequences or remove negative consequences.

d. Group members believe the person has a special knowledge or skill and is trustworthy.

        e. Group members do what the person wants out of respect, liking, and wanting to be liked.

        f. A person can deliver negative consequences or remove positive consequences.

UNEQUAL RESOURCES EXERCISE

This exercise gives participants a chance to observe how groups (1) use resources that have been unequally distributed and (2) negotiate to obtain the resources they need. It is conducted with four groups, each having two to four members. If there are more persons than needed for the exercise, they may participate without being group members. Should more than one cluster of four groups participate, the coordinator may wish to add the element of competition between as well as within the clusters. The exercise should take less than one hour. The procedure for the coordinator is as follows:

1. Introduce the exercise as an experience with the use of resources needed to accomplish a task that have been distributed unequally among groups. Form the groups. For each cluster have at least two observers. Groups should be placed far enough away from each other so that their negotiation positions are not compromised by casual observation.
2. Meet briefly with the observers and discuss what they might focus upon. Any aspect of negotiation and problem solving can be observed.
3. Distribute an envelope of materials and a copy of the accompanying task sheet to each group. Explain that each group has different materials, but that each must complete the same tasks. Explain that the groups may negotiate for the use of materials and tools in any way that is agreeable to everyone. Emphasize that the first group to finish all the tasks is the winner. (If clusters are competing, there will be both a group winner and a cluster winner.) Give the signal to begin.
4. When the groups have finished, declare the winner. Then conduct a discussion on using resources, sharing, negotiating, competing, and using power. Ask the observers to participate in the discussion. Then ask the clusters to summarize its conclusions about the use of power that manifested itself during the exercise.

Group Materials

Group 1: scissors, ruler, paper clips, pencils, two 4-inch squares of red paper, and two 4-inch squares of white paper.

Group 2: scissors, glue, and two sheets each of gold paper, white paper, and blue paper, each 8½ by 11 inches.

Group 3: felt-tipped markers and two sheets each of green paper, white paper, and gold paper, each 8½ by 11 inches.

Group 4: five sheets of paper, 8½ by 11 inches—one green, one gold, one blue, one red, and one purple.

Unequal Resources Exercise Task Sheet

Each group is to complete the following tasks:

1. Make a 3-by-3-inch square of white paper.
2. Make a 4-by-2-inch rectangle of gold paper.
3. Make a 3-by-5-inch T-shaped piece of green and white paper.
4. Make a four-link paper chain, each link in a different color.
5. Make a 4-by-4-inch flag in any three colors.

The first group to complete all the tasks is the winner. Groups may negotiate with each other for the use of needed materials and tools on any mutually agreeable basis.

POWER POLITICS EXERCISE

The objective of this exercise is to examine the dynamics of negotiating for power. Group members with different amounts of power are to negotiate to form power coalitions with other group members. The exercise takes one and a half hours. Here is the procedure for the coordinator to follow:

1. Introduce the exercise as a situation in which different group members have different amounts of power and are negotiating to form power coalitions in order to complete a task. Divide the participants into groups of twelve. Each participant needs a pencil and a pad of paper for writing notes.
2. Hand out a copy of the accompanying instruction sheet to each participant and have them read it. Then hand out a slip of paper with a number on it to each participant. The numbers on the slips are to range from 100 to 1,200. Announce that there will be two rounds of negotiations before the first vote is taken. The first round will be a fifteen-minute period in which members write notes to one another. No verbal communication is permitted. Members may write as many notes to as many other members as they wish. Notes should include the names of the sender and the receiver. These notes are not to be read until the end of the fifteen-minute period. Give the signal to begin round 1.
3. At the end of fifteen minutes stop all note passing and allow members to read their notes. After they have done so, announce the beginning of round 2. The same rules apply. Round 2 lasts fifteen minutes.
4. At the end of round 2 ask the groups if they are ready to vote on their chairperson. If seven members want to vote, a vote is taken. All voting takes place by secret ballot. Members note the number of votes they control and how they commit them. If the group is not ready to vote, or if no one has enough votes to become chairperson, go to round 3.

5. In round 3 members may negotiate verbally with one another. There are no restrictions on negotiations during this round, which also lasts for fifteen minutes.

6. At the end of round 3 call for a vote. The vote is again by secret ballot. If no one has enough votes to become chairperson, allow ten-minute free-negotiation period. Then take a final vote.

7. Have the groups discuss their experience, using the following questions as guides:

    a. What deals were made for the 100 units of patronage? How was power used in making those deals?

    b. What negotiation strategies were used?

    c. How did members make their decision about whom to commit their votes to? What criteria did they use to make the decision?

    d. What were the feelings and reactions of the members to the experience?

    e. What feelings arose from the unequal distribution of votes? How did it feel to control a small number of votes? How did it feel to control a large number of votes?

    f. How did members create allies and develop power blocs? What strategies did they use?

    g. Who felt powerful? Who felt powerless?

    h. What conclusions can you make about the use of power? (Write these on newsprint to share with other groups.)

Power Politics Exercise Instruction Sheet

This is a game of power politics. Your group is to become the governing body of a political party, and you and the other group members must select a general chairperson. This is a crucial decision for the party. The person you elect will have extensive power and control over who gets how much patronage from the party. He or she will have 100 units of patronage to distribute among deserving members of the group. Members of your group may negotiate for votes and the distribution of the patronage. Each of you controls a different number of votes. One member controls 100 votes, a second controls 200, a third controls 300, and so on, with one member controlling 1,200 votes. The number of votes you have is on a slip of paper that will be given to you by the coordinator of the exercise. Keep this slip. *Do not show it to any other group member.* You may commit your votes to any member you wish; you may also split your votes among several members if you so desire. A member must receive 4,000 votes to become chairperson.

POWER AND PROBLEM SOLVING

In the two previous exercises the resources of the group were distributed unequally among its members. This will be the case with most of the problems a group faces. Yet because resources are unequally distributed does not mean that there are members who are powerless. Every group member has some power; every group member is able to influence other group members in some way. Different group members will have different bases of power: some, for example, may have a high degree of informational power, whereas others may have legitimate power. How a group manages the element of influence in member relationships has an important bearing on group effectiveness.

The effectiveness of any group is improved when (1) power is relatively balanced among its members, and (2) power is based upon competence, expertise, and information. Influence needs to be generally balanced or equal among all group members. A member's commitment to implementing a group decision depends upon her believing that she has influenced the decision. The ability of the group to solve problems increases as all group members come to feel that they share equally in influencing the direction of the group effort, and as the group climate becomes relatively free of domination by a few of the most powerful members. When members have equal power they are more cooperative in their interactions and more responsive to the cooperative initiatives of other members. Studies have found that even within organizations the satisfaction of subordinates increases when they believe they can influence particular aspects of the organization's decision making. Unequal power interferes with the trust and communication necessary for managing group conflicts constructively. Thus, the problem-solving ability of a group is improved when the group has flexible power patterns that in the long run equalize influence among group members.

A group's decisions are invariably of higher quality when power is based upon competence, expertise, and relevant information—not upon authority or popularity. The problem-solving capacity of many groups is seriously damaged when the member with the most authority is most influential at a time that calls for expertise and accurate information as the bases of power. The participation and involvement of all group members are dependent upon their being able to share the bases of power that will enable them to influence the decisions made by the group.

When power is not distributed equally among group members, or when the use of authority dominates and expertise and informational bases of power are ignored, group effectiveness is undermined. The next exercise deals with the unequal distribution of power and the consequences it can have for both high- and low-power group members.

POWER TO THE ANIMALS EXERCISE

The objective of this exercise is to examine the interaction among groups of different power as they negotiate with one another. The exercise takes two hours. The coordinator should read the accompanying instructions regarding the distribution of marbles and then follow this procedure:

1. Introduce the exercise as one that highlights interaction among groups having unequal power. Divide the class into groups of twelve. Explain that within each group

are three mammals, four birds, and five fish; the status of the members in each group is determined by how well they negotiate—for marbles. (Even if there are more than twelve participants in a group, keep the number of mammals under five.) Hand out a copy of the general instructions to every participant.

2. Distribute twelve bags of marbles randomly within each group. Make sure that the members understand their instructions. Give them time to examine what marbles they have, warning them not to let other group members see the marbles. Then begin negotiation session 1, which is to last five minutes.

3. During the negotiation session place on newsprint three headings: "Mammals," "Birds," and "Fish." After five minutes stop the negotiating and have the participants compute their scores. Take the three highest scores and place them, along with the persons' initials, under the heading "Mammals." (Even if there are more than twelve participants in a group, keep the number of mammals under five.) Place the next four scores, together with the persons' initials, under the heading "Birds." Place the remaining five scores, with the persons' initials, under the heading "Fish." Have each person make a name tag indicating what he is and put it on.

4. Begin negotiation session 2. After five minutes end it and ask for scores. Read just the individual scores, placing the three highest in the mammals column, the next four in the birds column, and the next five in the fish column. Members who change columns on the basis of their score will have to exchange their name tags.

5. Conduct negotiation session 3 in the same way.

6. Conduct negotiation session 4 in the same way.

7. Announce that the mammals now have the authority to make the rules for the exercise and that although anyone else can suggest rules, the mammals will decide which ones will be implemented. Inform the mammals that they may make any rules they wish, such as a rule that all marbles must be redistributed so that everyone has equal points, or a rule that all fish and birds must give mammals the marbles they ask for whether they want to or not. Have the mammals record their rules on newsprint.

8. After the new rules are established, conduct negotiation session 5. Then allow five minutes for the mammals to discuss and make any rule changes.

9. Repeat this cycle twice. Then give the birds and the fish copies of the list of strategies for influencing a high-power group. The birds and the fish have ten minutes to discuss the strategies and decide which ones to adopt. Then continue with another negotiation session.

10. After a variety of strategies have been tried by the birds and the fish, or when they refuse to continue, conduct a discussion of the experience. The following questions may be used as guides:
    a. What were your feelings and your reactions to the experience?
    b. Are there any parallels between the system set up by the game and the system in which we live?
    c. Would it have made much difference if the members who were fish had been the mammals?
    d. Were the mammals acting with legitimate authority?
    e. Are there any parallels between the exercise and the relations among racial groups, rich and poor, and adults and students?
    f. What negotiation strategies were used?

g. What feelings arose from the unequal distribution of power? How did it feel to have high power? How did it feel to have low power?

h. How did the strategies for changing the high-power group work? What contributed to their effectiveness or ineffectiveness?

i. What conclusions about the use of power can be made from your experiences in the exercise?

Distribution of Marbles

1. The total number of marbles needed is seventy-two (six times the number of group members).

2. The number of green marbles needed is five (the number of mammals plus two).

3. The number of yellow marbles needed is ten (the number of birds plus the number of fish plus one).

4. The number of red, white, and blue marbles needed is fifty-seven, nineteen of each.

Give each participant a bag of six marbles. Five bags are to contain one green marble, one yellow marble, and four marbles randomly selected from the colors red, white, and blue. Three bags are to contain one yellow marble and five marbles randomly selected from the colors red, white, and blue. The remaining four bags are to contain a random assortment of red, white, and blue marbles. These twelve bags are to be distributed at random within each group.

General Instructions

In this exercise there are three levels of power, based on marbles in each group. Group members have the chance to progress from one level of power to another by obtaining marbles through negotiation. The three members who get the most power will be declared the winners when the exercise ends. You will be given six marbles each. The scoring system for the marbles is given below. Additional points are awarded if a member is able to get several marbles of the same color:

Color	Points	Number of a kind	Points
Green	50	⑥	50
Yellow	25	⑤	30
Red	15	④	20
White	10	③	10
Blue	5		

For example, a person's total score if she had six green marbles would be 300 (6 × 50) plus 50 (for six of a kind), or 350 points.

The rules for negotiation are as follows:

1. You have five minutes to improve your score.
2. You improve your score by negotiating with other group members.
3. Members must be holding hands to have an agreement.
4. Only one-for-one trades are legal. Two for one or any other combination is illegal.
5. Once a member touches the hand of another member, a marble of unequal value (or color) must be traded. If two members cannot make an agreement, they will have to hold hands for the entire negotiating round.
6. There is no talking unless hands are touching. This rule must be strictly followed.
7. Members with folded arms do not have to negotiate with other members.
8. All marbles must be hidden. This rule must be strictly followed.

Strategies for Influencing a High-power Group

1. Build your own organizations and resources in order to make the low-power group less vulnerable.
2. Form coalitions.
3. Change the attitudes of high-power group members through education or moral persuasion.
4. Use existing legal procedures to bring pressures for change.
5. Search for ways in which to make high-power group members dependent upon the low-power group.
6. Use harassment techniques to increase the high-power group's costs of sticking with the status quo.

UNEQUAL POWER

When the distribution of power within a group is obviously unequal, both the high- and the low-power members have troubles. As we have seen, overall group effectiveness suffers, the gains members receive from being members decrease, and severe maintenance problems result. In discussions of theory and research pertaining to high and low power, the usual reference is to our society rather than to a small, problem-solving group. Yet the same dynamics between high-power and low-power persons can be found in a group of any size, even one as large as our society. In the previous exercise you yourself experienced, depending on your marbles, what it means to have a great deal of power or very little power. Compare your experience with the following discussions of high- and low-power group members.

High-Power Members

Life generally seems good for high-power persons. Everything goes right, every problem is easily solved, everyone seems to like and appreciate them and everything they do. High-power persons are typically happy with their situation and tend not to see how much the use of power is involved in their relationships. They are convinced that low-power persons really do like them, that everyone communicates honestly with them, that no one hides information from them, and that they are really seen as "nice" persons. When this enjoyable world is threatened by dissatisfaction expressed by low-power persons, however, high-power persons tend not to react benevolently. They are hard to move toward cooperation, conciliation, and compromise, and they will largely ignore the efforts of their low-power groupmates to increase cooperative problem solving. To them, low-power persons somehow never learn to "know their place"; they insist on "rocking the boat" out of ignorance and spite.

There are at least two strategies that high-power group members use to make it more difficult for low-power members to reduce the differences in power between them (Jones and Gerard, 1967). The first is to institute norms or rules in the group that legitimize their power and make wrong any attempt by others to change the status quo. As you may have noticed in the previous exercise, the first action taken by most groups who attain power is to make their holding of it legitimate and to establish regulations and norms that make illegitimate any change in the existing power relationships. For example, in most communities the white power structure has established strong norms as to where minority-group members may live, what occupations they may have, and where they must go to school—as well as procedures for making both whites and nonwhites believe that the status quo is "legitimate" and "right." This strategy may be described as the "power-defines-justice" strategy, or the "might-is-right" strategy.

The second strategy high-power members employ to solidify their position is to make the risk of attempting to change the status quo so great that the low-power members are deterred from trying to do so. They can invoke this strategy by establishing severe penalties against those who might attempt to change the status quo, and by offering the low-power members a variety of benefits or rewards on the condition that they refrain from rebelliousness. Of the two, the second seems to be more effective. The threat of punishment has never worked effectively to deter behavior, but the paternalistic leadership that tries to keep everyone happy has been applied successfully in combating labor and racial unrest in many parts of the country. This strategy may be defined as the "this-hurts-me-more-than-it-will-hurt-you" strategy, or the "if-only-you-would-behave-neither-of-us-would-go-through-this-suffering" strategy.

In America, high power is believed to result in arrogance and corruption. "Power corrupts" is a common household saying, and most persons have seen the arrogance of those who have more power than they do (often secretaries in the office of their boss). There are many exceptions to these correlations, of course, but perhaps not nearly as many as high-power persons like to believe.

Halle (1967) makes the interesting suggestion that the greater a person's power, the more insufficient it is likely to seem, simply because the claims upon it increase faster than the power to fulfill them. The Ford Foundation, for example, though by far the richest of American foundations, is undoubtedly the most inadequately endowed in terms of the expectations it is called on to meet. High power may also have difficulty in handling small problems: it may become easier to drop an atom bomb on a mosquito than to use a can of bug spray.

A number of research studies have examined the effects of high power on group members. Kipnis (1972) found that powerful group members (1) made more attempts to influence the behavior of the low-power members, (2) devalued the performance of the low-power members, (3) attributed the efforts of the low-power members to their own use of power rather than to the low-power members' motivations to do well, (4) viewed the low-power members as objects of manipulation, and (5) expressed a preference for the maintenance of psychological distance from the low-power members. Participants who were randomly assigned to central positions in a communication network (the more powerful positions) not only viewed themselves as powerful but also rated themselves as more capable than the participants who were randomly assigned peripheral positions (Stotle, 1978). Tjosvold (1978) notes that high-power group members (1) feel more secure than low-power members, (2) underestimate the low-power members' positive intentions, (3) devalue the low-power person, (4) are inattentive to the communications of the low-power person, (5) are unresponsive to cooperative gestures by the low-power members, and (6) attempt to protect their superior power by rejecting demands for change. High-power group members also seem uninterested in learning about the intentions and plans of low-power members (Tjosvold and Sagaria, 1978).

Low-Power Members

Group members subjected to the power of another generally find such a relationship threatening and debilitating. Tjosvold (1978) observes that members with low power are apt to feel frustrated and uncertain about their future goal facilitation because they depend heavily on the unpredictable behavior of the high-power members. These feelings of uncertainty and anxiety provoke (1) increased vigilance and attempts to understand and predict the high-power members' behavior, (2) distorted perceptions of the positive intent of the high-power members toward them, (3) attraction to, mixed with fear of, the high-power members, (4) stifling of criticism of the high-power members, (5) unwillingness to clarify one's position to the high-power members, (6) ingratiation, conformity, flattery, and effacing self-presentation so as to induce the high-power members to like and to reward them, and (7) the expectation of exploitation (low-power members tend to believe that because they have no retaliatory capability they are vulnerable and helpless and will be exploited). Low-power members have been found to direct much of their communication and attention to high-power members and to keep on good terms with them.

On the other hand, low-power group members have been found to resist attempts by high-power members to control them. Tjosvold (1978) notes that low-power members have been found to defy threats, to counter-threaten, to refuse to comply with an influence attempt even when resistance is costly, to dislike the high-power members, and to perceive the relationship as competitive. Johnson and Allen (1972) found that low-power group members who believed they were equal to their high-power peers felt underre-warded and attempted to obtain increased rewards from the group while emphasizing the incompetence, uncooperativeness, lack of generosity, and unfairness of the high-power members. In addition, they disliked their high-power peers.

Deutsch (1969) assumes that the goal of low-power members is to estab-lish authentic, cooperative, equal-power relationships with the high-power members. He states that the ability of low-power members to offer and engage in authentic cooperation means that they are aware that they are neither helpless nor powerless, even though they are at a disadvantage. Cooperative action requires a recognition that a person has the capacity to "go it alone" if necessary; unless a person has the freedom to choose not to cooperate, there can be no free choice to cooperate. Thus, the low-power members in a group need to build enough cohesiveness and strength to function independently of the high-power members if this is necessary. In addition, the high-power members must be motivated to cooperate with the low-power members. This means that the latter must find goals that are important to the high-power members, especially goals they cannot accomplish without the coopera-tion of the low-power members.

Deutsch (1969) notes that a variety of strategies for influencing high-power members are available to low-power members. By building their own organizations and developing their own resources, low-power members not only can make themselves less vulnerable to exploitation, but can add to their power by providing themselves with alternatives that preclude their being dependent solely upon the high-power members. Low-power members can add to their power by allying themselves with third parties. Another strategy is to try to use existing legal procedures to bring pressures for change. Further, low-power members can search for attachments with the high-power members that, if made more obvious, could increase the latter's positive feel-ings toward or outcome dependence upon the low-power members. Low-power members can try to change the attitudes of those in high power through education or moral persuasion. Finally, the low-power members can use ha-rassment techniques in order to increase the high-power members' costs of staying with the status quo. In planning how to increase their power in relation to the high-power members, low-power members of a group should first clarify their goals, then completely inventory their resources, and finally study how to make the high-power members more aware of their dependence on them and of their compatibility (if any) of goals.

You may check your understanding of this section by answering the following questions (answers at the end of the chapter):

Match the strategies with the group members who use them:

1. They find that goals important to the other-power members cannot be accomplished without them.

    a. High-power members

2. They try to change attitudes through education or moral persuasion.

    b. Low-power members

3. They make rules that legitamize power.

4. They punish attempts to change things.

5. They try to develop good relations with the other-power members.

True   False   **6.** High-power persons are usually eager to cooperate and compromise.

True   False   **7.** The greater a person's power, the more sufficient it is likely to seem.

True   False   **8.** High-power people tend to feel that it is their superb leadership that is the cause of low-power people doing well rather than low power motivation.

True   False   **9.** High-power people are generally unresponsive to cooperative gestures by low-power people and reject demands for change.

True   False   **10.** Low-power people seldom resist attempts by high-power people to control them.

POWER AND CONFLICT

An intimate relationship exists between power and conflict. The use of power is always present in personal and group interaction. Group conflict does not exist, however, unless a group member wants something to happen that she does not have the power to make happen. If a person wants group members to do something and has the power to make them do it, there is no conflict.

Also, if the person wants group members to do something and they want to do it, then even though she does not have the power to make sure they do it there is no conflict. But if a person wants other group members to do something they do not want to do and she does not have enough power to overcome their unwillingness, then a state of conflict exists. The successful attempt to use power can often end a conflict. The successful attempt to influence the group is one that helps resolve conflicts, whereas the unsuccessful attempt can increase the conflict. Conflicts are also increased when the desire to influence is not matched by the capacity to influence.

The destructive management of conflict is characterized by less and less mutual influence among group members. In a conflict situation that is being badly managed, informational power and expertise power are apt to be rejected because each participant sees the other as being untrustworthy and as trying to use his knowledge or expertise for personal goals. Hostility and distrust undermine legitimate power. The emphasis on differences among group members decreases mutual referent power. Reward power can arouse suspicions of bribery or suggest that one is attempting to increase another's dependence upon him. When the bases for these kinds of influence deteriorate, those with power begin to rely more and more on the use of coercive power.

The use of a coercive power base is a destructive way to manage a conflict for many reasons. It exacerbates the conflict, thereby increasing hostility, resentment, lies, threats, retaliation, revenge, and distrust. Threats often lead to aggression and counter-threats. Coercion and threats can sometimes cut short or control a conflict simply by getting behavioral compliance or by forcing a group member to leave the situation, but it will never lead to a productive resolution and cooperation. Communication decreases and becomes less reliable. Mutual influence also decreases, and the likelihood of a mutually satisfying settlement is diminished. Thus, whenever possible, attempts to exercise influence through the use of a coercive power base should be avoided in conflicts. One central strategy to resolve or control a conflict is to reestablish mutual influence among all those in the group.

Here is a test of your understanding of this section (answers at the end of the chapter):

1. In which instance does conflict exist?
    a. A person wants the other group members to do something and has the power to make them do it.
    b. A person wants other group members to do something and does not have the power to make them do it, but they want to do it.
    c. A person wants other group members to do something they don't want to do, and doesn't have enough power to make them do it.

True   False   **2.** The successful use of power can end a conflict.

True   False   **3.** In a conflict situation that is badly managed, information and expertise are apt to be the only forms of power accepted.

True   False   **4.** The use of coercive power lessens the conflict.

True   False   **5.** The more punishment is used, the less chance there is of an agreement being reached.

True   False   **6.** A central strategy to resolve a conflict is to reestablish mutual influence in the group.

FEMALES AT SUMMER CAMP EXERCISE

The purpose of this exercise is to provide an opportunity for a discussion as to how groups form, how leadership is developed, and how power is used within peer groups. It achieves this purpose by examining the interrelationships among ten female college students at summer camp. The procedure is as follows:

1. Form groups of six members. One member volunteers to be an observer. The task of the observer is to record the nature of leadership and power within the group as they complete the task.

2. Each participating group member (five in all) are given the description of two of the females (ten in all). The group as a whole is given a copy of the Characteristics Chart. The task of the group is to answer the following questions:
  a. Who are the members of each subgroup?
  b. Who is the leader of each subgroup?
  c. What characterizes the interactions among members of different subgroups?
  Each group is to decide by concensus the answers to these questions with all members indicating that they know the answers to the questions and can explain how the group arrived at their conclusions.

3. When the group has finished Step 2, write a description of leadership that includes answers to the following questions:
  a. What leadership qualities do the females identified as leaders have?
  b. How do the leaders of the subgroups exercise their leadership?
  Each group is to agree by consensus to all the points included in their written description of leadership.

4. When the group has finished Step 3, write a description of power as it relates to social systems that includes the answers to the following questions:
  a. How do the females exert influence on each other?
  b. What bases of power do the females use?
  Each group is to agree by consensus to all the points included in their written description of power and influence.

5. The groups should share their descriptions of leadership and power with each other in a discussion involving the entire class.

Characteristics of Females at the Summer Camp

Characteristics	Girls									
	Virginia	Renee	Pat	Debbie	Janice	Dianne	Gail	Cindy	Cathy	Heidi
Religion	Catholic	Catholic	Nonsectarian	Methodist	Presbyterian	Baptist	Christian	Baptist	Catholic	Baptist
Attendance	Frequent	Occasional	Never	Frequent	Rare	Frequent	Occasional	Occasional	Occasional	Frequent
College major	Math	Education	Business Mgt.	Home Ec.	Accounting	History	Pre-Law	Languages	Home Ec.	Music
Grade average	B	C	A	B	A	B	A	B	C	C
Family income	Medium	Medium	Medium	Low	High	Medium	High	Medium	Low	Low

Females at Summer Camps Exercise Descriptions

Virginia is a social girl who often talks to others. She is quite attractive and dresses well. She dates often. When she has problems, she shares them with Renee or Pat. She sometimes borrows clothes from them. At night she is usually in her room or in Cathy's room. She sometimes sneaks out of camp at night and always gets back without being caught. She shares the food and liquor that she sneaks into the camp with Renee, Cathy, and sometimes Janice.

Renee is a fairly attractive, rather insecure person. She smokes and drinks. She dates occasionally, often double-dating with Cathy. She borrows clothes from Virginia and Debbie. At night she is usually in Virginia or Cathy's room and confides in them. At times she sneaks out of camp at night and is helped by Virginia to get back in. She shares food and liquor with Cathy and Virginia.

Pat is a clear-headed girl with a perceptive mind. She does not drink and is fairly traditional in her ideas. She is quiet and seldom dates; she never double-dates. She loans clothes to Janice, Virginia, Gail, and Heidi, but does not borrow them. She is a good listener and others confide in her but she does not reciprocate. At night she can be found in her own room but she is often accompanied by one of the other girls.

Debbie is a rather wild girl who dates frequently, occasionally double-dating with Janice. She seems mostly interested in boys—her main topic of conversation. She shares clothes with Virginia and Janice, and at night can usually be found in one of their rooms. At times she sneaks out of camp at night and is helped to get back in by Virginia. She shares food with Janice, Virginia, and occasionally Cathy. She confides in Janice.

Janice is an outgoing girl who is quite attractive and dresses well. She dates often and sometimes double-dates with Debbie. When she has problems she goes to see Pat. She borrows clothes from Pat or Debbie. At night she is usually in her own room. She is a good talker and is successful in debating most of the other girls. She is well-versed in clothes, dating and men, and has lots of spending money. She shares food from home with Debbie, Virginia, and Gail.

Dianne is a neat, well-groomed, modest girl with strong moral convictions. She seldom dates and does not smoke or drink. She is very active in church work and attends several times a week. When she has a personal problem, she goes to see Pat or her minister. She lends clothes to Cindy. At night she is usually in her own room. She likes to read and has been known to remind the girls about quiet hours, which has caused some resentment from Janice and Renee.

Gail is a wealthy, well-traveled, sophisticated girl who seems to relate well to everyone on a casual level. She dates occasionally but never double-dates. She sometimes borrows clothes from Pat, with whom she shares her problems. She is mature and understanding of others but does not seem to form very close friendships. At night she can be found in the rooms of Pat or Dianne. She shares food with Dianne, Pat, and sometimes Janice.

Cindy is a very shy girl who seldom dates. She doesn't smoke or drink. She occasionally goes to a movie with Dianne, sometimes Heidi. At night she can be found in Dianne's or Janice's room. She shares food with Dianne or Janice. She avoids Renee and Virginia.

Cathy is a rather loud, chunky girl. She often swears and is heard telling dirty jokes. She occasionally double-dates with Renee. She likes to smoke and drink. She shares her problems with Virginia and Renee. At night she is in her own room or Virginia's room. She shares food with Virginia, Renee, and sometimes Debbie.

Heidi is an overweight girl who tries to be friendly with everyone. She goes out of her way to run errands and otherwise try to please the other girls. She does not smoke, drink, or date. She attends movies with Cindy or Dianne. She does not dress well and Pat is the only one who will lend her clothes. At night she is either in her own room or Pat's or Dianne's room. She shares her problems with Pat or Dianne. She shares food with Dianne, Cindy, Gail, and Pat.

GROUP-POWER EXERCISES

1. With your classmates, form groups of five. Place all the change the group members have in a hat. Decide who in the group gets all the money. Discuss the experience.
2. Stand by the walls of the room with your classmates. Each of you pick a spot in the center of the room in which you would like to sit. At a signal from a coordinator, go sit in that spot. Once all of you are settled, discuss your experience with the nearest person.
3. Stand in the circle with your classmates, touching fingertips with the person on either side. Pick a spot in the room to which you would like the group to go. Do not talk. When the signal is given, try to get the group to move to your chosen spot. Discuss what you have learned with a partner.
4. Stand in a circle with your classmates. Each member helps with one hand to hold a sheet of paper. No verbal communication is allowed. At the signal the paper suddenly becomes ''power.'' See what happens and discuss.
5. Pair up with a classmate. Sit in chairs facing each other. You have five minutes to decide, nonverbally, who is going to sit on the floor. At the end of that time one person *must* be on the floor. See what happens and discuss.
6. Sit in a circle with your classmates. Each of you close your eyes and imagine you live in a small rural village. You have been handed an important message to deliver to someone in a much more powerful neighboring village. You begin to walk to the other village. You pass a girl on a bridge. You pass a man on a bicycle. You pass a family having a picnic. You hear the sound of birds singing, you see trees moving in the breeze, you smell the grass and the earth. Rounding a bend, you suddenly come upon a wall. It continues in both directions as far as you can see. The village you need to get to is beyond the wall. For a few minutes think of what happens. Then open your eyes and share stories of what happened at the wall. Discuss, from the standpoint of power.

7. Sit in a circle with your classmates. Each of you close your eyes and picture the group in which you are a member. In your fantasy, begin a game of follow-the-leader. At first see yourself as the leader and note what happens among the followers. Now shift leaders and see someone else at the head of the line. Keep going until all the members of your group have had a chance to be the leader. Then open your eyes and discuss the following questions: What kinds of things did different persons lead the group to do? What feelings did you imagine among the followers? How did you picture the group behaving when you were the leader? Who seemed the most "natural" in the role? Who seemed the least "natural" in the role?

8. Divide into groups of four with your classmates. Make a picture or collage of power, using available resources—magazines, pencils, paints, crayons, newspapers, and so forth. At the end of thirty minutes discuss the picture of each group. If Polaroid cameras are available, instead of making a picture of power go out and take a picture of power. Then come back and discuss.

9. This exercise is for a group that has been working together on a task. Arrange yourselves in a line according to how powerful you see yourselves, from most powerful to least powerful. Before beginning mark one end of the line as the spot for the most powerful person so that all members will know how to arrange themselves. After the line has stabilized ask if anyone wants to move to a different location. Discuss self-perceptions and perceptions of others. How does your power as perceived by other members compare with how you see it? Were there disagreements among members about who is the most powerful? Does the group have certain biases about power, such as the richest person being seen as the most powerful?

YOUR POWER BEHAVIOR

You have now participated in a series of exercises on power as well as having read a summary of much of the current theory and research on the use of power. Power has been discussed in several previous chapters. At this point, form a group with two of your classmates. Discuss what you have learned about yourself and your behavior in power situations. What are your feelings when you are being opposed and have to rely upon power to further your goals? How do you feel when others quickly conform to what you wish them to do? How do you react when others force you to comply to their wishes? What basis of power do you usually rely upon? Have you ever been manipulated or conned? If so, what did it feel like? Any question about power and its use should be discussed if it increases your understanding of yourself and the other members of your group. Write down your conclusions about yourself and your use of power.

SUMMARY

You should now have a good understanding of power and how it can help or hinder a group. You have experienced high- and low-power situations and know the dangers of having either high or low power. In the next chapter you will learn more about how groups hold together and direct the behavior of their members.

ANSWERS

Page 345—1. b; 2. a; 3. b; 4. a; 5. a; 6. b; 7. a; 8. b; 9. a; 10. b; 11. true; 12. false; 13. false; 14. true; 15. false; 16. true; 17. false; 18. true; 19. false; 20. false; 21. false; 22. true; 23. true; 24. true; 25. false.

Page 351—1. c; 2. f; 3. b; 4. e; 5. d; 6. a.

Page 362—1. b; 2. b; 3. a; 4. a; 5. b; 6. false; 7. false; 8. true; 9. true; 10. false.

Page 363—1. c; 2. true; 3. false; 4. false; 5. true; 6. true.

9

Cohesion, Member Needs, Trust, and Group Norms

BASIC CONCEPTS TO BE COVERED IN THIS CHAPTER

In this chapter a number of concepts are defined and discussed. The major ones are listed below. The procedure for learning these concepts is as follows:

1. The class forms heterogeneous groups of four.
2. Each group divides into two pairs.
3. The task for each pair is to:
   a. define each concept, noting the page on which it is defined and discussed.
   b. make sure that both members of the pair understand the meaning of each concept.
4. In each group, members compare the answers of the two pairs. If there is disagreement, they look up the concept in the chapter and clarify it until they all agree on the definition and understand it.

Concepts

1. group cohesion
2. inclusion needs
3. control needs
4. affection needs
5. open relationship
6. trust
7. trusting behavior
8. trustworthy behavior
9. openness
10. acceptance
11. support
12. cooperative intentions
13. group norms
14. social comparison
15. conformity

GROUP COHESION

In order to function effectively a group has to cohere, or, to put it in several other ways, "hang together," generate a "we feeling" among members, or have a positive emotional climate. The most frequently used term to describe a sense of member liking for and commitment to the group is *cohesiveness*. *Group cohesion* is the extent to which the influences on members to remain in the group are greater than the influences on members to leave the group. It is the sum of all the factors influencing members to stay in the group. When group members like one another and wish to remain in one another's presence, the group is cohesive.

Group cohesion is determined by the assessment of group members of the desirable and undesirable consequences of group membership. The more favorable the outcomes members can expect from membership, the more they will be attracted to the group. The outcomes expected from membership in a given group depend on such factors as the nature of the group and its goals, how clearly the goals are stated, how clear the procedures (or paths) are for achieving the goals, how likely it is that the goals will be successfully achieved, the past successes of the group in achieving its goals, how well the group members cooperate with each other, how constructively conflicts among members are managed, the attitude similarity of group members, and whether membership in other groups would provide greater benefits. Group cohesion is constantly changing because different members are attracted to the group to different degrees and the same member's attraction toward the group will vary at different times. Each event that occurs in the group alters the cohesion of the group to some extent.

The level of group cohesion is indicated in several ways. Attendance by group members, whether members arrive on time, the trust and support present among group members, the amount of individuality accepted in the group, the amount of fun members have—all may reflect the cohesion of the group. Cohesion can also be measured just by asking members whether they like one another, whether they want to continue their membership, and whether they are sure they can work effectively with the other group members in the future, and through sociometric devices.

A variety of research studies indicate that group cohesiveness has several definite consequences upon a group (Cartwright, 1968; Watson and Johnson, 1972). As cohesiveness increases, so too does the capacity of a group to keep its members—and the longer the group keeps its members, the greater the likelihood that it will achieve its goals. Highly cohesive groups are characterized by low turnover in membership and low absenteeism. It is less likely to be disrupted when one member does decide to leave. As cohesiveness increases, there is a corresponding rise in the participation of all group members—and the greater the participation of members, the more resources are available to the group to enhance goal accomplishment.

As cohesiveness increases, members also become more committed to the group's goals, accept assigned tasks and roles more readily, and conform to group norms more frequently. Members of cohesive groups put a greater value on the group's goals and stick more closely to the group's norms than do members of groups lacking cohesion. They are also more eager to protect the group's norms by putting pressure on or rejecting those who violate them. They are more loyal to the group and more willing to work toward a common goal. Unlike members of loosely assembled groups, members of cohesive groups take on group responsibilities more often, persist longer in working toward difficult goals, are more motivated to accomplish the group's tasks (if for no other reason than to live up to the expectations of their fellow group members), and are more satisfied with the work of the group. When the norms of a group favor productivity, those groups that are highly cohesive are more productive in accomplishing goals and in completing assigned tasks. Moreover, group members communicate more frequently and effectively in highly cohesive groups. Their interaction is more friendly, cooperative, and democratic. They are more likely to influence one another in making decisions, to be more willing to listen to other members, to be more willing to accept the opinions of the other members, and to be more willing to be influenced by other members. They are also more willing to endure pain or frustration on behalf of the group and more willing to defend the group against external criticism or attack. Finally, they are more satisfied with the group.

Highly cohesive groups are a source of security for members: they serve to reduce anxiety and to heighten self-esteem. Members of highly cohesive groups experience greater security and relief from tension in the group than do members of noncohesive groups. The awareness that one is liked, accepted, and valued and that others hold similar goals and values is an important aspect of psychological health. A person's acceptance by other group members is related in an important way to his participation in the group—the greater the group's acceptance, the more likely he is to participate, and the acceptance of the group becomes much more important psychologically *after* a person has disclosed himself to the group through participation. Acceptance and approval are of utmost importance for any group member.

Although cohesive groups may show greater acceptance, intimacy, and understanding, there is also evidence that they allow greater development and expression of hostility and conflict than do noncohesive groups. Unless antagonism is openly expressed and conflicts are openly resolved, persistent and impenetrable hostile attitudes may develop that will increasingly hamper effective member cooperation and interaction. The result of a hostile attitude is often an avoidance of and an irrational dislike for the ideas of other members—and a refusal to communicate with them. At the most fundamental level, a person simply does not enjoy being with someone she dislikes, and the resulting lack of communication bars chances for the conflict to be resolved. These circumstances have been found to apply between groups as well as between members of a group. Cohesiveness affects such behavior because when the degree of cohesiveness is considerable, the members must mean enough to one another to be willing to bear the discomfort of working through the conflict. Regardless of how angry members of a cohesive group may become with one another, they are more apt to continue communication, which enables the group to resolve conflicts and capitalize upon controversies, both of which increase its productivity. Not only are members of cohesive groups better able to express hostility, but there is also evidence that they are better able to express hostility toward the leader (Pepitone and Reichling, 1955; Wright, 1943). All in all, cohesiveness in a group results in a better group, one in which members work more cooperatively on their tasks and resolve group difficulties.

How can a group increase its cohesion? There are several ways of doing so:

1. Structuring cooperation among members: One of the most predictable outcomes of cooperative interaction is that group members will like each other and value their membership in the group. Since cooperation is discussed at length in Chapter 4, it will not be discussed here.
2. Successfully meeting the personal needs of members: For a group to be cohesive, the members' needs for mutual inclusion, mutual influence, and mutual affection among themselves must be met.
3. Maintaining a high level of trust among members: Without a high level of trust, a group cannot be cohesive.
4. Promoting group norms that encourage the expression of individuality, trusting and trustworthy behavior, and concern and affection among group members: For a group to be cohesive, group members need to understand how to implement appropriate norms within the group.

Meeting the personal needs of group members, building and maintaining a high level of trust, and implementing appropriate group norms will all be discussed in this chapter.

QUIZ

Check your reading of this section by answering the following questions. Answers are on page 399.

True   False   1. Group cohesion is the result of all forces acting as a deterrent on negative behavior.

True   False   2. Cohesion rarely changes in a group.

True   False   **3.** You can tell if a group has cohesion by whether members like each other and want to stay in the group.

True   False   **4.** Cohesion can be built into a group by structuring cooperation, trust, and acceptance of individuality.

True   False   **5.** Highly cohesive groups will have low membership turnover and high absenteeism.

True   False   **6.** Highly cohesive group members stick closely to the group norms.

True   False   **7.** Member of highly cohesive groups work harder.

True   False   **8.** Members influence each other less in highly cohesive groups.

True   False   **9.** Members have more anxiety and less self-esteem in highly cohesive groups.

True   False   **10.** Highly cohesive groups have more expressed hostility and conflict.

YOUR COHESION BEHAVIOR EXERCISE (I)

How does your behavior affect group cohesion? When you want to increase group cohesion what do you do? How would you describe your behavior in influencing group cohesion? The following questions should help you reflect upon how your behavior influences the cohesion of the groups to which you belong. Answer each question as honestly as possible.

1. I try to make sure that everyone enjoys being a member of the group.
   Never   1 : 2 : 3 : 4 : 5 : 6 : 7 : 8 : 9   Always

2. I disclose my ideas, feelings, and reactions to what is currently taking place within the group.
   Never   1 : 2 : 3 : 4 : 5 : 6 : 7 : 8 : 9   Always

3. I express acceptance and support when other members disclose their ideas, feelings, and reactions to what is currently taking place in the group.
   Never   1 : 2 : 3 : 4 : 5 : 6 : 7 : 8 : 9   Always

4. I try to make all members feel valued and appreciated.
   Never   1 : 2 : 3 : 4 : 5 : 6 : 7 : 8 : 9   Always

5. I try to include other members in group activities.
   Never   1 : 2 : 3 : 4 : 5 : 6 : 7 : 8 : 9   Always

6. I am influenced by other group members.
   Never   1 : 2 : 3 : 4 : 5 : 6 : 7 : 8 : 9   Always

7. I take risks in expressing new ideas and my current feelings.
   Never   1 : 2 : 3 : 4 : 5 : 6 : 7 : 8 : 9   Always

8. I express liking, affection, and concern for other members.

    Never 1 : 2 : 3 : 4 : 5 : 6 : 7 : 8 : 9 Always

9. I encourage group norms that support individuality and personal expression.

    Never 1 : 2 : 3 : 4 : 5 : 6 : 7 : 8 : 9 Always

These questions focus upon several ways of increasing group cohesion. The first question describes a general attempt to keep cohesion high. Questions 2 and 3 pertain to the expression of ideas and feelings and the support for others expressing ideas and feelings; such personal participation is essential for cohesiveness and for the development of trust. Questions 4 and 8 also focus upon support for, and liking of, other group members. Question 5 refers to the inclusion of other members, and question 6 takes up one's willingness to be influenced by other members. Questions 7 and 9 center on the acceptance of individuality within the group. All these factors are important for group cohesion. Discuss your answers with another group member. Then add all your answers together to get a total cohesion score. Keep your responses to these questions in mind as you proceed through this chapter.

MEMBER NEEDS AND GROUP DEVELOPMENT

Persons need other persons. A person is a social being who depends on other individuals for his humanness (Johnson, 1973). All human beings, because they live in a society, must establish a social balance between themselves and their associates. This social nature of humankind gives rise to certain interpersonal needs. Three are basic: inclusion, control, and affection (Schutz, 1958). Every group, no matter what its purpose or who its members are, has to deal with these three needs. The *inclusion* need centers in membership—who is "in" and who is "out," who is included and who is excluded, who belongs and who does not, who is part of togetherness and who is not. Some members want the group to be very inclusive; other members want it to be loosely knit. The *control* need pertains to power relations in the group—who has influence over the other group members, who has authority. Some members will want a great deal of influence; others may not want to influence anyone. The *affection* need has to do with how close the relations in the group are. Some members may want a close, warm group; others may want a cool and distant group atmosphere.

The need for inclusion is the need persons have to keep a satisfactory relationship between themselves and others in terms of interaction and belongingness. This is the membership issue of groups. Some persons like to be with others all the time; others seek much less contact, preferring privacy. Membership behavior has two aspects: trying to include other members in what is taking place within the group, and wanting other members to try to include you. Because inclusion involves the process of forming relationships, it usually comes first in the life of a group. A person with little need for inclusion may be called undersocial; he tends to be introverted and withdrawn. The oversocial person is at the opposite extreme: she tends toward extroversion. During the membership phase of the group's formation and development, it is important for each member to answer the question "Who am I with these other persons?" When all have a sense of identification with the group, the membership issue is resolved. A group observer will notice this when statements shift from "I" and "others" to "we."

Control problems usually follow those of inclusion in the development of a group. Once a group has formed, it begins to differentiate among members. Different members take or seek different roles, and power struggles and influence often become central issues. The need for control is the need members have to keep a satisfactory relation among themselves in terms of power or influence. Every person has a need to control her environment to some degree so that it will be predictable for her. Ordinarily this amounts to controlling others, because people are the main agents that threaten an individual's environment and create an unpredictable and uncontrollable situation. This need for control varies from wanting to control one's entire environment, including all the persons around one, to wanting to control no one in any situation, no matter how appropriate control would be. A person who is extremely low on control—an "abdicrat"—tends to be submissive and does not accept power and responsibility in her interpersonal behavior. She drifts toward the subordinate position, in which she will not have to take responsibility for making decisions; someone else will take charge. A person who is extremely high on control—an "autocrat"—is very dominating. She wants to be at the top of a power hierarchy, and is afraid people will not be influenced or controlled by her and will therefore come to dominate her. The person in the middle feels comfortable in giving or in receiving influence, whichever fits the situation. There are two aspects of control in a group: the degree to which one controls others and the degree to which one wants to be controlled. Often, issues of control are centered in decision making. This is evidenced by members asking "Does it make any difference if I am here or not?" Every member has a preference as to the degree to which she needs to control or influence other members and the degree to which she wishes to be controlled or influenced by other members. If leadership is distributed throughout the group, all members will control and be controlled.

Affection is based on the building of emotional ties. As a consequence, it is usually the last phase to emerge in the development of a group. In this inclusion phase, members' control needs require them to encounter one another, decide to continue their relationship, and work out how they will be related. To continue the group relationship, members must form ties of affection; they must embrace one another in order to form a lasting bond. The need for affection is the need a person has to keep a satisfactory relationship between himself and others in terms of love and affection. At one extreme are people who like close relationships with every person they meet. At the other extreme are those who prefer their personal relationships to be impersonal and distant, perhaps friendly but not close and intimate. Affection also has two aspects: the degree to which a person expresses affection toward others and the degree to which a person wants others to express affection toward him. In a group the issue is one of members feeling valued and respected; being accepted is a vital part of membership in the group. Members may ask, "How much do I care for these others and how much do they care for me?" Many times this question is answered in the moments after a task is completed successfully by the group—when each member feels he has been working with good people, when there is an awareness of warm feelings and pride in "our" accomplishments. At other times it is answered just with feelings of affection and satisfaction in being together.

You can check your understanding of this section by answering the following questions (answers at the end of the chapter):
Match the needs with their definitions:

____ **1.** Inclusion
____ **2.** Control
____ **3.** Affection

a. The need to keep a satisfactory relationship in terms of power and influence

b. The need to keep a satisfactory relationship in terms of belonging and interacting

c. The need to keep a satisfactory relationship in terms of liking and loving

True False **4.** The two aspects of membership behavior are wanting other members to include you and wanting to be included by other members.

True False **5.** The two aspects of control are the degree to which you control others and the degree to which others control you.

True False **6.** The two aspects of affection are the degree to which you express affection toward others and the degree to which you want others to express affection toward you.

True False **7.** Inclusion involves the process of forming relationships.

True False **8.** Everyone needs to control his environment.

True False **9.** If leadership is distributed throughout the group, some members will control and others will be controlled.

True False **10.** Inclusion needs require persons to confront each other and work out how they will be related.

INCLUSION, CONTROL, AND AFFECTION EXERCISE

The purpose of this exercise is to provide direct experiences involving inclusion, control, and affection within a group setting. The exercise highlights the impact on group cohesiveness of meeting or frustrating personal needs. It may be conducted within two hours. The procedure for the coordinator is as follows:

1. Introduce the exercise as a microlab on the three needs of inclusion, control, and affection. A brief review of the preceding discussion of these needs may be helpful. Explain that the exercise has three rounds.

2. *Round 1:*

   a. Have the participants mill around the room for a while and then form groups of three. They are then to decide individually who was the most influential in bringing the triad together, point at that person, and talk about how they decided to be together.

   b. Have the participants again mill around the room. While they are doing this ask them to close their eyes, and find the other two members of their triad. When all the group have reformed, have them talk about the experience.

   c. Give each triad two minutes to eliminate one of its members. The person eliminated from the group should move to the end of the room and sit quietly, reflect on his feelings, and not interact with the others. Publicly interview the "orphans" to find out what kind of decision-making process resulted in their being selected as the one to leave the threesome.

   d. Ask the pairs to select a new person to join them. They may not claim back the person they have just eliminated. At your signal, pairs should move to the end of the room and claim the person they want to join them.

   e. Combine the triads into groups of six and have them share their feelings about their experiences so far.

3. *Round 2:*

   a. Have the triads decide on who in their group is to be A, who is to be B, and who C—and then reflect on how they made their decisions. Who influenced the decisions the most?

   b. Without talking, the C's, are to pose as a statue. The A's are then to continue building the statue by assuming a posture in harmony with the C's. Prohibit talking while this is going on. The B's are to complete the statue by assuming a pose in harmony with the C's and the A's. Now break up the statue. Have the group members talk with one another about the nonverbal interaction that took place while they were creating the statue, and about how they influenced one another by the poses they assumed.

   c. Allow the triads two minutes to again decide which one of them will leave the group. The "singles" are to gather at the far end of the room for instructions. Tell the pairs to sit knee to knee with each other, talk to each other about their feelings and reactions to the exercise thus far, or to hold a conversation about whatever interests them both. Instruct the singles (out of hearing of the pairs) to pick a pair, approach it, and watch in what ways they are or are not included by the pair. When all or most of the singles have become part of an ongoing conversation, stop the participants and have a general discussion on the experiences of the "newcomers."

   d. Ask the triads to join in groups of six and talk about their feelings and reactions to round 2.
4. *Round 3:*
   a. Ask each triad to quickly find something that makes it distinct from all others in the room, and announce what they have picked.
   b. Have each member recall an impressive moment of quiet beauty and share that memory with the others in their triad.
   c. Give each triad two minutes to decide which one of its members shall leave. Have those cast adrift gather in the center of the room and sit quietly on the floor; the pairs are to form a circle around them. Inform the pairs that they are to decide, talking in whispers, (1) whether to pick anyone from the center and (2) if they do, who it should be (it cannot be their former triad member). Ask the singles to decide (1) whether to pick a new group to join and (2) which group it should be (it cannot be their former group). Ask all participants to make a clear decision and stick to it. At your signal, all participants are to demonstrate the choice they have made. Those who are left (individuals or pairs who did not choose and were not chosen), if any, are to be interviewed about the result of their choice and the feelings they are having about their immediate situation. Then ensure that everyone is in a triad.
   d. Have the triads form groups of six and discuss their feelings and reactions to round 3.
5. Ask the participants to reflect on the experiences of all three rounds and share what they have learned with the other members of their final triad. They should use the following questions as a guide:
   a. What feelings do you remember having throughout the exercise?
   b. What was happening around each feeling? Were there any patterns of reaction in the various situations?
   c. When approaching a new group how did you usually feel?
   d. When approaching a new group what was your usual behavior?
   e. When eliminating a member of your group how did you usually feel?
   f. When being eliminated from a group how did you usually feel?
   g. When receiving affection how did you usually feel?
   h. When influencing a decision how did you usually feel and behave?
   i. When being influenced how did you usually feel and behave?

MORE INTERPERSONAL-NEEDS EXERCISES

The eleven exercises that follow also deal with the three interpersonal needs of group members. Each outlines the procedure for a coordinator to follow. In all exercises participants are part of one group, except where noted otherwise.

Inclusion Exercises

1. After the group members have had some time together indicate that the center of the room is for those who definitely feel a part of the group. Then have group members place themselves in the room in relation to how they feel. To obtain further information, ask them to stand nearest the persons to whom they feel closest. They should then share feelings and perceptions about their placement.

2. When someone indicates that he feels excluded from the group, ask the other members to stand in a circle with their arms around each other's waist. The excluded person, who is outside the circle, is to try to get inside. After he succeeds in doing so—or after he has tried very hard to do so—discuss his feelings of trying to get inside the circle and the feelings of those who were part of the circle. Have the participants exchange views on what they learned about the group and how it deals with inclusion and exclusion.

Affection Exercises

1. Ask each group member to think of an imaginary, meaningful gift for each of the other members. Each member then describes the gifts she has selected.
2. Ask group members to focus on one another with three statements: (1) When I look at you I see . . . ; (2) I wish you would . . . ; and (3) What I really like about you is. . . .
3. Ask the group to stand in a circle and give itself a big hug.

Control Exercises

1. Ask the participants to pick an imaginary spot in the center of the room that is theirs. At the signal, each is to try to sit on his spot. Once settled, the group members are to turn to a neighbor and discuss the experience.
2. Ask group members to stand in a circle and touch fingertips with the person on either side. Then ask each member to pick a spot in the room to which she would like the group to go. Make it clear to the group members that they must keep fingertip contact and that they may not talk. At the signal, everyone tries to get the group to her chosen spot. Discuss what members learned about the group and how it deals with the control issue.

Cohesion Exercises

1. Divide the participants into several groups. Give each group fifteen minutes to develop and construct a group symbol, such as a flag or a drawing of the group, and to develop several group traditions that will be carried out in the future. Ask the groups to share these symbols and traditions with one another. Then ask the groups to analyze the effect these activities have had upon cohesion.
2. Review the exercises in the previous chapters. Find exercises in which participants were asked to indicate their satisfaction with the group, their liking for group members, their desire to continue as a member of the group, and other indexes of group cohesion.

3. Divide participants into groups of four to six. Have group members sit with their back to the center of their group and talk about their impressions of the group. They should then sit facing one another with their eyes closed and discuss who the members of the group are. Ask them to open their eyes, look at one another's hands, and discuss the most significant things that have recently happened to group members. Then ask them to lie down with their head toward the center of the group and their shoulders touching and describe what they were doing when they were ten and what they were doing when they were fifteen. Have them raise one arm and have a group hand dance. Then have them discuss what effect each procedure and topic had upon group cohesion. Finally, ask them to say good-bye in a nonverbal way.

THE LEVEL OF ACCEPTANCE IN YOUR GROUP EXERCISE

What is the level of acceptance in your group? The purpose of this exercise is to provide a way in which the level of acceptance in your group may be assessed and discussed. The procedure is as follows:

1. With the other members of your group, fill out the questionnaire below. Questionnaires should be unsigned so that no one's responses can be identified.
2. Tabulate the results in the summary table that follows the questionnaire.
3. Discuss the conclusions that can be drawn from the results. Consider these two questions:
   a. What is contributing to the present high or low level of acceptance in the group?
   b. How may the level of acceptance in the group be increased?

Questionnaire: Level of Acceptance

Think about the ways in which the members of your group normally behave toward you. In the parentheses in front of the statements below, place the number corresponding to your perceptions of the group as a whole, using the following scale:

5 = They *always* behave this way.
4 = They *typically* behave this way.
3 = They *usually* behave this way.
2 = They *seldom* behave this way.
1 = They *rarely* behave this way.
0 = They *never* behave this way.

My fellow group members:

1. (——) . . . . are completely honest with me.
2. . . . . .(——) . . . . understand what I am trying to communicate.

3. . . . .(———) . . . . . interrupt and ignore my comments.
4. . . . .(———) accept me just the way I am.
5. (———) . . . . tell me when I bother them.
6. . . . . .(———) . . . . don't understand things I say or do.
7. . . . .(———) . . . . . are interested in me.
8. . . . .(———) make it easy for me to be myself.
9. (———) . . . . don't tell me things that would hurt my feelings.
10. . . . . .(———) . . . . understand who I really am.
11. . . . .(———) . . . . . include me in what they are doing.
12. . . . .(———) evaluate whether I am acceptable or unacceptable.
13. (———) . . . . are completely open with me.
14. . . . . .(———) . . . . immediately know when something is bothering me.
15. . . . .(———) . . . . . value me as a person, apart from my skills or status.
16. . . . .(———) accept my differences or peculiarities.

      (———) Authenticity with me
         (———) Understanding of me
            (———) Valuing of me
               (———) Accepting of me

Total the number of points in each column. Statements 3, 6, 9, and 12 are reversed in the scoring—subtract from 5 the rating given to each before placing the remainder in each column.

SUMMARY TABLE: LEVEL OF ACCEPTANCE

Score	Authenticity	Understanding	Valuing	Accepting
0–4	_____	_____	_____	_____
5–8	_____	_____	_____	_____
9–12	_____	_____	_____	_____
13–16	_____	_____	_____	_____
17–20	_____	_____	_____	_____

HOW TRUSTING AND TRUSTWORTHY I AM EXERCISE

When you are attempting to build a relationship with someone there is always the risk that the person will react in a rejecting and competitive way. In order for two group members to trust each other, each has to expect the other to be trustworthy and each has to engage in trusting behavior. This exercise allows you to compare the way you see your trust-building behavior in the group with the way other members see it. The procedure is as follows:

1. Complete the questionnaire below. Score your responses.
2. Then make a slip of paper for each member of your group. Fill out each slip as

shown below, rating the members from 1 (low) to 7 (high) on how open and accepting you perceive him or her to be.

```
┌─────────────────────────────────────────┐
│  Member receiving feedback:   Edythe     │
│  1. Openness and sharing:        3       │
│  2. Acceptance, support,                 │
│       and cooperativeness:       6       │
└─────────────────────────────────────────┘
```

Base your rating on how you think the person has behaved during the entire time your group has met together.

3. Hand each member his or her slip. If there are six members in your group, you should receive five ratings of yourself, and each of the other members should likewise end up with five slips. Compute an average of how the other members see your behavior by adding all your ratings for openness and dividing up the number of slips and then doing the same with your ratings for acceptance.

4. In the diagram at the end of the exercise your average openness and acceptance by (1) drawing a dotted line for the results of the feedback slips you received and (2) drawing a solid line for the results of your questionnaire.

5. Discuss with the other group members how similar your perception and their perceptions of your openness and acceptance are. If there is a difference between the two, ask the group to give you more specific feedback about your trust-building behavior in the group. Then discuss how to build trust with others in situations outside the group.

Questionnaire

Here is a series of statements about your behavior in your group. Address each as honestly as you can. There are no right or wrong answers. It is important for you to describe your behavior as accurately as possible.

1. I offer facts, give my opinions and ideas, and provide suggestions and relevant information in order to promote the group discussion.
   Never 1 : 2 : 3 : 4 : 5 : 6 : 7 Always

2. I express my willingness to cooperate with other group members and my expectations that they will also be cooperative.
   Never 1 : 2 : 3 : 4 : 5 : 6 : 7 Always

3. I am open and candid in my dealings with the entire group.
   Never 1 : 2 : 3 : 4 : 5 : 6 : 7 Always

4. I give support to group members who are on the spot and struggling to express themselves intellectually or emotionally.
   Never 1 : 2 : 3 : 4 : 5 : 6 : 7 Always

5. I keep my thoughts, feelings, and reactions to myself during group discussions.
   Never 1 : 2 : 3 : 4 : 5 : 6 : 7 Always

6. I evaluate the contributions of other group members in terms of whether their contributions are useful to me and whether they are right or wrong.
Never   1 : 2 : 3 : 4 : 5 : 6 : 7   Always

7. I take risks in expressing new ideas and my current feelings during a group discussion.
Never   1 : 2 : 3 : 4 : 5 : 6 : 7   Always

8. I communicate to other group members that I am aware of, and appreciate, their abilities, talents, skills, and resources.
Never   1 : 2 : 3 : 4 : 5 : 6 : 7   Always

9. I offer help to anyone in the group in order to bring up the performance of everyone.
Never   1 : 2 : 3 : 4 : 5 : 6 : 7   Always

10. I accept and support the openness of other group members, support them for taking risks, and encourage individuality in them.
Never   1 : 2 : 3 : 4 : 5 : 6 : 7   Always

11. I share any sources of information or other resources I have with the other group members in order to promote the success of individual members and the group as a whole.
Never   1 : 2 : 3 : 4 : 5 : 6 : 7   Always

12. I often paraphrase or summarize what other members have said before I respond or comment.
Never   1 : 2 : 3 : 4 : 5 : 6 : 7   Always

13. I level with other group members.
Never   1 : 2 : 3 : 4 : 5 : 6 : 7   Always

14. I warmly encourage all members to participate, recognizing them for their contributions, demonstrating acceptance of and openness to their ideas, and generally being friendly and responsive to them.
Never   1 : 2 : 3 : 4 : 5 : 6 : 7   Always

Reverse the scoring (subtract from 7 the rating given and place the remainder in the spaces provided) of questions 5 and 6. Then add the scores in the following way:

Openness and Sharing	*Acceptance and Support*
1. ___	**2.** ___
3. ___	**4.** ___
5. ___	**6.** ___
7. ___	**8.** ___
9. ___	**10.** ___
11. ___	**12.** ___
13. ___	**14.** ___
Total ___	**Total** ___

If you have a score of 21 or over, you are trusting or trustworthy, whichever the case might be. If you have a score of less than 21, you are distrustful or untrustworthy, whichever the case may be.

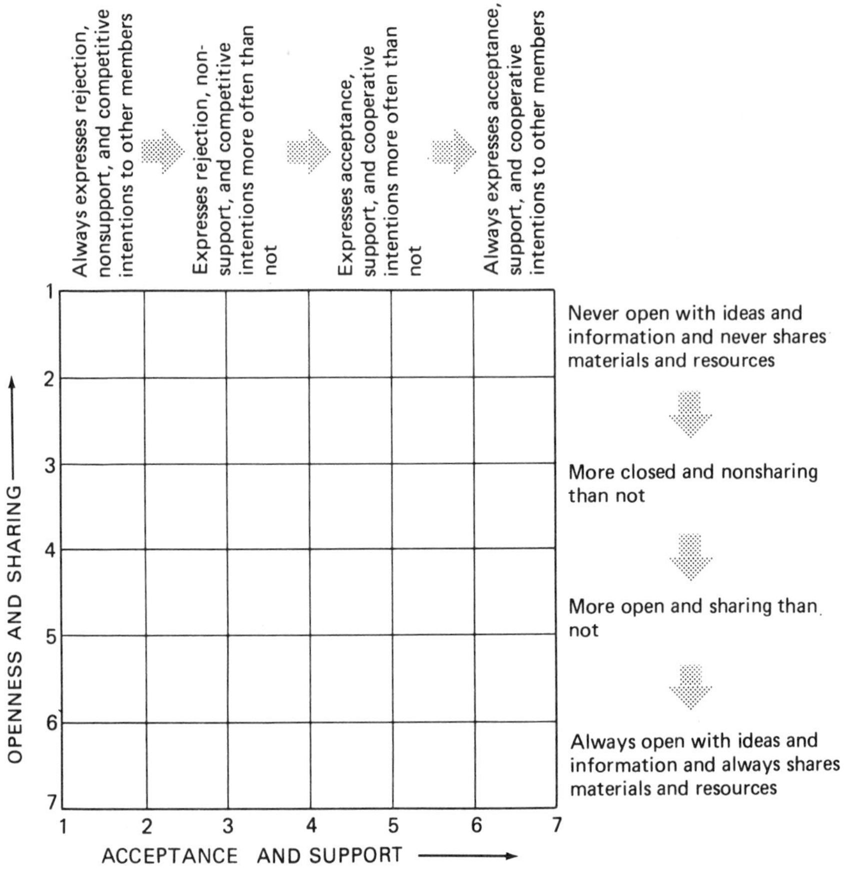
Always expresses rejection, nonsupport, and competitive intentions to other members
Expresses rejection, nonsupport, and competitive intentions more often than not
Expresses acceptance, support, and cooperative intentions more often than not
Always expresses acceptance, support, and cooperative intentions to other members
Never open with ideas and information and never shares materials and resources
More closed and nonsharing than not
More open and sharing than not
Always open with ideas and information and always shares materials and resources
OPENNESS AND SHARING
ACCEPTANCE AND SUPPORT
1
2
3
4
5
6
7

Johnson Trust Diagram, Part One

Johnson Trust Diagram, Part Two

	High Acceptance, Support, and Cooperative Intentions	*Low Acceptance, Support, and Cooperative Intentions*
High Openness and Sharing	Trusting and trustworthy	Trusting but untrustworthy
Low Openness and Sharing	Distrustful but trustworthy	Distrustful and untrustworthy

PRACTICING TRUST-BUILDING SKILLS EXERCISE

This exercise is aimed at providing you with an opportunity to practice the trust-building skills that are needed in order for relationships to grow and develop. Here is the procedure:

1. With your classmates form groups of six members. Choose one member to observe.
2. Complete the task outlined below.
3. Discuss the following questions in your group:
    a. Who engaged in what types of trust-building behaviors?
    b. What feelings do members of the group have about their participation in the group?
    c. Was trust increased or decreased by participation in this exercise?

Observation Sheet

1. Contributes ideas				
2. Describes feelings				
3. Paraphrases				
4. Expresses acceptance and support				
5. Expresses warmth and liking				

Trusting behaviors = 1 and 2
Trustworthy behaviors = 3, 4, and 5

Task

Working as a group, estimate the number of persons in your city (or school) who possess each of the following genetic traits. Establish the frequency of occurrence of each genetic trait, first in your group and then in the entire room. On the basis of the percentage of occurrence in your group and the room, estimate the number of persons in your city (or school) who possess each trait.

1. Dimples in the cheeks versus no dimples.
2. Brown (or hazel) eyes versus blue, gray, or green eyes.
3. Attached versus free earlobes (an earlobe is free if it dips below the point where it is attached).
4. Little-finger bend versus no bend. (Place your little fingers together with your palms toward you. If your little fingers bend away from each other at the tips, you have the famous little-finger bend.)
5. Tongue roll versus no tongue roll (if you can curl up both sides of your tongue to make a trough, you have it; it's not contagious).

6. Hairy versus nonhairy middle fingers (examine the back of the middle finger on each hand and look for hair between the first and second knuckles).

7. Widow's peak versus straight or curved hairline (examine the hairline across your forehead and look for a definite dip or point of hair extending down toward your nose).

OPEN VERSUS CLOSED RELATIONSHIPS EXERCISE

Are the relationships among group members open or closed? The purpose of this exercise is to provide participants with an opportunity to reflect on and discuss this question. The procedure is as follows:

1. Read carefully the accompanying diagram of open and closed relationships.
2. Working by yourself, write down answers to the following questions:
   a. How open are your relationships with other group members?
   b. Are there relationships within the group you wish to make more open?
   c. Are there relationships within the group you wish to make more closed?
   d. What actions are needed to make a relationship more open?
   e. What actions are needed to make a relationship more closed?
3. Meet as a group and discuss each of these questions. Arrive at a group consensus on the answers to questions *d* and *e*.
4. Each group shares its conclusions about open and closed relationships with the rest of the class.

For a more complete discussion of open and closed relationships, see Johnson (1981).

DEVELOPING AND MAINTAINING TRUST

An essential aspect of increasing a group's cohesion is developing and maintaining a high level of trust among group members. The development and maintenance of trust is discussed at length in Johnson (1981), and will therefore be reviewed only briefly at this point. If possible, readers should review the treatment of trust in that text before going ahead with this chapter.

Why is trust important? Trust is a necessary condition for stable cooperation and effective communication. The higher the trust the more stable the cooperation and the more effective the communication. A group member will more openly express his thoughts, feelings, reactions, opinions, information, and ideas when the trust level is high. When the trust level is low, group members will be evasive, dishonest, and inconsiderate in their communications. Group members will more honestly and frequently announce their cooperative intentions and contribute to a cooperative effort when they believe they are dealing with highly trustworthy persons. Cooperation and group

Open and Closed Relationships

Closed ◄- - - - - - - - - - - - - - - - - - - ►Open

	Closed		Open	
Content being discussed	The content is of concern to no one (weather talk).	The content consists of technical aspects of work.	The content consists of the ideas and feelings of one person.	The content consists of the relationship between the two persons.
Time reference	No time reference (jokes and generalizations).	Distant past or future being discussed.	Recent past or future being discussed.	The immediate "here and now" being discussed.
Awareness of your sensing, interpreting, feeling, intending	You never listen to yourself and try to ignore, repress, and deny feelings and reactions.		You are constantly aware of what you are sensing, the interpretations you are making, your feelings, and your intentions about acting on your feelings.	
Openness with own ideas, feelings, reactions	Your statements are generalizations, abstract ideas, intellectualizations; feelings are excluded as irrelevant and inappropriate and nonexistent.		Your personal reactions such as attitudes, values, preferences, feelings, experiences, and observations of the present are stated and focused upon; feelings are included as helpful information about the present.	
Feedback from other people	Feedback from others is avoided, ignored, not listened to, and perceived as being hostile attacks on your personality.		Feedback from others is asked for, sought out, listened to, and used to increase your self-awareness; it is perceived as being a helpful attempt to add to your growth and effectiveness.	
Acceptance of yourself	You believe that once you are known you will be disliked and rejected and, therefore, you hide your "real" self and try to make the impression you think will be most appreciated by other people.		You express confidence in your abilities and skills; can discuss your positive qualities without bragging and without false modesty; you understand how you have used your strengths in the past to achieve your goals and are confident you will do so again in the future.	
Openness to others' ideas, feelings, reactions	You avoid and disregard others' reactions, ideas and feelings; you are embarrassed and put off by others' expressions of feelings; you reject other people and try to one-up and better them; you refuse to hear their feedback on their reactions to your behavior.		You listen to and solicit others' reactions, ideas, and feelings; you are interested and receptive to what others are saying and feeling; you express a desire to cooperate fully with them; you make it clear that you see their value and strengths even when you disagree with them; you ask others for feedback on their perceptions of your behavior.	
Acceptance of other people	You evaluate the other person's actions, communicate that the other is unacceptable, show disregard for the other as a person.		You react without evaluation to the other's actions, communicate that the other is acceptable, value the other as a person.	

effectiveness rest upon every member's sharing resources, giving and receiving help, dividing the work, and contributing to the accomplishment of mutual goals. Such behaviors will occur when there is trust that everyone else is contributing to the group's progress and not using members' openness and sharing of resources for personal rather than group gain.

What is trust? Making a choice to trust another member involves the perception that the choice can lead to gains or losses, that whether you will gain or lose depends upon the behavior of the other member, that the loss will be greater than the gain, and that the other member will probably behave in such a way that you will gain rather than lose. Sounds complicated, doesn't it? In fact there is nothing simple about trust: it is a complex concept and difficult to explain. An example may help. Imagine you are part of a small group that is supposed to decide which teachers to rehire for next year. You begin to contribute to the discussion, knowing you will gain if you contribute good ideas that other members accept but will lose if your ideas are laughed at and belittled. Whether you gain or lose depends upon the behavior of the other group members. You will feel more hurt if you are laughed at than you will feel satisfaction if your ideas are appreciated. Yet you expect the other group members to consider your ideas and accept them. The issue of trust is expressed in the question every member asks: "If I openly express myself, will what I say be used against me?"

In a goal-oriented group the crucial elements of trust are openness and sharing on the one hand and acceptance, support, and cooperative intentions on the other. Cooperative group work requires openness and sharing, which in turn are determined by the expression of acceptance, support, and cooperative intentions in the group. *Openness* is the sharing of information, ideas, thoughts, feelings, and reactions to the issue the group is pursuing. *Sharing* is the offering of your materials and resources to others in order to help them move the group toward goal accomplishment. *Acceptance* is the communication of high regard for another person and his contributions to the group's work. *Support* is the communication to another person that you recognize her strengths and believe she has the capabilities she needs to manage productively the situation she is in. *Cooperative intentions* are the expectations that you are going to behave cooperatively and that every group member will also cooperate in achieving the group's goals. From these definitions, *trusting behavior* may be defined as openness and sharing and *trustworthy behavior* may be defined as the expression of acceptance, support, and cooperative intentions. In considering members' trustworthy behavior, you should remember that accepting and supporting the contributions of other group members does not mean that you agree with everything they say. You can express acceptance and support for the openness and sharing of other members and at the same time express different ideas and opposing points of view. This is an important point in building and maintaining trust.

QUIZ

Check your reading of this section by answering the following questions. Answers are on page 399.

True   False   **1.** Trust is necessary for stable cooperation and effective communication.

True   False   **2.** An ingredient of trust is the awareness that you are taking a chance of gaining or losing by it.

Match the following elements of trust with their definitions:

____ **3.** The communication of high regard for another person and his contributions to the group.

____ **4.** Offering your materials and resources to others to help obtain the goal.

____ **5.** The expectation that you and the group members will help each other.

____ **6.** Sharing information, ideas, thoughts, feelings, and reactions to the issue.

____ **7.** Openness and sharing with others.

____ **8.** Expressing acceptance, support, and cooperative intentions.

____ **9.** Communicating that you recognize another person's strengths and believe she is capable.

a. Openness
b. Sharing
c. Acceptance
d. Support
e. Cooperative intentions
f. Trusting behavior
g. Trustworthy behavior

NORM EXERCISE 1

With your classmates divide into triads and list five "dos" and five "don'ts" for group members. Then meet as one group and have each triad present its list. As a group decide which three "dos" and which three "don'ts" affect group cohesion the most.

NORM EXERCISE 2

Several behaviors are listed below. For each one please indicate how appropriate or inappropriate you think it would be as a norm for your group. Write the number that shows your best estimate of how the group would feel: *5* if the behavior is definitely appropriate as a norm, *4* if the behavior is somewhat appropriate, *3* if it is questionable, *2* if it is somewhat inappropriate, and *1* if it is definitely inappropriate.

____ **1.** Said little or nothing in most meetings.

____ **2.** Talked about the details of her sex life.

____ **3.** Brought up problems he had with others who weren't in the group.

____ **4.** Kissed another group member.

____ **5.** Asked for reactions or feedback ("How do you see me in this group?").

____ **6.** Talked mostly about what was going on in the group.

____ **7.** Frequently joked.

____ **8.** Pleaded for help.

____ **9.** Challenged other members' remarks.

____ **10.** Said she was not getting anything out of being in the group.

____ **11.** Described his reactions to what was taking place in the group.

____ **12.** Highlighted opposition among ideas.

____ **13.** Formed a contract with another member about the use of each other's resources in meeting both their needs and goals.

____ **14.** Refused to be bound by a group decision.

____ **15.** Asked for the goal to be clarified.

____ **16.** Noted competition in the group and asked how it could be reduced.

____ **17.** Gave advice to other group members about what to do.

____ **18.** Interrupted a dialogue between two members.

____ **19.** Told another member that she was unlikable.

____ **20.** Was often absent.

____ **21.** Shouted with anger at another member.

____ **22.** With strong feelings, told another member how likable he was.

____ **23.** Tried to manipulate the group to get her own way.

____ **24.** Hit another group member.

____ **25.** Acted indifferently to other members.

____ **26.** Dominated the group's discussion for more than one session.

____ **27.** Encouraged other group members to react to the topic being discussed.

____ **28.** Tried to convince members of the rightness of a certain point of view.

____ **29.** Talked a lot without showing his real feelings.

____ **30.** Told the group off, saying that it was worthless.

____ **31.** Showed she had no intention of changing her behavior.

____ **32.** Resisted the suggestions of other members about procedures.

_____ **33.** Commented that the decision-making procedure was not appropriate to the nature of the decision.

_____ **34.** Asked that the causes of a group problem be analyzed.

_____ **35.** Expressed affection for several group members.

After reacting to these items the members of your group may think of other behavioral norms to include. Once all members have rated the group norms, the group should discuss them and decide how each affects the cohesion of the group.

GROUP NORMS

To build and maintain a high level of cohesiveness within a group, members must value individuality, encourage trusting and trustworthy behavior, foster cooperativeness, and promote the expression of affection and support among group members. The way in which these positive actions by members become implemented and stabilized in a group is for the actions to be supported by norms that indicate what behaviors are expected of good group members.

The _norms_ of a group are the group's common beliefs regarding appropriate behavior for members; they tell, in other words, how members are expected to behave. They are the prescribed modes of conduct and belief that not only guide the behavior of group members, but help group interaction by specifying the kinds of responses that are expected and acceptable in particular situations. All groups have norms, set either formally or informally. A group of students that often parties together, for example, will have common ideas about what is acceptable and unacceptable behavior at a party, about what is expected of everyone. More formally organized groups, such as classrooms, will have norms about absence, tardiness, accomplishment of assigned work, and appropriate times to speak. In any group some norms specify the behavior expected of all group members and others apply only to persons in specific roles. In the classroom, for instance, some norms govern both the teacher's and the students' behavior but others may apply only to the teacher or only to the students. Because norms refer to the expected behavior sanctioned (rewarded or punished) by a group, they have a specific "ought to" or "must" quality: group members must not disrupt the group's work, group members ought to participate in discussions, and so on. The norms of any group vary in importance. Those that are less important for the objectives and values of the group usually allow for a greater range of behavior and bring less severe pressures for members to conform than do norms that are highly relevant to group functioning.

For a group norm to influence a person's behavior, the person must recognize that it exists, be aware that other group members accept and follow the regulation, and accept and follow it himself. At first a person may confirm to a group norm because the group typically rewards conforming behavior and punishes nonconforming behavior. Later the person may internalize the norm and conform to it automatically, even when no other group members are present. A regulation that all members should be on time for group meetings, for example, becomes a norm only to the extent that the individual group member accepts it, sees other group members accepting it, and sees them enforce the regulation among themselves.

Group norms help a group maintain behavioral consistency among its members. They provide a basis for predicting the behavior of other members and serve as guides for a member's own behavior. Norms thus help each group member anticipate how the others are going to behave in repetitive situations, and they reduce ambiguity concerning appropriate behavior within the group. Norms are formed only with respect to matters that have some significance for the group. Norms may apply to all members or only to certain members. Norms vary in the degree to which they are accepted by the group members. Some norms allow for more deviation by members than others. Some norms require strict adherence to a rule; others permit a wide range of behavior that is regarded as acceptable.

Norms cannot be imposed on a group, but rather develop out of the interaction among members. Norms are social products. This was demonstrated ingeniously by Muzafer Sherif (1935). When a fixed point of light is viewed in total darkness, it appears to move spontaneously; a perceptual phenomenon known as the autokinetic effect. Sherif utilized this phenomenon in studying how group norms develop and how group members come to form coherent, shared beliefs about novel events. Sherif asked participants, first individually and then in groups, to note how much the light moved. When tested in groups the participants coalesced in their judgments on the amount of movement. Once a group decision was made about how much the light was moving, the norm persisted even when the group was not present. Individual participants used the group judgment as a frame of reference within which to evaluate the perceived movement of the light. Many of the judgments and values of individual group members that seem to be their own are shaped in part by the judgments of their fellow group members.

Another classic study on the impact of group norms on the beliefs and values of group members was conducted by Newcomb (1943), who followed the college career of students at Bennington College. The students, all females from mostly well-to-do and politically conservative families, lived in a community where most of the faculty and older students were somewhat amaterialistic and politically liberal. A majority of the Bennington students became progressively more liberal over their careers, but some did not. Newcomb was able to relate the student's ultimate political orientation to the group she identified with—liberal, if she thought of herself as foremost a member of the campus community, and conservative, if her primary identification was with her family. This study served as the basis on which the study of referenced groups began.

The more cohesive the group, the more influence it will have on the behavior, judgments, and attitudes of its members. Members of cohesive groups rely on each other for defining their social reality. That is, when they *cannot* test a belief or perception against physical reality they will validate it on the basis of the consensual agreement of other group members—social reality. Festinger (1954) developed a theory of social comparison based on this phenomenon. The norms of a group may be so strong that new leaders coming into the group need to accommodate themselves to the well-established customs and traditions. Let's take a closer look at this issue of conformity to group norms.

CONFORMING TO GROUP NORMS

Group norms vary both in the degree to which conformity is required and in the degree of conformity to a particular group norm by members in different situations. In our society conformity has acquired a generally negative connotation. People often see it as a blind, unreasoning, slavish adherence to the patterns of behavior established by others, or to the demands of authority. Even among social psychologists there is a common conception of conformity as agreement with the majority or for the sake of agreement. Conformity to group norms is frequently viewed as a violation of one's principles in order to obtain group acceptance, or a selling out of one's individuality in order to get ahead. Much of the research on conformity is based on behaviors such as lying about one's perceptions or beliefs. Conforming to group norms, however, frequently improves the functioning of a group at no expense to the individual's principles or beliefs. Conforming to a classroom norm that one should provide help and assistance to classmates, for example, is beneficial for the group and the students involved. There are conditions under which conformity to group norms may violate important values and principles of an individual, and other conditions under which it will support these values and beliefs.

The classic studies on conformity under group pressures were conducted by Solomon Asch (1956). Asch was born in 1907 in Poland. He arrived in the United States at age thirteen. In 1928 he received a B.S. degree from City College of New York. In 1932 he received a Ph.D. degree from Columbia University. He was an unusually independent person and of him it has often been said that it took the least conformant of social psychologists to defend conformity and to point out that an essential feature of social life is the willingness to trust the observations of others. In his experimental studies on conformity he asked participants to choose which of several lines came closest in length to a line they had just seen. There was an obvious right answer. Yet each participant found himself faced with most or all of his fellow group members (group size ranged from three to fifteen) agreeing on an obviously wrong answer. The participant was thus faced with a conflict: accepting the evidence of her own eyes or going along with the group's perception.

Sixty-eight percent of the individual estimates remained independent; 32 percent were deflected part or all of the way to the unanimous judgment of the fellow group members. One fourth of the participants made no concessions to the unanimous majority; one third conformed in half or more of the trials. Whether the majority consisted of three or fifteen members made little difference, as long as it was unanimous. If one other member agreed with the participant, the tendency to err in the direction of the majority estimate dropped from 32 percent to 10 percent. If the participant reported his estimates secretly, furthermore, the promajority errors were fewer. The results of the Asch experiments were somewhat shocking, as they seemed to indicate that many persons would go along with an erroneous group judgment even when they knew it was false. Henry David Thoreau once said, "As for conforming outwardly, and living your own life inwardly, I do not think much of that." Most social psychologists reacted to the results of Asch's studies as if they agreed with Thoreau.

In discussing conformity to group norms we must differentiate two dimensions: conformity–anticonformity and independence–dependence (Allen 1965; Hollander and Willis, 1967). The conformers and anticonformers both react to the group norm and base their behavior on it: the conformers agree with the norm, the anticonformers disagree with the norm, and both behave accordingly. An independent person, on the other hand, does not give undue importance to the group norm in making her judgment.

Not all behavior is covered by group norms. Not many groups care what foods their members eat or whether they prefer one type of drink to another. Group norms deal primarily with the behavior affecting the accomplishment of the group's task and the ability of the group to maintain itself over time. In general, the more relevant the individual's behavior to the accomplishment of the group's task and the maintenance of the group, the more the pressures toward conformity. Many years ago observers in industrial organizations noted that members of male work groups typically established production standards (norms) that were adhered to by most members (Homans, 1950; Roethlisberger and Dickson, 1939). When a worker deviated too much from the standard he was subjected to ridicule and other sanctions. If he produced too much he was referred to as a "speed king" or a "rate-buster"; if he produced too little, he was a "chiseler." Schachter (1951), Emerson (1954), and Schachter and his associates (1954) all found in their studies of deviation from group norms that the more relevant the deviation to the purposes of the group, the greater the rejection of the deviant by the group. Festinger (1950) and Allen (1965) concluded that there will be greater pressures to conform to task-related norms if goal attainment depends on the coordinated behavior of the group members. Raven and Rietsema (1957) found that the clearer the group goal and the path to the goal are to the group members, the stronger the pressures toward uniformity in task behavior will be. In general, nonconforming behaviors are accepted if they are perceived by the group's members as potentially improving the group's ability to accomplish its task and maintain itself; they are not accepted if they interfere with group maintenance and task accomplishment.

NORMS AND POWER

Group norms often serve as substitutes for influence among group members (Thibaut and Kelley, 1959). Both the weaker and the stronger members tend to gain from having mutually acceptable norms that introduce regularity and control into their relationship without making direct interpersonal application of power necessary. The high-power members do not encounter the resistance and lack of wholehearted cooperation that often come from applying power in forceful ways. And the low-power members have more of a chance to influence the high-power members through the norms that specify their expected behavior and the limits of the use of power. Norms are a protection against the capricious or inconsistent use of influence by high-power members, but they also free the high-power members from constantly checking the behavior of low-power members to make sure they are conforming. Norms carry weight because they embody some of the personal power given up by group members. Individuals let themselves be influenced by norms in ways that they would never permit themselves to be influenced by others, for norms often take on the characteristics of moral obligations. At the very least, conformity to group norms is a requirement for continued membership in the group.

At this point stop and think about your group. What group norms serve as a substitute for the use of power? Ask other group members what their answers are to this question. Try to build a set of conclusions about how norms influence group members and serve as a substitute for the direct application of power.

IMPLEMENTATION OF GROUP NORMS

There are several ways in which norms can be started in a group (Johnson, 1970). One frequent method is for a member to state it directly and tell other members to accept it. A member might say, for example, "I think we should express our feelings openly about this topic" and tell other members to do so. Norms can also be initiated through modeling, wherein members learn to conform to a group norm by watching others conform. Modeling is discussed in Johnson (1970; 1979). Norms can also be imported from other groups. People usually learn cultural norms of social responsibility (you should help someone who is in need of help), fair play (don't kick someone when he's down), and reciprocity (if someone does you a favor, you should do her a favor in return) from others, and these norms can be incorporated into one's own group. All in all, however, perhaps the most effective way of starting group norms is through group discussion.

Johnson (1970) has presented a set of general guidelines for the establishment and support of group norms:

1. For members to accept group norms, they must recognize that they exist, see that the other members accept and follow them, and feel some internal commitment to them.

2. Members will accept and internalize norms to the extent that they see them as helping accomplish the goals and tasks to which they are committed. It is helpful, therefore, for a group to clarify how conformity to a norm will help goal accomplishment.

3. Members will accept and internalize norms for which they feel a sense of ownership. Generally, members will support and accept norms that they have helped set up.

4. Group members should enforce the norms on each other immediately after a violation. Enforcement should also be as consistent as possible.

5. Appropriate models and examples for conforming to the group norms should be present. Members should have the chance to practice the desired behaviors.

6. Cultural norms that promote goal accomplishment and group maintenance and growth should be imported into the group.

7. Because norms exist only to help group effectiveness, they should be flexible so that at any time more appropriate norms can be substituted.

In your group review the material in this section. Then divide into groups of three and plan how to implement at least two norms in the group. Then reconvene as a large group and discuss any topic of interest while each triad attempts to implement its norms into the group.

QUIZ

Check your reading of this section by answering the following questions. Answers are on page 399.

True False 1. Norms refer to common beliefs that tell members how they are expected to behave in the group.

True False 2. Group norms build and keep group cohesion.

True False 3. All groups have norms.

True False 4. Group norms are the same for all members.

True False 5. Norms can be imposed on a group or can develop out of group interaction.

True False 6. Conforming to group norms usually means sacrificing individual principles and beliefs.

True False 7. Conformers agree with the group norm and anticonformers are independent of the group norm.

True False **8.** Nonconforming behaviors that are seen as helping in task accomplishment will be accepted by the group.

True False **9.** Norms are protection against the whims of high-power members.

True False **10.** Norms can be started in a group by members who model them.

YOUR COHESION BEHAVIOR EXERCISE (II)

In this chapter we have defined the nature of group cohesion and discussed a variety of ways to build and maintain an acceptable level of cohesiveness in a group. The first method was to highlight the mutual dependence of members in achieving joint goals and cooperating in order to do so. The second method was to ensure that all members' needs for mutual inclusion, influence, and affection are met. The third method was to build a high level of trust among group members and to ensure that all members engage in both trusting and trustworthy actions. The final method was to initiate group norms that encourage the expression of individuality and of concern and affection among members.

Review your experiences in the exercises and your conclusions from reading the material in this chapter. At this point, how would you describe your behavior in terms of building and maintaining a high level of cohesion in the group? How would other members describe it? What skills do you still need to develop to be able to build and maintain a high level of cohesion in the groups to which you belong? Think about these questions. Write down your responses. Then meet in a group of three and review one another's answers. Add anything that will be of help to the other members of your triad. Then share your overall conclusions with the rest of the class.

SUMMARY

In this chapter you learned about and practiced group cohesion, member needs, trust, and group norms. A cohesive group can be an extremely dynamic and effective force, particularly in solving problems effectively, as you will find out in the next chapter.

ANSWERS

Page 374—1. false; 2. false; 3. true; 4. true; 5. false; 6. true; 7. true; 8. false; 9. false; 10. true.

Page 378—1. b; 2. a; 3. c; 4. true; 5. false; 6. true; 7. true; 8. true; 9. false; 10. false.

Page 391—1. true; 2. true; 3. c; 4. b; 5. e; 6. a; 7. f; 8. g; 9. d.

Page 398-1. true; 2. true; 3. true; 4. false; 5. false; 6. false; 7. false; 8. true; 9. true; 10. true.

10

Problem Solving

INTRODUCTION

Every chapter of this book deals with some aspect of solving group problems effectively. The adequacy of group problem solving is the primary focus of group skills. Before we proceed further in examining the problem-solving process, it may be helpful to define several key concepts. For our purposes, a *problem* may be defined as a discrepancy or difference between an actual state of affairs and a desired or ideal state of affairs. *Problem solving* is the process of resolving the unsettled matters, of finding an answer to a difficulty; it is a process that results in a solution to a problem, and it involves changing the actual state of affairs until it is identical with the desired state of affairs. Thus, there are four concerns in solving a problem: (1) determining the actual or current state of affairs; (2) specifying the desired state of affairs; (3) determining the best means of moving the group from the actual to the desired state of affairs; and (4) doing so. Problem solving requires both an idea about where the group should be and correct information about where it is now. Every group, furthermore, can be evaluated on the basis of its problem-solving adequacy. *Problem-solving adequacy* has four elements: (1) general agreement about the desired state of affairs; (2) structures and procedures for producing, understanding, and using relevant information about the actual state of affairs; (3) structures and procedures for inventing possible solutions, for deciding upon and implementing the best solution, and for evaluating its effectiveness in having permanently eliminated the problem; and (4) accomplishing these three activities without deteriorating—preferably while augmenting—the effectiveness of the group's problem-solving capabilities.

You can test your understanding of this section by answering the following questions (answers at the end of the chapter):

1. A problem is defined as a:
   a. difference of opinion between group members.
   b. difference between the actual and ideal state of affairs.
   c. process that results in a solution to the problem.
2. Problem solving is defined as:
   a. resolution of differences of opinion between group members.
   b. difference between the actual and ideal state of affairs.
   c. process that results in a solution to the problem.
3. What are the four parts of solving a problem?
   a. solving the problem
   b. giving up and going home
   c. figuring out the current state of affairs
   d. figuring out the desired state of affairs
   e. figuring out how to change the current state to the desired state
   f. figuring out how to gather the resources necessary for solving the problem
   g. having the members solve the problem by themselves

YOUR PROBLEM–SOLVING BEHAVIOR (I)

When your group is struggling with a problem, how do you behave? Before reading the subsequent discussion of problem solving, consider this question for a moment. The analytical statements below should be helpful.

1. When a problem comes up in a meeting, I try to make sure it is thoroughly explored until everyone understands what the problem is.
   Never   1 : 2 : 3 : 4 : 5 : 6 : 7   Always
2. I ask why the problem exists and what the causes are.
   Never   1 : 2 : 3 : 4 : 5 : 6 : 7   Always
3. I tend to accept the first solution that is proposed by a group member.
   Never   1 : 2 : 3 : 4 : 5 : 6 : 7   Always
4. When a group decides which solution to adopt and implement, I make certain it is clear what the decision is, who should carry it out, and when it should be carried out.
   Never   1 : 2 : 3 : 4 : 5 : 6 : 7   Always
5. I do not take the time to really study or define the problem the group is working on.
   Never   1 : 2 : 3 : 4 : 5 : 6 : 7   Always
6. I tend to propose answers without really having thought through the problem and its causes carefully.
   Never   1 : 2 : 3 : 4 : 5 : 6 : 7   Always

7. I make sure that the group discusses the pros and cons of several different solutions to a problem.
    Never   1 : 2 : 3 : 4 : 5 : 6 : 7   Always

8. I tend to let decisions remain vague in terms of what they are and who will carry them out.
    Never   1 : 2 : 3 : 4 : 5 : 6 : 7   Always

9. I push for definite follow-ups on how decisions reached at earlier meetings have worked out in practice.
    Never   1 : 2 : 3 : 4 : 5 : 6 : 7   Always

10. I know if the results of the group's work are worth the effort.
    Never   1 : 2 : 3 : 4 : 5 : 6 : 7   Always

FIVE STEPS IN PROBLEM SOLVING

There are five basic steps in the problem-solving process: (1) defining the problem, (2) diagnosing how big it is and what causes it, (3) formulating alternative strategies or plans for solving it, (4) deciding upon and implementing the most desirable strategies, and (5) evaluating the success of the strategies used. Every step in this process is vitally important for different reasons, and the steps are all interrelated. How the problem is defined at the start, for example, may affect how committed the group members are to implementing the strategies decided upon. Of the statements above, two deal with each step: statements 1 and 6 pertain to defining the problem, 2 and 7 to diagnosing the problem, 3 and 8 to formulating alternative strategies, 4 and 9 to deciding upon and implementing strategies, and 5 and 10 to evaluating the success of the strategies. Some statements are worded in such a way that they should be scored positively; the others should be scored negatively. Think about the self-analysis you made through these statements, and how it contributes to the problem-solving adequacy of a group. Then continue reading this chapter.

Defining the Problem

The clearer and more accurate the definition of the problem, the easier it is to complete the four other steps in the problem-solving process. The discussion of group goals in Chapter 4 is relevant to defining the problem in order to begin the problem-solving sequence. A problem exists, as we have just noted, where there is a difference between the actual and the desired state of affairs. Accordingly, the definition of a problem begins with getting everyone in the group to agree on what the desired state of affairs is. The next objective is to obtain valid information about the existing state of affairs. The difference between the desired and actual state of affairs should be thoroughly discussed, because it is from the awareness of this discrepancy that the commitment to solve the problem is built. Because problem-solving groups often progress too quickly toward a solution to a problem without first getting a clear, consensual definition of the problem itself, members of the group should see to it that everyone understands what the problem is before going on to the next step. The direction a group first takes in defining a problem may keep it from finding a successful solution (Maier, 1930). Therefore, the group should be careful not to agree prematurely on the definition of the problem.

Defining whose situation is within the resources of the group is perhaps the hardest step of the problem-solving process. Here is a suggested procedure:

1. List a series of statements about the problem. Describe it as concretely as possible by mentioning persons, places, and resources. There should be as many different statements of the problem as the members are willing to give. Write them on a blackboard where everyone can see them. Avoid arguing about whether the problem is perfectly stated.
2. Restate each problem statement so that it includes a description of both the desired and actual state of affairs. Take out alternative definitions that are beyond the resources of the group to solve, and choose the definition that the group members agree is most correct. The problem should be important, solvable, and urgent.

For a discussion of how to define an interpersonal problem, see Johnson (1981). In assessing how a group has defined a problem, the following questions may be helpful:

1. Is the problem clearly defined?
2. How specific is the problem definition? Is it overly abstract? How is the actual situation different from the desired situation?
3. Does the definition allow for alternatives or does it imply a single solution? Does it mistake a solution or goal for the problem?
4. Is the problem stated in a way that does not arouse defensiveness?
5. Who initiated the problem statement? Who clarified it?
6. Do all members agree with the problem statement? Did the group ascertain agreement?

Here is a quick test of your understanding of this section (answers at the end of the chapter):

True   False   1. The first step in problem-solving is to get valid information about the present state of affairs.

True False **2.** Problem-solving groups often progress too quickly toward a solution to the problem.

True False **3.** The direction a group first takes in defining a problem may keep it from finding a successful solution.

True False **4.** Defining a workable problem is one of the easiest steps of the problem-solving process.

5. You are in a group with a problem that needs a workable definition. Being the expert in the group, you are asked to lead the group in doing this. Write down the two procedures you will undoubtedly follow:

a. _____

b. _____

Diagnosing the Problem

The second step in the problem-solving process is diagnosing the dimension and causes of the problem. The objective here is to identify the nature and magnitude of the forces helping the group to move toward the desired state of affairs as well as the forces hindering this movement. Determining what forces are acting upon the problem situation is called *force-field analysis* (Lewin, 1945; Myrdal, 1944). Force-field analysis sees the problem as a balance between forces working in opposite directions—some helping the movement toward the desired state of affairs and others restraining such movement. This balance is the actual state of affairs, a "quasi-stationary equilibrium" that can be altered through changes in the forces. Figure 10.1 illustrates the basic notion of force-field analysis.

The ideal state of affairs toward which the group is working is on the right side of Figure 10.1 and is represented by a plus sign. The worst state of affairs, on the left side of the figure, is represented by a minus sign. The vertical line in the middle signifies the current state of affairs. On any problem numerous forces are at work, some restraining change and others helping change.

FIGURE 10.1 Force-field analysis.

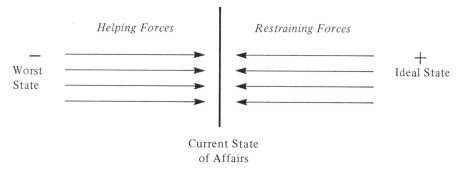

Helping Forces   Restraining Forces

— Worst State   + Ideal State

Current State
of Affairs

There are two basic steps for a group to follow in doing a force-field analysis:

1. Make up lists of forces by first brainstorming all the helping forces and then all the restraining forces. The lists should include all possible forces, whether psychological, interpersonal, organizational, or societal. If a force seems to be a complex of variables, list each variable separately. Avoid critical judgment; it is essential that every member's ideas be publicly requested and aired.

2. Rank the forces according to the importance of their effect on the present situation. Agree on the most important helping and restraining forces, which may total from three to six each. Rate the important forces according to how easily they can be increased or decreased, and avoid spending time discussing those that the group cannot influence with their current resources.

Without defining a problem correctly and specifically, it cannot be adequately diagnosed. And without an accurate and precise diagnosis of the forces involved, the alternative strategies for the solution of the problem cannot be formulated.

Here is a quick check of your comprehension of this section (answers at the end of the chapter):

1. Force-field analysis sees the problem as:
   a. a movement toward a desired state of affairs.
   b. something out of a science-fiction story.
   c. a balance between helping and hindering forces working in opposite directions.
   d. a balance between helping and hindering forces working in similar directions.

2. You did a brilliant job in helping your group define its problem in a workable way. The members are so impressed with your expertise that they have asked you to again lead the group, this time in a force-field analysis of the problem. Consequently, you confidently lead the group in the two major steps of a force-field analysis, which are:
   a. _____
   b. _____

A PROBLEM–DIAGNOSIS PROGRAM

This program is designed to help you diagnose a problem that involves persons working together in a group. The program consists of separate steps, each of which contains a complete and separate idea, question, or instruction. Be sure that you understand and complete each step before going on to the next one.

1. Identify the problem you wish to work on. Describe the problem as you now see it. _____

_____

_____

_____

2. Most problem statements can be rephrased so that they describe two things:
   a. the situation as it is now
   b. the situation as you would like it to be (the ideal)
   Restate your problem situation in these terms. _____

_____

_____

_____

3. Most problem situations can be understood in terms of the forces that push toward and against improvement—in other words, the helping forces and restraining forces (see Figure 10.1). It is useful to analyze a problem by making lists of the helping and restraining forces affecting a situation. Think about these now, and list them. Be sure to list as many as you can, not worrying at this point about how important each one is. Use additional paper if you need to.

Helping Forces	*Restraining Forces*
_____	_____
_____	_____
_____	_____
_____	_____
_____	_____

4. Review the two lists. Underline those forces that seem to be the most important right now, and that you think you might be able to influence constructively. Depending on the problem, there may be one specific force that stands out, or there may be two or three helping forces and two or three restraining forces that are particularly important.

5. Now, for each restraining force you have underlined list some possible courses of action that you might be able to plan and carry out in order to reduce the effect of the force or eliminate it completely. Brainstorm. List as many action steps as possible, without worrying about how effective or practical they would be. You will later have a chance to decide which are the most appropriate.

Restraining force A: _____

Possible action steps to reduce this force: _____

_____

_____

Restraining force B: _____

Possible action steps to reduce this force: _____

_____

_____

Restraining force C: _____

Possible action steps to reduce this force: _____

_____

_____

6. Now do the same with each helping force you underlined. List all the action steps that come to mind that would increase the effect of each helping force.
Helping force A: _____

Possible action steps to increase this force: _____

_____

_____

_____

Helping force B: _____

Possible action steps to increase this force: _____

_____

_____

_____

Helping force C: _____

Possible action steps to increase this force: _____

_____

_____

_____

7. You have now listed some action steps that might change the key forces affecting your problem situation. Review these possible action steps and underline those that seem promising.

8. List the steps you have underlined. Then, for each action step list the materials, persons, and other resources available to you for carrying out the action.

Action Steps	*Resources Available*
_____	_____
_____	_____
_____	_____
_____	_____
_____	_____

9. Review the list of action steps and resources and think about how each might fit into a comprehensive plan of action. Take out those items that do not seem to fit into the overall plan, add any new steps and resources that will round out the plan, think about a possible sequence of action, and outline that sequence: _____

10. Plan a way of evaluating the effectiveness of your action program as it is implemented. Then list the evaluation procedures you will use. _____

11. You now have a plan of action for dealing with the problem situation. The next step is for you to implement it.

Formulating Alternative Strategies

The third step in problem solving is identifying and drawing up alternative ways to solve the problem. Creativeness, divergent thinking, opposition among ideas, and inventiveness are essential for this phase; these are discussed in Chapter 6. Each alternative solution needs to be concretely specified. The theory of force-field analysis is a particularly useful way to specify alternative strategies for solving a problem. According to this theory, changes in the present situation will occur only as the helpful and restraining forces are changed so that the level where they are balancing is altered. There are two basic methods for changing the equilibrium point between the two sets of forces: increasing the strength or number of the helping forces and decreasing the strength or number of the restraining forces. Of the two, the preferable strategy is to get rid of the restraining forces or reduce their strength. Experience has shown that as pressure is applied to the present situation in the form of increases in the helping forces, natural resistances also increase, reducing the effectiveness of that strategy. Reducing the restraining forces, therefore, is usually the more effective of the two strategies. The fewer the forces acting upon the present situation, furthermore, the lower the tension level of the persons involved in the situation.

Often, persons who use force-field analysis try to reduce restraining forces and increase helping forces at the same time. When this can be done, it is very effective. One way of intervening simultaneously with both types of forces is to change a restraining force so that it becomes a helping force.

The resistance of group members to changes desired by other members is a typical restraining force in a problem-solving situation. One of the most successful strategies for changing the direction of this force is to involve the resisting members in diagnosing the problem situation and planning the solutions (Watson and Johnson, 1972). People enjoy and affirm the changes they make themselves, and resist changes imposed upon them by others. Involvement of resisters in the diagnosing and planning of change often means a more difficult planning process, but it virtually guarantees their commitment to the proposed changes. It also helps clear up any misunderstandings and differences of opinion before the strategies are implemented, and it uses the resources of the "opposition."

Force-field analysis is useful for two reasons. First, it avoids the error of a single-factor analysis of a problem: using it will keep attention on the problem situation until a number of relevant factors are identified. Second, by helping to identify a number of problem-related factors it gives group members several points at which they may intervene in their attempt to produce a change. Because any change is the result of a number of factors, an effective strategy of change involves several actions that are directed toward several of those factors. When several factors are modified at the same time, permanent improvement is more likely.

In specifying alternative strategies for change, group members should think of as many ways as possible in which the forces holding the group from moving toward the desired state might be reduced. They should obtain ideas from everyone in the group. If group members do not have many ideas, outside consultants can always be invited to lend assistance. Bringing in an expert who knows a lot about the substance of the problem is often extremely helpful at this point. Group members should try to take each restraining force in turn and think up ways to reduce its strength or to eliminate it altogether. Brainstorming is useful, and divergent thinking should be encouraged.

In determining how well your group has formulated alternative strategies, you may find the following questions helpful:

1. Does a persistent "set" inhibit idea production? Do members feel free to produce deviant ideas?
2. Do dominant members or coalitions stifle the ideas of other members?
3. Is the group comfortable with silence?

4. Does the group direct its attention toward soluble aspects of the problem, or does it endlessly attempt a solution to an insoluble aspect?

5. Are ideas combined or improved to produce still other ideas?

6. Do all members participate? Are minority opinions given a full hearing?

7. Do the group atmosphere and norms encourage expression of disagreement?

8. Are some members overly protective of their own ideas?

9. Does the group have appropriate methods for testing ideas?

10. Does the group search for both the positive and the negative consequences that might be attached to various alternatives?

Here are four questions to check your understanding of this section (answers at the end of the chapter):

1. According to the theory of force-field analysis, changes in the present situation will happen only when:
   a. the forces are changed so that the level where they are balancing is changed.
   b. the forces are changed so that the helping ones balance the hindering ones.
   c. the forces are seen as agents that help in the problem-solving process.
   d. force is used.

2. The most effective way to change the force field is to:
   a. increase the strength of the helping forces.
   b. decrease the strength of the hindering forces.
   c. decrease the strength of both forces.

3. When people are a restraining force, a successful strategy is to:
   a. ignore them until they give in.
   b. explain to them why they are wrong.
   c. involve them in planning the solution.

4. Force-field analysis is useful for two reasons:
   a. it avoids single-factor analysis of a problem.
   b. it avoids use of standard solutions to a problem.
   c. it produces permanent change.
   d. it gives the group more than one point where it can attempt to produce a change.
   e. it gives the group the best solution to the problem.

Deciding Upon and Implementing Strategies

Once all the possible strategies have been identified and formulated in specific terms, the group needs to select the strategies it will implement. This procedure involves two central aspects of problem solving: decision making and decision implementation. *Decision making* is a process that results in a choice among alternative courses of action; it is discussed at length in Chapter 3. *Decision implementation* is the execution of the decision; it is also discussed in Chapter 3. Decision making requires alternatives from which a group can choose, and decision implementation requires internal commitment by group members to the decisions made. During this fourth step in the problem-solving process the group should use critical judgment and convergent thinking to build concrete plans for implementation. The following points may be helpful to a group that is deciding upon and implementing strategies:

1. Select the alternatives that seem best. List three positive values in adopting each alternative.
2. List the materials and other resources needed to implement each strategy. The cost of implementation in terms of time, people, and material resources should be specified.
3. Evaluate how realistic each strategy is; the necessary variables should be within the power of the group members to influence.
4. Weigh the probabilities for success against the cost of implementation.
5. Try to anticipate all the barriers to implementation and how the group members will handle them.
6. Put the ideas and actions of each strategy into a time sequence and estimate specific dates for the actions to occur.
7. Assign responsibilities to group members for implementing the strategies.
8. Begin taking the first steps.

The following questions may be useful in assessing how well your group has decided upon and implemented a strategy:

1. Did premature voting occur?
2. Were all the members ready for a decision? Was there adequate testing of ideas?
3. Did the group make any effort to summarize its progress?
4. How was the decision made? What method was used?
5. Were the feelings of the members adequately explored?
6. How did the group handle conflict? Was it smoothed over or brought into the open?
7. Did the group explore the possible consequences of the decision from the points of view of those outside the group?
8. Was there a detailed plan of action?
9. Did the group assign responsibilities for various action steps?

10. Did the group pause for reality testing, refinement, and replanning? Did it anticipate potential problems in implementation?

11. Are all of the members committed to the decision? Which members appear to have reservations?

12. Did the group allow time for a critical examination of its process of arriving at the decision?

Evaluating the Success of the Strategies

The fifth and final step in problem solving is evaluating the success of the strategies the group has decided to implement. To do that, the group members must figure out (1) whether the strategies were successfully implemented and (2) what the effects were. The first activity is sometimes called process evaluation because it deals with the process of implementing a strategy; the second is called outcome evaluation because it involves assessing the consequences of implementing the strategy. Planners should establish ways in which to judge the effectiveness of their actions in implementing the strategy, and review their progress as each action step occurs. The major criterion in assessing the outcome of an implemented strategy is whether the actual state of affairs is closer to the desired state of affairs than it was before the strategy was carried out.

If the group finds that its strategies have been successfully implemented, but have failed to bring the current situation substantially closer to the ideal state of affairs, it may develop new strategies until it finds one that is effective. The solution of one set of problems, however, often brings other problems into the open, and in trying out various strategies the group may find that it has not been working for the solution of the most critical problem in the situation. The result of the evaluation step, therefore, should be to show the group what problems have been solved and to what extent, what problems still need to be solved, and what new problems have come up. Evaluation should result in a new definition of a problem, a rediagnosis of the situation, and the beginning of a new problem-solving sequence.

BLOCKS TO PROBLEM-SOLVING EFFECTIVENESS

There are eight blocks to problem-solving effectiveness to which group members should be alerted:

1. *Lack of clarity in stating the problem.* Much of the initial effort of groups engaged in solving a problem is directed toward orienting members to what the problem is. This is an extremely important phase of problem solving, and the group should devote sufficient time and effort to identifying the problem, defining it, and thereby getting the members involved in and com-

mitted to solving it. Often, groups are doomed to failure when they inadequately define their problem.

2. *Not getting the needed information.* When information is minimal the definition of the problem will be inadequate, fewer alternative strategies for the solution will be generated, and the potential consequences of those alternatives will not be properly explored. The result is relatively low-grade solutions. Great emphasis must be placed on fact finding if a group is to solve a problem effectively.

3. *Poor communication within the group.* Poor communication among group members has the same effect as lack of information—with the added problem that it makes it difficult to implement any action that requires coordination among members. Effective communication among all group members is necessary for effective problem solving.

4. *Premature testing of alternative strategies, or premature choice.* For most of us ideas are fragile creations, easily blighted by a chill, or even indifferent, reception. As groups proceed in their problem-solving activities they must avoid all tendencies to evaluate each idea as it comes along. Instead, they should create an atmosphere that supports the presentation and the pooling of a wide assortment of ideas. Only then can the group critically evaluate the alternatives.

5. *A critical, evaluative, competitive climate.* A supportive, trusting, cooperative atmosphere is necessary for solving problems successfully. If group members are afraid of the way in which other members are evaluating their ideas, effective problem solving is destroyed.

6. *Pressures for conformity.* Pressures for conformity and compliance slow the development of different ideas. Divergent thinking as well as convergent thinking are necessary for sound problem solving.

7. *Lack of inquiry and problem-solving skills.* Some groups may need special training in how to use inquiry and problem-solving methods to their advantage. Training may be provided by an expert member of the group, or the group may wish to call in a consultant.

8. *Inadequate motivation.* Any problem-solving group must be motivated to solve its problems. If the group members are not motivated, they must be persuaded to see the importance of the problem and the necessity for seeking a solution. Members who leave work to others clearly lack motivation.

Here are two quick questions to check your comprehension (answers at the end of the chapter):

1. Because of your brilliant and knowledgeable leadership, the group is now ready to evaluate the success of its strategies. To do so, what two things must it figure out?

    a. _____

    b. _____

2. After the evaluation the group realized that the problem was not success- fully solved. In an attempt to keep them from blaming your leadership you search desperately for possible blocks to problem-solving effectiveness. These blocks are:

a. _____

b. _____

c. _____

d. _____

e. _____

f. _____

g. _____

h. _____

GROUPTHINK AND PROBLEM SOLVING

As we saw in Chapter 3, group performance in problem-solving activities is much better than individual performance. This superiority is not to imply, of course, that group performance is always successful. For example, studies by Janis (1971) indicate that under certain conditions a phenomenon called "groupthink" can prevent effective problem solving. Janis studied the groups advising presidents of the United States and found that powerful social pres- sures brought to bear whenever a dissident began to voice his objections to what otherwise appeared to be a group consensus. He also found group norms that bolstered morale at the expense of critical thinking. One of the most common norms was that members should remain loyal to the group by sticking with the policies to which the group had already committed itself, even when those policies were obviously working out badly and had unin- tended consequences that disturbed the conscience of each member. Group- think is a problem-solving process in which proposals are accepted without scrutiny of the pros and cons of the alternatives, and in which considerable suppression of opposing thoughts takes place. The suppression of opposition, however, takes on a rather unique form: a dissenting member is not shouted down; rather, each group member decides himself that his misgivings are not relevant and should be set aside. Janis lists eight main symptoms of groupthink:

1. Most or all of the members of the group share an illusion of being invulnera- ble that gives them some degree of reassurance about obvious dangers and leads them to become overoptimistic and willing to take extraordinary risks. It also causes them to fail to respond to clear warnings of danger.

2. The group collectively constructs rationalizations in order to discount warnings and other forms of negative feedback that would, if taken seriously, lead members to think again about their assumptions each time they recommitted themselves to past decisions.

3. Members have an unquestioning belief in the moralness of their group. This belief results in a tendency to ignore the ethical consequences of their decisions.

4. Group members hold stereotyped views of the leaders of enemy groups. They assume that these persons are either so evil that genuine attempts to negotiate differences with them are unwarranted, or so weak or stupid that they cannot deal effectively with whatever attempts, however risky, the group makes to defeat their purposes.

5. The group applies direct pressure to any member who momentarily expresses doubts about any of the group's shared illusions, or who questions the validity of the arguments supporting a policy alternative favored by the majority.

6. Members avoid deviating from what appears to be group consensus. They keep silent about their misgivings and even minimize to themselves the importance of their doubts. A great deal of self-censorship takes place within the group.

7. Members share an illusion of unanimity within the group about almost all judgments expressed by members who speak in favor of the majority view.

8. Members sometimes appoint themselves as "mindguards" to protect the leader and themselves from adverse information that might break the complacency they share about the effectiveness and morality of past decisions.

Janis also lists six poor decision-making practices of groups that are caught in the trap of groupthink:

1. The group limits its discussions to a few alternative courses of action (often only two) without an initial survey of all the other alternatives that might be worthy of consideration.

2. The group fails to reexamine the course of action initially preferred by the majority after they learn of risks and drawbacks they had not considered originally.

3. The members spend little or no time discussing whether there are covert gains they may have overlooked, or ways in which to reduce the seemingly prohibitive costs of rejected alternatives.

4. The group makes little or no attempt to get information from experts within its own organization, members who might be able to supply more precise estimates of potential losses and gains.

5. Members show positive interest in facts and opinions that support their preferred policy and tend to ignore facts and opinions that do not.

6. Members spend little time considering how their chosen policy might be hindered by bureaucratic inertia, sabotaged by political opponents, or temporarily derailed by common accidents. They fail to work out contingency or alternative plans to cope with foreseeable setbacks that could endanger the overall success of their decision.

To check your understanding of groupthink you may wish to answer the questions below (answers at the end of the chapter):

1. Groupthink is a process whereby:
   a. everyone in the group thinks of ways to solve the problem.
   b. proposals are accepted without careful consideration of alternatives.
   c. proposals aren't accepted until every alternative is considered.
   d. a considerable amount of evaluation takes place.

2. The suppression of opposition in groupthink takes the form of:
   a. a member's ideas being shouted down.
   b. a member deciding that his ideas aren't relevant.
   c. a member deciding that others' ideas aren't relevant.
   d. an authority making the decisions.

3. Four symptoms of groupthink are:
   a. Members think they are invulnerable.
   b. Members agree with the authority who makes the decision.
   c. Members have stereotyped views of enemy leaders.
   d. Members avoid deviating from what seems to be group consensus.
   e. Members have stereotyped views of other members.
   f. Members are surprised when things go wrong.
   g. Members don't question the group's basic assumption.

4. Three poor decision-making practices of groupthink are:
   a. The group limits itself to only a few alternatives.
   b. The group does not reexamine its initial course of action.
   c. The group cannot decide on an alternative.
   d. The group does not consult experts.
   e. The group ignores facts that support their preferred policy.

CLIMATE

Another critical aspect of effective group problem solving is the climate or atmosphere in the group. Group climate is primarily a consequence of its goal structure and the orientation of its members. Climates can be either cooperative or competitive. Review Table 4.1 (on page 161), which lists the effects of cooperative and competitive group climates on group problem solving.

GROUP MEMBERSHIP

Groups can be composed either of persons who are much alike (homogeneous) or persons who are different from one another (heterogeneous). There is a good deal of evidence to show that heterogeneous groups are superior to homogeneous groups in solving problems effectively and in arriving at creative solutions. The usual explanation for the superiority of heterogeneous groups is that they generate a wider variety of ideas about, and different possible approaches to, the problem. Effective groups must not only have a diversity of viewpoints and backgrounds to consider, they must also provide conditions under which these varied viewpoints can be heard. One of the most effective barriers to hearing all points of view in a group is the tendency of members to evaluate suggested solutions as they appear, one by one, instead of waiting until all suggestions are in and then making their choice. An evaluation-free period of idea production can lead to a solution of high quality if the members can avoid focusing on particular strategies before exploring many possible solutions. The appearance of creative solutions to problems is enhanced by the diversity of opinion represented in the group—as long as the conflict among opinions is managed constructively.

Opposition and a diversity of viewpoints are essential for effective problem solving. These differences bring about involvement, creativity, and high-quality solutions. Controversy among ideas is a prerequisite for effective problem solving, and the best way to structure it into the group is by having a heterogeneous membership.

YOUR PROBLEM–SOLVING BEHAVIOR (II)

Before concluding this chapter on problem-solving procedures you may find it helpful to once again review your own behavior in problem-solving groups and determine how you now behave and how you would like to behave. You may also wish to make some plans for eliminating differences between the two. With your classmates divide into groups of three. As a group, take each problem-solving step and write down the task and maintenance behaviors most needed in each. Note the behaviors that are typically yours and the behaviors in which you rarely, if ever, engage. Within your group, decide how each person can behave in the future to further the problem-solving process of the groups to which she belongs.

SUMMARY

In going through this book, you and your group have read much material, and practiced and developed many group skills. You now have the satisfaction of knowing that not only are you wiser than you were before, but you are also more capable of translating that wisdom into actions that will be of continued use to you.

ANSWERS

Page 402: 1: b; 2: c; 3: c, d, e, f

Page 404: 1: false; 2: true; 3: true; 4: false; 5: (a) List a series of problem statements. (b) Rephrase the statements to include a description of both the desired and the actual states of affairs.

Page 406: 1: c; 2: (a) Make up lists of helping and hindering forces by brainstorming. (b) Rank the forces in order of the importance of their effect on the present situation.

Page 411: 1: a; 2: b; 3: c; 4: a, d

Page 414: 1: (a) whether the strategies were successfully implemented; (b) what the effects of the strategies were on the problem; 2: (See pages 413–414.)

Page 417: 1: b; 2: b; 3: a, c, d, g; 4: a, b, d

11

Leading Learning and Discussion Groups

THE NATURE OF LEARNING GROUPS

Many groups have as their purpose the promotion of learning among group members. Group learning occurs in all sorts of educational settings, from preschool programs to postgraduate seminars, from athletic teams to special conferences, from consumer-education meetings to wilderness-survival programs. In one's school, career, leisure, and community life, participation in discussion groups is a pervasive experience. Discussion groups are one of the most important and versatile educational tools available, and as such are heavily used.

A *learning group* is a group whose purpose is to ensure that group members learn specific subject matter, information, knowledge, skills, and procedures. Learning is the primary purpose of the group. The whole point of having a discussion is to promote the learning of the members, and if such learning is not taking place, the group cannot be considered productive. The terms *learning group* and *discussion group* will be used interchangeably throughout this chapter.

There are three types of interaction within a discussion group: the interaction between the coordinator and the group members, the interaction between the group members and the curriculum materials, and the interaction among group members. Both the coordinator's role and the curriculum have received a great deal of attention in instructional theory (see Johnson, 1979), but the member–member interaction patterns have been largely ignored and often mismanaged by educators. This chapter will focus on the structuring of constructive interaction among group members so as to ensure maximal learning by all members.

Despite the pervasiveness of learning in groups in our society, educators receive very little specific training on how to conduct discussion groups in ways that maxmize members' learning. The all-too-common practice of simply asking group members to sit around a table and carry on a "meaningful" discussion is all too often unproductive. One major difficulty is that although people spend much of their lives talking with one another, most persons have failed to develop the abilities and attitudes necessary for carrying on a worthwhile discussion for the purpose of learning new information, knowledge, skills, and procedures. People tend to be self-conscious, to be overly concerned with what others may think of their ideas, to listen carelessly to others, and to look for others to provide direction and leadership.

The development of a productive learning group must be preceded by the conscious development of an effective group. In order to be effective, a learning group must have the following elements:

1. a clear, cooperative goal structure
2. accurate two-way communication among members
3. widespread distribution participation and leadership among group members
4. the use of consensus to arrive at answers, solutions, and decisions
5. power and influence based on expertise and access to information and social skills, not on authority
6. the frequent occurrence of controversy
7. the open confrontation and negotiation of conflicts of interest among members and between the group members and the coordinator
8. high cohesiveness
9. high trust among members
10. a climate of acceptance and support among members and between the group members and the coordinator
11. group norms promoting individual responsibility and accountability, helping and sharing, and achievement
12. generally high group and interpersonal skills among members.

In other words, an effective learning group must possess all of the characteristics of an effective group listed in Chapter 1 and throughout this book. Discussion-group members must be taught the fundamental skills and attitudes necessary for group effectiveness if they are to learn anything in a discussion group. They must know how to build an effective group.

In recent years there has been considerable development of effective procedures for structuring cooperative learning groups (Johnson and Johnson, 1975, 1978). These procedures will be summarized in this chapter. Readers interested in further study are referred to Johnson and Johnson (1975).

Also available are two handbooks containing cooperatively structured lessons for classes from preschool through adult education (Chasnoff, 1979; Lyons, 1980), a movie demonstrating the use of cooperative learning groups (Johnson and Johnson, 1980), and a newsletter for educators wishing to exchange ideas with others interested in the use of cooperative learning procedures (*Reporting on Cooperative Learning*).

In this chapter we shall first discuss the stages of development of cooperative learning groups. We then outline the basic procedures for structuring productive learning groups. Finally, we discuss the role of the coordinator in ensuring that learning groups operate successfully.

THE STAGES OF DEVELOPMENT OF LEARNING GROUPS

Learning groups typically move through seven stages. These stages were derived from the application to cooperation learning groups of the stages of group development identified by Tuckman (1965). Tuckman reviewed approximately fifty studies on group development conducted in a wide variety of settings. Although the descriptions of the stages the groups went through varied widely on the surface (some studies identifying three stages and others identifying seven or eight), Tuckman found a surprising amount of agreement beneath the diversity. He identified four stages: forming, storming, norming, and performing. During the forming stage, there is a period of uncertainty in which members try to determine their place in the group and the procedures and rules of the group. During the storming stage, conflicts begin to arise as members resist the influence of the group and rebel against accomplishing the task. During the norming stage, the group establishes cohesiveness and commitment, discovering new ways to work together and setting norms for appropriate behavior. Finally, during the performing stage the group develops proficiency in achieving its goals and becomes more flexible in its patterns of working together. Virtually all the studies that Tuckman reviewed, however, involved group leaders who were passive and nondirective and who made no attempt to intervene in the group process. In most learning groups there is an instructor or coordinator who tries to ensure that the group functions productively.

In applying Tuckman's conclusions to cooperative learning groups, the authors (with the help of Roger Johnson and a number of other colleagues) identified seven stages of development: (1) defining and structuring procedures and becoming oriented, (2) conforming to procedures and getting acquainted, (3) recognizing mutuality and building trust, (4) rebelling and differentiating, (5) committing to and taking ownership for the goals, procedures, and other members, (6) functioning maturely and productively, and (7) terminating. Each of these stages is discussed in turn.

Defining and Structuring Procedures and Becoming Oriented

When a discussion group begins, the members are usually concerned about what is expected of them and what the goals of the session are. Group members want to know what is going to happen; what is expected of them; whether or not they will be accepted, influential, and liked; how the group is going to function; and who the other group members are. Group members expect the coordinator to explain how the group is to function in a way that reassures them that their personal needs will be met. When a learning group first meets, therefore, the coordinator defines the procedures to be used, assigns participants to groups, communicates the task, establishes the cooperative interdependence among members, and generally organizes the group and announces the beginning of the group's work.

Conforming to Procedures and Getting Acquainted

As group members follow the prescribed procedures and interact around the task, they become acquainted with one another and familiarize themselves with the procedures until they can follow them easily. They learn the strengths and weaknesses of the other group members. During this stage the group members are dependent on the coordinator for direction and clarification of the goals and procedures of the group. It is also during this stage that the coordinator stresses the following group norms: (1) taking responsibility for one's own learning and the learning of the other members of the group, (2) providing help and assistance to other members, (3) responding to other members in an accepting, supportive, and trustworthy way, (4) making decisions through consensus, and (5) confronting and solving problems in group functioning. During this stage the goals and procedures of the group are the coordinator's. The group members conform to the prescribed procedures and interact with each other, but they are not personally committed to the group's goals and each other.

Recognizing Mutuality and Building Trust

The third stage of group development is marked by group members (1) recognizing their cooperative interdependence and (2) building trust among themselves. A sense of mutuality is built as group members recognize that they are in fact interdependent and that they are in a sink-or-swim-together situation. Members begin to take responsibility for each other's learning and appropriate behavior. They accept and internalize the reality that if *they* wish to do well, they have to ensure that all other group members learn the assigned material, complete the assigned work, and participate actively in discussions.

Trust is built through disclosing one's thoughts, ideas, conclusions, and feelings, and having the other group members respond with acceptance, support, and reciprocation of the disclosures. Trust is discussed at length in Chapter 9 and in Johnson (1981). While a group is in this stage, it is important that all members engage in trusting behavior and respond to other members with trustworthiness.

Rebelling and Differentiating

The fourth stage of group development is marked by group members (1) rebelling against the coordinator and the procedures and (2) differentiating themselves from each other through disagreements and conflicts. On the road to maturity a group will go through a period (sometimes short, sometimes long) of challenging the authority of the coordinator. It is an ordinary occurrence and should be expected. This swing toward independence contrasts sharply with the dependence demonstrated by students during Stage 2. Many group members may have the attitude that learning is a passive process in which they can slip by without doing much work. Participation in a cooperative learning group requires students to take responsibility for their own learning and the learning of the other members of their group, and to participate actively in the group's work. Sometimes group members will resist these responsibilities and attempt to return to the more traditional passive, self-centered, minimal-effort student role. Students may say things like, "Do I have to help Roger," "I don't like working in groups," "I won't work in groups unless I can work with my friends," "I'm not going to help her," "Why should I teach these dummies? That's your job," "I've learned the material, that's all I should be expected to do." Group members may wish to test and challenge the coordinator's sincerity and commitment to the procedures. Students may say things like, "It's not fair that I don't get an 'A' just because the other members didn't do their share," "I'm the only one doing my work," "Can't you get Roger out of our group?" and "You are being unjust and unfair by requiring me to take responsibility for the learning of the other group members." Students may become "counter-dependent" and attempt to establish their independence by doing just the opposite of what the group-learning procedures call for.

On the road to group maturity members will almost inevitably go through a period of bickering with one another. In developing close and committed relationships there is first an effort to get to know each other and then often a pulling back in order to differentiate oneself from the other group members. Students may begin to say things to each other like, "I don't have to do what you say," "Just because you want to do it that way doesn't mean that I want to do it that way," "I can say no to you," "Can we disagree and still be friends?," "We don't have to like each other just because we work together," and "I'm tired of doing it your way, I want us to do it my way." Relationships among group members are often built through a cycle of becoming friendly, establishing independence through disagreement and conflict, and then committing oneself to a relationship. Differentiating is important for group members to establish boundaries where they stop and the other members begin and to establish their autonomy as individual and separate members of the group (Johnson, 1979, 1980).

The coordinator can expect both rebellion against the discussion group procedures and conflict among group members as a natural and expected stage of group development. She will want to deal with both in an open and accepting way. Some advice for doing so includes: (1) Do not tighten control and try to force conformity to prescribed procedures, reason and negotiate; (2) Confront and problem-solve when students become counter-dependent and rebellious, (3) Mediate conflicts among members helping the group establish members' autonomy and individuality, (4) Work toward students taking ownership of the procedures and committing themselves to each other's success. Coordinating a learning group at this stage is like teaching a child to ride a bicycle; one runs along side to prevent the child from falling but one must let loose so the child can learn to balance on his own.

Committing to and Taking Ownership for the Goals, Procedures, and Other Members

During this stage, dependence on the coordinator and conformity to the prescribed procedures are replaced by dependence on the other members of the group and personal commitment to the collaborative nature of the experience. The "changing hands" from the coordinator's group to our group that began in the previous stage is finalized in this stage. The group becomes "ours" rather than "hers." Group norms become internalized and group members enforce the norms on themselves; the coordinator no longer has to enforce the norms and encourage group members to cooperate with each other. The norms and procedures become internally imposed rather than externally imposed. Motivation to learn becomes intrinsic rather than extrinsic. Members become committed to the cooperative procedures and accept responsibility for maximizing the learning of all group members.

Group members also become personally committed to each other in this stage of group development. They become concerned about each other's welfare and learning, provide support and assistance (not because the coordinator wants them to but because they care about each other), believe that they can rely on the support and assistance of other group members, and truly become friends.

Functioning Maturely and Productively

As members' commitment to one another and to the cooperative accomplishment of the group's goals increases, the group achieves maturity, autonomy, and productivity. A definite sense of group identity emerges as the group becomes a mature working unit possessing the skills and attitudes necessary for effective collaboration in maximizing all members' learning. Group members can work together to achieve a variety of learning tasks and can deal with controversy and conflicts of interest in constructive ways. The group's attention alternates between task and maintenance concerns. Group members clearly collaborate to achieve the group's goals while ensuring that their relationships with each other are maintained at a high quality level. The group can do without the assistance of the coordinator in managing problems that arise. The coordinator becomes a consultant to the group rather than a directive leader. The relationships among group members continue to improve, as does the relationship between the coordinator and the members.

In the maturely functioning group, all members participate and are influenced by each other according to the expertise and information each possesses. The actions of one group member truly substitute for the actions of other members as the group moves harmoniously, through a division of labor toward maximizing the learning of all members. Members freely ask for and give help and assistance. There is a sense of pride in the group's achievements and a sense of gratitude to other members for their contributions to the group's success. Members feel good about the group's efforts, each other, and themselves. Controversy is encouraged and looked forward to, and conflicts of interest are openly confronted and resolved. Leadership is shared and viewed as the responsibility of all members. All the group's decisions concerning the answers to problems being studied are made by consensus. All the criteria for effective groups are met.

Many discussion groups never reach this stage. Either the coordinator does not have the skills to establish the cooperative interdependence within the group or the group members do not have the group skills needed to function maturely. In order to establish an autonomous, productive, and mature discussion group, the coordinator manages each previous stage of development competently while at the same time ensures that members are mastering the group skills they need in order to interact effectively.

Terminating

The life of every group is finite. The learning group eventually ends and the members go their separate ways. The more mature and cohesive the learning group, and the stronger the emotional bonds that have been formed among group members, the more potentially upsetting the termination period is. The ending of the group may be painful for members and the coordinator alike. Nevertheless, group members deal with the problems of separating so that they can leave the group experience behind them and move on to new experiences.

Length of Each Stage

Not all stages last the same amount of time. Many groups move very quickly through the first five stages, spend considerable time functioning maturely, and then terminate quickly. The average amount of time discussion groups tend to spend in each stage is presented in Figure 11.1.

Summary

The coordinator of a discussion group must, therefore: (1) introduce, define, and structure the learning group, (2) clarify procedures, reinforce members for conforming to the procedures, and help members become acquainted, (3) emphasize and highlight the cooperative interdependence among group members and encourage their engaging in both trusting and trustworthy behaviors, (4) accept the rebellion by and differentiation among group members as a normal process and use confrontation and constructive negotiation to help members establish their independence from each other and the prescribed procedures, (5) facilitate the members' committing themselves to and taking ownership for the group's goals, procedures, and other members, (6) be a consultant to the group providing needed material and informational resources for the group to function effectively; and (7) signal termination and help the members move on to future groups.

Another view of the coordinator's role is contained in the next section. There are a number of basic procedures the coordinator of a discussion group needs to carry out in building a productive group. These procedures further clarify the role of the coordinator.

FIGURE 11.1 Stages of Group Development

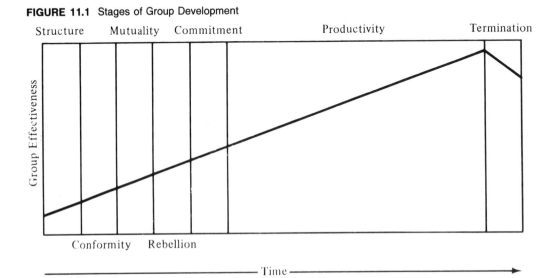

CHANGE OF OWNERSHIP FROM COORDINATOR
TO GROUP MEMBERS

For a discussion group to be successful, the group members must commit themselves to the goals and procedures of the group. Group members need to come to believe that it is *their* goals the group is working toward and it is *their* procedures the group is using. The group members will then believe that it is *their* success when they are productive. The "changing of hands" of perceived ownership of goals and procedures from coordinator to group members is a gradual process that takes place as the group matures. Very briefly, during the first two stages the goals and procedures are basically the coordinators', as the coordinator explains the goals and procedures of the discussion group and reinforces group members for engaging in appropriate task and maintenance actions. When group members begin to recognize their mutuality and build trust the changing of hands begins. The rebellion is an essential aspect of the group members beginning to restate the goals and procedures in their terms and take ownership for them. Through the final three stages the group members perceive the group's goals and procedures as being essentially theirs, not the coordinators'.

BASIC PROCEDURES FOR STRUCTURING
DISCUSSION GROUPS

In conducting productive group discussions, the coordinator must follow certain basic procedures. These procedures ensure that the group is structured cooperatively and that the members have the needed group skills to function effectively. Many times learning groups are assumed to be cooperative when they are not. Cooperation is *not* having participants sit side by side and exchange comments as they learn. A learning group is *not* cooperative if members are instructed to learn on their own and help the slower members. Cooperation is *not* having group members share materials before a competitive examination. Cooperation is much more than being physically near other persons, discussing material with other members, helping other members, or sharing materials with other members, although each of these is an important aspect of cooperative learning.

The essence of cooperative learning is assigning a *group goal*, such as a single product (for example, answers to a single set of math problems, or a single report) or as high a group average on an examination as possible, and rewarding the entire group on the basis of the quality or quantity of their product according to a fixed standard of excellence. The coordinator, in other words, establishes a group goal and a criteria-referenced evaluation system and rewards group members on the basis of their group performance. The procedures for structuring an effective learning group are as follows.

Specify Objectives

As far as possible, the coordinator must specify the objectives for the learning group.

Select the Appropriate Group Size

The number of participants in a learning group has several important consequences for the success of the group. Optimum group size depends on the group's tasks, the composition of its members, the time available, the level of interpersonal and group skills of the members, and many other factors. Some of the more important effects of increasing group size are as follows (Johnson, 1980):

1. As the size of the group increases, the total resources of the group increase, but not the usable resources. The range of abilities, expertise, and skills available to the group increases with an increase in group size, as well as the sheer number of "hands" available for acquiring and processing information. The usable resource per member, however, will often increase at a slower rate than the total resources and will often not increase at all beyond a certain point. Adding a new member to a group of three will have more impact, for example, than adding a new member to a group of thirty.

2. As the size of the group increases, the heterogeneity of members increases. The probability that any given characteristic will appear increases as the size of the group increases, but the probability that all members have a given characteristic decreases as the size of the group increases.

3. As the size of the group increases, the opportunity for individual participation and reward decreases. The larger the group, the less opportunity each member has to participate in a discussion, the greater the feelings of threat and the greater the inhibition of impulses to participate, and the more a few members will dominate.

4. As the size of the group increases, the more the members' energy must be directed toward coordinating and assembling the contributions of the individual members.

5. As the size of the group increases, the less liked, supported, and valued individual members will be, and the greater the absenteeism, formality, conflict, and dissatisfaction with the group. The larger the group, the less the interpersonal regard among members may become.

6. As the size of the group increases, the clarity of members' perceptions of each other's degree of mastery of the material being learned will decrease.

Taken in its entirety, the evidence concerning group size indicates that the optimal size of learning groups might be from four to six members. Such a group is large enough to ensure diversity and a variety of resources, and small enough that everyone's resources will be utilized and everyone will participate and receive rewards for their contributions. In a group of this size the energy needed to coordinate members' contributions is minimized, acceptance and support among members are highlighted, and the achievement level of each member is perceived by other group members. When group members are very young, however, or when there is a marked lack of the interpersonal and group skills necessary for working productively with others, pairs or triads may be more productive than larger groups.

Assign Participants to Groups

Usually, the coordinator will wish to maximize the heterogeneity of learning groups. Although the research findings are not consistent, the overall weight of the evidence indicates that higher achievement by high-, medium-, and low-performing participants will result when they are placed in heterogeneous learning groups (Johnson, 1980a). Randomly assigning participants to groups usually ensures sufficient heterogeneity among members.

Arrange the Room

The design and arrangment of space and furniture in a room affects the learning of group members in two ways (Johnson, 1979). First, they communicate a symbolic message of what is expected. The way in which chairs are arranged, for example, is a message to participants: chairs in a row communicate a different message and expectation than chairs grouped in small circles. Second, room design can directly facilitate or interfere with learning. The way in which interior space is designed affects opportunities for social contact, patterns of participation in learning activities, patterns of communication among group members and between group members and the coordinator, the feelings (such as well-being, enjoyment, comfort, anger, and depression) of group members and the coordinator, the friendship patterns within the group, the ease of transition from one learning activity to another, the amount of time group members spend actually learning, the general morale of group members, the emergence of leadership, and the achievement of group members.

The design of the room is a tool that the coordinator can use to facilitate participant learning. In order to do so, the coordinator needs to know how to:

1. define patterns of work and social interaction through spatial arrangement, graphics, color, and physical boundaries.

2. utilize physical arrangements to maximize learning.

3. visually focus group members' attention on the coordinator, each other, or instructional materials, depending on the specific task.

4. control levels of noise in the room.

5. design patterns of circulation that will enable group members to have access to the social and material resources needed for learning.

Each of these factors is discussed in detail in Johnson (1979). In general, the coordinator will wish to cluster learning groups in such a way that they will not interfere with each other's functioning. Within the groups, members should be able to see the relevant materials, converse with each other, and exchange materials and ideas. Usually a circle is best; long or large tables should be avoided.

Distribute Materials

Materials need to be distributed among group members in such a way that all members participate and master the assignment. When a group is mature and experienced, and when group members have a high level of group and interpersonal skills, the coordinator may not have to arrange materials in any special way. When a group is new or when group members are not very skilled, there are at least three ways in which a coordinator may arrange and distribute materials to group members:

1. The coordinator may arrange the material like a jigsaw puzzle and give each group member one piece (Aronson, Blaney, Stephan, Sikes, and Snapp, 1978). A learning group, for example, could be writing a report on Abe Lincoln, each group member having material on a different part of his life. In order for the report to be completed, all group members will have to contribute their material and make sure it is incorporated into the report. Many of the exercises in Chapter 5 are set up in a jigsaw manner.

2. The materials may be structured as a controversy. Several of the controversy exercises in Chapter 6 are structured so that they may be used by learning groups. Since controversies were described in detail in that chapter, they will not be discussed here.

3. The materials may be structured in a game format and a tournament conducted among learning groups to see which group can learn the material the best and perform the best in the game. A procedure for developing instructional games is given by DeVries and Edwards (1973). They call their approach to structuring materials "Teams-Games-Tournament."

By arranging materials as a jigsaw puzzle or as a controversy, the coordinator creates a positive dependence of group members on each other for the information needed to complete the task. This resource interdependence of members ensures their collaboration.

Assign Roles

Cooperative interdependence may also be arranged through the assignment of complementary and interconnected roles to group members. One group member, for example, could be assigned the role of reading the assigned material to the entire group, another member could be assigned the role of recording the group's answers, another member could be given the role of making sure that all members actively participate, and another member could be given the role of making sure all group members understand and can explain the group's answers. The assignment of such roles creates a role interdependence among group members that ensures their collaboration. Through a division of labor created by the assignment of interdependent roles, group members become cooperatively interdependent and must work on the achievement of the group's goals together.

Explain the Cooperative Goal Structure and the Task

The task may be the successful completion of an assignment in any subject area. To explain the cooperative goal structure the coordinator will need to communicate that there is a group goal and a criteria-referenced evaluation system and that all group members will be rewarded on the basis of the quality of the group's work. The group goal answers the question "Why do I have to work cooperatively with other group members?" The goal needs to be set carefully with statements such as "I want only one set of answers from each group" or "Help each other with the spelling words because your score is the number of words the four of you spell correctly." Since Chapter 4 contains considerable discussion of the cooperative goal structure, we will not examine that topic here.

If there is more than one learning group, the coordinator may wish to structure intergroup cooperation by stating that bonus points will be awarded if all the groups reach a certain criterion of learning. It is also important that group members be able to receive accurate feedback on the level of their individual achievement. In this way the members and the group as a whole know who to give added assistance and support to. Individual accountability is an important aspect of cooperative learning.

It is often helpful to describe five or six cooperative actions expected of group members while they work together. "Make sure everyone in the group knows the material and can explain the rationale," "Make sure all group members participate actively and have their say," and "Argue your point of view and don't change your mind unless you are logically persuaded" are examples of reminders that group members need from time to time. It is also a good idea to let group members know you are going to be watching for specific cooperative actions while they work together.

Observe and Monitor the Behavior of Group Members

Just because the coordinator instructs group members to cooperate with each other does not mean that they will always do so. Much of the coordinator's time in cooperative learning situations is spent observing group members in order to see what problems they are having in working collaboratively. This book contains a variety of observation instruments and procedures that can be used for this purpose.

It is the monitoring and processing procedures that often motivate group members to engage in appropriate social skills while they are working together. The coordinator should keep in mind what member actions are to be observed, what observation and recording system he or she will use, and how the information gathered will be discussed and processed by group members.

Intervene to Teach Needed Group Skills

At times the coordinator becomes a consultant to the group in order to help it function more effectively. When it is obvious that group members lack certain group and interpersonal skills that they need in order to cooperate with each other, the coordinator will want to intervene in order to help the members learn these social skills. These skills, along with activities that may be used in teaching them, are covered throughout this book and in Johnson (1978; 1981). The specific process of teaching social skills is discussed in Chapter 1.

Evaluate the Quality and Quantity of Group Productivity

The quality and quantity of the learning of group members needs to be evaluated, by a criteria-referenced system. The procedures for setting up and using such an evaluation system are given in Johnson and Johnson (1975).

The product required from the group may be a report, the average of individual examination scores, or a single set of answers that all the group members agree to. One procedure that is effective in ensuring that all group members master the assigned material is the cooperative-test procedure used at the beginning of many of the chapters in this book to ensure that all group members understand the basic concepts in the chapter.

Assess How Well the Group Functioned

After the learning of the group members is evaluated, it is necessary to discuss how effectively the members worked together. At this point the results of the coordinator's monitoring should be communicated to the group members and discussed by them. The more precise the feedback given to each group member and the more thorough the group processing of the coordinator's observations, the more effectively the group will function next time. Often it is also helpful to have one member of the group observe each group session so that both the coordinator's and the member's observations can be discussed and used to improve the effectiveness of the group.

One important aspect of group life to discuss in the processing sessions is group maintenance. Groups are often exclusively task-oriented. Group sessions should be enjoyable, lively, and pleasant experiences. If no one is having fun, something is wrong. One of the major functions of controversy is to spark more involvement and enjoyment in a discussion. Group cohesion should be increasing with each session. Processing aspects of group functioning related to group maintenance usually improves the effectiveness of the group.

Another aspect of group life to assess is the attendance and preparation of group members. Members should attend a learning group regularly and come prepared. A productive group discussion is one in which members are present and prepared to discuss the material; only then can their resources be used fully. Absenteeism and lack of preparation, moreover, often demoralize other members. The greater the cooperativeness of group members, the more they will encourage and support each other's attendance and preparation.

Regular assessing of group functioning should be accepted as an integral part of group functioning. A productive group is one that realizes that there will be process problems and is willing to evaluate its progress in managing these problems effectively. By assessing the group's functioning members learn what they must do to improve it and they gain a better understanding of how and when to contribute to its needs. Group skills, in other words, are improved through the processing of the coordinators' observations.

Finally, regular processing sessions facilitate the development of the group to higher levels of maturity.

THE COORDINATOR'S ROLE: FINAL NOTES

For every discussion group there is usually a designated leader, or coordinator. Often this person is the teacher or the educator in charge of the instructional program. The responsibilities of such a person are hard to define specifically because he needs to promote discussion without controlling or dominating it; he needs to promote a process in which a group of persons learn from their discussion and interaction with one another. Some of the coordinator's responsibilities are to introduce the discussion session; to be a task-oriented timekeeper who keeps the group moving so that it does not get sidetracked or bogged down; to restate and call attention to the main ideas of the discussion so that learning is focused; to promote a climate of acceptance, openness, warmth, and support to facilitate learning; and to know when to provide a sense of closure.

Though all group members are responsible for behaving in ways that help one another learn, the coordinator may be more qualified than most other members to use four particular types of helpful behaviors. The first is the instructional behavior of resource expert. In most cases the coordinator will best know the materials, information, and readings that are most relevant and helpful for the group. Her second type of helpful behavior is that of a teacher—teaching the members the group skills they need to function effectively in a discussion group. The coordinator may hold skill sessions in which members are given practice in fulfilling different functions in the group, or in which she makes periodic evaluations of the present functions and those needed to improve the quality of the group's performance. The third behavior is that of a process observer. As such, the coordinator must not only diagnose the present functioning of the group, but intervene in the group in ways that improve its effectiveness. The observation skills the coordinator needs in order to diagnose group effectiveness and questionnaires helpful in gathering members' perceptions of current group functioning are presented in previous chapters of this book. The intervention skills the coordinator needs in order to improve group functioning are also covered in previous chapters.

Finally, the coordinator may be the keeper of the group's physical structure. It is the discussion leader who will check to see that the group is sitting fairly close together in a circle without tables or desks between members, in a comfortable, pleasant room—perhaps with refreshments. This task is a vital part of promoting a productive session, for the physical setting can do much to help or obstruct learning in a discussion group.

In addition to these responsibilities, there are other ways in which a coordinator can assist the group. During any single discussion session the coordinator can be helpful, for example, in (1) beginning a discussion session, (2) keeping it going, and (3) ending it. As we have seen, in the early part of a session members are usually concerned about what is expected of them and what the goals of the session are. A discussion of these points provides a basis for orienting and directing group members. Furthermore, as the meeting progresses the coordinator may occasionally test whether the group clearly knows what the goals are. Group members also need to know clearly the coordinator's responsibilities and why he is there. A coordinator never wants to be in the position of having all group maintenance and goal accomplishment left up to him. One of the easiest ways to make sure that all members will fulfill the responsibilities expected of them is to have the coordinator's role well defined.

Another part of beginning a discussion is setting a helpful climate. As we have noted, group members will not "open up" until they feel secure in expressing their attitudes and ideas and know they won't be ignored, ridiculed, criticized, or otherwise embarrassed by the other group members. Some of the ways in which a coordinator can promote a free and friendly climate are by helping members become better acquainted; dispensing with unnecessary formalities, such as raising hands for permission to speak; listening attentively to what each group member is saying; not evaluating the contributions of members or commenting on every contribution made; ruling out preaching, teaching, and moralizing; and avoiding forcing members into participation before they are ready.

A good discussion leader is prepared with several questions and stimulating comments for beginning a discussion, though she should not be in a hurry to use them. One of the critical points in a discussion group's development is freeing the members from dependence upon the coordinator's ideas and direction. Silence, therefore, should not disturb the coordinator. Many a discussion never got started because the coordinator didn't stop talking long enough for the group to "pick up the ball."

During the discussion the coordinator should help establish norms of participation by all members, model good communication skills, promote member-to-member interaction, and maintain the group's direction and agenda. He can encourage productive participation by watching the signs of a member's efforts to be heard and giving her an opportunity to contribute; by being wary of those too eager to talk, as they can monopolize all the group's time; by encouraging and supporting all members who participate; by summarizing and clarifying the contributions; and by not dominating the discussion or commenting too frequently. Above all, a coordinator should show enthusiasm for the discussion and a sincere interest in the group members.

Often in a discussion group one member will obstruct the functioning of the group. And almost as often the other members will not be able to solve the problem constructively: they either support the obstructer or reject him—both of which are undesirable. The coordinator, then, may have to intervene if the situation is to be handled productively. The skills in handling interpersonal conflicts are discussed in Chapters 6 and 7 in this book and in Johnson (1981). The important point for the group to remember in such a situation is that the conflict must be processed, negotiated, and resolved to everyone's satisfaction.

A coordintor needs to be concerned with how the meeting is ended. A few minutes before the group discussion is scheduled to close, or when it appears that the group has exhausted the subject, the session can be concluded with a summary of the significant points by a member or the coordinator. This summary should be brief, but it should not be a last-minute statement given to the tune of moving chairs and scuffling feet. The summary is vital because it leaves the group with a sense of achievement, it clarifies group thinking, and it tests the conclusions of the summarizer against those of other group members. After the summary the group should evaluate how it has functioned as a group. Finally, the coordinator may express her appreciation to the group. If the group is to meet again, she may wish to explain where and when. And if a final report is required, it should be presented before the fine points of the discussion are forgotten.

Leading Growth Groups

INTRODUCTION

In the past twenty years there has been an explosion in people's participation in growth groups. It is estimated that over five million Americans have at one time or another participated in some type of group activity aimed at personal growth or change. Several million more are members of self-help groups, and tens of thousands have participated in counseling and psychotherapy groups. Special group experiences have been designed to help improve marriages, to bridge the gap between parents and children, to strengthen the communion and unity that have characterized religious organizations in the past, to help people handle conflict more constructively, and to increase people's ability to meditate, "center," and communicate through touch. Training in human relations has become mandatory for potential teachers, and intercultural experiences between minorities and whites are frequently offered as a means of improving teaching and cross-cultural relations. There are sensitivity groups, encounter groups, confrontation groups, personal-growth groups, strength groups, consciousness-raising groups, and such a variety of other groups that no one can keep up with current labels. All such groups are generally referred to as *growth groups* in this book. With such a demand for small-group experiences, and with such an expansion in the types of group experiences available, it is difficult to conceive of a book on groups that does not cover growth groups.

To be an effective growth-group leader a person needs to: (1) understand the unique powers of group experiences, (2) understand the events within groups that promote participant change and growth, (3) understand the goals of growth groups, and (4) perform competently a certain set of skills needed to lead a growth group. Each of these aspects of facilitating personal growth in a group context will be discussed in this chapter. We shall also discuss how one becomes a group facilitator and how the feelings, intuition, and conceptual frameworks of growth-group leaders are related.

THE SOCIAL–SKILLS BASIS OF PERSONAL GROWTH

Jane is a college sophomore who lives in a dorm. She is seeking to participate in a growth group because of her shyness. After a year and a half of college she has made only one friend and finds it hard to talk even to her roommate. Jane is very anxious about approaching others, and she lacks the small-group and interpersonal skills she needs in order to interact effectively with others. A social-skills training approach would focus on teaching Jane how to initiate a conversation, how to show interest in another person, and how to build and maintain a relationship. The existence of Jane's anxiety is not ignored, but instead of focusing only on reducing the anxiety a growth group leader assumes that the anxiety will decrease as Jane acquires more effective skills in relating to others.

Most participants enter growth groups hoping to develop or refine certain skills in relating to others. It is their interpersonal interactions that have led them to depression, anger, anxiety, guilt, capriciousness, and other conflictive feelings. If they could resolve their conflicts with others, influence others in the ways they wish, or manage their feelings constructively, they would do so. Through either a lack of small-group and interpersonal skills or an inability to utilize the social skills they have, participants seek the help of a growth group.

It is our interpersonal relationships that provide the warmth, caring, support, and collaboration that give life its excitement and potential for joy and personal fulfillment. And it is in these relationships that both the origin of and the solution to participants' problems can usually be found. Psychological health can be defined as the ability of a person to build and maintain cooperative relationships with family, neighbors, friends, and fellow employees (Johnson, 1979, 1980b). The quality of one's relationships depends largely on one's interpersonal competence. Interpersonal and small-group skills form the basic nexus between the individual and others, and if participants are to cope with the stresses, strains, and conflicts involved in building and maintaining productive and fulfilling relationships, they must have a modicum of these skills. The underlying purpose of most growth groups, therefore, is to help participants achieve some kind of behavioral and cognitive change that increases their competence in managing their interpersonal relationships so that they can lead more productive, self-enhancing, and fulfilling lives. The advantages of and procedures for increasing one's interpersonal and small-group skills in a growth group form the body of this chapter.

THE UNIQUE POWERS OF GROUP EXPERIENCES

Some persons seek isolation and privacy while they try to think through their problems and decide how they are going to improve their relationships. Others seek out a friend or a counselor and discuss their problems and plans in a dyad. Groups, however, have several unique advantages over solitary contemplation and dyadic discussion for those who want to grow, develop, and change. These unique capacities of groups are as follows.

1. Groups provide a more heterogeneous social setting in which interpersonal skills may be learned, mastered, and integrated into one's behavioral repertoire. Whereas in a dyad only one relationship has to be maintained, in a group several relationships have to be maintained and increased concern about rejection and exclusion for inappropriate behavior may result. In a dyad there is acceptance by only one person; in a group there may be acceptance by many persons. Different persons provoke different feelings and reactions, and in a group more feelings and reactions are generated. In a dyad there is one person to compare oneself with; in a group there are several. The greater number of relationships available in the group provide a richness and potential for learning not possible in a dyad or a solitary situation.

2. Groups generate a sense of community, belonging, support, acceptance, and assistance that eases the pain associated with therapeutic exploration and encourages risk taking in achieving growth goals (Lieberman, Lakin, and Whitaker, 1968). Groups offer a member acceptance by a number of persons, no matter what the member's history or behavior outside of the group. They provide the supportive climate that permits members to take risks and to reveal themselves. They provide the public esteem and acceptance that form the basis for increased self-esteem and self-acceptance. Members' confidence in their ability to grow and change may increase as they feel their groupmates become committed to assist and support them in doing so.

3. Groups influence the behavioral and attitudinal patterns of members. A group is able to influence its members in a variety of ways beyond what one other person in a dyad can do. Social pressure to engage in more constructive behavior is greater in a group setting, the social approval of a number of persons is a more powerful reward than the social approval of one person, the authenticating affirmation of one's peers is more powerful than that of one person, and the threat of expulsion by a whole group is more powerful punishment than the threat of expulsion by one person. Within a group there are group norms that members will be influenced to conform to, and in a growth group the norms will encourage growth and the mastery of more constructive ways of behaving and thinking. Within a group there are a number of persons to identify with and imitate, whereas in a dyad there is only one.

4. Groups may induce and then reduce powerful feelings (Lieberman, Lakin, and Whitaker, 1968). Growth groups provide an environment in which participants may experience previously terrifying feelings with a new sense

of acceptance. By finding that the previously feared feelings are not overwhelming or that the feared consequences do not occur, the participant has a corrective emotional experience. The wider variety of persons and the more diverse interpersonal events that take place within a group enable the group to induce more powerful emotions. Yet the support and acceptance within the group makes it likely that the emotions will not be completely overwhelming or terrorizing. The experiencing and discussing of the emotions in a supportive and caring environment usually reduces them and decreases their influence on the participant's future behavior and thinking.

5. Groups require the use of a wide variety of interpersonal skills and competencies. While contemplating problems by oneself, there are no interpersonal skills being used. Discussing problems with one person requires some interpersonal skills. But discussing problems and trying out new behaviors in a group requires a far broader range of interpersonal skills and competencies. Listening to others discuss their problems and helping them experiment with more constructive ways of behaving and thinking requires skills and competencies that may never be apparent in a dyadic relationship.

6. Groups provide opportunities for participants to understand and help their peers. In helping other group members to understand their destructive behavioral and attitudinal patterns and facilitating their experimentation with more constructive ways of behaving and thinking, participants build self-esteem, self-insight, and increased interpersonal competence. Helping others is also an important opportunity for altruistic behavior that may be absent from their daily lives. By working to understand others in the group and by caring for the personal struggles that other members are going through, participants gain in a variety of ways.

7. Groups provide a variety of perspectives that stimulate insight into and understanding of one's problems and behavior. By providing labels for the participant's thoughts, feelings, and experiences and by helping the participant reflect on his interactions with them, the other group members help him understand his actions. A group adds to any insight achieved by a member through its consensual validation of the insight.

8. Groups provide sources of comparison for participants (Lieberman, Lakin, and Whitaker, 1968). Members of growth groups often compare their attitudes toward their parents, spouses, children, and friends; their feelings about events within the group; the things that makes them sad, happy, guilty, and angry; the ways each member typically deals with and expresses anger and affection; and so on. Such comparisons occur naturally within a group and facilitate possible new ways of feeling, perceiving, and behaving.

9. Groups provide a variety of sources of feedback (Lieberman, Lakin, and Whitaker, 1968). Within a group a person is provided the opportunity to engage in behavior or express observations and feelings, note the consequences of doing so, and hear from other members about her impact on them. In a group setting, participants can test their behavior and seek feedback from a variety of persons.

10. Groups provide a remedial environment for the solution of problems. It is within relationships that problems develop and people learn maladaptive patterns of thinking and behaving. A growth group enables participants to work on their problems immediately within a remedial environment. Besides understanding their problems, participants may take immediate corrective steps in their relationships with other members.

11. Groups provide the constructive peer relationships needed for healthy social and cognitive development (Johnson, 1980b). Peer relationships are an absolute necessity for healthy development, and group settings provide access to constructive relationships that may be absent in participants' lives.

EVENTS THAT PROMOTE PARTICIPANT CHANGE

Within growth groups there are a series of events that promote participant change (Leiberman, 1980). Some of these events directly promote change; others reduce blocks to change. The events are as follows.

1. Change is promoted by the emotional expression of positive and negative feelings toward other group members and about important life events. Participants may express feelings toward other group members. They may also express feelings that they had previously blocked and thereby unburden themselves of an emotional restraint. If participants do not feel free to express positive and negative feelings such as caring and anger in the group, their ability to learn from each other and from their experiences in the group is markedly reduced. Unless participants are free to express both negative and positive feelings toward each other openly and directly, the road to change will be blocked.

2. Change is promoted by the experiencing of intense positive and negative emotions, whether or not they are expressed. Events within the group may unleash feelings certain participants have been previously unable or unwilling to experience. As we have seen, participants may find that such feelings are not overwhelming or that the feared consequences do not occur. Thus, a corrective emotional experience may result even when the feelings are not overtly expressed. Participants may learn a new acceptance of feelings they were previously afraid of.

3. Change is promoted by the observation of other group members having significant emotional experiences. Participants often have beneficial experiences by observing other members having corrective emotional experiences. Other members' emotional experiences may clarify issues for a participant, who may then make use of the experiences in his own problematic areas.

4. Change is promoted by the inculcation of hope and a decrease in

demoralization. To be demoralized is to be disheartened, bewildered, confused, disordered, and deprived of courage. The demoralized participant feels isolated, hopeless, and helpless. Group situations can generate events that inspire hope in participants, feelings that one can change, and beliefs that one can influence the causes of one's problems. Seeing other members in the group who have successfully grappled with problems or who have changed as a result of their participation in the group is one such event.

5. Change is promoted by the decrease in participants' egocentrism and the increase in their perspective-taking abilities. Through exchanges of ideas about problems and solutions within a context where participants feel understood and accepted, participants will be more aware of and open to other perspectives. Group leaders may also structure perspective-reversal situations in which participants switch positions and argue each other's point of view or take the perspective of a significant person outside of the group, such as a mother, boss, or spouse.

6. Change is promoted by self-disclosure, the realization that others have similar feelings, and insight into one's problems. In growth groups self-disclosure consists of the explicit communication of information (a) that a participant believes other group members would be unlikely to acquire unless she told it to them, and (b) that she considers so highly private that she would exercise great caution regarding whom she told it to. Self-disclosure to a group of peers is quite different from self-disclosure to one other person. It feels less dramatic and is a less anxiety-laden action to reveal private information to a single person than to a group. The significance of self-disclosure is not what is disclosed, but rather the response of other members to what one has said. The therapeutic and growth value of self-disclosure lies in the sense of well-being, the trust and confidence in other human beings, and the acceptance by other members that one obtains after disclosing anxiety-producing information to the group and receiving a caring and supportive response from the other members. Self-disclosure can be cathartic when participants discover that no one is shocked by their deeply hidden secrets that have always made them feel ashamed, guilty, depressed, or angry. When several members of a group engage in self-disclosure on similar problems, they feel considerable relief when they discover that they are not the only ones who have reacted the way they have and who experience the feelings they do. There are times when discovering the similarities in their experiences, reactions, actions, and feelings reassures participants that they are normal. Finally, the disclosure of anxiety-producing information to a group facilitates the achievement of insight into one's problems and the dynamics of the situations being discussed.

In summary, self-disclosure helps provide participants with insight into their problems as they organize and think through their experiences in order to share them with others. It creates a sense of relief when participants discover that their problems are not unique and that they are not inherently evil for feeling and behaving as they do. It releases and frees one from anxiety-producing feelings when no one is shocked or horrified by them. Finally, self-disclosure that results in understanding and acceptance by others promotes a sense of personal well-being and trust in others.

7. Change is promoted by experimentation with new behavior and by feedback received from others. The availability of immediate information about how one is perceived by peers is unique to the group situation. There seems to be a basic human need to know how one stands with one's peers and how one is perceived by others. The feedback participants receive from other group members is an important ingredient in increasing their self-awareness and self-esteem. The nature and value of constructive feedback is discussed at length in Johnson (1981) and Johnson (1978). Along with feedback, growth groups offer participants the opportunity to experiment with new patterns of behavior under low-risk conditions. Having experimented with new behavior patterns in the group, the participants will feel able to engage in the new behaviors in the outside world. Participants must feel that the group setting is safe enough for them to try out new ways of behaving, and they must identify problem areas and new ways of behaving in order to experiment with new behaviors. Feedback is a vital part of experimentation, for the participants need to find out how other members perceive the effectiveness of the new behavioral patterns they are trying out.

8. Change is promoted by other group members modeling constructive behavior and attitude patterns the participants wish to master. One of the best ways to learn new patterns of behaving and thinking is seeing them demonstrated by others. An important element of change, and of the maintaining of changes, is the internalization of how other participants and the group leader would have handled problem situations. Observing others use specific competencies to solve problems and relate more effectively to others can lead to considerable reflection and the discovery of alternative ways to achieve a goal.

9. Change is promoted by cognitive insight into one's problems, behavior patterns, and attitude patterns. Both increased understanding of oneself and the conscious implementation of interpersonal skills depend on cognitive learning. In their classic study of growth groups Lieberman, Yalom, and Miles (1973) found that it was self-disclosure involving some sort of cognitive mastery or understanding—not self-disclosure in and of itself—that was related to positive change. Many types of growth groups emphasize the learning of specific cognitive skills and frameworks as part of positive change.

ESTABLISHING THE GOALS OF A GROWTH GROUP

When participants join a growth group both they and the group's leader have a set of goals for the group. The participants may wish to improve the state of their feelings or find a more meaningful career. The leader may wish to improve the participants' general interpersonal functioning, or even teach growth dynamics. Assuming that the goals of the participants and those of the group leader do not completely overlap, the two must negotiate a set of goals that they can mutually commit themselves to achieving. When participants and the leader have different goals, the goals may initially be cooperative (working to achieve the participants' goals facilitates the accomplishment of the leader's goals, and vice versa) or competitive (working to achieve the participants' goals interferes with the accomplishment of the leader's goals, and vice versa). In order for the growth group to be successful, the leader and the participants need to negotiate a set of cooperatively structured goals.

Some of the common goals leaders of growth groups may have are: (1) to facilitate participants' acquisition of self-enhancing patterns of attitudes and behaviors, (2) to facilitate participants' psychological health, (3) to increase participants' skills and competencies for creating humanizing relationships, (4) to increase participants' interpersonal effectiveness, and (5) to promote participants' self-actualization. Let's look briefly at each of these goals.

Self-enchancement

Many participants may have developed patterns of behaviors and attitudes that decrease their ability to build and maintain effective relationships with others. These patterns create and sustain negative and self-destructive consequences and ultimately lead to a more painful and troubled life. If a person has no opportunity to change, her self-defeating patterns of attitudes and behaviors will affect all aspects of her life. One of the goals of leaders of growth groups, then, is to help participants identify their self-defeating and self-destructive attitudinal and behavioral patterns and change them to self-enhancing patterns.

Psychological Health

It is within interpersonal relationships that psychological illness or health is developed. *Psychological health* can be defined as the ability to be aware of and manage effectively one's cooperative interactions with others (Johnson, 1980b). In order to build and maintain the relationships so necessary for psychological health, individuals need to develop (Johnson, 1979):

1. a generalized interpersonal trust in the affection and support of others.
2. the perspective-taking abilities needed for an understanding of how a situation appears to another person and how that person is reacting cognitively and affectively.
3. a meaningful direction and purpose in life, a sense of "where I am going"

that is valued by others and similar to the goals of the significant persons in one's life.

4. an awareness of meaningful cooperative interdependence with others.

5. an integrated and coherent sense of personal identity.

Humanizing Relationships

Humanizing relationships reflect the qualities of kindness, mercy, consideration, tenderness, love, concern, compassion, responsiveness, and friendship. One goal of most group leaders is to create humanizing relationships within the group and to help participants build the competencies they need to form such relationships outside the group.

Interpersonal Effectiveness

Interpersonal and group skills are based on a person's interpersonal effectiveness. *Interpersonal effectiveness* may be defined as the extent to which the consequences of a person's behavior match his intentions (Johnson, 1981). When two participants interact, for example, they have no choice but to make some impression on each other. When they make the impression they want, their interpersonal effectiveness is high; when they make an impression they do not want, their interpersonal effectiveness is low. All the group skills discussed in this book and the interpersonal skills discussed in Johnson (1981) are relevant to interpersonal effectiveness.

Self-actualization

Self-actualization may be defined as the psychological need for growth, development, and utilization of potential (Maslow, 1954). A self-actualizing participant will be moving toward the full use of her talents, capacities, and potentialities. Self-actualization involves both self-development and self-utilization: one develops potentialities and then uses them in order to actualize oneself.

LEADING A GROWTH GROUP

Groups are uniquely suited to helping persons grow and change in constructive ways. As we have seen, a number of events may take place in a growth group that facilitate participant growth and help achieve the group's goals. But if these events are·in fact to take place, the group leader needs several sets of complex skills:

1. establishing the conditions for modifying participants' patterns of behavior and attitudes

2. being a resource expert on how to learn and change within a group
3. teaching needed interpersonal and small-group skills
4. modeling the constructive use of small-group and interpersonal skills
5. ensuring that members are provided with constructive confrontations and feedback
6. helping define and diagnose the problems of participants
7. making sure that members are provided with opportunities for self-disclosure and experimentation with new attitude and behavior patterns
8. promoting corrective or reparative emotional experiences within the group
9. engineering a problem-solving process with which participants can address their concerns
10. negotiating changes in participants' patterns of attitude and behaviors
11. engineering an effective group
12. establishing and enforcing a contract with participants
13. carrying out the executive functions of the group.

Each of these sets of skills is discussed in turn.

Establishing Conditions for Participant Change

This set of skills consists of establishing the conditions for change, helping participants change, and then stabilizing the new and more appropriate patterns of behavior and attitudes. Establishing the conditions for change is discussed in detail in Johnson (1980b). These conditions are as follows:

1. A sufficient level of trust among group members to ensure that participants feel free to self-disclose, experiment with new patterns of thinking and behaving, and give and receive feedback. This includes a warm and supportive climate in which participants feel free to take risks.
2. A reduction of participants' egocentrism and the encouragement of their viewing problems and behavior patterns from a variety of perspectives.
3. A reduction of participants' demoralization and an increase in their sense of control and influence over themselves and their lives.
4. The promotion of positive identification by the participant with other members who have the skills and competencies she needs in order to solve the problems she is experiencing.

Being a Resource Expert

An effective group leader must have the skills to act as a resource expert, an educator using inquiry and experiential methods, and a diagnoser of personal, interpersonal, and group dynamics. Any growth-group facilitator should be skilled in the use of inquiry and experiential methods of learning, a subject discussed in Chapter 1 and Appendix A. Almost all types of growth groups emphasize inquiry into the experiences of the group members. This inquiry is usually based upon diagnoses of the personal, interpersonal, and group dynamics being experienced. To make such diagnoses, the facilitator applies a conceptual framework based upon theory and research to the behavior of the group members. And to apply such a framework, the facilitator must have expertise in one of the behavioral sciences, such as psychology or sociology. The presentation of conceptual frameworks enables members not only to gain insight into their behavior and their internal reactions to what occurs within the group, but to understand more fully the interpersonal and group dynamics they are involved in. Thus, a facilitator must have a solid knowledge of one of the behavioral sciences, an expertise in inquiry and experiential-learning methods, and the ability to use his knowledge and expertise to help the members understand what they are experiencing. Leiberman, Yalom, and Miles (1973) found that the most effective leaders had a great ability to present conceptualizations that gave meaning to the experiences the members were undergoing. This one ability was the most important variable in promoting member learning that they found in their study. Such conceptualizations are especially useful to members after the group experience has ended, when they are able to use them to understand more fully their day-to-day interpersonal and group situations. The conceptualizations presented in this book and in Johnson (1981) are examples of the types of conceptual frameworks a facilitator must be able to communicate to members.

Teaching Group and Interpersonal Skills

One of the major keys to decreasing self-defeating behavior and increasing self-enhancing behavior is improving participants' group and interpersonal skills. It is often because participants lack social skills or are unable to utilize effectively the group and interpersonal skills they do have that they seek out a growth group to participate in. Improving participants' competency in and utilization of social skills can best be done in a group setting. In order to begin skill teaching growth-group leaders need to ask themselves questions such as these:

1. What are the group and interpersonal skills every person needs in order to function effectively in our society and lead a fulfilling and self-enhancing life? These skills are detailed in this book and in Johnson (1978; 1981).
2. What interpersonal and group skills are participants failing to utilize effectively?
3. What interpersonal and group skills do participants lack?

4. Will the learning and utilization of the apparently needed group and inter-personal skills reduce participants' self-defeating and self-destructive be-havior and thinking and increase their ability to create for themselves a more productive, self-enhancing, and fulfilling life?

In some growth groups interpersonal and group skills are taught directly through exercises like the ones contained in this book. In other growth groups the skill building is conducted through reflection on members' interactions and relationships. Leading growth groups requires the capacity to facilitate the social-skill learning of the participants. Since such skill learning is dis-cussed in depth in Chapter 1 and Appendix A, it will not be discussed here.

Modeling the Constructive Use of Social Skills

A fourth set of skills required of a facilitator consists of modeling the behaviors she hopes members will learn from their group experience. Social-learning theory (Bandura, 1969) emphasizes the importance of modeling desired be-haviors and then reinforcing group members (for example, giving recognition and approval for imitating the facilitator); this procedure is probably the most effective way to teach new skills. The behaviors a facilitator may model are discussed in this book and in Johnson (1981). Such behaviors would include, for example, sending and receiving communications, self-disclosure, giving and receiving feedback, experimenting with alternative behaviors, and expressing acceptance and support for others. A willingness to model desired skills means that the facilitator will take an active part in interacting with other group members. Some research indicates that activeness on the part of the facilitator is to be preferred to passiveness (which, when it pertains to members, is associated with anxiety, dissatisfaction, silence, poor atten-dance, discontinuance, and lack of learning), except when the activeness turns into domination (Bierman, 1969). Peters (1966), in addition, found that mem-bers who imitate the facilitator learn more from growth groups than those who do not. Thus, the facilitator may want to be the "ideal member" in the group in order to promote members' skill development. Finally, it should be noted that simply being an "authentic person" does not necessarily enable the facilitator to systematically present effective skills to be imitated by group members; a facilitator must be interpersonally effective in order to model desired skills.

Providing Constructive Confrontations and Feedback

The facilitator must be able to make sure that members are provided with constructive feedback and confrontations. Helpful feedback is the sharing, upon request, of a description of how a person sees another person's behavior and its consequences, and a description of how the person is reacting to the other person's behavior. A confrontation is a deliberate attempt to help another person examine the consequences of some aspect of his behavior; it is an invitation to engage in self-examination. A confrontation originates from a desire to involve oneself more deeply with the person one is confronting, and it is intended to help the person behave in more fruitful or less destructive ways. The specific skills of feedback and confrontation are presented in Johnson (1981). The point to keep in mind when facilitating feedback and confrontations is the difference among the behavior being observed, the conceptual framework the observer is using, and the inferences and interpretations made about the person engaging in the behavior. A facilitator should never let group members confuse these three elements of giving feedback and confronting other members. The actual behavior being observed will be the same to all group members (assuming that the observations are valid), but the conceptual frameworks used to understand the behavior and to make interpretations and inferences about it can be widely disparate. Selling other group members on one interpretation of what is taking place is a much different activity from arriving at a consensus of what behavior is taking place.

Defining and Diagnosing Participants' Problems

Creating meaning for participants by labeling feelings and events that they undergo and attributing meaning to experiences occurring within the group is a fundamental activity of leaders of growth groups. The increased understanding of participants resulting from such leader behavior reduces their fear and anxiety concerning emotional and interpersonal experiences and provides them with cognitive tools that they can use in becoming more effective persons. In helping participants understand their feelings and experiences, the leader must be careful about the way in which she attributes the causes of their problems and must pay attention to the resulting sense of personal control experienced by participants.

A participant's problems may be attributed to something within the participant (internal causation) or something outside of the participant (external causation). Causes may also be viewed as stable (incapable of change) or unstable (capable of change). Depending on the problem and the situation, a leader may wish to help the participant view a problem as having stable, external causes or unstable, internal causes. When a person is deeply depressed about a perceived failure, for example, the leader may wish to help him focus on the external, unstable causes of the failure. But when he succeeds, the leader may wish to emphasize the internal, stable causes of the success in order to improve his self-esteem.

Participants' problems should usually be defined in ways that increase their sense of personal control in solving them. Most individuals seem to seek a sense of control over their lives. A belief that one is in control of her life makes the world more predictable to her and she tends to react more positively to the events that take place around her and the experiences she has. One of the reasons for severe depressions following major illnesses such as heart attacks is assumed to be the feeling that one has lost control over one's life (Glass, 1977). A belief in one's control over events affects performance on tasks (Glass and Singer, 1972), judgments of the pleasantness of one's surroundings and mood (Rodin, Solomon, and Metcalf, 1978), the positiveness of our reactions (Glass, 1977), how active, sociable, and vigorous we are (Langer and Rodin, 1976), and our general health and length of life (Rodin and Langer, 1977). The facilitator of a growth group will usually want to define and diagnose participants' problems in ways that maximize their sense of control over their lives.

Group leaders should also define participants' problems in ways that maximize their sense of freedom in solving them. Brehm (1966; 1972) has proposed the concept of psychological reactance to explain some of the reactions individuals have to a loss of control or freedom of choice. *Reactance* is a motivational state that is aroused whenever persons feel that their freedom has been abridged or threatened. Threats to personal freedom motivate persons to take actions that will help them regain their freedom and control. This motivation to regain freedom can be used to change self-defeating to self-enhancing patterns of attitudes and behavior. Being placed in a dependent position, on the other hand, can lead to a significant drop in later performance when one is asked to behave independently on one's own (Langer and Benevento, 1978).

Confusion over their feelings and actions increases participants' anxiety and fear concerning their problems. A necessary skill of a growth-group leader, then, is to help participants apply to their actions and feelings insights and meaningful interpretations that will increase their sense of personal control and freedom.

Ensuring Opportunities for Self-Disclosure and Experimentation

Many of the important experiences in growth groups come directly from participants' self-disclosures and experimentation with new patterns of thinking and behaving. An important function of the group leader, therefore, is to ensure that opportunities to do so are present in the group.

Promoting Reparative Emotional Experiences

The facilitator needs to be able to promote corrective or reparative emotional experiences in the group. Highly personalized and relevant learning often arouses emotions—anxiety while the learning is taking place and happiness and satisfaction when it is achieved. To give and receive feedback, to confront and be confronted, to experiment with new behaviors, to bring out personal concerns to be problem-solved—all promote considerable emotional reaction. High levels of warmth, anger, frustration, and anxiety are found in most growth-group experiences. A facilitator may stimulate emotional reaction by confronting group members, by supporting attempts to experiment with alternative behaviors, by promoting feedback and problem solving, by disclosing highly personal material about herself, and by expressing warmth and support for the members of the group. The most effective leaders in the Leiberman, Yalom, and Miles (1973) study engaged in a moderate amount of emotionally stimulating behavior. Though emotional experiences do not mean that learning will take place, genuine learning is often accompanied by emotionality. The facilitator needs to be certain that the members not only experience deep emotion but also are helped to look at the experience objectively, in such a way as to give it meaning for the future. She should emphasize reflection as well as experience and guide members in applying their present experiences. In managing the emotionality of the group, the facilitator must also moderately stimulate learning that arouses emotions and provide conceptualizations that will promote learning from emotional experiences.

Engineering a Problem-Solving Process

Facilitators need to be able to engineer a problem-solving process with which participants can address their concerns. This subject has been discussed in Chapter 10 of this book as well as in other chapters. In such a problem-solving process it may be important to bring in information about the person's past behavior and feelings as well as his behavior and feelings in the group (Lieberman, Yalom, and Miles, 1973).

Negotiating Changes in Participants' Patterns of Attitudes and Behaviors

Another set of skills for leaders of growth groups consists of helping participants clarify their current attitude and behavior patterns, determining how those patterns are affecting the participants' feelings and interactions with others, strengthening constructive patterns of attitudes and behaviors, and changing destructive patterns that lead to self-defeating cycles of behavior and cause such feelings as guilt, depression, anxiety, fear, anger, and resentment. Encouraging participants to actively take the perspectives of others with whom they are involved, communicating warmth and understanding, highlighting conflict between desired consequences and actual behavior and thinking, and initiating problem-solving discussions are all ways in which a group leader may facilitate participants' mastery of more self-enhancing patterns of attitudes and behaviors. For a more thorough discussion of these methods, see Johnson (1980b) and Johnson and Matross (1977).

Engineering an Effective Group

The facilitator should be able to engineer an effective group. All the skills discussed in this book are useful here. Only in a growth group that is effective can the learning of members take place. The cohesion of the group; group norms that favor moderate emotional intensity, confrontation, and supportive peer control; the distribution of participation and leadership; the quality of communication; the management of conflict—these and all the other aspects of group effectiveness are extremely important for productive growth groups. A facilitator must be able to promote effective group behavior among the members.

Establishing and Maintaining a Contract

It is sometimes useful for a facilitator to have a clear contract with participants concerning their responsibilities as group members. The contract might provide, for example, that members are (1) to be completely open to the group about both past and current behavior, (2) to take responsibility for themselves once they enter the group and not blame others or circumstances for their predicaments, and (3) to get involved with the other group members and cooperate in increasing their learning. When an explicit contract is made, the facilitator becomes the "keeper of the contract" and should see to it that it is enforced.

Carrying Out Executive Functions

Finally, a facilitator may have a variety of executive functions to carry out. Organizing the group, arranging for facilities in which it is to meet, providing it with needed materials, and conducting an evaluation of its success—all of which require a range of administrative and evaluative skills—may be the responsibilities of the facilitator.

BECOMING A FACILITATOR

In the past two decades more and more persons have wanted to become qualified to conduct growth groups. One does not have to be a qualified growth-group facilitator to conduct inquiry- and experiential-learning activities. This book has organized material on group skills so that many different types of educational ventures can use it in the absence of a highly qualified staff. Yet being skilled in conducting inquiry- and experiential-learning activities does not mean that a person is qualified to conduct growth groups.

A person interested in being a facilitator should ask himself four basic questions. The first question is "Do I have an adequate training in a behavioral science?" A facilitator should have a background in an applied behavioral science (such as social psychology) that places a heavy emphasis upon interpersonal relations and group dynamics. Ideally, he should have a basic knowledge of personality theory, psychopathology, group processes, and interpersonal dynamics. Ideally, he should be connected with some organization, institution of higher education, or other agency that confirms his professional status. A serious commitment to growth groups should be part, but not all, of his professional activity. He should clearly know his intentions and goals as a facilitator, and he should understand all the ramifications of the client–facilitator relationship. A familiarity with the research on growth groups is also necessary.

The second question is "How much experience have I had as a participant and a facilitator in growth groups?" Larkin (1972) recommends that before a person can legitimately function as a facilitator she should have had a three-year training sequence something like this:

1. Participate as a member in at least two growth groups.
2. Observe group meetings of at least five growth groups and meet after the sessions with their facilitator to discuss the interactions of members and other relevant processes.
3. Co-lead five groups with experienced facilitators.
4. Lead five groups as sole facilitator, but be observed and discuss with the observer functioning in the facilitator role.
5. Undergo either psychotherapy or some equivalent sustained experiential self-study.
6. Be evaluated by well-qualified local facilitators who not only focus upon your general fitness of character and your preparation, but review with care evaluations others have made of you and their recommendations.
7. Keep up to date by periodically becoming involved in local seminars, supervision by more experienced professionals, and discussions of the ethics of the facilitator's role and function.

The third question is "What is my personal level of sensitivity, self-awareness, self-understanding, and self-actualization?" No matter how much training a person has as a facilitator, if he is not self-aware and self-understanding, he will not be able to resist indulging his own personal needs for such things as power and positive responses from participants. The personal qualities of sensitivity to and respect and liking for others are crucial for facilitators. Finally, Maslow (1962) states that a need-deficient person tends to see others in terms of the ways in which they can be of use; the self-actualized person, who is freer and more disinterested, is able to stand off and see others as they are—unique persons with their own problems who can be helped in various ways by various means.

The final question is "Am I certified by a professional organization?" There are many professional organizations that to some extent certify members as being competent as growth-group facilitators. Also, many states license or certify practicing psychologists. A serious facilitator will take the time and trouble to become certified by a professional organization or licensed by her state.

FEELINGS, INTUITION, AND CONCEPTUAL FRAMEWORKS

One major requisite of an effective facilitator is the ability to assess accurately his feelings, intuition, and conceptual frameworks. To a capable, well-trained, and experienced facilitator the three become integrated. Among poorly trained and inexperienced facilitators feelings and intuition may be given a "mystical" sense of rightness and followed blindly as a form of emotional anarchy. Though this issue is closely related to the discussion of creativity in Chapter 6, it is important enough to be reviewed briefly at this point.

A person's feelings are great sources of information about what is happening within the group and what sorts of problems are occurring in the relationships among members. But feelings are not infallible. They are susceptible to bias, distortion, and misunderstanding, especially in situations where the person is threatened, defensive, anxious, or tense. Moreover, all people have their blind spots, and in certain situations, or under certain conditions, their feelings can be a reflection of their own fears and anxieties rather than of what is actually taking place in the group. It is important, therefore, for a facilitator to "calibrate" herself on the validity and reliability of her feelings in different situations, in response to different types of events, and under different conditions. When a person becomes highly emotional, she should be cautious about relying on the accuracy of her feelings, because it is then that they are most susceptible to distortion and bias. Understanding oneself and the potential causes of various feelings is important in learning when to take action on the basis of one's intuitions and feelings.

Awareness of one's feelings and knowledge of the areas in which one can trust one's feelings lead to the issue of intuition as a base for judging what is taking place in the group and how and when to intervene in certain situations. Hunches often prompt a facilitator to intervene without his being able to explain the basis of its appropriateness. Intuition is a preconscious process: the person does not know quite how the conclusions or impulses were determined. Intuitive thinking characterisically does not advance in careful, well-defined steps; the person has an emotional and cognitive reaction to the total situation and arrives at an answer. He rarely can provide an adequate account of how the answer evolved, and he may be unaware of just what aspects of the problem situation he is responding to. Intuition results from an immersion in the group process and among the members, and from a strong identification with and empathy for what is occurring in the group. The greater the familiarity a person has with the issues that concern the group, the greater the likelihood of his intuitions being correct. A wide understanding of and acquaintance and empathy with both human nature and the nature of the group members will enhance one's intuition about the participants more than factual knowledge will. Experience in calibrating one's intuitive abilities is needed because one will find that one's intuition, like one's emotions, is sound on certain types of issues but misleading on others.

The overuse of intuition in leading growth groups has several shortcomings. Facilitators who through lack of training or self-discipline do not have conceptual frameworks from the behavioral sciences or the skills to use such frameworks in gathering information about what is taking place in the group and among its members are ignoring these shortcomings. First, hunches often confuse observation with inference; a facilitator begins defending her intuitive inferences as if they were observations and facts. One cannot, for example, *prove* that a member is projecting his feelings into others. Second, facilitators may overrate the validity of their personal observations, believing them more accurate than they usually are. Research on rumors and testimony, for example, indicates that quite often eyewitnesses' perceptions, memory, and inferences are completely inaccurate even though they are convinced that they know exactly what happened. Third, the history of medicine and clinical psychology gives overwhelming evidence of the folly of treatments based upon intuition. For several centuries, for example, it was intuitively obvious not only that the insane were possessed by demons but that all diseases were in the blood and a sick person, therefore, could be cured by bleeding. What was intuitively obvious yesterday is often laughed at today. Fourth, the research on self-fulfilling prophecies indicates that people quite often engage in behavior that makes an originally false conclusion or perception become valid. Thus, a facilitator whose intuition is wrong may misunderstand a situation but set in action certain dynamics that create the very situation she is trying to correct but that confirm her original false intuition. A fifth shortcoming is that a person's intuitions give her no adequate basis for knowing whether they are accurate. The major fallacy in intuitive thought is not that it may be inaccurate (though we know that many hunches turn out to be mistaken); a person's intuitions may be quite accurate. It is rather that no basis exists for knowing if it is right or wrong. A facilitator who takes action on the basis of her intuition takes action before she can verify whether or not the action is appropriate. Finally, it must be recognized that intuition represents an internal logic based upon one's culture and frame of reference. Intuitive judgments about another culture or another frame of reference can be very misleading.

The need to use feelings and intuitions as a basis for action within the group, even though the dangers of doing so are recognized, reflects the necessity of conceptual frameworks and data-gathering skills that can be used to verify hunches. Facilitators must have the ability to clarify their intuitions to the degree that they are able to formulate hypotheses that can be verified or disproved. It is through conceptualizing what is happening within the group and among its members that the facilitator usually derives effective interventions. It is through the facilitator's communication of his conceptualizations, furthermore, that much of the learning of members takes place. Although facilitators vary in how much they rely on behavioral-science conceptualizations and how much they rely on their feelings and intuitions, all have some conceptualization of what is taking place. One always has a set of assumptions from which to operate; the only question is how well formulated and explicit the conceptual framework is, and how systematically it is used to verify one's hunches.

A conceptual framework is nothing more than a way of looking at pieces of behavior in order to make some kind of sense out of them. Individual behaviors, when examined one by one, often have little or no value to the observer. When the pieces are conceptually connected, however, they become understandable and useful. The facilitator uses a conceptual framework to see the connections among and meaning of the individual behaviors of group members. All conceptualizations involve understanding relationships, grasping inherent meaning, or comprehending a structure. The value of conceptualization is that it provides an instrument for decision making. A facilitator is able to use her theoretical system to bring her interventions under rational control. She plans her actions in accordance with a system of related hypotheses rather than on the basis of an intuited procedure. The knowledge now available in the behavioral sciences provides facilitators with the means of organizing their perceptions, making observations systematically in order to promote member learning, checking out their hunches, and communicating their expertise to the members. There is no way to overemphasize the importance to facilitators of explicit conceptual schemes that they can use systematically in helping members learn from their experiences.

As with intuition, however, if facilitators use *only* their conceptualizations, their effectiveness may suffer. Their behavior in a group may become uncreative and overly structured. They may be pretending that the group is at a level of sophistication and knowledge that it is not, and they will be repressing their capacity for the kind of creativity that provides insights and alternative solutions to the problems the group faces. Though conceptual frameworks do help organize observations and do aid understanding and communication, they do not always help facilitators to draw upon the creativity they need in order to arrive at insights into members' behavior and put fire and zest into their own growth and actualization.

An effective facilitator should be aware of and accept his feelings. He should use them to spark his intuition about what is taking place in the group and among its members. He should also have expertise in using conceptual frameworks to verify hunches, to systematically observe member behavior, and to communicate with members in ways that facilitate their learning. Intuition and theory are both necessary and useful in generating effective interventions within a growth group. Neither should be slighted; neither should be overvalued when employed separately.

GROWTH GROUPS AND PARTICIPANT ANXIETY

During the past twenty years there have been allegations that growth groups create levels of anxiety that are potentially damaging psychologically (Gottschalk, 1966). These allegations have not been supported by evidence. To determine how anxious college students are before and after participating in a growth group, Johnson, Kavanagh, and Lubin (1973), in two separate studies, compared the anxiety level of participants in a growth group with their anxiety level before and after taking a final examination in a course in group dynamics. They found that participant anxiety at the beginning of the growth group was less than that experienced before a final examination, and that participant anxiety after the growth group was over was considerably less than that experienced after a final examination. Participating in a growth group, then, seems less stressful than taking course examinations.

13

Epilogue

Group skills and knowledge are vital for creating effective groups, which in turn are vital for developing a high quality of life and psychological health. As noted in Chapter 1, groups are of incalculable importance in the life of every person and skills in group membership are absolutely essential for effective functioning within any society, family, organization, or relationship. We are not born with these skills, they must be developed. You have now completed a variety of experiences aimed at increasing your group skills and knowledge. It is hoped that you are now more skillful in leading decision-making activities to accomplish group goals. During such activities, it is hoped that you will be able to promote effective communication, controversy, conflict management, mutual influence, and other aspects of group effectiveness. It is also hoped that you will be able to apply your increased skills and knowledge in a variety of groups and under a variety of conditions. You may wish to repeat many of the exercises in this book to reinforce your knowledge and to reread much of the material to gain a more complete understanding of how to utilize group skills. There are, however, two concluding exercises that may be helpful in applying the material covered in this book to the memberships you hold in groups.

TERMINATING A GROUP EXERCISE

The goals of this exercise are to (1) complete any unfinished business in a group, (2) relive and remember the positive group experiences the group has had, (3) synthesize what group members have received from being part of the group, and (4) describe and express constructively group members' feelings about the termination of the group.

The theme of the exercise is that though every group ends, the things you as a member have given and received, the ways in which you have grown, the skills you have learned, all continue with you. Terminating relationships may be sad, but the ways in which you have grown within your relationships with other group members can be applied to group situations in the future. Here is the procedure for the group to follow in the exercise:

1. Discuss the topic, "Is there anything that needs to be resolved, discussed, dealt with, or expressed before the group ends?"
2. Discuss these questions: "What have been the most significant experiences of the group? What have I gotten out of being a member of the group? How has being a part of this group facilitated my growth as a person? What skills have I learned from being in this group?" As alternatives to a discussion, group members might make a painting, a collage, or a poem describing their experiences.
3. Discuss how you feel about the group winding up its activities and what feelings you want to express about the termination. Personal styles of handling the dissolution of a group may be discussed. If you cannot discuss this issue, the following alternatives may generate a productive discussion:
   a. Each of you in turn says good-bye. to the group and leaves. Each of you then spends five minutes thinking about your feelings and returns to express anything you wanted to but did not express before.
   b. Each of you nonverbally shows how you felt when you first joined the group and then shows nonverbally how you feel now.
4. As a closing exercise, stand up in a close circle. You are all to imagine that you have the magical power to give anything you wish to another group member. You are then to give the person on your right a parting gift, each taking your turn so that everyone in the group can hear what the gifts are. Examples of what individuals might give are moonbeams, a flower, a better self-concept, an ability to commit oneself to a relationship, comfort with conflict, more empathy with others, the perfect love affair, and so on. When giving the gift, extend your hands as if actually passing something to the other person.
5. Have a group hug.

SELF-CONTRACT EXERCISE

Write a description of yourself as a group member. Mention all the strengths and skills you can think of and mention the areas in which you need to increase your skills. Then make a contract with yourself to make some changes in your life; the contract can involve starting something new, stopping something old, or changing some present aspect of your life. It should involve applying your group skills to the actual group situations you are now facing, or working to develop certain skills further. It may involve joining new groups and terminating old group memberships. In making the contract, pick several group memberships you now have and set a series of goals concerning how you will behave to increase your effectiveness and satisfaction as a group member. Write the contract down, place it in an envelope, address the envelope to yourself, and open it three months later.

Appendix A

Conducting Skill-Training Exercises

A TYPICAL SKILL-TRAINING SESSION

Before discussing how to conduct a skill-training session it may be helpful to review the overall structure of a group exercise. A typical session would involve the following procedures:

1. Participants are presented with an introduction by a coordinator, who then conducts a warm-up discussion. The introduction should include the objectives of the session, an outline of what will happen, and a description of the specific skills with which the participants will be concerned during the exercise: The warm-up discussion sets the stage for the exercise, engenders participant involvement, and promotes some sort of emotional connection among participants. The warm-up could take the form of a brief exchange of current feelings among participants or an interesting anecdote about group skills told by the coordinator. The expectations of the participants should be set at this point.

2. The exercise is then conducted.

3. After the exercise is completed, the participants are asked to conceptualize, analyze, and summarize their experience. This step may be structured through discussion questions or data feedback about how each person and the group behaved. The personal learnings of each participant, their application to his life, and the theoretical principles into which the participants gained insight as a result of their experience can be focused upon.

4. In a general session participants should talk over the experience and summarize their ideas about their experience. The coordinator should integrate

appropriate theory and cognitive frameworks into the participants' statements. The emphasis at this point is upon integrating the important learnings, theory, and research with their experiences.

5. The coordinator should then discuss the issues of applying the learnings and skills to the participants' specific life situations.

6. An evaluation of the success of the session in accomplishing its objectives should be made.

7. At the end of the session a sense of closure needs to be provided by the coordinator. This may be achieved by a short, fun, involving experience. Or the coordinator may simply say that the training exercise is over.

DESIGNING A SKILL-TRAINING SESSION

A skill-training program could involve any number and combination of the exercises presented in this book. It could consist of a single exercise or of several exercises drawn from different chapters. It could last a few minutes or several days. Whatever the length of the session and the number of exercises used, the basic design of the training process is the same. The following elements need to be considered when the coordinator designs a skill-training session:

1. The coordinator–participant relationship must be examined. Useful questions to be cleared up include: What is the purpose of the session? Why is the coordinator conducting it? What is the contract between the coordinator and the participants? What is the relationship between the coordinator and the participants? Your motivation as coordinator, hidden agendas (if any), explicit and implicit assumptions about the session and the participants, and your limitations and competencies should be reviewed. It is also helpful to know the following information about the participants:
   a. Expectations: What do the participants hope, believe, or fear will happen or not happen?
   b. Experience: What kind of previous training have the participants had?
   c. Relevance: How might the learnings be used after the session?
   d. Relationships: What are the participants' past and future relationships with each other?
   e. Needs: What specific learnings, and what general kinds of learnings, do the participants want or need?
   f. Vital data: sex, age, marital status, general attitudes, physical or emotional problems and pressures, back-home support possibilities, and so on.
   g. Motivation: What is the level of the participants' motivation?
   h. Recruitment: How were the participants recruited? Did they all voluntarily agree to attend the session?

2. The desired outcomes of the session should be specified; they are usually discussed as objectives or goals. They should specify who is to be trained and what is to be the direction and magnitude of the desired learning. Clearly specified goals are useful when you are deciding upon the components of the session and its evaluation. All the criteria for clear goals given in Chapter 4 are of importance when you are stating the session's objectives. Participants should be able to spell out the learnings they will try to achieve.

3. Detail the constraints on the session. These include the time periods available, the location, the facilities, and your range of competencies.

4. Generate a list of alternative exercises and activities that can be used in the skill-training session. These alternatives may include a variety of exercises and theory sessions. This list can be put together from two sources: the desired outcomes of the session and the resources and preferences of the coordinator(s). All the exercises in this book and in *Reaching Out* are possibilities.

5. Make a tentative design for the session. Evaluate it in terms of these questions:

    a. Is it appropriate for accomplishing the desired outcomes?

    b. Are the activities within your range of competencies?

    c. Is there an opportunity for participants to express their needs or expectations or both?

    d. Does it enable the participants to make the transition from the "outside" world to the session and back to the "outside" world?

    e. Does it encourage the transfer of learnings?

    f. Does it have high personal relevance for the participants, and will it enable them to function better in their day-to-day life?

    g. If there is more than one coordinator, does it allow time for you to check signals with each other?

    h. Are high- and low-tension activities appropriately placed within the design?

    i. Are the assumptions about the skill and background of the participants appropriate?

    j. Does the overall design provide a sense of continuity, appropriate transitions among activities, a good "flow"?

    k. Are participants able to see the relationship between the exercises and the desired outcomes of the session?

    l. Does it allow for a logical flow of experiences?

    m. Does it offer flexibility in case of unexpected and emerging needs.

    n. Is it consistent with the principles of experiential learning?

    o. Is there opportunity for ongoing participant feedback and evaluation?

    p. Are you prepared to recognize and deal with unanticipated learning outcomes?

    q. Are all the necessary materials and facilities available?

6. Make sure you are highly committed to the final design. If there is more than one coordinator, assign responsibilities. Arrange for the materials and facilities.

7. If there is more than one coordinator, assess how you function as a staff. See if any team development needs to take place among the staff before the skill-training session begins.

EVALUATION

Evaluation is the process of determining how successful—or unsuccessful—a group was in achieving its goal or objective. In the case of a skill-training session it is the process by which evidence is gathered about whether the desired outcomes of the session were accomplished, what unanticipated learnings were accomplished, how the activities involved in the session contributed to its success or failure, and what the coordinator(s) could do to improve their competencies. In an evaluation there must be a clear, operational statement of the desired outcomes, ways to measure how nearly the desired outcomes were achieved and what activities and coordinator behaviors contributed to the session's success or failure, time for the participants to give feedback on the effectiveness of the session, and time following the session for the data to be analyzed and conclusions drawn.

In evaluation it is helpful to know such things as the emotional reactions of the participants (how they feel now), the specific or significant learnings the participants have obviously achieved, the amount of increased participant competence in performing the skills, what sort of future experiences the participants now see the need for, the degree to which the desired outcomes were accomplished, the participants' reactions to various parts of the session, and what the coordinator(s) did that was helpful or unhelpful to the participants.

A variety of data-collection procedures can be used by the coordinator(s) to evaluate a session: interviews, general statements made by the participants, questionnaire responses, observation of how skills were applied, and so on. All sessions do not have to be evaluated at a high level of proficiency, but more than the general impressions of the coordinator(s) should be used. At the very least, the coordinator(s) should be able to direct the same session in the future in a more effective and efficient way.

HELPFUL GUIDELINES

In conducting the exercises in this book the coordinator will have a set of general responsibilities. These include:

1. organizing the materials, procedures, and facilities she will need in order to manage the exercise.

2. introducing, ending, and tying together the experiences involved in the exercise.

3. keeping time in a task-oriented way in order to prevent the participants from getting sidetracked.

4. restating and calling attention to the main learnings of the exercise, which include relating the experiences to the theory.

5. setting a climate of experimentation, acceptance, openness, and warmth so that participants will be encouraged to try out new skills and improve their competencies.

6. serving as an anchor point by being reliable, knowledgeable, trustworthy, and responsible.

7. modeling the skills he wishes to teach.

8. following the general outlines of experiential learning.

9. being enthusiastic about the value of the exercise.

10. knowing and understanding the material well.

11. making sure everyone understands her instructions and responsibilities.

12. being sensitive to the differences in participation, needs, and styles of the participants.

13. remaining flexible so that the preplanned procedures do not interfere with the participants' learning.

14. enjoying himself and making sure that he also learns and benefits from the exercises.

Appendix B

Ethics of Experiential Learning

All learning activities require a code of ethics, either implicit or explicit. A great deal of attention has been paid to the ethics of growth-group leaders, but little consideration has been given to the ethics of conducting experiential-learning activities. Some of the ethical issues relevant to the type of skill-training exercises included in this book are as follows.

The most serious ethical issue involved in teaching group skills is determining the value and necessity of such cognitive and behavioral changes for the participants. Attempting to teach another person carries with it a responsibility not to work against that person's best interests and needs. It should also be noted that the only way to promote ethical standards in teaching–learning relationships is for the teachers to enforce their code of ethics on themselves and to use good judgment in what they do. As long as a teacher's behavior is based on care, respect, and regard for participants, ethical violations will be minimized. Persons leading experiential-learning activities must therefore develop a personal code of ethics to which they hold themselves accountable. The following points should provoke some thought as to what that personal code of ethics might include.

THE CONTRACT: INFORMED CONSENT AND MUTUAL AGREEMENT

1. The coordinator's intentions and objectives should be clearly communicated to the participants. The participants should understand that they are going to participate in an experiential exercise in which they will be

expected to examine their own behavior and the behavior of others, and analyze the behaviors for purposes of learning.

2. The nature of the contract should be easily understood by the coordinator and the participants. The number of experiences, the length of each session, and the appropriateness and the objectives of each exercise should be agreed on.

3. The point at which the contract is terminated should be clear to both the coordinator and the participants.

THE ACTIVITIES

1. The participants' freedom of choice should be respected. Participation should be voluntary. A participant's freedom to choose whether or not to become involved in an exercise or part of an exercise should be respected. This freedom includes advising the participants on how they can say "no" to the instructions of the coordinator.

2. The coordinator should have an explicit reason for conducting the exercise and be prepared to state it publicly.

3. Only exercises the coordinator is competent to direct should be conducted. If the coordinator lacks certification and competence in psychotherapy, for example, exercises aimed at exposing deep psychodynamics of participants should not be held (and there are no such exercises in this book).

4. The coordinator should present relevant theory and research when it is appropriate to the participants' learning and increased effectiveness.

5. The coordinator should be constantly aware of his behavior styles and personal needs, and deal with them productively in the performance of his role. He should also be aware of the impact of his needs and style on the participants.

6. The coordinator should assess all experiences by discussing the participants' feelings and reactions to them and by asking the participants what can be learned from the experiences. Adequate time must be programmed into the design of the session for this purpose.

7. The coordinator should not initiate confrontations between participants, which may damage their future relationship. This does not mean that coordinators should discourage risk taking in giving feedback, the making of honest disclosures, or attempts to face conflicts and improve the relationship. It simply means that confrontations should originate with the participants, not the coordinator.

8. If any personal information is revealed, the coordinator should make sure that the possibility of it being used in any way to damage the participants is minimized.

9. Ideally, the coordinator should be able to recognize symptoms of serious psychological stress and be able to make responsible decisions when such problems arise. At the very least, the coordinator should know where emergency psychological services are available.

10. Sessions should be evaluated in such a way that the coordinator receives feedback that will improve her performance. The sessions should be open to scrutiny by competent professionals interested in the effectiveness of experiential learning.

11. Follow-up interviews with the participants should be made possible so that the impact of the sessions on them can be assessed and their feelings and reactions to the sessions discussed.

THE COORDINATOR'S KNOWLEDGE, SKILLS, AND NEEDS

1. What the coordinator does needs to be based on empirically validated knowledge. Folklore, superstition, common sense, fads, popular gimmicks, and personal experiences are not adequate bases for teaching others. The coordinator should thoroughly understand the principles of experiential learning, the steps of skill development, and the knowledge that the exercise is designed to teach.

2. In addition to knowledge, the coordinator should have some experience in conducting exercises and some skills in helping participants reflect on their behavior, and that of others and learn from it. Knowing the steps of experiential learning is not enough: the coordinator should also have some skills and competencies in applying the principles of experiential learning.

3. At any time during the exercises the coordinator should be able to explain the theory she is operating by and the way in which current activities relate to the theory. This does not mean that the coordinator will not use her intuition and impulses when conducting an exercise, but she should be able to reconstruct the theory behind her intuitive actions.

4. The coordinator should be aware of his behavior style and personal needs and deal with them productively in the performance of the teaching role. He should also be aware of the impact of his personal needs and styles on the participants.

FINAL NOTES

The ability of most of you to conduct and coordinate experiential-learning exercises should improve if you apply the material in this book with intelligence and caution. If you are interested in other skill-building exercises, see Johnson (1978; 1981). You do not have to be a skilled teacher to conduct the exercises contained in this book, but constant concern for increasing your knowledge and skills in experiential learning is helpful.

The preceding statements are meant to be guidelines, not rigid rules. The only effective way to enforce ethical standards in educational activities is for the persons conducting the educational problems to enforce their code of ethics on themselves and use good judgment in what they do. Again, as long as a coordinator's behavior is based on care, respect, and regard for the participants, ethical violations will probably be avoided. It is hoped that the above guidelines will be provocative in helping the users of this book build a personal code of ethical conduct.

Appendix C

How to Compute a Group Average

To find a group average, simply total the individual scores of the group members and divide by the number of members in the group. Here is an example:

Members	Score
Tom	5
Jane	6
Dennis	4
Pat	7
Roger	3
David	6
Edythe	6
Dale	5
8 members	42

$$\text{Average} = 5.25$$
$$8\overline{)42.00}$$

Appendix D

Answers

FURNITURE FACTORY EXERCISE: SOLUTION
(See page 68)

The more directly Mr. Day involves the workers in the change, the more likely they are to support the change.

a. 5
b. 1
c. 3
d. 4
e. 2

HOLLOW SQUARE EXERCISE (See page 77)

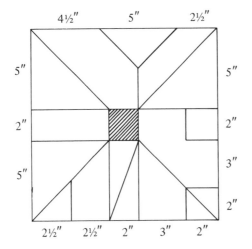

WINTER SURVIVAL EXERCISE (See page 111)

Background Information for Coordinator

None of the information here should be given to participants until after they have completed the decision-making parts of the exercise. Mid-January is the coldest time of the year in Minnesota and Manitoba. The first problem the survivors face, therefore, is to preserve their body heat and protect themselves against its loss. This problem can be met by building a fire, minimizing movement and exertion, using as much insulation as possible, and constructing a shelter.

The participants have just crash-landed. Many individuals tend to overlook the enormous shock reaction this has upon the human body, and the death of the pilot and copilot increases the shock. Decision making under such conditions is extremely difficult. Such a situation requires a strong emphasis upon the use of reasoning, not only for making decisions, but also for reducing the fear and panic every survivor would naturally feel. Shock is manifested in feelings of helplessness, loneliness, and hopelessness as well as in fear. These feelings have brought about more fatalities than perhaps any other cause in survival situations. Through the use of reasoning, hope for survival and the will to live can be generated. Certainly the state of shock means that the movement of the survivors should be at a minimum and that an attempt to calm them should be made.

Before taking off, a pilot always has to file a flight plan. The flight plan contains the vital information regarding the flight, such as the course, speed, estimated time of arrival, type of aircraft, and number of persons on board. Search-and-rescue operations would begin shortly after the failure of the plane to appear at its destination at its estimated time of arrival.

The twenty miles to the nearest known town is a long walk even under ideal conditions, particularly if one is not used to walking such distances. Under the circumstances of being in shock, being dressed in city clothes, and having deep snow in the woods and a variety of water barriers to cross, to attempt to walk out would mean almost certain death from freezing and exhaustion. At temperatures of minus twenty-five to minus forty the loss of body heat through exertion is a very serious matter.

Once the survivors have found ways in which to keep warm, their immediate problem is to attract the attention of search planes and search parties. Thus, all the items the group has salvaged must be assessed for their value in signaling the group's whereabouts.

WINTER SURVIVAL EXERCISE: ANSWER KEY

Item	Experts' Ranking	Your Ranking	Difference Score
Ball of steel wool	2		
Newspapers (one per person)	8		
Compass	12		
Hand ax	6		
Cigarette lighter (without fluid)	1		
Loaded .45-caliber pistol	9		
Sectional air map made of plastic	11		
Twenty-by-twenty-foot piece of heavy-duty canvas	5		
Extra shirt and pants for each survivor	3		
Can of shortening	4		
Quart of 100-proof whiskey	10		
Family-size chocolate bar (one per person)	7		
Total			

Explanation of Answer Key

The following ranking of the survivors' items was made on the basis of information provided by Mark Wanvig and Roger Johnson and supplemented by Rutstrum (1973). Wanvig was an instructor in survival training for three years in the reconnaissance school in the 101st Division of the U.S. Army and later an instructor in wilderness survival for four years at the Twin City Institute for Talented Youth. He is now conducting wilderness-survival programs for Minneapolis teachers. Johnson is a national expert on environmental education.

1. *Cigarette lighter (without fluid)*. The gravest danger facing the group is exposure to the cold. The greatest need is for a source of warmth and the second greatest need is for signaling devices. This makes building a fire the first order of business. Without matches something is needed to produce sparks to start a fire. Even without fluid the cigarette lighter can be used to produce sparks. The fire will provide not only warmth but also smoke for daytime signaling and firelight for nighttime signaling.

2. *Ball of steel wool*. To make a fire, the survivors need a means of catching the sparks made by the cigarette lighter. Steel wool is the best substance with which to catch a spark and support a flame, even if it is a little wet.

3. *Extra shirt and pants for each survivor*. Clothes are probably the most versatile items one can have in a situation like this. Besides adding warmth to the body they can be used for shelter, signaling, bedding, bandages, string when unraveled, and tinder to make fires. Even maps can be drawn on them. The versatility of clothes and the need for fires, signaling devices, and warmth make these items third in importance.

4. *Can of shortening*. This item has many uses—the most important being that a

mirrorlike signaling device can be made from the lid. After shining the lid with the steel wool, the survivors can use it to produce an effective reflector of sunlight. A mirror is the most powerful tool they have for communicating their presence. In sunlight, a simple mirror can generate five to seven million candlepower. The reflected sunbeam can be seen beyond the horizon. Its effectiveness is somewhat limited by the trees, but one member of the group could climb a tree and use the mirror to signal search planes. If the survivors had no other means of signaling than this, they would still have a better than 80-percent chance of being rescued within the first twenty-four hours.

Other uses for this item are as follows: The shortening can be rubbed on exposed areas of the body, such as the face, lips, and hands, for protection from the cold. In desperation it could be eaten in small amounts. When melted into an oil the shortening is helpful in starting fires. When soaked into a piece of cloth, melted shortening will produce an effective candlewick. The can is useful in melting snow to produce drinking water. Even in winter water is important, as the body loses water in many ways, such as through perspiration, respiration, and shock. This water must be replenished, because dehydration affects one's ability to make clear decisions. The can is also useful as a cup.

5. *Twenty-by-twenty-foot piece of heavy-duty canvas.* The cold makes some form of shelter necessary. The canvas can be part of a shelter, protecting the survivors from the wind and possible snow. Spread on a frame and secured, it could make a good tent as well as a ground cover. Rigged as a wind screen, it could hold heat. Its squareness, contrasting with the surrounding terrain, might also be spotted in an air search, and this makes it an important signaling device.

6. *Hand ax.* The survivors need a continuous supply of wood in order to maintain the fire. The ax is useful in obtaining wood, and also for clearing a sheltered campsite, cutting boughs for ground insulation, and constructing a frame for the shelter.

7. *Family-size chocolate bars (one per person).* To gather wood for the fire and to set up signals, the survivors need energy. The chocolate will supply the energy to sustain them for some time. Because it contains mostly carbohydrates, it supplies energy without making digestive demands upon the body.

8. *Newspapers (one per person).* The newspaper can be used for starting a fire. It will also serve as an insulator: when rolled up and placed under the clothes around a person's legs and arms, it provides dead-air space for extra protection from the cold. The survivors can use the paper for recreation by reading it, memorizing it, folding it, or tearing it. They can roll it into a cone and yell through it as a signal device. They can also spread it around an area to help signal a rescue party.

9. *Loaded .45-caliber pistol.* The pistol provides a sound-signaling device. (The international distress signal is three shots fired in rapid succession.) There have been numerous cases of survivors going undetected because they were too weak to make a loud enough noise to attract attention. The butt of the pistol can be used as a hammer. The powder from the shells will assist in fire building. By placing a small bit of cloth in a cartridge emptied of its bullet, one can start a fire by firing the gun at dry wood on the ground. At night the muzzle blast of the gun is visible, and this provides another means of signaling.

The pistol's advantages are counterbalanced by its dangerous disadvantages. Anger, frustration, impatience, irritability, and lapses of rationality may increase as the group waits to be rescued. The availability of a lethal weapon is a substantial danger to the group under these conditions. Although the pistol could be used for hunting, it would take a highly skilled marksman to kill an animal with it. Even then the animal would have to be transported through the snow to the crash area, which would probably consume more energy than would be advisable.

10. *Quart of 100-proof whiskey.* The only uses of the whiskey are as an aid in fire building and as a fuel. A torch could be made from a piece of clothing soaked in the whiskey and attached to an upright pole. The danger of the whiskey is that someone might try to drink it when it is cold. Alcohol takes on the temperature it is exposed to, and a drink of it at minus thirty degrees Fahrenheit would freeze a person's esophagus and stomach and do considerable damage to the mouth. Drinking it warm would cause dehydration. Alcohol, furthermore, mixes badly with cold because it dilates the blood vessels in the skin. This results in chilled blood being carried back to the heart, which in turn chills the heart and contributes to a rapid loss of body heat. An intoxicated person is much more likely to get hypothermia than a nonintoxicated person. The bottle may be used to store heated water.

11. *Compass.* Because the compass may also encourage some survivors to try to walk to the nearest town, it too is a dangerous item. The only redeeming feature of the compass is the possible use of its glass top as a reflector of sunlight to signal search planes, but this would be the least effective of the potential signaling devices available. That it might tempt survivors to walk away from the crash site makes it the least desirable of the twelve items.

12. *Sectional air map made of plastic.* This item is dangerous because it will encourage individuals to attempt to walk to the nearest town—thereby condemning them to almost certain death.

DANGERS OF SOME COMMON DRUGS: EXPERT'S RANKING* (See page 118)

To score your individual or group's ranking, take the absolute difference between your rank and the expert's rank (ignoring plus or minus signs), then total the difference scores. The lower the total score, the more accurate the ranking. Since research is continually being conducted on these drugs, and since the expert's ranking is somewhat dated, you may wish to consult with local experts concerning their ranking of the dangerousness of these drugs.

Item	Experts' Ranking	Your Ranking	Difference Score
Alcohol	1		
Barbiturates and hypnotics	2		
Cigarette smoking (tobacco)	8		
Glue sniffing	5		
Speed (methamphetamine and dexedrine)	4		
Heroin, codeine, morphine, and other opiates	6		
marijuana	9		
cocaine	3		
LSD and other hallucinogens	7		_____
Total			

* This exercise is based on information given in Samuel Irwin, *Drugs of Abuse: An Introduction to Their Actions and Potential Hazards* (Beloit, Wisc.: Student Association for the Study of Hallucinogens, 1973).

1. Alcohol has high potential for psychological and physical dependence, greatly impairs judgment and coordination (a leading cause of driving accidents), increases aggressiveness and violent behavior, often produces marked social deterioration, and causes irreversible damage to the brain, liver, and other body tissues. The withdrawal symptoms (delirium tremens) from alcohol abuse are also often life-threatening and difficult to treat. It is possible to die from an overdose of alcohol. The dangers of alcohol increase when used in combination with other drugs.

2. Barbiturates have high potential for psychological and physical dependence, greatly impair memory, judgment, vigilance, and coordination; produce marked social deterioration as well as mental deterioration; can be taken intravenously; increase aggressiveness and violent behavior; and, when taken in coma-producing dosages, result in tissue damage. Hypnotics are similar to alcohol and barbiturates in their overall effects and dependence liability. There is a greater danger of death from overdose from hypnotics than from barbiturates.

3. Cocaine impairs memory, judgment, vigilance, and perception. It can lead to both physical and mental deterioration as well as social deterioration. It increases tendencies toward violence. Special hazards include the possible use of unsterile materials to inject cocaine into one's bloodstream (which may lead to hepatitis and septicemia), the rapid loss of control after taking the drug, and the possibility of death by overdose. Cocaine is even more physiologically addicting than "speed."

4. Methamphetamine and dexedrine (called "speed") have high psychological dependence liability (they are too pleasurable). They also predictably produce a paranoid-schizophrenic state with greatly impaired judgment, excitement, and a tendency for violence after repeated use of doses three or more times what a physician might prescribe. Users are tempted to seek more intense effects by taking the drugs by injection. This leads to further impairment of functioning, a high probability of loss of control, great physiological impairment from loss of sleep and appetite, a possibility of hepatitis (serious inflammation of the liver) or septicemia (infection by bacteria) from the use of unsterile materials, and a probable need for protective hospitalization.

5. Glue sniffing (with toluene as the solvent) is considerably less dangerous than previously thought. But although its effects last only a short time, it can produce a sudden loss of control and consciousness, leading to possible death from respiratory depression and arrest. There is evidence for tissue damage with solvents such as gasoline, benzene, and chloroform, but not with toluene.

6. Heroin and related narcotics (codeine) do not impair coordination and judgment in normal doses, do not produce tissue damage, and are more likely to inhibit aggressive behavior. When taken intravenously, these drugs are potentially very addictive, both psychologically and physically, and their continued use can lead to social deterioration. But the physical dependence would be of little consequence if the drugs were freely available, and sufficient tolerance develops to the depressant effects so that it is possible to function more productively under the influence of heroin than with alcohol or barbiturates. The main danger from heroin (or morphine) is acute respiratory failure and death from overdosage during initial use, as a very narrow margin exists then between the effective dose and the lethal dose. Since illicit supplies vary greatly in potency, this represents a serious danger. Because unsterile materials are often used for injection, there is also the possibility of developing hepatitis and septicemia.

7. LSD-25 and other hallucinogens (mescaline, for example) can cause psychotic reactions, but such occurrences are relatively rare (less than 1 percent of volunteers in

clinical settings have prolonged adverse reactions, and the rate for the general population of illicit users is probably less than 5 percent). LSD is not an addictive drug in the usual sense; it is taken intermittently, and its use is usually gradually discontinued. The hallucinogens produce no physical dependence, but pose hazards in the psychosocial realm, triggering psychotic or depressive reactions in susceptible individuals, and opening up the possibility of flashbacks of LSD-like effects even months after the last dose (attributed by some clinicians to hysterical reactions associated with unresolved conflicts). For some, the LSD experience can profoundly modify personal attitudes and life-style, not necessarily detrimentally. The lethal dose is so high that no human deaths have been reported from overdosage.

8. Cigarette smoking causes a high incidence of irreversible tissue damage (to lungs, heart, and blood vessels), and cancer formation accompanying prolonged use of cigarettes is common. These hazards greatly reduce the life span and often debilitate the individual long before death.

9. Marijuana causes fewer untoward reactions from its use requiring treatment or hospitalization than any other type of psychoactive drug. Also, marijuana is more prone to reduce aggressiveness than to increase it. Psychological dependence on the drug is not as great a hazard as it is with alcohol; there is little tolerance development, no danger of physiological dependence, and no significant tissue damage associated with its use. In small and moderate doses, there seems to be only minor impairment of judgment or coordination, and hallucinogeniclike effects are relatively difficult to achieve by smoking (they can occur when the drug is taken orally, a route that leads to a much less predictable drug effect). As with LSD, the lethal dosage of marijuana is so high that it is extremely difficult to kill oneself from overdosage.

THEY'LL NEVER TAKE US ALIVE EXERCISE:
ANSWER KEY (See page 121)

Item	Experts' Ranking	Your Ranking	Difference Score
swimming	5		
railroads	7		
police work	11		
home appliances	9		
alcohol	2		
nuclear power	12		
smoking	1		
motor vehicles	3		
pesticides	15		
handguns	4		
bicycles	8		
firefighting	10		
mountain climbing	13		
vaccinations	14		
surgery	6	_____	
Total			

BROKEN SQUARES EXERCISE: DIRECTIONS FOR
MAKING A SET OF SQUARES (See page 148)

For each five-member group you will need a set of five envelopes containing pieces of cardboard that have been cut in different patterns and that, when properly arranged with pieces from some of the other four envelopes, will form five squares of equal size. To prepare a set, cut out five cardboard squares of equal size, approximately six by six inches. Place the squares in a row and make them as below, penciling the letters *a, b, c,* etc., lightly so that they can later be erased.

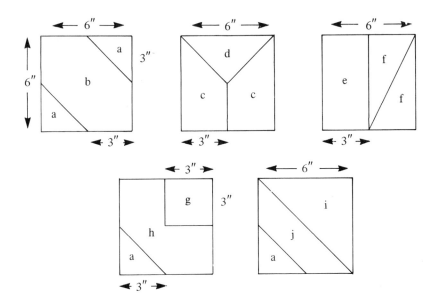

The lines should be so drawn that when the pieces are cut out, all pieces marked *a* will be exactly the same size, the pieces marked *c* will be the same size, and the pieces marked *f* will be the same size. By using multiples of three inches, several combinations will be possible that will enable participants to form one or two squares, but one combination is possible that will form five squares six by six inches.

After drawing the lines of the six by six inch squares and labeling them with the lowercase letters, cut each square as marked into smaller pieces to make the parts of the puzzle.

Mark the five envelopes *A, B, C, D,* and *E,* and distribute the carboard pieces among them as follows:

Envelope A has pieces i, h, e.
Envelope B has pieces a, a, a, c.
Envelope C has pieces a, j.
Envelope D has pieces d, f.
Envelope E has pieces g, b, f, c.

Erase the penciled letter from each piece and write on it instead its appropriate envelope letter. This relabeling will make it easy, when a group has completed the task, to return the pieces to the proper envelope for later use.

GOAL STRUCTURES EXERCISE: ANSWERS
(See page 151)

Squares: 40
Biangles: 11
Triangles: 18

BEWISE COLLEGE PROBLEM: SOLUTION
(See page 189)

Name	Background	Education Degree	Teaching Experience	Public-Relations Experience	Administrative Experience
David Wolcott	Black American	Master's	13 years	*none*	8 years
Roger Thornton	*Upper-class family*	B.A., master's	7 years	9 years; politician	16 years
Edythe Holubec	Community-center director	*none*	8 years	2 years	7 years
Frank Pierce	Neighborhood-center worker; community relations	Master's	*none*	14 years	14 years
Helen Johnson	Childhood in slums	B.A., master's	4 years	5 years	15 years
Keith Clement	Volunteer work; author of a book	B.A.	5 years	13 years	*none*

Andrews College is the smallest college in the state, and therefore it had a completely black-American student body in 1952.

As is evident from the table, all candidates but Helen Johnson are disqualified because they lack one of the qualifications outlined in the data sheets.

SOLSTICE-SHENANIGANS MYSTERY: SOLUTION

The Solstice Shenanigans Mystery Exercise appears on page 195. The painting by Artisimisso was stolen by Mr. Handsome, who took it with him when he left the party at 9:50. He took the painting because he was a kleptomaniac.

LIEPZ AND BOUNZ EXERCISE: SOLUTION

The Liepz and Bounz Exercise is on page 196. David jogged from Farmland to Muncie in 1 (5/5) jumpz.

SQUARE ARRANGEMENT I: ONE-WAY COMMUNICATION (See page 208)

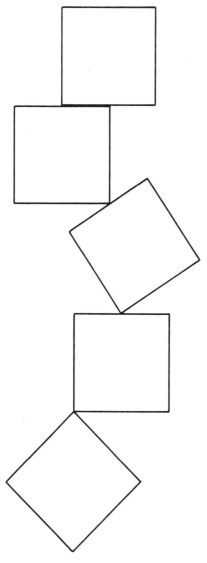

Instructions: Study the arrangement above. With your back to the group members, instruct them on how to draw the squares. Begin with the top square and describe each in succession, taking particular note of the placement of each in relation to the preceding one. No questions are allowed.

SQUARE ARRANGEMENT II: TWO-WAY COMMUNICATION (See page 208)

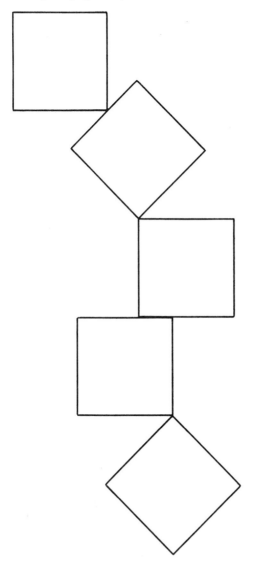

Instructions: Study the arrangement above. Facing the group, instruct the members on how to draw the squares. Begin with the top square and describe each in succession, taking particular note of the placement of each in relation to the preceding one. Answer all questions from participants and repeat your descriptions if necessary.

The Stranded in the Desert Exercise appears on page 237.

Item	Experts' Ranking	Your Ranking	Difference Score
magnetic compass	12		
20-by-20 feet piece of light blue heavy duty canvas	7		
book, *Plants of the Desert*	10		
rear-view mirror	1		
large knife	5		
flashlight (four battery size)	8		
one jacket per person	2		
one transparent plastic ground cloth (6-by-4-feet) per person	4		
loaded .38-caliber pistol	9		
one two-quart plastic canteen full of water per person	3		
accurate map of the area	11		
large box of kitchen matches	6		
Total			

Score your group's ranking by finding the absolute difference between your ranking and the experts' ranking. An absolute difference is found by recording the difference between the two rankings while ignoring all plus or minus signs. After finding all the absolute differences, sum them. The lower your total score, the more accurate your ranking.

Stranded in the Desert: Rationale for Experts' Ranking

The group has just been through a traumatic situation that has had a shocking impact on all members. The fact that your adviser and the driver were killed would increase the shock reaction. Most, if not all, members of your group need to receive treatment for shock. Five of the more important problems for your group are as follows (Nesbitt, Pond, & Allen, 1959). One vital problem for the group members is dehydration from exposure to the sun, from bodily activity (causing perspiration and respiration), and from the hot dry air circulating next to the skin. To prevent dehydration the group members should: (1) remain calm to reduce loss of moisture through respiration, (2) wear as many clothes as you can to reduce the loss of moisture through perspiration and having the dry desert air circulate next to your skin (by wearing sufficient clothes to keep the desert air away from your skin you can lengthen your survival time by at least a day), (3) stay in the shade, (4) minimize movement, especially during the day, and (5) drink as much water as you can. Any activity that increases heartbeat, respiration, and perspiration will speed up dehydration. Taking care to remain calm and in the shade, the group could probably survive three days without water. The need for clothes makes the jackets important. The need for shade makes the canvas important. To survive you must keep your body properly hydrated either with adequate water or by keeping body heat production down and keeping desert heat (from sun, air, and ground reflection) out. Once the jackets are on and the sunshade is up, everyone should be as calm and inactive as possible.

Another vital problem is signalling search parties of your whereabouts so that you may be rescued. The items that may be used to signal your presence are the mirror, the canvas, the flashlight, the revolver, and a fire (matches). The mirror is the most important signalling device the group has. As Nesbitt, Pond, and Allen (1959) state, "A signal mirror is the best, the simplest, the most important piece of survival equipment ever invented for the desert." In sunlight the mirror can generate five to seven million candle power of light, which may be seen beyond the horizon. It pays to flash the mirror at the horizon even when no plane is in view; search planes have turned toward a mirror flash even when the survivors have neither seen nor heard them. The canvas, when spread out to make a shelter, not only can reduce the temperature underneath it by as much as 20 degrees, but it can also be easily spotted from the air because it contrasts with the terrain. The flashlight provides a reliable and quick night signalling device. The pistol is an important sound signalling device, since speech becomes seriously impaired due to dehydration. In the desert setting there have been numerous occurrences of searchers not detecting the people they were looking for because the survivors could not make loud enough noises to attract the searchers' attention. There are important disadvantages to having the revolver in the hands of a group member who may become hysterical due to the trauma of the situation or delusional due to dehydration. Finally, building a fire at night and using smoke columns during the day will help attract the attention of searchers. "A column of smoke by day, a pillar of fire by night" is a Biblical quotation worth remembering for desert signalling.

The third major problem is obtaining as much drinkable water as possible. The water you have in your canteens is enough to keep you rational for a while, but not enough to extend your survival time. That is, the water in the canteens is enough to hold off the effects of dehydration for a while; without water, within 24 hours you can expect to have impatience, nausea, and sleepiness interfere with rational decision-making. The only way in which you may obtain purified water to drink from the shallow water hole nearby is to build a solar still. The still is built by stretching the ground-clothes a few inches above the waterhole and tilting them so that they drain into the canteens. The knife is helpful in cutting the stakes necessary to arrange the ground-clothes. When the sun shines through the plastic onto the water, condensation forms on the underside of the plastic. This moisture is distilled and purified water.

The fourth problem is protecting yourself from the cold at night. Although the desert is hot during the day, it still gets cold at night. The jackets become important to protect the group members from the cold, as do the matches (to build a fire), and the canvas (to provide a shelter).

The fifth problem is gathering food if the group is not rescued in the first few days. It is important not to eat protein, as it takes considerable water to digest protein and flush out the waste products. The book on plants will be helpful in obtaining food. Hunting for animals, furthermore, would cause dehydration and would do far more harm than good.

If the group decides to walk out, traveling only at night, all members will probably be dead by the second day. They will have walked less than thirty-three miles during the two nights. If group members decide to walk during the day, they will probably be dead by the next morning, after walking less than twelve miles. For the group to walk out, having just gone through a traumatic experience that has had a considerable impact on the body, having few if any members who have walked forty-five miles before, and having to carry the canvas and wear the jackets to prevent dehydration, would be disastrous. One further fact of great importance: Once the members start walking, they will be much harder to spot by search parties. The compass and the map, therefore, are not helpful to the group's survival.

FALLOUT SHELTER EXERCISE: ANSWERS*
(See page 246)

__1__ Containers of water. (The average person would need at least 1 quart of liquid per day. Each person should be allowed to drink according to need since studies have shown that nothing is gained by limiting the liquids below the amount demanded by the body. Two weeks is probably the maximum time needed to stay in the shelter. After that, other sources of water could be found.)

__2__ Canned and dried foods. (Enough food should be on hand to feed everyone for two weeks, if possible. However, most people can get along on about half as much food as usual and can survive for several days without any. Therefore, this is not as important as the water.)

__3__ 1 large and 1 small garbage can with lids. (Next to water and food, the next most important concern is sanitation. Poor sanitation will attract diseases and vermin. The small garbage can can be used as a toilet and the large garbage can can be used to store garbage and human wastes until they can be taken outside and buried. Burial of the garbage is important to prevent spread of disease by rats or insects.)

__4__ First-aid kit and iodine and medicines. (Useful if anyone gets hurt or falls ill; should include medicine for anyone with chronic illness. The iodine can be used to sterilize water.)

__5__ Battery powered radio. (Useful for obtaining information about what is happening outside the shelter and for information on when it is safe to come out. Useful for contact with outside world.)

__6__ Soap and towels. (Useful and important for sanitation.)

__7__ Liquid chlorine bleach. (Useful for sprinkling in the toilet to keep down odors and germs; it could also be used to sterilize any water which has become cloudy and thereby might contain bacteria.)

__8__ Matches and candles. (They would help illuminate the shelter and thus make it more comfortable, particularly since there is not likely to be any natural source of light or electricity available.)

__9__ Blankets. (They would be used for heat and comfort; would be of important but moderate use.)

__10__ Flashlight and batteries. (Useful for illumination.)

* This exercise is based on information in *Protection in the Nuclear Age.* (Washington, D.C.: Department of Defense, Defense Civil Preparedness Agency, Feb. 1977.)

_11_ Cooking and eating utensils. (Useful in preparing and serving foods, but not essential.)

_12_ Broom. (Useful for brushing radioactive fallout off anyone who had to leave the shelter for emergency reasons before they reentered.)

_13_ Canned heat stove. (Useful if a heat supply is needed, however, it can only be used if there is adequate ventilation for the fumes; it could be dangerous.)

_14_ Geiger Counter. (Unnecessary. It could be used to check level of radiation outside the shelter to determine when it is safe to emerge, but the same information and more can be obtained from the radio. Also, fallout particles are visible and the radiation from them is given off quickly, so danger from radiation could be reduced by waiting 24—48 hours after the large particles have stopped falling.)

_15_ Foam fire extinguisher. (Useful for fighting fires outside the shelter but could not be used within the shelter because of danger from the fumes.)

CREATIVITY PROBLEM: SOLUTION (See page 269)

The solution of this problem is based upon the creative insight of going outside the obvious boundaries of the dots.

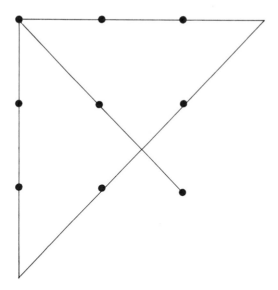

JOE DOODLEBUG EXERCISE: HINTS (See page 269)

1. Joe does not always have to face the food in order to eat it.
2. Joe can jump sideways and backward, as well as forward.
3. Read the problem again: Joe was moving east when the food was presented.

JOE DOODLEBUG EXERCISE: SOLUTION (See page 269)

At the moment Joe's master set down the food, Joe had already jumped once to the east. He therefore has to jump sideways three times more to the east, and once sideways back to the west, landing on top of the food. He can now eat.

MAKING A PROFIT EXERCISE: BUYER PROFIT SHEET

The Making a Profit Exercise appears on page 293.

Oil		Gas		Coal	
Price	*Profit*	*Price*	*Profit*	*Price*	*Profit*
A	$4,000	A	$2,000	A	$1,000
B	3,500	B	1,750	B	875
C	3,000	C	1,500	C	750
D	2,500	D	1,250	D	625
E	2,000	E	1,000	E	500
F	1,500	F	750	F	375
G	1,000	G	500	G	250
H	500	H	250	H	125
I	0	I	0	I	0

The nine prices for each commodity are represented by the letters A to I. Next to each price is the profit you would make for reselling each commodity if you bought it at that price.

You can say anything you wish during negotiations, but you may *not* show this profit sheet to the seller you are negotiating with.

MAKING A PROFIT EXERCISE: SELLER PROFIT SHEET

Oil		Gas		Coal	
Price	*Profit*	*Price*	*Profit*	*Price*	*Profit*
A	0	A	0	A	0
B	125	B	250	B	500
C	250	C	500	C	1,000
D	375	D	750	D	1,500
E	500	E	1,000	E	2,000
F	625	F	1,250	F	2,500
G	750	G	1,500	G	3,000
H	875	H	1,750	H	3,500
I	$1,000	I	$2,000	I	$4,000

The nine prices for each commodity are represented by the letters A to I. Next to each price is the profit you would make for each commodity if you sold it at that price.

You can say anything you wish during negotiations, but you may *not* show this profit sheet to the buyer you are negotiating with.

BATTLESHIP EXERCISE: MODEL FOR COORDINATOR
(See page 317)

	A	B	C	D	E	F	G	H	I	J
1										
2										
3										
4				1						
5			1	3	1					
6			1	5	1					
7			1	5	1					
8			1	3	1					
9				1						
10										

References

ALLEN, V. L. Situational factors in conformity. In L. Berkowitz (ed.), *Advances in experimental social psychology* (Vol. 2). New York: Academic Press, 1965.

ALLPORT, F. *Social psychology*. Boston: Houghton Mifflin, 1924.

ALLPORT, G. W., and POSTMAN, L. J. The basic psychology of rumor. *Transactions of New York Academic Sciences*, Series II, 1945, *8*, 61–81.

ARGYRIS, C. *Intervention theory and method*. Reading, Mass.: Addison-Wesley, 1970.

ARONSON, E. *The social animal*. San Francisco: W. H. Freeman, 1972.

ARONSON, E., BLANEY, N., STEPHAN, C., SIKES, J., and SNAPP, M. *The jigsaw classroom*. Beverly Hills, Calif.: Sage, 1978.

ASCH, S. E. Studies of independence and conformity: A minority of one against a unanimous majority. *Psychological Monographs*, 1956, *70*, 416.

BACH, G. R., and WYDEN, P. *The intimate enemy*. New York: Morrow, 1969.

BAHN, C. The interaction of creativity and social facilitation in creative problem solving (doctoral dissertation, Columbia University, 1964). *Dissertation Abstracts International*, 1964. (University Microfilms No. 65-7499).

BALDERSTON, G. *Group incentives, some variations in the use of group bonus and gang piece work*. Philadelphia: University of Pennsylvania Press, 1930.

BALES, R. F. *Interaction process analysis*. Reading, Mass.: Addison-Wesley, 1950.

———. Some uniformities of behavior in small social systems. In G. E. Swanson, T. M. Newcomb, and E. L. Hartley (eds.), *Readings in social psychology*. New York: Holt, 1952.

BALES, R. F., and BORGATTA, E. F. Size of group as a factor in the interaction profile. In A. P. Hare, E. F. Borgatta, and R. F. Bales (eds.), *Small groups*. New York: Knopf, 1955.

BANDURA, A. Vicarious processes: A case of no-trial learning. In L. Berkowitz (ed.), *Advances in experimental social psychology* (Vol. 2). New York: Academic Press, 1965.

———. *Principles of behavior modification*. New York: Holt, Rinehart & Winston, 1969.

BARNLUND, D. C. A comparative study of individual, majority and group judgment. *Journal of Abnormal and Social Psychology,* 1959, *58,* 55.

BARON, R. S., BARON, P. H., and MILLER, N. The relation between distraction and persuasion. *Psychological Bulletin,* 1973, *80,* 310–323.

BARTLETT, F. C. *Remembering.* Cambridge: Cambridge University Press, 1932.

BASS, B. *Leadership, psychology, and organizational behavior.* New York: Harper & Row, 1960.

BAVELAS, A. Morale and training of leaders. In G. Watson (ed.), *Civilian morale.* Boston: Houghton Mifflin, 1942.

————. A mathematical model for group structures. *Applied Anthropology,* 1948, *7,* 16–30.

BAVELAS, A., HOSTORF, A., GROSS, A., and KITE, W. Experiments on the alteration of group structure. *Journal of Experimental Social Psychology,* 1965, *1,* 55–70.

BECKHARD, R. *Organizational development.* Reading, Mass.: Addison-Wesley, 1969.

BECKHARD, R., and LAKE, D. G. Short and long-range effects of a team development effort. In H. A. Hornstein, B. A. Benedict, W. W. Burke, R. Lewicki, and M. G. Gindes (eds.), *Strategies of social intervention: A behavioral science analysis.* New York: Free Press, 1971.

BEISECKER, T. Communication and conflict in interpersonal negotiations. Paper presented to the Speech Communication Association, New York, 1969.

BEKHTEREV, W. Die ergebnisse des experiments auf dem gebiet der kollektiven reflexologie. *Zeitschrift für Angewandte Psychologie,* 1924.

BENNETT, E. Discussion, decision, commitment and consensus in "group decision." *Human Relations,* 1955, *8,* 251.

BERLYNE, D. Uncertainty and conflict: A point of contact between information-theory and behavior-theory concepts. *Psychological Review,* 1957, *64,* 329–339.

————. Notes on intrinsic motivation and intrinsic reward in relation to instruction. In J. Bruner (ed.), *Learning about learning* (Cooperative Research Monograph No. 15). Washington, D.C.: U.S. Department of Health, Education and Welfare, Office of Education, 1966.

BERSCHEID, E., and WALSTER, E. Physical attractiveness. In L. Berkowitz (ed.), *Advances in experimental social psychology* (Vol. 7). New York: Academic Press, 1974.

BIERMAN, R. Dimensions for interpersonal facilitation in psychotherapy in child development. *Psychological Bulletin,* 1969, *72,* 338–352.

BLAKE, R. R., and MOUTON, J. S. Comprehension of own and outgroup positions under intergroup competition. *Journal of Conflict Resolution,* 1961, *5,* 304–310.

————. Comprehension of points of commonality in competing solutions. *Sociometry,* 1962, *25,* 56–63.

————. The intergroup dynamics of win-lose conflict and problem-solving collaboration in union-management relations. In Muzafer Sherif (ed.), *Intergroup relations and leadership.* New York: John Wiley, 1962.

————. *Building a dynamic corporation through grid organization development.* Reading, Mass.: Addison-Wesley, 1969.

————. The fifth achievement. *Journal of Applied Behavioral Science,* 1970, *6,* 413–426.

BLANCHARD, F. A., WEIGEL, R. H., and COOK, S. W. The effect of relative competence of group members upon interpersonal attraction in cooperating interracial groups. *Journal of Personality and Social Psychology,* 1975, *32,* 519–530.

BOLEN, L., and TORRANCE, E. An experimental study of the influence of locus of control, dyadic interaction, and sex, on creative thinking. Paper presented at the American Educational Research Association, San Francisco, April 1976.

BONNER, H. *Group dynamics: Principles and applications.* New York: Ronald Press, 1959.

BOTKIN, B. *A Treasury of American Anecdotes.* New York: Random House, 1957.

BROWN, B. The effects of the need to maintain face on interpersonal bargaining. *Journal of Experimental Social Psychology,* 1968, *4,* 107–122.

BURKE, P. Leadership role differentiation. In C. McClintock (ed.), *Experimental social psychology.* New York: Holt, Rinehart & Winston, 1972.

BURKE, R. Methods of resolving interpersonal conflict. *Personnel Administration,* 1969 (July), 48–55.

———. Methods of resolving superior–subordinate conflict: The constructive use of subordinate differences and disagreements. *Organizational Behavior and Human Performance,* 1970, *5,* 393–411.

BUYS, C. Humans would do better without groups. *Personality and Social Psychology Bulletin,* 1978, *4,* 123–125.

BYRNE, D. Attitudes and attraction. In L. Berkowitz (ed.), *Advances in experimental social psychology* (Vol. 4). New York: Academic Press, 1969.

CARTWRIGHT, D. A field theoretical conception of power. In D. Cartwright (ed.), *Studies in social power.* Ann Arbor: University of Michigan, Institute for Social Research, 1959.

———. The nature of group cohesiveness. In D. Cartwright and A. Zander (eds.), *Group dynamics: Research and theory* (3rd ed.). New York: Harper & Row, 1968.

CARTWRIGHT, D., and ZANDER, A. (eds.). *Group dynamics: Research and theory* (3rd ed.). New York: Harper & Row, 1968.

CASSEL, R., and SHAFER, A. An experiment in leadership training. *Journal of Psychology,* 1961, *51,* 299–305.

CATTELL, R. New concepts for measuring leadership, in terms of group syntality. *Human Relations,* 1951, *4,* 161–184.

CHASNOFF, R. (ed.). *Structuring cooperative learning: The 1979 handbook.* Minneapolis: J & J Book Co., 1979.

CHERTKOFF, J. and ESSER, J. A review of experiments in explicit bargaining. *Journal of Experimental Social Psychology,* 1976, *12,* 464–487.

CHESLER, M., and FRANKLIN, J. Interracial and intergenerational conflict in secondary schools. Paper presented at the Annual Meeting of the American Sociological Association, Boston, August 1968.

CHRISTIE, R., and GEIS, F. *Studies in Machiavelianism.* New York: Academic Press, 1970.

COCH, L., and FRENCH, J. R. P. JR. Overcoming resistance to change. *Human Relations,* 1948, *1,* 512–533.

COHEN, M., and MARCH, J. *Leadership and ambiguity.* New York: McGraw-Hill, 1974.

COX, C. *The early mental traits of three hundred geniuses.* Stanford, Calif.: Stanford University Press, 1926.

DANCE, F. E. X. The "concept" of communication. *Journal of Communication,* 1970, *20,* 201–210.

DAVID, G. A., and HOUTMAN, S. E. *Thinking creatively: A guide to training imagination.* Madison: Wisconsin Research and Development Center for Cognitive Learning, 1968.

DECECCO, J., and RICHARDS, A. *Growing pains: Uses of school conflict.* New York: Aberdeen Press, 1974.

DeCecco, J., and Richards, A., Civil war in the high schools. *Psychology Today,* 175, 9 (November), 51–81.

Deutsch, M. A theory of cooperation and competition. *Human Relations,* 1949, 2, 129–152.

————. Trust and suspicion. *Journal of Conflict Resolution,* 1958, 2, 265–279.

————. The effect of motivational orientation upon trust and suspicion. *Human Relations,* 1960, *13,* 123–139.

————. Cooperation and trust: Some theoretical notes. In M. R. Jones (ed.), *Nebraska Symposium on Motivation.* Lincoln: University of Nebraska Press, 1962.

————. Conflicts: Productive and destructive. *Journal of Social Issues,* 1969, *25,* 7–43.

————. *The resolution of conflict.* New Haven: Yale University Press, 1973.

————. Equity, equality, and need: What determines which value will be used as the basis of distributive justice? *Journal of Social Issues,* 1975, *31,* 137–149.

————. Education and distributive justice: Some reflections on grading systems. *American Psychologist,* 1979, *34,* 391–401.

Deutsch, M., Canavan, D., and Rubin, J. The effects of size of conflict and sex of experimenter upon interpersonal bargaining. *Journal of Experimental Social Psychology,* 1971, *7,* 258–267.

Deutsch, M., and Lewicki, R. "Locking in" effects during a game of chicken. *Journal of Conflict Resolution,* 1970, *14,* 367–378.

DeVries, D., and Edwards, K. Learning games and student teams: Their effects on classroom process. *American Educational Research Journal,* 1973, *10,* 307–318.

Diesing, P. *Reason in society.* Urbana: University of Illinois Press, 1962.

Douglas, A. *Industrial peacemaking.* New York: Columbia University Press, 1962.

Dunnette, M. D., Campbell, J., and Jaastad, K. The effect of group participation on brainstorming effectiveness of two industrial samples. *Journal of Applied Psychology,* 1963, *47,* 30–37.

Eichler, G., and Merrill, R. Can social leadership be improved by instruction in its technique? *Journal of Educational Sociology,* 1933, *7,* 233–236.

Emerson, R. Deviation and rejection: An experimental replication. *American Sociological Review,* 1954, *19,* 688–693.

Falk, D., and Johnson, D. W. The effects of perspective-taking and egocentrism on problem solving in heterogeneous and homogeneous groups. *Journal of Social Psychology,* 1977, *102,* 63–72.

Fay, B. *Benjamin Franklin: The apostle of modern times.* Boston: Little, Brown, 1929.

Feshback, S. Aggression. In P. Mussen (ed.), *Carmichael's Manual of Child Psychology* (Vol. 2). New York: John Wiley, 1970.

Festinger, L. Informal social communication. *Psychological Review,* 1950, *57,* 271–292.

————. A theory of social comparison processes. *Human Relations,* 1954, *7,* 117–140.

————. *A theory of cognitive dissonance.* Evanston, Il.: Row, Peterson, 1957.

Fiedler, F. E. A contingency model of leadership effectiveness. In L. Berkowitz (ed.), *Advances in experimental social psychology* (Vol. 1). New York: Academic Press, 1964.

————. *A theory of leadership effectiveness.* New York: McGraw-Hill, 1967.

————. Style of circumstance: The leadership enigma. *Psychology Today,* 1969, *2*(10), 38–46.

Flanders, N. Some relationships among teacher influence, pupil attitudes, and achievement. In B. Biddle and W. Ellena (eds.), *Contemporary research on teacher effectiveness.* New York: Holt, Rinehart & Winston, 1964.

Fox, D., and Lorge, I. The relative quality of decisions written by individuals and by groups as the available time for problem solving is increased. *Journal of Social Psychology*, 1962, *57*, 227–242.

Frankfort, H., Frankfort, H., Wilson, J., and Jacobsen, T. *Before philosophy.* Baltimore: Penguin, 1949.

Freeman, E. *Social psychology.* New York: Holt, 1936.

French, J. R. P., and Coch, L. Overcoming resistance to change. *Human Relations,* 1948, *1*, 512–532.

French, J. R. P., and Raven, B. H. The basis of social power. In D. Cartwright (ed.), *Studies in social power.* Ann Arbor: University of Michigan Press, 1959.

Friedlander, F. The impact of organizational training laboratories upon the effectiveness and interaction of ongoing groups. *Personnel Psychology*, 1967, *20*, 289–308.

———. A comparative study of consulting processes and group development. *Journal of Applied Behavioral Science*, 1968, *4*, 377–399.

Gardin, J., Kaplan, K., Firestone, I., and Cowan, G. Proxemic effects on cooperation, attitude, and approach-avoidance in a prisoner's dilemma game. *Journal of Personality and Social Psychology*, 1973, *27*, 13–18.

Gibb, J. R. Defensive communication. *Journal of Communication*, 1961, *11*, 141–148.

Giffin, K. The contribution of studies of source credibility to a theory of interpersonal trust in the communication process. *Psychological Bulletin*, 1967, *68*, 104–121.

Glidewell, J. C. *Group emotionality and productivity.* Doctoral dissertation, University of Chicago, 1953.

Goldman, M. A comparison of individual and group performance for varying combinations of initial ability. *Journal of Personality and Social Psychology*, 1965, *1*, 210–216.

Gordon, K. Group judgments in the field of lifted weights. *Journal of Experimental Psychology*, 1924, *7*, 398–400.

Gordon, W. *Synectics.* New York: Harper & Row, 1961.

Gump, P. Environmental guidance of the classroom behavioral system. In B. Biddle and W. Ellena (eds.). *Contemporary Research on Teacher Effectiveness.* New York: Holt, Rinehart & Winston, 1964.

Halle, L. J. Overestimating the power of power. *The New Republic,* June 10, 1967, 15–17.

Harrison, R. Impact of the laboratory on perceptions of others by the experimental group. In C. Arygyris (ed.), *Interpersonal competence and organizational effectiveness.* Homewood, Il.: Richard D. Irwin, 1962.

Hersey, P., and Blanchard, K. Management of organizational behavior: Utilizing human resources (3rd ed.). Englewood Cliffs, N.J.: Prentice-Hall, 1977.

Hoffman, L. R. Conditions for creative problem solving. *Journal of Psychology*, 1961, *52*, 429–444.

Hoffman, L. R., Harburg, E., and Maier, N. R. F. Differences and disagreement as factors in creative problem solving. *Journal of Abnormal and Social Psychology*, 1962, *64*, 206–214.

Hollander, E. P., and Willis, R. H. Some current issues in the psychology of conformity and nonconformity. *Psychological Bulletin*, 1967, *68*, 62–76.

Homans, G. *The human group,* New York: Harcourt, Brace, 1950.

———. *Social behaviors: Its elementary forms.* New York: Harcourt, Brace, & World, 1961.

Horwitz, M. The recall of interrupted group tasks: An experimental study of individual motivation in relation to group goals. *Human Relations,* 1954, *7*, 3–38.

HOVLAND, C. I., LUMSDAINE, A. A., and SHEFFIELD, F. D. *Experiment on mass communication.* Princeton, N.J.: Princeton University Press, 1949.

HOWELLS, L., and BECKER, S. Seating arrangement and leadership emergence. *Journal of Personality and Social Psychology,* 1962, *64,* 148–150.

IKLE, F. *How nations negotiate.* New York: Harper & Row, 1964.

ILLING, H. C. G. Jung on the present trends in group psychotherapy. *Human Relations,* 1957, *10,* 77–84.

JANIS, I. L. Group think. *Psychology Today,* 1971, *5*(6), 43–46; 74–76.

JANIS, I., and MANN, L. *Decision making.* New York: Free Press, 1977.

JOHNSON, D. W. *The social psychology of education.* New York: Holt, Rinehart & Winston, 1970.

———. Role reversal: A summary and review of the research. *International Journal of Group Tensions,* 1971, *1,* 318–334. (a)

———. The effectiveness of role reversal: The actor or the listener. *Psychological Reports,* 1971, *28,* 275–282. (b)

———. The effects of warmth of interaction, accuracy of understanding, and the proposal of compromises on the listener's behavior. *Journal of Counseling Psychology,* 1971, *18,* 207–216. (c)

———. The effects of the order of expressing warmth and anger upon the actor and the listener. *Journal of Counseling Psychology,* 1971, *18,* 571–578. (d)

———. The effects of role reversal on seeing a conflict from the opponent's frame of reference. Unpublished manuscript, University of Minnesota, 1972.

———. *Contemporary social psychology.* Philadelphia: Lippincott, 1973.

———. The affective side of the schooling experience. *Elementary School Journal,* 1973, *73,* 306–313.

———. Communication and the inducement of cooperative behavior in conflicts. *Speech Monographs,* 1974, *41,* 64–78.

———. Cooperativeness and social perspective taking. *Journal of Personality and Social Psychology,* 1975, *31*(2), 241–244.

———. Distribution and exchange of information in problem solving dyads. *Communication Research,* 1977, *4,* 283–298.

———. *Human relations and your career: A guide to interpersonal skills.* Englewood Cliffs, N.J.: Prentice-Hall, 1978.

———. *Educational psychology.* Englewood Cliffs, N.J.: Prentice-Hall, 1979.

———. Group processes: Influences on student–student interaction on school outcomes. In J. McMillan (ed.), *Social psychology of school learning.* New York: Academic Press, 1980a.

———. Attitude Modification Methods. In F. Kanfer and A. Goldstein (eds.), *Helping People Change.* New York: Pergamon Press, 1980b.

———. *Reaching out: Interpersonal effectiveness and self-actualization* (2nd ed.). Englewood Cliffs, N.J.: Prentice-Hall, 1981.

JOHNSON, D. W., and ALLEN, S. Deviation from organizational norms concerning the relations between status and power. *Sociological Quarterly,* 1972, *13,* 174–182.

JOHNSON, D. W., and JOHNSON, R. T. Instructional goal structure: Cooperative, competitive, or individualistic? *Review of Educational Research,* 1974, *44,* 213–240.

———. *Learning together and alone: Cooperation, competition, and individualization.* Englewood Cliffs, N.J.: Prentice-Hall, 1975.

————. Cooperative, competitive and individualistic learning. *Journal of Research and Development in Education,* 1978, *12,* 3–15.

————. Conflict in the classroom: Controversy and learning. *Review of Educational Research,* 1979, *49,* 51–70.

————. *Belonging* (movie). Minneapolis: J & J Book Co., 1980.

JOHNSON, D. W., and JOHNSON, R. T. (eds.). Social interdependence in the classroom: Cooperation, competition, individualism. *Journal of Research and Development in Education,* 1978, *12* (Fall).

JOHNSON, D. W., JOHNSON, R. T., and SKON, L. The effects of cooperative, competitive, and individualistic conditions on student achievement on different types of tasks. *Contemporary Educational Psychology,* 1979, *4,* 99–106.

JOHNSON, D. W., KAVANAGH, J., and LUBIN, B. Tests, T-groups, and tension. *Comparative Group Studies,* 1973, *4,* 81–88.

JOHNSON, D. W., and LEWICKI, R. J. The initiation of superordinate goals. *Journal of Applied Behavioral Science,* 1969, *5,* 9–24.

JOHNSON, D. W., MARUYAMA, G., JOHNSON, R. T., NELSON, D., and SKON, L. Effects of cooperative, competitive, and individualistic goal structures on achievement: A meta-analysis. *Psychological Bulletin,* 1981, *89,* 47–62.

JOHNSON, D. W., McCARTY, K., and ALLEN, T. Congruent and contradictory verbal and nonverbal communications of cooperativeness and competitiveness in negotiations. *Communication Research,* 1976, *3,* 275–292.

JOHNSON, R. T. Personal communication on inquiry procedures in discovery learning, 1972.

JONES, E. E., and GERARD, H. B. *Foundations of social psychology.* New York: John Wiley, 1967.

KELLEY, H. H., and STAHELSKI, A. J. Social interaction basis of cooperators' and competitors' beliefs about others. *Journal of Personality and Social Psychology,* 1970, *16,* 66–91.

KERR, N., ATKIN, R., STASSER, G., MEEK, D., HOLT, R., and DAVIS, J. Guilt beyond a reasonable doubt: Effects of concept definition and assigned decision rule on the judgments of mock jurors. *Journal of Personality and Social Psychology,* 1976, *34,* 282–294.

KIPNIS, D. Does power corrupt? *Journal of Personality and Social Psychology,* 1972, *24,* 33–41.

KOSTICK, M. M. An experiment in group decision. *Journal of Teacher Education,* 1957, *8,* 67–72.

LABARRE. W. *The ghost dance.* New York: Delta, 1972.

LAKIN, M. *Interpersonal encounter: Theory and practice in sensitivity training.* New York: McGraw-Hill, 1972.

LATANE, B., WILLIAMS, K., and HARKINGS, S. Many hands make for light work: The causes and consequences of social loafing. *Journal of Personality and Social Psychology,* 1975, *37,* 822–832.

LAUGHLIN, P. Social combination processes of cooperative problem-solving groups on verbal intellective tasks. In M. Fishbein (ed.), *Progress in social psychology* (Vol. 1). Hillsdale, N.J.: Lawrence Erlbaum, 1980.

LAUGHLIN, P. R., BRANCH, L. G., and JOHNSON, H. H. Individual versus triadic performance on a unidimensional complementary task as a function of initial ability level. *Journal of Personality and Social Psychology,* 1969, *12,* 144–150.

LAWRENCE, P., and LORSCH, J. *Organization and environment: Managing differentiation and integration.* Cambridge: Harvard University, Division of Research, Graduate School of Business Administration, 1967.

LEAVITT, H. Some effects of certain communication patterns on group performance. *Journal of Abnormal and Social Psychology,* 1951, *46,* 38–50.

LEIBERMAN, M. A., YALOM, I. D., and MILES, M. B. *Encounter groups: First facts.* New York: Basic Books, 1973.

————. Group Methods. In F. Kanfer and A. Goldstein (eds.), *Helping People Change.* New York: Pergamon Press, 1980.

LEVINE, J., and BUTLER, J. Lecture vs. group decision in changing behavior. *Journal of Applied Psychology,* 1952, *36,* 29–33.

LEVI—STRAUSS, C. *The Raw and the cooked: Introduction to a science of mythology* (Vol. 1). New York: Harper & Row, 1969.

LEWIN, K. *A dynamic theory of personality.* New York: McGraw-Hill, 1935.

————. Forces behind food habits and methods of change. *Bulletin of the National Research Council,* 1943, *108,* 35–65.

————. Psychology and the process of group living, Bulletin SPPSI. *Journal of Social Psychology,* 1943, *17,* 113–131.

————. Dynamics of group action. *Educational Leadership,* 1944, *1,* 195–200.

————. Group decisions and social change. In T. M. Newcomb and E. L. Hartley (eds.), *Readings in social psychology.* New York: Holt, 1947.

————. *Field theory in social science.* New York: Harper, 1951.

————. Studies in group decision. In D. Cartwright and A. Zander (eds.), *Group dynamics: Research and theory.* Evanston, Ill.: Row, Peterson, 1953.

LEWIN, K., DEMBO, T., FESTINGER, L., and SEARS, P. Level of aspiration. In J. M. V. Hunt (ed.), *Personality and the behavior disorders.* New York: Ronald Press, 1944.

LEWIN, K., and GRABBE, P. Conduct, knowledge, and acceptance of new values. *Journal of Social Issues,* 1945, *1,* 56–64.

LEWIN, K., LIPPITT, R., and WHITE, R. K. Patterns of aggressive behavior in experimentally created "social climates." *Journal of Social Psychology,* 1939, *10,* 271–299.

LEWIS, S., and PRUITT, D. Organization, aspiration level, and communication freedom in integrative bargaining. *Proceedings of the 79th Annual Convention of the American Psychological Association,* 1971, *6,* 221–222.

LOMBARDO, M., and McCALL, M. Leaders on line: Observations from a simulation of managerial work. Paper presented at the Sixth Biennial Leadership Symposium, "Leadership: Beyond Establishment Views," October 1980, Southern Illinois University at Carbondale.

LONDON, P. *Behavior control.* New York: Harper & Row, 1969.

LORD, R. Functional leadership behavior: Measurement and relation to social power and leadership perceptions. *Administrative Science Quarterly,* 1977, *22,* 114–133.

LOWRY, N., and JOHNSON, D. W. Effects of controversy on epistemic curiosity, achievement, and attitudes. *Journal of Social Psychology,* 1981, *115,* 31–43.

LYONS, V. (ed.). *Structuring cooperative learning: The 1980 handbook.* Minneapolis: J & J Book Co., 1980.

MAIER, N. R. F. Reasoning in humans: I: On direction. *Journal of Comparative Psychology,* 1930, *10,* 115–43.

MAIER, N. R. F., and HOFFMAN, L. R. Financial incentives and group decision in motivating change. *Journal of Social Psychology,* 1964, *64,* 369–378.

MAIER, N. R. F., and SOLEM, A. R. The contribution of a discussion leader to the quality of group thinking: The effective use of minority opinions. *Human Relations,* 1952, *5,* 277–288.

MANN, R. A review of the relationship between personality and performance in small groups. *Psychological Bulletin,* 1959, *56,* 241–270.

MARROW, A. *Making management human.* New York: McGraw-Hill, 1957.

MASLOW, A. H. *Motivation and personality.* New York: Harper & Row, 1954.

———. *Toward a psychology of being.* Princeton, N.J.: Van Nostrand, 1962.

McDAVID, J., and HARARI, H. *Social psychology: Individuals, groups, societies.* New York: Harper & Row, 1968.

McGREGOR, D. The human side of enterprise. New York: McGraw-Hill, 1967.

———. *The professional manager.* New York: McGraw-Hill, 1967.

McGUIRE, W. Inducing resistance to persuasion. In Berkowitz, L. (Ed.), *Advances in experimental social psychology* (Vol. 1). New York: Academic Press, 1964, 192–232.

———. The nature of attitudes and attitude change. In B. Lindsey and E. Aronson (eds.), *Handbook of social psychology* (Vol. 3). Reading, Mass.: Addison-Wesley, 1969.

MICHENER, H., and BURT, M. Components of "authority" as determinants of compliance. *Journal of Personality Psychology,* 1975, *31,* 606–614.

MICHENER, H., and LAWLER, E. Endorsement of formal leaders: An integrative model. *Journal of Personality and Social Psychology,* 1975, *31,* 216–223.

MILLS, T. *The sociology of small groups.* Englewood Cliffs, N.J.; Prentice-Hall, 1967.

MOEDE, W. *Experimentelle massenpsychologie.* Leipzig: S. Hirzel, 1920.

MORTON, R. B., and WRIGHT, A. A critical incidents evaluation of an organizational training laboratory. Working paper, Aerojet General Corporation, 1964.

MOSCOVICI, S., and DOISE, W. Decision making in groups. In C. Nemeth (ed.), *Social psychology: Classic and contemporary integrations.* Chicago: Rand McNally, 1974.

MOSCOVICI, S., and ZAVALLONI, M. The group as a polarizer of attitudes. *Journal of Personality and Social Psychology,* 1969, *12,* 125–135.

MYERS, D., and LAMM, H. The group polarization phenomenon. *Psychological Bulletin,* 1976, *83,* 602–627.

MYERS, R. *Some effects of seating arrangements in counseling.* Doctoral dissertation, University of Florida, 1969.

NEMETH, C. Interaction between jurors as a function of majority vs. unanimity decision rules. *Journal of Applied Social Psychology,* 1977, *7,* 38–56.

NESBITT, P., POND, A., and ALLEN, W. *The survival book.* New York: Funk & Wagnalls, 1959.

NEWCOMB, T. *Personality and social change.* New York: Dryden, 1943.

PELZ, E. Some factors in "group decision." In E. Maccoby, T. Newcomb, and E. Hartley (eds.), *Readings in social psychology.* New York: Holt, 1958.

PENNINGTON, D., HARAVEY, F., and BASS, B. Some effects of decision and discussion on coalescence, change, and effectiveness. *Journal of Applied Psychology,* 1958, *42,* 404–408.

PEPINSKI, P., HEMPHILL, J., and SHEVITZ, R. Attempts to lead, group productivity, and morale under conditions of acceptance and rejection. *Journal of Abnormal and Social Psychology,* 1958, *57,* 47–54.

PEPITONE, A. *Responsibility to the group and its effects on the performance of members.* Doctoral dissertation, University of Michigan, 1952.

PEPITONE, A. (ed.). *Children in cooperation and competition.* Lexington, Mass.: Lexington Books, 1980.

PEPITONE, A., and REICHLING, G. Group cohesiveness and the expression of hostility. *Human Relations,* 1955, *8,* 327–339.

PETERS, D. R. *Identification and personal change in laboratory training.* Doctoral dissertation, Massachusetts Institute of Technology, 1966.

PFEFFER, J., and SALANCIK, G. *The external control of organizations.* New York: Harper & Row, 1978.

PRESTON, M., and HEINTZ, R. Effects of participatory vs. supervisory leadership on group judgement. *Journal of Abnormal and Social Psychology,* 1949, *44,* 345–355.

PRUITT, D., and JOHNSON, D. W. Mediation as an aid to face saving in negotiation. *Journal of Personality and Social Psychology,* 1970, *14,* 239–246.

RADKE, M., and KLISURICH, D. Experiments in changing food habits. *Journal of the American Dietetics Association,* 1947, *23,* 403–409.

RAFALIDES, M., and HOY, W. Student sense of alienation and pupil control orientation of high schools. *The High School Journal,* 1971, *55*(3), 102.

RAVEN, B. H., and KRUGLANSKI, A. W. Conflict and power. In P. Swingle (ed.), *The structure of conflict.* New York: Academic Press, 1970.

RAVEN, B. H., and RIETSEMA, J. The effects of varied clarity of group goal and group path upon the individual and his relation to his group. *Human Relations,* 1957, *10,* 29–44.

RAWLS, J. *A theory of justice.* Cambridge: Harvard University Press, 1971.

Reporting on Cooperative Learning (biannual newsletter). Minneapolis: J & J Book Co.

Report of the National Advisory Commission on Civil Disorder. New York: Bantam, 1968.

RIECKEN, H. Some problems of consensus development. *Rural Sociology,* 1952, *17,* 245–252.

ROBBINS, S. *Managing organizational conflict.* Englewood Cliffs, N.J.: Prentice-Hall, 1974.

ROETHLISBERGER, F. J., and DICKSON, W. J. *Management and the worker.* Cambridge: Harvard University Press, 1939.

ROGERS, C. R. Towards a theory of creativity. In P. Vernon (ed.), *Readings in creativity.* London: Penguin, 1970.

ROKEACH, M. The nature and meaning of dogmatism. *Psychological Review,* 1954, *61,* 194–204.

———. *The open and closed mind.* New York: Basic Books, 1960.

———. *Beliefs, attitudes, and values.* San Francisco: Jossey-Bass, 1968.

RUBIN, J., and BROWN, B. *The social psychology of bargaining and negotiation.* New York: Academic Press, 1975.

RUTSTRUM, C. *The new ways of the wilderness.* New York: Collier, 1973.

SARACHEK, G. Greek concepts of leadership. *Academy of Management Journal,* 1968, *11,* 39–48.

SCHACHTER, S. Deviation, rejection, and communication. *Journal of Abnormal and Social Psychology,* 1951, *46,* 190–207.

SCHACHTER, S., et al., Cross-cultural experiments on threat and rejection. *Human Relations,* 1954, *7,* 403–439.

SCHEIN, E. H. *Process consultation.* Reading, Mass.: Addison-Wesley, 1969.

SCHELLING, T. C. *The strategy of conflict.* Cambridge: Harvard University Press, 1960.

SCHNEIDER, J. The cultural situation as a condition for the achievement of fame. *American Sociological Review,* 1937, *2,* 480–491.

SCHUTZ, W. C. *Firo: A three dimensional theory of interpersonal behavior.* New York: Holt, Rinehart & Winston, 1958.

SHAW, M. A comparison of individuals and small groups in the rational solution of complex problems. *American Journal of Psychology,* 1932, *44,* 491–504.

———. Communication networks. In L. Berkowitz (ed.), *Advances in experimental social psychology* (Vol. 1). New York: Academic Press, 1964.

———. *Group dynamics.* New York: McGraw-Hill, 1976.

———. *The psychology of group norms.* New York: Harper, 1936.

———. *The psychology of social norms.* New York: Harper, 1936.

———. *In common predicament.* Boston: Houghton Mifflin, 1966.

SHERIF, M., and SHERIF, C. *An outline of social psychology.* New York: Harper & Row, 1956.

———. *Social psychology.* New York: Harper & Row, 1969.

SIMON, H. *Administrative behavior: A study of decision-making processes in administrative organization* (3rd ed.) New York: Free Press, 1976.

SIMONTON, D. Was Napolean a military genius? Score: Carlyle 1, Tolstoy 1. *Psychological Reports,* 1979, *44,* 21–22.

SKON, L., JOHNSON, D. W., and JOHNSON, R. Cooperative peer interaction versus individual competition and individualistic efforts: Effects on the acquisition of cognitive reasoning strategies. *Journal of Educational Psychology,* 1981, *73,* 83–92.

SMITH, K., JOHNSON, D. W., and JOHNSON, R. T. Can conflict be constructive? Controversy versus concurrence seeking in learning groups. *Journal of Educational Psychology,* 1981, *73,* 651–663.

SMITH, M. Social situation, social behavior, and social group. *Psychological Review,* 1945, *52,* 224–229.

SOUTH, E. Some psychological aspects of committee work. *Journal of Applied Psychology,* 1927, *11,* 348–368, 437–464.

STEIN, M. I. The creative individual. Manuscript, 1968.

STEINZOR, B. The spatial factor in face-to-face discussion groups. *Journal of Abnormal and Social Psychology,* 1950, *45,* 552–555.

STEVENS, C. M. *Strategy and collective bargaining negotiation.* New York: McGraw-Hill, 1963.

STOGDILL, R. *Individual behavior and group achievement.* New York: Oxford University Press, 1959.

———. *Handbook of leadership.* New York: Free Press, 1974.

STOTLE, J. Power structure and personal competence. *Journal of Social Psychology,* 1978, *38,* 72–83.

STRODTBECK, F., and HOOK, L. The social dimensions of a twelve man jury table. *Sociometry,* 1961, *24,* 397–415.

TERMAN, L., and ODOR, M. *The gifted child grows up.* Stanford, Calif.: Stanford University Press, 1947.

THIBAUT, J. W., and KELLY, H. H. *The social psychology of groups.* New York: John Wiley, 1959.

TJOSVOLD, D. Threat as a low-power person's strategy in bargaining: Social face and tangible outcomes. *International Journal of Group Tensions,* 1974, *4,* 494–510.

———. Low-power person's strategies in bargaining: Negotiability of demand, maintaining face, and race. *International Journal of Group Tensions,* 1977.

———. Alternative organizations for schools and classrooms. In D. Bart-Tal and L. Saxe (eds.), *Social psychology of education.* Washington, D.C.: Hemisphere, 1978.

TJOSVOLD, D., and SAGARIA, D. Effects of relative power of cognitive perspective-taking. *Personality and Social Psychology Bulletin.* 1978, *4,* 256–259.

TORRANCE, E. Some consequences of power differences in decision making in permanent and temporary three-man groups. *Research Studies, State College of Washington,* 1954, *22,* 130–140.

———. Group decision making and disagreement. *Social Forces,* 1957, *35,* 314–318.

TREFFINGER, D., SPEEDIE, S., and BRUNNER, W. Improving children's creative problem solving ability: The Purdue creativity project. *The Journal of Creative Behavior,* 1974, *8,* 20–29.

TRIANDIS, H., BASS, A., EWEN, R., and MIEKSELE, E. Teaching creativity as a function of the creativity of the members. *Journal of Applied Psychology,* 1963, *47,* 104–110.

VILLASENOR, V. *Jury: The people vs. Juan Corona.* New York: Bantam, 1977.

WALTON, R. *Interpersonal peacemaking.* Reading, Mass.: Addison-Wesley, 1969.

WALTON, R. E., and MCKERSIE, R. B. *A behavioral theory of labor negotiations.* New York: McGraw-Hill, 1965.

WATSON, G. Do groups think more effectively than individuals? *Journal of Abnormal and Social Psychology,* 1928, *23,* 328–336.

———. Do groups think more effectively than individuals? In G. Murphy and L. Murphy (eds.), *Experimental social psychology.* New York: Harper, 1931.

WATSON, G., and JOHNSON, D. W. *Social psychology: Issues and insights* (2nd ed.). Philadelphia: Lippincott, 1972.

WHYTE, W. *Street corner society.* Chicago: University of Chicago Press, 1943.

WIGGAM, A. The biology of leadership. In H. Metcalf (ed.), *Business leadership.* New York: Pitman, 1931.

WOODS, F. *The influence of monarchs.* New York: MacMillan, 1913.

WRIGHT, M. E. The influence of frustration upon social relations of young children. *Character and Personality,* 1943, *12,* 111–112.

ZAJONC, R. Compresence. In P. Paulus (ed.), *Psychology of group influence.* Hillsdale, N.J.: Lawrence Erlbaum, 1980.

ZANDER, A. The psychology of group process. In A. Inkeles, J. Coleman, and R. Turner (eds.), *Annual review of sociology* (Vol. 5). Palo Alto, Calif.: Annual Reviews Inc., 1979.

———. The origins and consequences of group goals. In L. Festinger (ed.), *Retrospections on social psychology.* New York: Oxford University Press, 1980.

ZANDER, A., and ARMSTRONG, W. Working for group pride in a slipper factory. *Journal of Applied Social Psychology,* 1972, *2,* 293–307.

ZDEP, S., and OAKES, W. Reinforcement of leadership behavior in group discussion. *Journal of Experimental Social Psychology,* 1967, *3,* 310–320.

ZELENY, L. Experimental appraisal of a group learning plan. *Journal of Educational Research,* 1940, *34,* 37–42.

ZENGER, J. P. As cited in D. G. Lake, M. R. Ritvo, and G. M. St. L. O'Brien, Applying behavioral science: Current projects. *Journal of Applied Behavioral Science,* 1969, *5,* 385.

ZILLER, R. Group size: A determinant of the quality and stability of group decision. *Sociometry,* 1957, *20,* 165–173.

Index